University Casebook Series

December, 1980

ACCOUNTING AND THE LAW, Fourth Edition (1978), with Problems Pamphlet (Successor to Dohr, Phillips, Thompson & Warren)

George C. Thompson, Professor, Columbia University Graduate School of Business.
Robert Whitman, Professor of Law, University of Connecticut.
Ellis L. Phillips, Jr., Member of the New York Bar.
William C. Warren, Professor of Law Emeritus, Columbia University.

ACCOUNTING FOR LAWYERS, MATERIALS ON (1980)

David R. Herwitz, Professor of Law, Harvard University.

ADMINISTRATIVE LAW, Seventh Edition (1979), with 1979 Problems Supplement (Supplement edited in association with Paul R. Verkuil, Dean and Professor of Law, Tulane University)

Walter Gellhorn, University Professor Emeritus, Columbia University.
Clark Byse, Professor of Law, Harvard University.
Peter L. Strauss, Professor of Law, Columbia University.

ADMIRALTY, Second Edition (1978), with Statute and Rule Supplement

Jo Desha Lucas, Professor of Law, University of Chicago.

ADVOCACY, see also Lawyering Process

ADVOCACY, INTRODUCTION TO, Third Edition (1981)

Board of Student Advisers, Harvard Law School.

AGENCY, see also Enterprise Organization

AGENCY–ASSOCIATIONS–EMPLOYMENT–PARTNERSHIPS, Second Edition (1977)

Abridgement from Conard, Knauss & Siegel's Enterprise Organization.

ANTITRUST AND REGULATORY ALTERNATIVES (1977), Fifth Edition

Louis B. Schwartz, Professor of Law, University of Pennsylvania.
John J. Flynn, Professor of Law, University of Utah.

ANTITRUST SUPPLEMENT—SELECTED STATUTES AND RELATED MATERIALS (1977)

John J. Flynn, Professor of Law, University of Utah.

BIOGRAPHY OF A LEGAL DISPUTE, THE: An Introduction to American Civil Procedure (1968)

Marc A. Franklin, Professor of Law, Stanford University.

BUSINESS ORGANIZATION, see also Enterprise Organization

BUSINESS PLANNING (1966), with 1980 Supplement

David R. Herwitz, Professor of Law, Harvard University.

UNIVERSITY CASEBOOK SERIES—Continued

BUSINESS TORTS (1972)

Milton Handler, Professor of Law Emeritus, Columbia University.

CIVIL PROCEDURE, see Procedure

CLINIC, see also Lawyering Process

COMMERCIAL AND CONSUMER TRANSACTIONS, Second Edition (1978)

William D. Warren, Dean of the School of Law, University of California, Los Angeles.
William E. Hogan, Professor of Law, Cornell University.
Robert L. Jordan, Professor of Law, University of California, Los Angeles.

COMMERCIAL LAW, CASES & MATERIALS ON, Third Edition (1976)

E. Allan Farnsworth, Professor of Law, Cornell University.
John Honnold, Professor of Law, University of Pennsylvania.

COMMERCIAL PAPER, Second Edition (1976)

E. Allan Farnsworth, Professor of Law, Columbia University.

COMMERCIAL PAPER AND BANK DEPOSITS AND COLLECTIONS (1967), with Statutory Supplement.

William D. Hawkland, Professor of Law, University of Illinois.

COMMERCIAL TRANSACTIONS—Text, Cases and Problems, Fourth Edition (1968)

Robert Braucher, Professor of Law Emeritus, Harvard University, and
The late Arthur E. Sutherland, Jr., Professor of Law, Harvard University.

COMPARATIVE LAW, Fourth Edition (1980)

Rudolf B. Schlesinger, Professor of Law, Hastings College of the Law.

COMPETITIVE PROCESS, LEGAL REGULATION OF THE, Second Edition (1979), with Statutory Supplement

Edmund W. Kitch, Professor of Law, University of Chicago.
Harvey S. Perlman, Professor of Law, University of Virginia.

CONFLICT OF LAWS, Seventh Edition (1978), with 1980 Supplement

Willis L. M. Reese, Professor of Law, Columbia University, and
Maurice Rosenberg, Professor of Law, Columbia University.

CONSTITUTIONAL LAW, Fifth Edition (1977), with 1980 Supplement

Edward L. Barrett, Jr., Professor of Law, University of California, Davis.

CONSTITUTIONAL LAW, Tenth Edition (1980)

Gerald Gunther, Professor of Law, Stanford University.

CONSTITUTIONAL LAW, INDIVIDUAL RIGHTS IN, Third Edition (1981)

Gerald Gunther, Professor of Law, Stanford University.

CONTRACT LAW AND ITS APPLICATION, Second Edition (1977)

Addison Mueller, Professor of Law Emeritus, University of California, Los Angeles.
Arthur I. Rosett, Professor of Law, University of California, Los Angeles.

UNIVERSITY CASEBOOK SERIES—Continued

CONTRACT LAW, STUDIES IN, Second Edition (1977)

Edward J. Murphy, Professor of Law, University of Notre Dame.
Richard E. Speidel, Professor of Law, University of Virginia.

CONTRACTS, Third Edition (1977)

John P. Dawson, Professor of Law Emeritus, Harvard University, and
William Burnett Harvey, Professor of Law and Political Science, Boston University.

CONTRACTS, Third Edition (1980), with Statutory Supplement

E. Allan Farnsworth, Professor of Law, Columbia University.
William F. Young, Professor of Law, Columbia University.

CONTRACTS, Second Edition (1978), with Statutory and Administrative Law Supplement (1978)

Ian R. Macneil, Professor of Law, Cornell University.

COPYRIGHT, Unfair Competition, and Other Topics Bearing on the Protection of Literary, Musical, and Artistic Works, Third Edition (1978)

Benjamin Kaplan, Professor of Law Emeritus, Harvard University, and
Ralph S. Brown, Jr., Professor of Law, Yale University.

CORPORATE FINANCE, Second Edition (1979), with 1980 New Developments Supplement

Victor Brudney, Professor of Law, Harvard University.
Marvin A. Chirelstein, Professor of Law, Yale University.

CORPORATE READJUSTMENTS AND REORGANIZATIONS (1976)

Walter J. Blum, Professor of Law, University of Chicago.
Stanley A. Kaplan, Professor of Law, University of Chicago.

CORPORATION LAW, BASIC, Second Edition (1979), with Documentary Supplement

Detlev F. Vagts, Professor of Law, Harvard University.

CORPORATIONS, see also Enterprise Organization

CORPORATIONS, Fifth Edition—Unabridged (1980)

William L. Cary, Professor of Law, Columbia University.
Melvin Aron Eisenberg, Professor of Law, University of California, Berkeley.

CORPORATIONS, Fifth Edition—Abridged (1980)

William L. Cary, Professor of Law, Columbia University.
Melvin Aron Eisenberg, Professor of Law, University of California, Berkeley.

CORPORATIONS, THE LAW OF: WHAT CORPORATE LAWYERS DO (1976)

Jan G. Deutsch, Professor of Law, Yale University.
Joseph J. Bianco, Professor of Law, Yeshiva University.

CORPORATIONS COURSE GAME PLAN (1975)

David R. Herwitz, Professor of Law, Harvard University.

CREDIT TRANSACTIONS AND CONSUMER PROTECTION (1976)

John Honnold, Professor of Law, University of Pennsylvania.

CREDITORS' RIGHTS, see also Debtor-Creditor Law

UNIVERSITY CASEBOOK SERIES—Continued

DECEDENTS' ESTATES (1971)

Max Rheinstein, late Professor of Law Emeritus, University of Chicago.
Mary Ann Glendon, Professor of Law, Boston College.

DECEDENTS' ESTATES AND TRUSTS, Fifth Edition (1977)

John Ritchie, Professor of Law Emeritus, University of Virginia.
Neill H. Alford, Jr., Professor of Law, University of Virginia.
Richard W. Effland, Professor of Law, Arizona State University.

DECEDENTS' ESTATES AND TRUSTS (1968)

Howard R. Williams, Professor of Law, Stanford University.

DOMESTIC RELATIONS, see also Family Law

DOMESTIC RELATIONS, Third Edition (1978) with 1980 Supplement

Walter Wadlington, Professor of Law, University of Virginia.
Monrad G. Paulsen, Dean of the Law School, Yeshiva University.

DYNAMICS OF AMERICAN LAW, THE: Courts, the Legal Process and Freedom of Expression (1968)

Marc A. Franklin, Professor of Law, Stanford University.

ELECTRONIC MASS MEDIA, Second Edition (1979)

William K. Jones, Professor of Law, Columbia University.

ENTERPRISE ORGANIZATION, Second Edition (1977), with 1979 Statutory and Formulary Supplement

Alfred F. Conard, Professor of Law, University of Michigan.
Robert L. Knauss, Dean of the School of Law, Vanderbilt University.
Stanley Siegel, Professor of Law, University of California, Los Angeles.

EQUITY AND EQUITABLE REMEDIES (1975)

Edward D. Re, Adjunct Professor of Law, St. John's University.

EQUITY, RESTITUTION AND DAMAGES, Second Edition (1974)

Robert Childres, late Professor of Law, Northwestern University.
William F. Johnson, Jr., Professor of Law, New York University.

ESTATE PLANNING PROBLEMS (1973), with 1977 Supplement

David Westfall, Professor of Law, Harvard University.

ETHICS, see Legal Profession, and Professional Responsibility

EVIDENCE, Fourth Edition (1981)

David W. Louisell, late Professor of Law, University of California, Berkeley.
John Kaplan, Professor of Law, Stanford University.
Jon R. Waltz, Professor of Law, Northwestern University.

EVIDENCE, Sixth Edition (1973), with 1980 Supplement

John M. Maguire, late Professor of Law Emeritus, Harvard University.
Jack B. Weinstein, Professor of Law, Columbia University.
James H. Chadbourn, Professor of Law, Harvard University.
John H. Mansfield, Professor of Law, Harvard University.

EVIDENCE (1968)

Francis C. Sullivan, Professor of Law, Louisiana State University.
Paul Hardin, III, Professor of Law, Duke University.

FAMILY LAW, see also Domestic Relations

FAMILY LAW (1978), with 1981 Supplement

Judith C. Areen, Professor of Law, Georgetown University.

FAMILY LAW: STATUTORY MATERIALS, Second Edition (1974)

Monrad G. Paulsen, Dean of the Law School, Yeshiva University.
Walter Wadlington, Professor of Law, University of Virginia.

FEDERAL COURTS, Sixth Edition (1976), with 1980 Supplement

Charles T. McCormick, late Professor of Law, University of Texas.
James H. Chadbourn, Professor of Law, Harvard University, and
Charles Alan Wright, Professor of Law, University of Texas.

FEDERAL COURTS AND THE FEDERAL SYSTEM, Hart and Wechsler's Second Edition (1973), with 1981 Supplement

Paul M. Bator, Professor of Law, Harvard University.
Paul J. Mishkin, Professor of Law, University of California, Berkeley.
David L. Shapiro, Professor of Law, Harvard University.
Herbert Wechsler, Professor of Law, Columbia University.

FEDERAL PUBLIC LAND AND RESOURCES LAW (1981)

George C. Coggins, Professor of Law, University of Kansas.
Charles F. Wilkinson, Professor of Law, University of Oregon.

FEDERAL RULES OF CIVIL PROCEDURE, 1980 Edition

FEDERAL TAXATION, see Taxation

FOOD AND DRUG LAW (1980)

Richard A. Merrill, Dean of the School of Law, University of Virginia.
Peter Barton Hutt, Esq.

FUTURE INTERESTS (1958)

Philip Mechem, late Professor of Law Emeritus, University of Pennsylvania.

FUTURE INTERESTS (1970)

Howard R. Williams, Professor of Law, Stanford University.

FUTURE INTERESTS AND ESTATE PLANNING (1961), with 1962 Supplement

W. Barton Leach, late Professor of Law, Harvard University.
James K. Logan, formerly Dean of the Law School, University of Kansas.

GOVERNMENT CONTRACTS, FEDERAL (1975), with 1980 Supplement

John W. Whelan, Professor of Law, Hastings College of the Law.
Robert S. Pasley, Professor of Law Emeritus, Cornell University.

HOUSING—THE ILL-HOUSED (1971)

Peter W. Martin, Professor of Law, Cornell University.

INJUNCTIONS (1972)

Owen M. Fiss, Professor of Law, Yale University.

INSTITUTIONAL INVESTORS, 1978

David L. Ratner, Professor of Law, Cornell University.

INSURANCE (1971)

William F. Young, Professor of Law, Columbia University.

INTERNATIONAL LAW, see also Transnational Legal Problems and United Nations Law

INTERNATIONAL LEGAL SYSTEM (1973), with Documentary Supplement

Noyes E. Leech, Professor of Law, University of Pennsylvania.
Covey T. Oliver, Professor of Law, University of Pennsylvania.
Joseph Modeste Sweeney, Professor of Law, Tulane University.

INTERNATIONAL TRADE AND INVESTMENT, REGULATION OF (1970)

Carl H. Fulda, late Professor of Law, University of Texas.
Warren F. Schwartz, Professor of Law, University of Virginia.

INTERNATIONAL TRANSACTIONS AND RELATIONS (1960)

Milton Katz, Professor of Law, Harvard University, and
Kingman Brewster, Jr., Professor of Law, Harvard University.

INTRODUCTION TO LAW, see also Legal Method, On Law in Courts, and Dynamics of American Law

INTRODUCTION TO THE STUDY OF LAW (1970)

E. Wayne Thode, late Professor of Law, University of Utah.
Leon Lebowitz, Professor of Law, University of Texas.
Lester J. Mazor, Professor of Law, University of Utah.

JUDICIAL CODE and Rules of Procedure in the Federal Courts with Excerpts from the Criminal Code, 1981 Edition

Henry M. Hart, Jr., late Professor of Law, Harvard University.
Herbert Wechsler, Professor of Law, Columbia University.

JURISPRUDENCE (Temporary Edition Hardbound) (1949)

Lon L. Fuller, Professor of Law Emeritus, Harvard University.

JUVENILE COURTS (1967)

Hon. Orman W. Ketcham, Juvenile Court of the District of Columbia.
Monrad G. Paulsen, Dean of the Law School, Yeshiva University.

JUVENILE JUSTICE PROCESS, Second Edition (1976), with 1980 Supplement

Frank W. Miller, Professor of Law, Washington University.
Robert O. Dawson, Professor of Law, University of Texas.
George E. Dix, Professor of Law, University of Texas.
Raymond I. Parnas, Professor of Law, University of California, Davis.

LABOR LAW, Eighth Edition (1977), with Statutory Supplement, and 1979 Case Supplement

Archibald Cox, Professor of Law, Harvard University, and
Derek C. Bok, President, Harvard University.
Robert A. Gorman, Professor of Law, University of Pennsylvania.

LABOR LAW (1968), with Statutory Supplement and 1974 Case Supplement

Clyde W. Summers, Professor of Law, University of Pennsylvania.
Harry H. Wellington, Dean of the Law School, Yale University.

UNIVERSITY CASEBOOK SERIES—Continued

LAND FINANCING, Second Edition (1977)

Norman Penney, Professor of Law, Cornell University.
Richard F. Broude, of the California Bar.

LAW AND MEDICINE (1980)

Walter Wadlington, Professor of Law and Professor of Legal Medicine, University of Virginia.
Jon R. Waltz, Professor of Law, Northwestern University.
Roger B. Dworkin, Professor of Law, Indiana University, and Professor of Biomedical History, University of Washington.

LAW, LANGUAGE AND ETHICS (1972)

William R. Bishin, Professor of Law, University of Southern California.
Christopher D. Stone, Professor of Law, University of Southern California.

LAWYERING PROCESS (1978), with Civil Problem Supplement and Criminal Problem Supplement

Gary Bellow, Professor of Law, Harvard University.
Bea Moulton, Professor of Law, Arizona State University.

LEGAL METHOD

Harry W. Jones, Professor of Law Emeritus, Columbia University.
John M. Kernochan, Professor of Law, Columbia University.
Arthur W. Murphy, Professor of Law, Columbia University.

LEGAL METHODS (1969)

Robert N. Covington, Professor of Law, Vanderbilt University.
E. Blythe Stason, late Professor of Law, Vanderbilt University.
John W. Wade, Professor of Law, Vanderbilt University.
Elliott E. Cheatham, late Professor of Law, Vanderbilt University.
Theodore A. Smedley, Professor of Law, Vanderbilt University.

LEGAL PROFESSION (1970)

Samuel D. Thurman, Dean of the College of Law, University of Utah.
Ellis L. Phillips, Jr., Professor of Law, Columbia University.
Elliott E. Cheatham, late Professor of Law, Vanderbilt University.

LEGISLATION, Third Edition (1973)

Horace E. Read, late Vice President, Dalhousie University.
John W. MacDonald, Professor of Law Emeritus, Cornell Law School.
Jefferson B. Fordham, Professor of Law, University of Utah, and
William J. Pierce, Professor of Law, University of Michigan.

LEGISLATIVE AND ADMINISTRATIVE PROCESSES (1976)

Hans A. Linde, Professor of Law, University of Oregon.
George Bunn, Professor of Law, University of Wisconsin.

LOCAL GOVERNMENT LAW, Revised Edition (1975)

Jefferson B. Fordham, Professor of Law, University of Utah.

MASS MEDIA LAW (1976), with 1979 Supplement

Marc A. Franklin, Professor of Law, Stanford University.

MENTAL HEALTH PROCESS, Second Edition (1976)

Frank W. Miller, Professor of Law, Washington University.
Robert O. Dawson, Professor of Law, University of Texas.
George E. Dix, Professor of Law, University of Texas.
Raymond I. Parnas, Professor of Law, University of California, Davis.

MUNICIPAL CORPORATIONS, see Local Government Law

NEGOTIABLE INSTRUMENTS, see Commercial Paper

NEW YORK PRACTICE, Fourth Edition (1978)

    Herbert Peterfreund, Professor of Law, New York University.
    Joseph M. McLaughlin, Dean of the Law School, Fordham University.

OIL AND GAS, Fourth Edition (1979)

    Howard R. Williams, Professor of Law, Stanford University
    Richard C. Maxwell, Professor of Law, University of California, Los Angeles.
    Charles J. Meyers, Dean of the Law School, Stanford University.

ON LAW IN COURTS (1965)

    Paul J. Mishkin, Professor of Law, University of California, Berkeley.
    Clarence Morris, Professor of Law Emeritus, University of Pennsylvania.

OWNERSHIP AND DEVELOPMENT OF LAND (1965)

    Jan Krasnowiecki, Professor of Law, University of Pennsylvania.

PARTNERSHIP PLANNING (1970) (Pamphlet)

    William L. Cary, Professor of Law, Columbia University.

PERSPECTIVES ON THE LAWYER AS PLANNER (Reprint of Chapters One through Five of Planning by Lawyers) (1978)

    Louis M. Brown, Professor of Law, University of Southern California.
    Edward A. Dauer, Professor of Law, Yale University.

PLANNING BY LAWYERS, MATERIALS ON A NONADVERSARIAL LEGAL PROCESS (1978)

    Louis M. Brown, Professor of Law, University of Southern California.
    Edward A. Dauer, Professor of Law, Yale University.

PLEADING AND PROCEDURE, see Procedure, Civil

POLICE FUNCTION (1976) (Pamphlet)

    Chapters 1–11 of Miller, Dawson, Dix & Parnas' Criminal Justice Administration, Second Edition.

PREVENTIVE LAW, see also Planning by Lawyers

PROCEDURE—Biography of a Legal Dispute (1968)

    Marc A. Franklin, Professor of Law, Stanford University.

PROCEDURE—CIVIL PROCEDURE, Second Edition (1974), with 1979 Supplement

    James H. Chadbourn, Professor of Law, Harvard University.
    A. Leo Levin, Professor of Law, University of Pennsylvania.
    Philip Shuchman, Professor of Law, University of Connecticut.

PROCEDURE—CIVIL PROCEDURE, Fourth Edition (1978), with 1980 Supplement

    Richard H. Field, late Professor of Law, Harvard University.
    Benjamin Kaplan, Professor of Law Emeritus, Harvard University.
    Kevin M. Clermont, Professor of Law, Cornell University.

PROCEDURE—CIVIL PROCEDURE, Third Edition (1976), with 1978 Supplement

    Maurice Rosenberg, Professor of Law, Columbia University.
    Jack B. Weinstein, Professor, of Law, Columbia University.
    Hans Smit, Professor of Law, Columbia University.
    Harold L. Korn, Professor of Law, Columbia University.

UNIVERSITY CASEBOOK SERIES—Continued

PROCEDURE—PLEADING AND PROCEDURE: State and Federal, Fourth Edition (1979)

David W. Louisell, late Professor of Law, University of California, Berkeley.
Geoffrey C. Hazard, Jr., Professor of Law, Yale University.

PROCEDURE—FEDERAL RULES OF CIVIL PROCEDURE, 1980 Edition

PROCEDURE PORTFOLIO (1962)

James H. Chadbourn, Professor of Law, Harvard University, and
A. Leo Levin, Professor of Law, University of Pennsylvania.

PRODUCTS LIABILITY (1980)

Marshall S. Shapo, Professor of Law, Northwestern University.

PRODUCTS LIABILITY AND SAFETY (1980), with Statutory Supplement

W. Page Keeton, Professor of Law, University of Texas.
David G. Owen, Professor of Law, University of South Carolina.
John E. Montgomery, Professor of Law, University of South Carolina.

PROFESSIONAL RESPONSIBILITY (1976), with 1979 Problems, Cases and Readings, Supplement, 1980 Statutory (National) Supplement, and 1980 Statutory (California) Supplement

Thomas D. Morgan, Professor of Law, University of Illinois.
Ronald D. Rotunda, Professor of Law, University of Illinois.

PROPERTY, Fourth Edition (1978)

John E. Cribbet, Dean of the Law School, University of Illinois.
Corwin W. Johnson, Professor of Law, University of Texas.

PROPERTY—PERSONAL (1953)

S. Kenneth Skolfield, late Professor of Law Emeritus, Boston University.

PROPERTY—PERSONAL, Third Edition (1954)

Everett Fraser, late Dean of the Law School Emeritus, University of Minnesota.
Third Edition by Charles W. Taintor, late Professor of Law, University of Pittsburgh.

PROPERTY—INTRODUCTION, TO REAL PROPERTY, Third Edition (1954)

Everett Fraser, late Dean of the Law School Emeritus, University of Minnesota.

PROPERTY—REAL PROPERTY AND CONVEYANCING (1954)

Edward E. Bade, late Professor of Law, University of Minnesota.

PROPERTY—FUNDAMENTALS OF MODERN REAL PROPERTY (1974), with 1980 Supplement

Edward H. Rabin, Professor of Law, University of California, Davis.

PROPERTY—PROBLEMS IN REAL PROPERTY (Pamphlet) (1969)

Edward H. Rabin, Professor of Law, University of California, Davis.

PROSECUTION AND ADJUDICATION (1976) (Pamphlet)

Chapters 12–16 of Miller, Dawson, Dix & Parnas' Criminal Justice Administration, Successor Edition.

PUBLIC REGULATION OF DANGEROUS PRODUCTS (paperback) (1980)

Marshall S. Shapo, Professor of Law, Northwestern University.

PUBLIC UTILITY LAW, see Free Enterprise, also Regulated Industries

REAL ESTATE PLANNING (1980), with 1980 Problems, Statutes and New Materials Supplement

Norton L. Steuben, Professor of Law, University of Colorado.

RECEIVERSHIP AND CORPORATE REORGANIZATION, see Creditors' Rights

REGULATED INDUSTRIES, Second Edition, 1976

William K. Jones, Professor of Law, Columbia University.

RESTITUTION, Second Edition (1966)

John W. Wade, Professor of Law, Vanderbilt University.

SALES (1980)

Marion W. Benfield, Jr., Professor of Law, University of Illinois.
William D. Hawkland, Chancellor, Louisiana State University Law Center.

SALES AND SALES FINANCING, Fourth Edition (1976)

John Honnold, Professor of Law, University of Pennsylvania.

SECURITY, Third Edition (1959)

John Hanna, late Professor of Law Emeritus, Columbia University.

SECURITIES REGULATION, Fourth Edition (1977), with 1980 Selected Statutes Supplement and 1980 Cases and Releases Supplement

Richard W. Jennings, Professor of Law, University of California, Berkeley.
Harold Marsh, Jr., Member of the California Bar.

SENTENCING AND THE CORRECTIONAL PROCESS, Second Edition (1976)

Frank W. Miller, Professor of Law, Washington University.
Robert O. Dawson, Professor of Law, University of Texas.
George E. Dix, Professor of Law, University of Texas.
Raymond I. Parnas, Professor of Law, University of California, Davis.

SOCIAL WELFARE AND THE INDIVIDUAL (1971)

Robert J. Levy, Professor of Law, University of Minnesota.
Thomas P. Lewis, Dean of the College of Law, University of Kentucky.
Peter W. Martin, Professor of Law, Cornell University.

TAX, POLICY ANALYSIS OF THE FEDERAL INCOME (1976)

William A. Klein, Professor of Law, University of California, Los Angeles.

TAXATION, FEDERAL INCOME (1976), with 1980 Supplement

Erwin N. Griswold, Dean Emeritus, Harvard Law School.
Michael J. Graetz, Professor of Law, University of Virginia.

TAXATION, FEDERAL INCOME, Second Edition (1977), with 1979 Supplement

James J. Freeland, Professor of Law, University of Florida.
Stephen A. Lind, Professor of Law, University of Florida.
Richard B. Stephens, Professor of Law Emeritus, University of Florida.

TAXATION, FEDERAL INCOME, Volume I, Personal Income Taxation (1972), with 1979 Supplement; Volume II, Taxation of Partnerships and Corporations, Second Edition (1980)

Stanley S. Surrey, Professor of Law, Harvard University.
William C. Warren, Professor of Law Emeritus, Columbia University.
Paul R. McDaniel, Professor of Law, Boston College Law School.
Hugh J. Ault, Professor of Law, Boston College Law School.

TAXATION, FEDERAL WEALTH TRANSFER (1977)

Stanley S. Surrey, Professor of Law, Harvard University.
William C. Warren, Professor of Law Emeritus, Columbia University, and
Paul R. McDaniel, Professor of Law, Boston College Law School.
Harry L. Gutman, Instructor, Harvard Law School and Boston College Law School.

TAXATION OF INDIVIDUALS, PARTNERSHIPS AND CORPORATIONS, PROBLEMS in the (1978)

Norton L. Steuben, Professor of Law, University of Colorado.
William J. Turnier, Professor of Law, University of North Carolina.

TAXES AND FINANCE—STATE AND LOCAL (1974)

Oliver Oldman, Professor of Law, Harvard University.
Ferdinand P. Schoettle, Professor of Law, University of Minnesota.

TORT LAW AND ALTERNATIVES: INJURIES AND REMEDIES, Second Edition (1979)

Marc A. Franklin, Professor of Law, Stanford University.

TORTS, Sixth Edition (1976)

William L. Prosser, late Professor of Law, University of California, Hastings College.
John W. Wade, Professor of Law, Vanderbilt University.
Victor E. Schwartz, Professor of Law, American University.

TORTS, Third Edition (1976)

Harry Shulman, late Dean of the Law School, Yale University.
Fleming James, Jr., Professor of Law Emeritus, Yale University.
Oscar S. Gray, Professor of Law, University of Maryland.

TRADE REGULATION (1975), with 1979 Supplement

Milton Handler, Professor of Law Emeritus, Columbia University.
Harlan M. Blake, Professor of Law, Columbia University.
Robert Pitofsky, Professor of Law, Georgetown University.
Harvey J. Goldschmid, Professor of Law, Columbia University.

TRADE REGULATION, see Antitrust

TRANSNATIONAL LEGAL PROBLEMS, Second Edition (1976), with Documentary Supplement

Henry J. Steiner, Professor of Law, Harvard University.
Detlev F. Vagts, Professor of Law, Harvard University.

TRIAL, see also Lawyering Process

TRIAL ADVOCACY (1968)

A. Leo Levin, Professor of Law, University of Pennsylvania.
Harold Cramer, of the Pennsylvania Bar.
Maurice Rosenberg, Professor of Law, Columbia University, Consultant.

TRUSTS, Fifth Edition (1978)

George G. Bogert, late Professor of Law Emeritus, University of Chicago.
Dallin H. Oaks, President, Brigham Young University.

TRUSTS AND SUCCESSION (Palmer's), Third Edition (1978)

Richard V. Wellman, Professor of Law, University of Georgia.
Lawrence W. Waggoner, Professor of Law, University of Michigan.
Olin L. Browder, Jr., Professor of Law, University of Michigan.

University Casebook Series

EDITORIAL BOARD

THE LAWYERING PROCESS:

NEGOTIATION

By

GARY BELLOW

Professor of Law, Harvard University

and

BEA MOULTON

Legal Services Corporation

Mineola, New York

THE FOUNDATION PRESS, INC.

1981

COPYRIGHT © 1981 By THE FOUNDATION PRESS, INC.

All rights reserved

Printed in the United States of America

Library of Congress Catalog Card Number: 81-67776

ISBN 0-88277-039-X

B. & M. Negotiation Pamph. UCB

INTRODUCTION

The following material is drawn from a larger work on lawyering skills and roles.[1] It is reorganized here to be used in a separate course on negotiation or as one piece of a broader examination of lawyering skills, whether in a clinical context or elsewhere in the law school curriculum. It could also be used to supplement materials used in substantive courses that include a focus on a negotiation-oriented practice, such as labor relations or personal injury litigation.

Our primary focus is on helping you reflect on and make sense of the skills a lawyer uses in negotiation and the related process of helping the client decide whether and on what terms to settle. Chapter One addresses the skills involved in bargaining with "adversaries"—in the formal sense of that term—and presents a framework for understanding what is involved in various stages of the negotiation process. Chapter Two, which includes most of what is a self-contained chapter on counseling in the larger work, focuses on the relationship with the client and the complex task of helping the client determine preferences and make decisions. In Chapter Three we turn to the ethical dimension of each of these areas of lawyer work.

Chapter One begins with excerpts from a variety of sources designed to encourage you to think about what is involved when a lawyer assesses a bargaining situation and becomes an active participant in it. For example, readings drawn from a commercial context and from game theory are offered as useful analogues in understanding the lawyer's tasks. Both Chapters One and Two also include short readings from fiction and journalistic accounts of actual bargaining or counseling situations. Readings from these sorts of materials are less likely to tell you how to do the task than to provide a framework for analyzing and reflecting on it. Our belief is that, although such questions are elusive, these readings offer a way of approaching them. We would suggest that in each subject area at least one class be devoted to such a general inquiry.

The introductory material in these two chapters is then followed by a more detailed analysis of the components of the task. It is best assigned piecemeal, in conjunction with a simulated performance and/or actual clinical experience. There are a number of collections of problem materials available, including two problem supplements to the longer work from which these readings are drawn, which contain a large number of exercises and several criminal and civil files.[2] Such

---

1. Bellow & Moulton, *The Lawyering Process: Materials for Clinical Instruction in Advocacy* © 1978, The Foundation Press.

2. *Id., Civil Problem Supplement* and *Criminal Problem Supplement,* © 1978, The Foundation Press.

exercises will help you develop a "feel" for the dynamics of the task involved and provide a structure for thinking about how the particular problems might be solved. The connection between reflection and action explored in such a context is central to your ability to improve and enlarge your own skills and understanding in the future.

Finally, we take up the ethical dimension of each of these tasks. Strategic choices inevitably have moral consequences and doing well may or may not involve doing good. It's our hope that you will look hard at the transcripts we've provided [3] in light of the Code of Professional Responsibility, your own experience with the task involved, and your own values and aspirations. It is well worth remembering how much of what we are becomes defined by how and what we do.

GARY BELLOW
BEA MOULTON

July, 1981

3. Videotapes of the transcripts are available from the American Bar Association's Consortium for Professional Education.

ACKNOWLEDGEMENTS

The problem with trying to list those who have helped us is the risk of omission. This work has been through many drafts and is, in a number of ways, the work of many hands. Its development parallels much of the debate, discussion, and experimentation that has accompanied the most recent efforts to introduce clinical education into the law school curriculum. It is impossible to distinguish between our involvement in that process and what we hope will be a contribution to it.

We owe a debt to scholars in a number of fields and many of our own colleagues, but first we would like to thank the people without whose help this book literally could never have been published: Donna Colletta of the Arizona State University College of Law, who typed and prepared many drafts and most of the final manuscript, and Cheryl Burg of the Harvard Law School, who also typed countless drafts. They have met our often unreasonable demands with grace, good humor and efficiency, and we would have been lost without them. They received substantial assistance from a number of others at both schools, including Carolyn Barone, Jeri Fitzgerald, Alice Fuhr, Mary O'Leary and Eileen Walker. In addition, Linda Beyer, Patricia Keairns, Fran Kendall, Iris Nissen, Virginia Stewart, Ellen Stone, and Dorothy Swanton helped out whenever they were asked, as did a number of other administrative and clerical personnel. We really are unable to name all those who assisted.

We also want particularly to thank Jeanne Kettleson, who made substantial contributions to a number of chapters, and had the temerity to teach with earlier drafts. She has consistently been a tough critic and a good friend.

As we have mentioned, we borrowed heavily from authors in a variety of fields. The list on the following pages only partially represents the debt we owe to a good many writers. Some of those whose writing we drew on gave us a considerable amount of personal help as well, including David Binder, Jeffrey Browne, John Cosier, Monroe Freedman, Charles Fried, Kenney Hegland, John Scanlan, George Shadoan, Tom Shaffer, William Simon and Andrew Watson. We also owe a debt to a number of people who actually worked on drafts or helped us work through some of the conceptual and pedagogical problems with which we struggled: Chris Argyris, Lee Bolman, Robert Condlin, John Cratsley, David Kaye, Bob Keeton, Jack Himmelstein, Michael Meltsner and Phil Schrag. Our failure to resolve these problems, of course, is our responsibility alone.

ACKNOWLEDGEMENTS

During the several years in which this work has been in progress, many teachers and lawyers—particularly those in the teaching fellow program at Harvard Law School—have taught or worked with students using these materials. Their comments and criticism have been most helpful. We want particularly to thank Mike Altman, Arthur John Anderson, David Barnhizer, Bob Bohn, Dorian Bowman, John Bowman, Clarissa Bronson, Barbara Buell, Barbara Burkett, Paul Collier, Nathan Crystal, Steve Fagan, Gene Fleming, Marty Gideonse, Dwight Golann, Jesse Goldner, Ann Greenberg, Rick Gross, Joe Harbaugh, Walter Heiser, Michelle Hermann, Rick Ireland, Rod Jones, Bill Joyner, Jeffrey Kobrick, Kenneth Kreiling, Nick Littlefield, Gary Lowenthal, Ken MacIver, Margorie McDiarmid, Kathy Mitchell, Fred Moss, Steve Morse, Steve Pepe, Mike Reiss, Dean Rivkin, David Rosenberg, Frank Samford, and Valerie Vanaman.

A number of other colleagues and friends have contributed in other ways, including Mike Brennan, Lou Brown, Hal Bruff, Edgar Cahn, Jean Cahn, Dick Carter, David Cavers, Phil Heymann, Earl Johnson, Rosabeth Kantor, Duncan Kennedy, Susan Kupfer, Marty Levine, Dorothy Nelson, Charles Nesson, Bill Pincus, Steve Rosenfeld, Frank Sander, Alan Stone, Sam Sutton, Roberto Unger and Lloyd Weinreb. In addition, throughout the years we have drawn on the experience of numerous others in legal aid and public defender practice, as well as on the insights of many other clinical teachers and students. The people in this category to whom we owe a real debt of gratitude are simply too numerous to name.

We also wish to thank Deans Willard Pedrick, Ernest Gellhorn and Alan Matheson of Arizona State and Dean Albert Sacks of Harvard; their cooperation and willingness to devote substantial resources to this project have in large part made it possible. Their support enabled us to employ a number of research assistants over the years, from whose efforts we have greatly benefitted: Frank Fanning, Mark Greenberg, Louraine Gutterman, Kathy Hillman, Virginia Richter, Nelson Rose, Layna Taylor, Glenda Ulfers, Karen Walker and especially Peter Puciloski, who kept working long after the money ran out.

Finally, we would like to thank the many authors and publishers who have given us permission to reprint copyrighted material. In addition to acknowledgements noted by special request on the first page of specific excerpts, we wish to thank the authors and publishers of the following materials:

ABA Project on Standards for Criminal Justice, Standards Relating to the Prosecution Function and the Defense Function. © 1971 by the American Bar Association. Reprinted with permission.

Benjamin, The Helping Interview, 2nd edition, 34-37, 103, 109-127. © 1974 by Houghton Mifflin Company. Used by permission.

ACKNOWLEDGEMENTS

Binder and Price, Legal Interviewing and Counseling, 147-53. © 1977. Reprinted with permission of West Publishing Company.

Bledstein, Culture of Professionalism, 87, 89-90, 91-92, 111-112. © 1976 by W. W. Norton & Co. Reprinted with permission.

Bross, Design for Decision, 34-38, 86-97, 103-116, 212-216. © 1953 by the MacMillan Company. Reprinted with permission.

Deutsch, "Conflicts: Productive and Destructive," 25 J. Social Issues, No. 1, 12-13, 23-24. © 1969 by the Society for the Psychological Study of Social Issues. Reprinted with permission of the publisher and the author.

Fisher, International Conflict for Beginners (abridged, from pages 11-72). © 1969 by Roger Fisher. Reprinted by permission of Harper & Row, Publishers, Inc.

Freedman, Lawyer's Ethics in an Adversary System, 43-49, 67-69, 71-75. © 1975 by the Bobbs-Merrill Co., Inc. Reprinted with permission. All rights reserved.

Freeman and Weihofen, Clinical Law Training, 13-15, 20-21. © 1972 by West Publishing Company. Reprinted with permission.

Freidson, Patients' Views of Medical Practice, 175-91. © 1961 by the Russell Sage Foundation. Reprinted with permission.

Fried, Medical Experimentation: Personal Integrity and Social Policy, 71, 73-75, 77, 101-03. © 1974 by Elsevier-North Holland Publishing Company. Reprinted with permission.

Goffman, Strategic Interaction, pp. 85, 89, 93-94, 99-105, 110-113. © 1969. Reprinted with permission of the University of Pennsylvania Press.

Green, The Other Government, 268-69, 272-89. © 1975 by Ralph Nader. Reprinted by permission of Grossman Publishers.

Hermann, Better Settlements Through Leverage, pp. 125-129, 133-135, 250-251. © 1965. Reprinted with permission of Lawyers Co-Operative Publishing Company.

Ilich, The Art and Skill of Successful Negotiation, 141-45. © 1973 by Prentice-Hall, Inc. Reprinted with permission of Prentice-Hall, Inc., Englewood Cliffs, New Jersey.

Johnson, Contemporary Social Psychology, 51-52, 55-58. © 1973. Reprinted with permission of J. B. Lippincott Company.

Karrass, The Negotiating Game, 56, 59-64, 66, 126-134, 141-145. © 1970 by Chester L. Karrass. Reprinted by permission of Thomas Y. Crowell Company, Inc.

ACKNOWLEDGEMENTS

Keeton, Trial Tactics and Methods, 2–3, 4, 42–44, 79–80, 303–05, 307–09, 311–17, 326–27. © 1973. Reprinted with permission of Little, Brown & Company and the author.

Latham, "Closing in on Agnew: The Prosecutor's Story," New York Magazine, 62 et seq., November 26, 1973. © 1973 by N.Y.M. Corporations. Reprinted with permission.

Lindblom, "The Science of Muddling Through," The Public Administration Review, 79, 80–87. © 1959. Reprinted with permission.

Matthews, "Negotiation: A Pedagogical Challenge," 6 Journal of Legal Education 94–96. © 1954. Reprinted with permission of the author and the Journal of Legal Education.

Muir, Police: Street Corner Politicians, 3–4, 44–45, 271–72. © 1977 by the University of Chicago. All rights reserved. Published 1977. Reprinted with permission of the University of Chicago Press and the author.

Nierenberg, Fundamentals of Negotiating, 133–37, 184–92. © 1973, 1971, 1968 by Gerard I. Nierenberg. Reprinted by permission of Hawthorn Books, Inc. All rights reserved.

Nizer, The Implosion Conspiracy, 195–98, 199–200. © 1973 by Doubleday & Company, Inc. Reprinted with permission.

Pierson, The Defense Attorney and Basic Defense Tactics, 228, 233–34, 247–48, 251–52. © 1956 by the Bobbs-Merrill Company, Inc. Reprinted by permission of the Michie Company.

Pruitt, "Indirect Communication and the Search for Agreement in Negotiation," 1 J.App. Social Psych. 205–11, 233–37. © 1971 by the Scripta Publishing Company. Reprinted with permission.

Rapoport, Strategy and Conscience, 19–21, 7–11. © 1964 by Anatol Rapoport. Reprinted by permission of Harper & Row Publishers.

Rosenthal, Lawyer and Client: Who's in Charge?, 7–10, 18–20, 169–70. © 1974 by Russell Sage Foundation, New York. Reprinted by permission.

Rubin, "A Causerie on Lawyers' Ethics in Negotiation," 35 Louisiana Law Review 577, 580–93. © 1975. Reprinted with permission of Louisiana Law Review.

Schelling, "An Essay on Bargaining," 46 Amer.Econ.Rev. 28, 287–89, 290–97, 299–301. © 1956. Reprinted in the Strategy of Conflict by Thomas Schelling. Reprinted with permission of the author and American Economic Association.

Sindell, Let's Talk Settlement, 382–85, 308. © 1963 by Matthew Bender. © 1968 by Joseph and David Sindell.

Solzhenitsyn, The Cancer Ward, 75–80. Translated by Rebecca Frank. Translation © 1968 by the Dial Press, Inc. Reprinted with permission of the Dial Press.

Statsky, Introduction to Paralegalism, 595, 598–600, 602–607. © 1974. Reprinted with permission of West Publishing Company.

Taylor, "Decision-Making and Problem-Solving," in Handbook of Organizations, 52–54, 56–58. © 1965. Reprinted by permission.

Traver, Anatomy of a Murder, 32, 35. © 1958. Reprinted with permission of St. Martin's Press.

Walton and McKersie, A Behavioral Theory of Labor Negotiations, 64–66, 93–95, 115–116. © 1965 by McGraw-Hill, Inc. Reprinted with permission of McGraw-Hill Book Company.

Watson, "The Lawyer as Counselor," 5 Journal of Family Law, 7, 9–12. © 1965. Reprinted with permission of the University of Louisville School of Law.

Weihofen, Legal Writing Style, 121–28. © 1961. Reprinted with permission of West Publishing Company.

Werchick, Settling the Case for Plaintiff, 4 American Jurisprudence, 293, 319–322, 363–365, 378. © 1966. Reprinted by permission of the copyright owner, Jurisprudence Publishers, Inc.

*

SUMMARY OF CONTENTS

*

TABLE OF CONTENTS

THE LAWYERING PROCESS:

NEGOTIATION

*

Chapter One

DEALING WITH ADVERSARIES

___

SECTION ONE. PRELIMINARY PERSPECTIVES

___

A. IMAGES AND FRAGMENTS

___

LATHAM, CLOSING IN ON AGNEW: THE
PROSECUTOR'S STORY

NEW YORK MAGAZINE (1973).

In March of 1972, George Beall had lunch with Robert Browne, the chief of the intelligence division of the Internal Revenue Service in Maryland .   .   .   at the Charcoal Hearth restaurant in Hopkins Plaza. Beall and Browne had had close professional relations for some time.

 Beall asked, more or less, where his office should go from here. Browne said that over the years I.R.S. had had many anonymous complaints about corruption in Baltimore County (a suburban jurisdiction which adjoins but does not include the city of Baltimore). Beall said that he, too, had heard rumors of payoffs and kickbacks. The two men decided to slice into Baltimore County and see what was there. . . .

    .   .   . [In] October, Robert Browne came up to George Beall's office and told him that .   .   .   [h]is agents had discovered that engineering and architectural firms which dealt with Baltimore County were generating large sums of cash. And cash goes with corruption the way needles go with narcotics.

George Beall says, "On that day the investigation shifted into second gear." The date was October 10, 1972. One year later, to the day, Spiro T. Agnew would cop a plea. . . .

Beall asked two young assistant attorneys, named Barney Skolnik and Tim Baker, to work on the investigation [and later added Ron Liebman, who had joined the U. S. Attorney's office in August] . . . .

* * *

With the help of the others, Tim Baker prepared a wave of long, complicated, detailed subpoenas. They were issued on January 4, 1973, and were returnable five days later. Twenty-six went to engineering and architectural firms. Another went to Baltimore County

itself, requesting county records for the years 1969, 1970, and 1971.
.   .   .   The documents [from the county alone] filled 120 filing
cabinets.   .   .   .

*   *   *

On February 9, only nineteen days after he had been sworn in for
a second term as the vice president of the United States, Spiro Agnew
made a move which   .   .   .   [created suspicions about his involvement in the case]   .   .   .   Agnew called Richard Kleindienst, who
was then attorney general, and told him that he was "concerned" and
"very nervous" about the investigation of corruption in Baltimore
County.   Kleindienst in turn called Beall and told him of the vice
president's discomfort.   Beall assured Kleindienst that Agnew was
not a target of the Baltimore County investigation.

The vice president's concern seems to have made its deepest impression on Tim Baker.   He says, "I think of myself as a Bobby Kennedy Democrat.   But I respected Agnew the way I respect Goldwater.
He did not have that chameleon quality like Nixon."   However, Agnew's call to Kleindienst changed his "whole attitude" toward the vice
president.   He says, "That persuaded me there must have been something."

Baker even considered attempting to bring obstruction-of-justice
charges against the vice president.   The others in his office convinced
him, however, that it was not a winnable case.   From that point on
.   .   .   Baker told the other prosecutors that eventually they were
going to find out what Agnew had done to be so nervous about.   His
partners kidded him about being so suspicious of a vice president.

*   *   *

[The investigation began to focus on] potential defendants.   The
prosecutors would say something like: "Your client is in a lot of
trouble.   But if he cooperates, he will end up substantially better off
than he would otherwise."

*   *   *

The prosecutors always emphasized that the first people to make
deals would get the best deals.   The corollary to this was that there
would come a time when no deals would be made at all.   The prosecutors liked to talk in metaphors.   When they used these metaphors on
lawyers, they smiled.   When they used them on prospective defendants, they didn't.

*   *   *

In the beginning, Skolnik, Baker, and Liebman would talk to
lawyers as a team.   Skolnik was teaching the junior prosecutors how
it was done.   .   .   .

.   .   .   From the defense side of the room, these two inexperienced prosecutors must have seemed almost fuzzy-checked.   To men
who were accustomed to measuring other men by how much money

they made, these underpaid children must have seemed about as threatening as office boys. But then these rich men would go home and they would not be able to get to sleep.

* * *

In early May, Steve Sachs [a lawyer representing potential defendant William Fornoff] returned to the federal courthouse. . . .

Sachs said something like: "Look, I know you've got A, B, and C; what else do you have?" Actually, A, B, and C were about all the prosecutors did have, but Skolnik was not about to confess as much to Sachs. Fornoff was therefore faced with what the prosecutors call "the black box phenomenon." The black box was the case against him and he did not know what was in it. Skolnik knew that it would be much harder to resist the pressure of unknown evidence, even if it were weak, than known evidence, even if it were strong. It was psychological warfare. It worked.

Skolnik gave Sachs a letter for his client to sign. The letter said that the client would come in, tell what he knew, supply corroborating documents, submit to cross examination, and that then and only then would the government make him an offer. Fornoff signed the letter. Skolnik had long known that it cut down on the chances for perjury if the defense lawyer told the client's story before the client himself told it, so Sachs told Fornoff's story for him, and then Fornoff came in and told it himself. The story implicated not only County Executive Dale Anderson, but also two engineering-firm executives named Lester Matz and Jerome Wolff.

* * *

One June 4, 1973, William Fornoff appeared before a judge and pleaded guilty to "impeding the enforcement" of federal tax laws by making cash deliveries to a "public official." It was obvious that Fornoff had copped a plea and was cooperating with the government. A lot of people had reason to be worried. Baltimore County Executive Dale Anderson had reason to fear that Fornoff had sold him to the prosecutors. Moreover, Lester Matz and Jerome Wolff had reason to fear that they had been sold also. They already knew what they would have to do if they did not want to go to jail for a long, long time.

* * *

Although the case against Agnew was still excruciatingly shaky, George Beall decided that he had better tell Washington about it. As soon as Elliot Richardson was sworn in as the new attorney general, Beall called his office and asked for an appointment.

* * *

[In his June 12 meeting with Richardson, Beall summarized the Baltimore County probe and told the attorney general about Agnew's repeatedly expressed concern about the investigation.] Beall added, somewhat cryptically, that his office had just received its first hint that Agnew had more to worry about than unfair publicity. The U. S. attorney chose to soft-pedal the Agnew connection, presenting it in the context of rumor and gossip. Richardson did not seem unduly concerned. After all, people were always making accusations against politicians. The attorney general said to keep in touch.

Beall returned to Baltimore where the next week his team of prosecutors began interviewing Lester Matz personally. The case against the vice president began to firm up. Matz, who was president of Matz, Childs, and Associates, told the prosecutors that his company had kicked back 5 per cent on engineering jobs and 2.5 per cent on surveying jobs to Agnew when he was county executive. When Agnew moved on to the governor's mansion, Matz said he had once delivered $20,000 to Agnew in a Manila envelope. When Agnew moved on to Washington, Matz said he had visited the vice president in the Executive Office Building and handed him $10,000 in an envelope. Matz said that he had returned home shaken because he had just paid off the vice president of the United States. Matz also gave the prosecutors corroborating documents—desk calendars, governor's agendas.

* * *

The second man to come aboard the Agnew boat was Jerome Wolff. His lawyer had approached the Baltimore prosecutors at about the same time Matz's attorney had—right after Fornoff copped a plea. But it had taken longer to negotiate a deal with Wolff than it had with Matz. . . . Wolff was president of Greiner Environmental Systems. He had also been Governor Agnew's road commissioner and had decided which firms would receive consulting contracts from the state. Wolff said that another man, I. H. (Bud) Hammerman II, then arranged payments from the favored companies. Wolff said the money was split three ways: 25 per cent for him, 25 per cent for Hammerman, and 50 per cent for Agnew.

After the prosecutors had listened to Wolff, Beall once again called the attorney general's office. . . . An appointment was scheduled for July 11. . . .

* * *

Richardson and the prosecutors talked about how they would proceed with the investigation in such a way as to minimize the danger that it would leak to the press. They developed an ingenious plan: the Baltimore prosecutors would henceforth concentrate their efforts on only those men who they were reasonably certain were guilty of involvement in the payoff network. There would be no fishing expeditions. Their reasoning was that guilty men were less likely to run to reporters than were innocent men.

* * *

In Baltimore the prosecutors finally persuaded I. H. (Bud) Hammerman to cooperate. When he finally started talking, it took him ten hours spread over two days to tell his story. Hammerman confirmed what Wolff had said about the payoffs which were split with Agnew 25–25–50. He said that he had had a code worked out whereby Agnew would call him and ask how many "papers" the investor had for him. Each "paper" meant $1,000 in cash. Hammerman was crucial to the investigation in several ways. He was crucial because of the evidence he provided against Agnew. He was also crucial because of Agnew's perception of who his friends were. When the vice president learned that Hammerman was cooperating with the prosecutors, he seemed to cave in psychologically.

*   *   *

Presidential Attorney Fred Buzhardt, acting as a go-between, called Richardson to say that Agnew's lawyers wanted to discuss a deal. The prosecutors were suspicious. They had not expected plea-bargaining to begin so early.

On September 12, Beall drove to Washington where he sat down with Richardson, Petersen, and three members of Agnew's legal team. The same group reconvened the next day. The two sides sized each other up.

The following Saturday, the Baltimore prosecutors returned to Washington for an all-day meeting in the attorney general's office. They proceeded to agree upon a dream deal. This would include full disclosure in writing of the prosecutors' evidence against Agnew, an oral confession in court by Agnew that he had accepted bribes, and a jail term for the vice president.

Once they had determined what they would ask for, they proceeded to attempt to agree upon priorities: what they would ask for first, second, third. This is where voices were raised. Richardson had always encouraged everyone to express his views, and everyone did.

Tim Baker's number one priority was a jail term for the vice president. The young prosecutor said that he wanted people to have confidence in their institutions, and he thought that required putting Spiro Agnew behind bars. He said that it "offended" him that the vice president had broken the law and "equal justice" required that he be locked up.

Barney Skolnik's first priority was to force the vice president to admit in open court that he had committed serious crimes. He was worried that, unless Agnew did make such a confession, many people would believe that he was at most a technical violator who had been unfairly treated by the government for improper reasons.

George Beall and Ron Liebman more or less agreed with Skolnik.

Elliot Richardson's number one priority was simple: resignation. He had said all summer that if Agnew were simply confronted with the evidence he would resign. But he had discovered that the vice president was not that kind of man. Now Richardson was willing to bargain to rid the country of the threat that this suspected felon might be thrust into the Presidency.

The following week, the plea-bargaining began in earnest with Agnew's attorneys. The Baltimore prosecutors returned to Washington. Negotiations generally followed this model: the ten-man Agnew debating society would meet in the attorney general's conference room, where each would argue for his own priorities. Then Richardson, Petersen, and Beall would go into the next room and meet with Agnew's lawyers.

The first round of plea-bargaining broke down, not over a jail term, as widely reported, but over how much wrongdoing Agnew would be willing to admit orally in court. This did not mean, however, that the Justice Department and Agnew's attorney agreed on what to do about jail. Rather, an impasse was reached before jail was put on the table for serious discussion.

These negotiations ended abruptly on Saturday, September 22, when *The Washington Post* ran a banner story which revealed that plea-bargaining was under way.

. . . [In a speech in Los Angeles,] the vice president said, "I will not resign if indicted. I will not resign if indicted," he seemed to be speaking directly to Richardson.

[He] accused the prosecution in general and Henry Petersen in particular of trying him in the press. . . . [One week later, on September 29, his attorney again made an overture concerning a plea.]

* * *

. . . [On] Sunday, October 7, the Baltimore prosecutors drove back to Washington for another meeting at the Justice Department. It was at this meeting that the Baltimore visitors first realized that a deal was probably going to be made with which they would not agree. Richardson told them that he was prepared to cave in on what Agnew would have to admit in open court. The attorney general also suggested that the Justice Department might make no recommendation either for or against jail. They would leave it up to the judge.

* * *

Barney Skolnik's was the loudest voice raised against the attorney general's softening position. Skolnik insisted that the vice president was "blackmailing" them and holding the country "hostage." The young prosecutor argued that no matter what Agnew said, he would have no choice but to resign if he were indicted.

The other Baltimore prosecutors generally agreed with Skolnik. They characterized Agnew's offer to resign as his "$100-chip," but they felt they could devalue that chip to the point of worthlessness by simply indicting him. They wanted to call his bluff.

* * *

Richardson listened . . . but did not alter his previously stated position. The attorney general even went so far as to add that he "might have to bite the bullet" on the issue of recommending no jail.

Skolnik stood up, coat off, hands on hips, and reviewed the "deal" in pejorative terms. The other Baltimore prosecutors seemed to feel as he did. They asked if Richardson would be willing to carry his deal into court personally and speak in the first person when explaining the deal to the judge. The attorney general at first resisted. For a while there seemed to be a real possibility that the Baltimore team could mutiny; they might refuse to appear in court and might even go so far as to take their case to the press.

Richardson said that he could understand why the prosecutors might not agree with certain components of the deal. He said they should not feel that they *had* to take it into court. He said that if they felt they had to dissociate themselves from the deal publicly, he would never hold it against them. Their careers would not suffer.

Richardson concluded by saying: "I did not come to the Justice Department with any idea that I was going to make friends." He told them that he expected to "get heat from both sides," from those who thought he had been too hard on Agnew and those who thought he had been too lenient. He added that he was also "prepared to take heat from you people."

The meeting ended.

* * *

Petersen, Beall, and Skolnik were sent to the Old Colony Motor Lodge in Alexandria to meet with Judge Walter Hoffman and Agnew's three lawyers. Once the Justice Department team said that Agnew would only have to make minimal admissions in court, jail quickly became the fulcrum of the negotiations. (Contrary to widely published reports, the written summary of the evidence was never sternly opposed by Agnew's attorneys.) The prosecutors said that the Justice Department would make no recommendation for or against jail. Agnew's defense team then turned to Judge Hoffman and asked him if he would be willing to promise no jail. The judge, who is not dumb, realized that if he promised no jail on his own, then he would be the one who would be criticized. Judge Hoffman therefore suggested somewhat ambiguously that he would be willing to let Agnew off without imprisonment only if the Justice Department so recommended. It quickly became apparent that there would be no deal made that day.

On Tuesday, October 9, Beall and Skolnik once again returned to Washington. Baker and Liebman stayed behind to take statements from Jerome Wolff and Lester Matz. There was another meeting in the attorney general's office. Emotions were high. Voices were raised.   Richardson said that his highest priority was getting Agnew out of office.   Skolnik yelled words like "blackmail."   People were shouting at each other about jail.   At this meeting Richardson agreed that he would be willing to appear in court and speak in the first person because he was the only one who believed in all of the provisions of the package.

This time, Richardson accompanied Petersen, Beall, and Skolnik when they went to meet the other side and the judge.   This meeting was held in the deputy attorney general's office at the Justice Department.   The attorney general told Judge Hoffman that he was not quite clear as to what the court's position was.   The judge said that unless the two sides could come to an agreement on punishment, he would not tell them what the sentence would be until they were all in the courtroom and the whole world was watching.   He hinted, however, that he would send Agnew to jail.   Agnew's lawyers reiterated that there would be no deal unless they could be promised in advance that their client would not be locked up.

Richardson said: "In that case I will recommend no jail."

* * *

Beall and Skolnik raced back to Baltimore, arriving at about 8 p. m.   The prosecutors launched into their night's work: writing what turned out to be a 40-page statement of the evidence against the vice president, which would be made a part of the record of the case. They took the statements which Baker and Liebman had been preparing and turned them into a third-person narrative.   They used scissors and a lot of tape to weave the four stories told by the four witnesses into one continuous drama of payoffs and corruption.

That night the prosecutors' wing took on the air of a newspaper city room.   They were working against a deadline.   The judge had told them that they had to deliver their statement of the evidence to Agnew's attorneys by eight o'clock the next morning.   Four secretaries worked all night with the prosecutors retyping the pasted-up drafts.   Then these freshly typed drafts were edited, rewritten, and retyped.   The statement went through about five drafts that night.

Richardson and Petersen arrived in the Baltimore courthouse at 1:30 a. m. and went to Beall's office to read the drafts as they came out of the typewriters.

At 4 or 5 a. m.—an hour suited to precipitate action—the young prosecutors marched into Beall's office and confronted Richardson. They asked him to include in his press-conference statement one sentence which would say that they had not concurred in the deal he had made.   Richardson utterly disarmed them by agreeing immediately.

At 7:15 a. m., the last page came off the typewriter.   They took time only to proofread about two-thirds of it.   Then they handed the statement of evidence to the U. S. marshals who were standing by.

. . . The marshals delivered the 40-page statement to Agnew's attorneys at 8:05 a. m., five minutes late.

The attorneys had to sign a letter before they were given the prosecutors' manuscript. The letter was a detail upon which Skolnik had insisted, because he still did not entirely trust the vice president or his men. At best he feared that Agnew's attorneys might attempt to edit the evidence. So the letter said that they were being given the 40 pages only to verify that they were an expanded version of a seven-page outline which they had already seen. At worst, he feared that the whole thing was a ruse to trick the prosecution into handing over its case to the defense well in advance of any trial. So the letter said that Agnew's lawyers would not back out of the deal at the last minute.

The Baltimore prosecutors arrived at their homes about the same time their typed pages were arriving in Washington, but none of them could go to sleep.

The prosecutors reassembled at the courthouse later that morning, and at 2 p. m. sharp they trooped upstairs to the courtroom. . . .

On cue, Spiro T. Agnew, who minutes before had resigned as the vice president of the United States, walked into the courtroom. For the first time, the prosecutors were sure that the deal was actually going to come off.

Ron Liebman stared at Agnew. The two of them were alumni of the same high school, Forest Park in Baltimore. Eleven months earlier, the young prosecutor had voted for Agnew. Now he had destroyed him. But this was the first time he had ever seen him.

THE TALE OF BRER RABBIT *

Brer Rabbit had got himself caught by Brer Fox and was well on his way to becoming evening dinner. Brer Rabbit was in a great deal of deep trouble. And all because he'd tried to win a fight with a tar baby.

There didn't seem much he could do about this one but he didn't seem concerned at all at being the Fox's dinner. He just said,

"Brer Fox—I don't mind if you eat me. But, oh, whatever you do—don't throw me in that briar patch."

Now Brer Fox was surely looking forward to eating his old enemy but he was curiouser and curiouser about Brer Rabbit's sweating and crying about being thrown into the briar patch.

And the more he questioned it the more Brer Rabbit wailed about how much he hated and feared that briar patch.

* This example of a very old negotiating tale was suggested by James White and Harry Edwards.

Pretty soon it did seem that Brer Rabbit would rather be eaten than be set among those briars.

I guess you know the rest.

———

2 SIDES SIT SILENTLY 4½ HOURS AT KOREAN TRUCE MEETING *

Panmunjom, Korea—(UPI)—The American general and the North Korean general glared at each other across the table and the only sound was the wind howling across the barren hills outside their hut.

Maj. Gen. James B. Knapp, negotiator for the United Nations Command (UNC), was waiting for Maj. Gen. Ri Choonsun of the Democratic People's Republic of North Korea to propose a recess.

They sat there, arms folded, for 4½ hours. Not a word. Finally, Gen. Ri got up, walked out and drove away.

It was the 289th meeting of the Korean Military Armistice Commission at the truce village of Panmunjom and set a record as the longest such meeting since the Korean War ended July 27, 1953.

The generals had been there 11 hours and 35 minutes. Neither ate or went to the toilet in all that time. Delegates to such meetings may leave the room only with a formal adjournment proposal.

Whichever side proposes a meeting usually proposes a recess. North Korea called yesterday's session. Ri never did propose a recess.

"In view of North Korea's rude and unwarranted conduct," Knapp said, "I consider this meeting to be terminated."

Before the 4½ hours of silence, Knapp called on North Korea to start a four-step de-escalation to ease tension along the Korean border. He promised reciprocation with a similar UNC program.

Knapp asked that North Korea:

—Remove from the North Korean part of the Demilitarized Zone all illegal weapons and unauthorized personnel.

—Immediately quit all attacks against South Korean and UNC forces.

—Reduce what Knapp said was the excessive size of North Korea's armed forces.

—Discontinue "polemic, bellicose, war-mongering public statements."

———

* *Silent Hostility at Panmunjom* (reprinted from the EVENING BULLETIN, Philadelphia, April 11, 1969, p. 10. By permission of UPI, New York, N. Y.).

NOTE

None of these bargaining situations involves what might be thought of as the typical negotiation in law practice. Few of us will be involved in cases as public or as idiosyncratic as the Panmunjom deliberations or the Agnew case. Nor will our goals and strategies often be as obvious to us—and as obscure to our opponents—as they were to Brer Rabbit. Nevertheless, the kind of choices that had to be made by the negotiators in these situations are invariably part of the bargaining process. Whether a lawyer's routine involves putting together complicated business transactions, settling personal injury claims, or engaging in repetitious plea bargaining, similar skills are required and similar influences are at work. What we want you to focus on here is your own understanding of this complex process.

First, ask yourself what is actually happening when parties negotiate with each other. What are the negotiators doing and thinking in each of the above cases? What are the sources of agreement on which they rely? Consider, for example, the function and significance of (i) the issues involved; (ii) the prior relationship between the bargainers; (iii) time and other constraints; (iv) the interests of third parties; (v) threats and promises; (vi) the available modes of communication; (vii) personal attributes. What will you make of these elements in your own work?

To negotiate effectively you will need, as in other tasks, a conceptual map of what takes place in the process. Yet lawyers bargain in many situations under many circumstances. What can be said about negotiation in general terms? Robert Mathews offers the following overview:

> Negotiation may be tentatively described . . . as a process of adjustment of existing differences, with a view to the establishment of a mutually more desirable legal relation by means of barter and compromise of legal rights and duties and of economic, psychological, social and other interests. It is accomplished consensually as contrasted with force of law. It may be achieved through the setting up of (1) a set of legal relations where none existed between the parties before (thus creating a primary relationship) or (2) a set of legal relations in substitution for and modification of a set already existing between the same parties (a secondary relationship). The first type exists in the area of contract law, is characteristically prospective; it is in fact 'consensual legislation' in that it establishes a set of standards for future regulation of the parties. The second type may exist in many areas of law—tort, contract or status—and is characteristically retrospective in that it readjusts in the light of current interests a set of legal rights and duties that are already in existence. It is in fact, then, 'consensual adjudication.'
>
> Put more simply, two parties who do not currently have a contract with each other may negotiate one. Its terms thereafter govern them in a fashion that may well be described as 'legislation by consent.'

While these terms are still operative these parties may become involved in a dispute as to their meaning or application. They resolve this dispute by negotiation; decide the meaning is X rather than Y. This is a determination as to what rights and duties the contract had previously established; it is 'adjudication by consent,' without recourse to the power of government.

In each of these cases the specie of trade is varied. Rights are surrendered or duties assumed for economic or psychological advantage. Considerations that relate to the environment of both parties or that are peculiar to the desires, needs, or disabilities or weaknesses of each separately, are secretly or openly weighed and exchanged. Whether the new relationship is primary in the sense of a new contract, or secondary in the sense of a re-expression or alteration of an old one, the culmination of the process ultimately represents an over-all bettering of position for each of the parties—a bettering, that is, within the framework of the strength or weakness of his bargaining capacity. Were this not so, the differences could never have been negotiated to agreement. No contract would have been entered into, or the dispute as to its terms would have been left to the force of law through litigation.

* * *

[To this process the parties bring their own . . . skills and insights. These relate to]: (1) positive advance of position; (2) onslaughts on opponent's position; (3) defensive protection of one's own position; and (4) behavior, manner, and command of data.

It may be said that illustratively an advance of position is furthered by such techniques as the logic of supporting data and presentation of argument; guidance of opponent to suggestion of concessions; excessive demands adequate for maneuver but within the area of plausibility; persuasion to accept abstract principles broad enough to comprise concrete demands; pressure through intimated or conjectured risk of loss through withdrawal of benefits, infliction of damage, appeal to public opinion, and reopening of issues tentatively accepted.

Illustrations of onslaughts upon opponent's position may relate to the weakening of either his bargaining power or his dialectical capacity. The former may be accomplished by indication of disabilities and predicaments and the latter by the use of diversionary devices such as misplaced emphasis, false issues, and false security; these latter may be attempted by deliberately induced confusion, loss of control through irritation, and the important factor of surprise.

There are certain obvious defensive measures, including the alternatives of rigid intransigence or resilient absorption or 'defense in depth,' plus mobility in adjustment to attack and the capacity to accomplish a shift to the offense.

The effectiveness of the use of each of these tactics is dependent upon three factors, each of which underlies and qualifies all negotiating skills. One is personal behavior in terms of poise, assurance, and mobility, all conveyed (or not) by voice and manner. Another is the capacity to evaluate the strength and weakness of the two positions, and to determine which interests may be wisely surrendered in return for comparable concessions by one's opponent. The third inheres in the subject matter rather than in the person. It concerns those major limitations which circumscribe the position of each negotiator—the degree of his client's desire or need (his economic, psychological or social position), the resultant burden of persuasion, and the factual or legal limitations within which free maneuver is possible. Both of these latter limitations are patently more restrictive in what has been referred to as an adjudicative determination than in a legislative one.[1]

There are, of course, many pitfalls in trying to reduce any complex subject to a limited number of propositions. For example, it may be true that a negotiator must be able "to evaluate the strengths and weaknesses of the two positions," but consider how you will go about actually accomplishing this complicated bargaining task. There are important features of every bargaining situation which circumscribe options, but distinguishing the given from the changeable is no simple matter. Nevertheless, you may find it surprisingly useful to compare Mathew's description to your own notions of what seems to be critical in this process.

Second, there is the ethical dimension of the process. Much that is asked of you in bargaining will surely give you pause, if you persist in trying to be both a good person and a good lawyer. After all, Brer Rabbit's strategy involved convincing Brer Fox of something that was not true—*i. e.,* that Brer Rabbit preferred being eaten to being thrown in the briar patch. Initial advantage and superior strength clearly favored Brer Fox, but he surely was "taken advantage of." What if the stakes aren't so high, or there is nothing to reduce disparities in skill and experience? Are there any limits on our license to press for the most advantageous settlement we can get in a bargaining situation? Lawyers negotiate without the formal protections of trial or the commitments which foster trust in other relationships. What keeps the process from becoming a free-for-all in which the parties are limited only by what they can get away with? In the Agnew case, for example, one member of the prosecution team insisted that the vice-president's attorneys sign a letter agreeing not to "back out of the deal" before they were given a summary of the evidence against their client. The prosecutors also refused to disclose the evidence they had against various defendants until those defendants had agreed to cooperate. How fair, proper and necessary did this strategy seem to you?

1. Mathews, *Negotiation: A Pedagogical Challenge,* 6 J.LEG.ED. 94–96 (1953). For readings on negotiation generally see SOCIAL CONFLICT: READINGS IN RULE STRUCTURES AND CONFLICT RELATIONSHIPS (P. Brickman ed. 1974); J. Rubin & B. Brown, THE SOCIAL PSYCHOLOGY OF BARGAINING AND NEGOTIATION (1975); CONFLICT RESOLUTION: CONTRIBUTIONS OF THE BEHAVIORAL SCIENCES (C. Smith ed. 1971). For discussion of negotiation in the legal context see H. Baer & A. Broder, HOW TO PREPARE AND NEGOTIATE CASES FOR SETTLEMENT (1967); H. Edwards & J. White, THE LAWYER AS A NEGOTIATOR (1977); J. Illich, THE ART AND SKILL OF SUCCESSFUL NEGOTIATION (1973); G. Nierenberg, FUNDAMENTALS OF NEGOTIATION (1973).

Some of you will insist that you want to avoid being manipulative as a negotiator, but think about what this means. Will you refuse to take into account the needs and attitudes of opposing counsel, or act in reference to them as you try to prevent initial disagreement from hardening into conflict? Will you be entirely open (*e. g.*, "I think you'd be a fool if you didn't take advantage of me on this . . .") because to do otherwise would be "calculating?" Some of you will have these feelings about manipulation, others will not. But all of you, if you aspire to being ethical, will face difficulties in matching your ethics to subtle distinctions in your behavior in this complex task.

Finally, there are the emotional aspects of the negotiating experience. What feelings and attitudes enable someone to remain silent in a face-to-face encounter for over four hours, or to apply the kind of incremental pressure which was exerted by the prosecutors in the Agnew case? What is the emotional legacy of such a controlled posture toward either oneself or others?

All of you have engaged in bargaining in which deception or even coercion has played a part. In your younger years, you undoubtedly persuaded parents to let you do some things they thought were ill-advised. And you have surely talked your way into opportunities or out of trouble throughout your school experience. In all these situations you used skill and knowledge of people. What sort of feelings about bargaining emerged in the process?

This question has two aspects. First, here, as elsewhere, success breeds success. Negotiators with high aspirations—with confidence about their probable success—work harder, are less satisfied with results, and generally get higher outcomes, even when they are less skilled than their opponents.[2] Conversely, the experience of failure, over time, becomes a self-fulfilling prophecy which itself defines the negotiator's initial expectations and satisfaction with lower results.[3] You might give some thought to your own experiences with these dynamics.

Second, bargaining is inevitably an interpersonal process. The kind of person you are obviously affects the kind of bargainer you will be. Christie and Geis offer the following observations about this relationship:

> We asked ourselves what abstract characteristics must someone who is effective in controlling others have? What kind of person should he be?
>
> The following characteristics struck us as being important:
>
> 1. *A relative lack of affect in interpersonal relationships.* In general . . . success in getting others to do what one wishes

---

2. *See generally* the studies summarized in C. Karrass, THE NEGOTIATING GAME 41–54 (1970).

3. *Id.* at 48–50.

them to do [is.] enhanced by viewing them as objects to be manipulated rather than as individuals with whom one has empathy. The greater the emotional involvement with others, the greater is the likelihood of identifying with their point of view. Once empathy occurs, it becomes more difficult to use psychological leverage to influence others to do things they may not want to do.

2. *A lack of concern with conventional morality.* Conventional morality is difficult to define, but most people think lying, cheating, and other forms of deceit are, although common, reprehensible. Whether manipulators are amoral or immoral . . . probably concerns them less than those who are manipulated . . . those who manipulate have an utilitarian rather than a moral view of their interactions with others.

3. *A lack of gross psychopathology.* The manipulator . . . takes an instrumentalist or rational view of others. Such a person may make errors in evaluating other individuals and the situation if his emotional needs seriously distorted his perceptions. Presumably, most neurotics and psychotics show deficiencies in reality testing and, by and large, fail in crucial ways in relating to others. Note that we are not suggesting that manipulators are the epitome of mental health; we are proposing that their contact with at least the more objective aspects of reality would have to be, almost by definition, within the normal range.

4. *Low ideological commitment.* The essence of successful manipulation is a focus upon getting things done rather than a focus upon long-range ideological goals. Although manipulators might be found in organizations of diverse ideologies, they [are] more involved in tactics for achieving possible ends than in an inflexible striving for an ultimate idealistic goal.[4]

How plausible is the view that there is a significant correlation between personality and negotiating outcomes? The studies that exist *suggest* (although they certainly don't establish) that the characteristics identified by Christie and Geis are associated with capacities common among effective negotiators. Do you possess these traits? What would it mean to you to have or develop such attitudes?

Related to all of these concerns is the problem of dealing realistically with power. In each of the excerpts set out earlier the bargainers had to effectively use and resist influence. Many of you will not handle this experience well. Some of you will misuse the leverage available to you. Others will be less able to resist pressure than would be expected from the objective circumstances.

There are many explanations for these variations. They may stem from untested assumptions about your adversary, or from discomfort with risk and contingency. The explanations are as extensive

4. R. Christie & F. Geis, STUDIES IN MACHIAVELLIANISM 3–4 (1970). For a consideration of other traits and variables, see V. Rubin & B. Brown, THE SOCIAL PSYCHOLOGY OF BARGAINING AND NEGOTIATION 157–96 (1975).

as human motivation itself. But whatever the source of such reactions, surely it will help to be in touch with your feelings in this situation as in others—to recognize that the emotions of anger, fear, or distrust that can well up in a negotiation cannot be ignored or denied.[5] If the feelings you experience in this task are different from what you expect or desire, you need to ask why. Hopefully, the following speculation on the process will help.

B. AN ORIENTING MODEL: NEGOTIATION AS EXCHANGE

Once again we find it useful to turn to a model—a set of simplifying assumptions to help you better understand an area of lawyer work. Bargaining is, essentially, a problem of exchange—of guiding the mixed motives of cooperation and competition toward agreement. This simple statement, however, should not obscure the complexities involved. Exchanges of desired "goods" are inevitably complicated by the exchanges of information that accompany them. What follows is one provocative description of the several levels of this process.

KARRASS, THE NEGOTIATING GAME

66, 127–34, 141–45, 56, 59–63 (1970).

[All negotiating can be thought of in terms of five bargaining subprocesses]:

Share bargaining. The process by which opponents share or ration the settlement range between themselves. If one gets more, the other gets less.

Problem-solving. The process by which both parties work together to solve each other's problems. In this process both gain at the same time.

Attitudinal bargaining. The process by which a mutually workable attitudinal relationship is developed to facilite negotiation.

In-group bargaining. The process by which a negotiator bargains with members of his own team and decision-making group to derive workable organizational objectives.

Personal bargaining. The process by which a negotiator makes a behavioral choice involving conflicting personal needs and goals.

[Each of these deserves some explanation.]

* * *

5. C. Malmquist, *Transference Phenomena Within the Negotiation Process* (1966) reprinted in H. Edwards & J. White, THE LAWYER AS A NE- GOTIATOR 165–70 (1977). *See also* THE STRUCTURE OF CONFLICT (P. Swingle, ed. 1970).

Share bargaining is concerned with issues involving the *division* of money, power or status   .   .   .   [It] always involves important conflicts of interest between parties [and]   .   .   .   a high degree of self-centeredness. If a party is to achieve high targets he must discover all he can about the opponent while hiding information about himself. Successful share bargaining involves intensive factfinding, analysis, secrecy and tact.   .   .   .

[Its] goal   .   .   .   [is] to find a settlement point that resolves the conflict of interest in one's own favor. In that light it makes little sense to say or do anything that might conceivably improve the bargaining position of the opponent.

In *every* negotiation [however] it is possible for both parties to help each other at no expense to themselves. If each understands the problems of the other and openly tries to solve these problems together, both can benefit. We call this the *problem-solving* process.   .   .   .

.   .   .   When an engineer and supplier work together to define specifications they are engaged in problem-solving bargaining. Other examples of problem-solving concern matters such as progress payments, system approvals and billing methods. It is not unusual for a buyer to issue a proposal request with an excess of standard and special clauses to protect his legal position. However, these terms may conflict with a supplier's business procedures and create unnecessary hardship. For example, if a seller's accounting system is on a monthly basis it may be expensive to provide cost reports weekly. In that case both parties may gain if they settle for a midmonth estimate and an accurate report monthly. The same potential for joint gain exists in other parts of the contract.

* * *

All that is necessary for success in [this type of bargaining] is adequate time, good will, open-mindedness and motivation. A supportive, nonjudgmental, communicative climate can help both parties find new ways to assist each other. Successful problem-solvers reveal rather than conceal; they show empathy rather than exploit. When such a climate prevails the potential for mutual gain will be large.

* * *

[*Attitudinal bargaining* is a third major process in negotiation.]

Relationships and attitudes between opponents are negotiable. The parties invariably start with preconceptions about the best way to act toward each other. The basis for these preconceptions have deep roots. As a person matures, his way of looking at the world and his feelings about it result in a relatively stable pattern of behavior. Beliefs, opinions and biases tend to be consistent with attitudes. Because attitudes are both emotional and rational they are hard to change. Nevertheless, a satisfactory negotiation cannot take place until both parties are willing to modify their attitudes sufficiently to engage in share and problem-solving processes.

* * *

The attitudinal-bargaining process assumes that desired relationships can be structured through negotiation with an opponent. Five relationships are basic to most bargaining situations. They are: 1) extreme aggression, 2) mild agression for deterrent purposes, 3) mutual accommodation, 4) open cooperation and 5) direct collusion with the opponent. In conducting [negotiation] it is necessary to decide which of these five relationships is [likely and] appropriate from a strategic standpoint [and to seek ways to develop them].

* * *

[Fourth, a negotiator must also strike a bargain with himself . . . . That is, engage in *personal bargaining* . . .]

An individual struggles to reconcile competing needs and goals by negotiating a suitable arrangement with the outside world. An exchange process goes on within him in which one need is traded for another. In the last analysis he chooses a pattern of behavior that he believes will provide the most satisfaction for the energy involved.

. . . The outcome of a negotiation may well depend upon how one party or the other reconciles [such] role-conflict.

* * *

[Finally, negotiators invariably] bargain for others as well as themselves. A man may transact business with a real-estate broker while away from his family, but they are as involved as though they were at the table. It is important to understand how a [negotiator] bargains with those he represents—that is, the people in his *own* organization or social group.

In a strict sense, organizations do not have objectives, but people within them do. Each member of a decision-making coalition has his own level of aspirations and a *personal definition* of the critical issues. The negotiator is but one member of the coalition that establishes group goals. Furthermore, each of the participants has an individual value system and represents a different degree of power, status and bargaining skill. What we normally call bargaining objectives is really an outcome of the *in-group* process.

* * *

[For example] there are [negotiators] who . . . concentrate on reducing the aspiration level of their own coalition instead of the opponent's. As a result they rarely fail to meet a target, for their wants are low from the start.

* * *

An appreciation of the in-group-bargaining process permits a negotiator to understand how an opponent makes strategic and tactical decisions. With this knowledge he may adjust his own plans to change the opponent's in-group values and expectations.

The Expected-Satisfaction Theory

[Within each of the bargaining subprocesses we have discussed, a negotiator seeks to satisfy his own needs and objectives; however, he can only do so by satisfying some of the needs and objectives of his opponent.   The expected-satisfaction theory posits that negotiated outcomes always reflect some degree of mutual satisfaction.]

Imagine for a moment that a tourist is entering a small grocery store in a Mexican village where prices are not marked. On the shelf are five dusty cans of Campbell's beans. The tourist loves these beans and has been without them for a long time. He would not object to buying all five at the right price, but would settle for one. From a price standpoint, the tourist would be delighted to pay 8¢, the normal California supermarket price, but is prepared to pay as much as 22¢ if necessary. As the price moves from 8¢ to 22¢ the tourist becomes less and less satisfied (shown in the diagram by three curved *solid* lines labeled "buyer high, buyer med and buyer low").

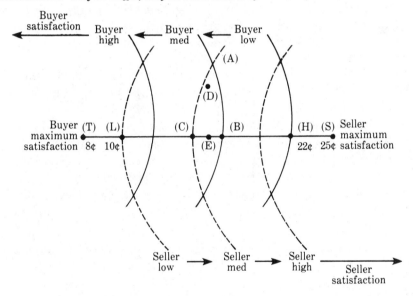

Proposal	Price	Average unit price, cents	Seller's* total profit, cents	Gain of loss of satisfaction, relative to proposal (A)	
				Buyer	Seller
(A)	1 for 15¢	15.0	5	—	—
(B)	3 for 45¢	15.0	15	None	Gain
(C)	5 for 55¢	11.0	5	Gain	None
(D)	2 for 28¢	14.0	8	Gain	Gain
(E)	5 for 63¢	12.6	13	Gain	Gain

*Seller's Cost=10 cents

Satisfaction Model of Negotiation

The grocer needs cash and would like to get rid of this slow-moving item. He operates on the principle that nothing must ever be sold at a loss, therefore he would rather do without a sale than sell at less than 10¢. The storekeeper is confident that sooner or later all five cans will be sold at prices between 10¢ and 25¢. As the price moves down from 25¢ the seller becomes less and less satisfied (shown in the diagram by three curved *dashed* lines labeled "seller high, seller med and seller low"). Any price between 10¢ and 22¢, the settlement range, will leave both parties more satisfied than if no deal is made.

The first question we should ask is whether there is a point of *equal* satisfaction for both. The second is whether there exists a point at which they will gain *equal* marginal satisfaction from the deal. The answer to both questions is, *not necessarily*.

The facts are that the grocer and tourist have entirely different value systems. The tourist has $100 in his wallet but refuses to be "taken" in any deal; he would rather walk away than pay 25¢ for a can of beans. The grocer *needs cash and every penny is important*, but he would rather do without than sell for less than 10¢. Furthermore, neither the tourist nor the grocer values the quality of Campbell's beans in the same way. Needless to say, there is no way to measure whether they can get equal satisfaction from the exchange. All that can be said is they will both gain satisfaction if the final price is between 10¢ and 22¢.

With that in mind let us now pick up the conversation at the point where both are considering whether to close the deal at 15¢ (shown as Proposal [A] in the diagram). At this price the grocer enjoys a 5¢ profit. Is this the best settlement for both parties? No.

The four proposals shown below are superior to Proposal (A):

Proposal (B)—If the grocer were wise, he would offer to sell three cans for 45¢, at which his profit would be 15¢. The tourist's average price would remain at 15¢. *This proposal would represent an improvement for the seller at no loss to the tourist.*

Proposal (C)—The tourist might counter with an offer to buy all five cans for 55¢, which would provide a large improvement for himself and still leave the grocer with the original 5¢ profit of Proposal (A).

Proposal (D)—If the above offer were refused, the tourist could propose to buy two cans for 28¢. In this case *both parties would be better off* because the grocer's profit would rise to 8¢ and the buyer's average cost fall to 14¢.

Proposal (E)—Finally, they would be wise to conclude a deal at five cans for 63¢, where the grocer earns 13¢ and the tourist pays only 12.6¢ per can. *There is no better deal possible for both in relation to the first offer.*

Proposals (B), (C) and (D) represent *trading*, or problem-solving, proposals. In each case an improved solution for one or both parties was possible by combining the needs of both in a package deal. Finally, a point was reached where they could no longer improve the satisfaction of one without hurting the other. If, in the example above, the grocer were to refuse the best offer and insist on 64¢ for five cans, then the tourist's unit cost would rise to 12.8¢ while the grocer's profit rose to 14¢. The grocer would benefit at the tourist's expense. Proposal (E) is therefore considered to be a share-bargaining proposal.

One more important point should be illustrated. Neither the tourist nor the grocer knows how much satisfaction he will get from the agreement. Each has *expectations* about the future. The grocer may make the deal, then see a 30¢-per-can tourist walk in a moment later. The tourist may open the cans and find them spoiled. The element of *expected satisfaction* is an integral part of every transaction. . . .

* * *

The Expected-Satisfaction Theory may be summarized in terms of seven basic propositions:

Proposition 1—Negotiation is not simply a good deal for both parties. While each must gain something, it is *improbable* that they will gain equally.

Proposition 2—No two value systems are likely to be the same. The grocer's concept of beans and money was not identical with the tourist's. Men have more or less the same needs *but achieve different degrees of satisfaction* from reaching goals.

Proposition 3—In *every* negotiation the potential exists for the parties to improve their *joint* satisfaction at no loss to either. The more intense the search for joint improvement, the more likely people will be to find superior solutions. This process of joint improvement is called *problem-solving* bargaining.

Proposition 4—In every negotiation there is a point reached at which the gains of one party are won at the loss of the other. This process of rationing is called *share* bargaining.

Proposition 5—All transactions are based upon *future expectations* of satisfaction. No two men are likely to estimate future satisfactions in the same way.

Proposition 6—In the last analysis it is not goods or money or services that people exchange in the process of negotiation but satisfaction. Material things represent only the more visible aspects of a transaction.

Proposition 7—A negotiator can only make assumptions about an opponent's satisfaction, expectations and goals. One important purpose of negotiation is to test these assumptions.

* * *

The Basic Principles of Power

Americans generally assume that the powerful party in a negotiation will exert the greatest influence. But we are beginning to wonder if this common-sense notion is true. . . . Power, like beauty, is to a large degree a state of mind.

* * *

One step in preparing for negotiation is to evaluate the power balance between opponents. Such an analysis is not possible unless the principles of power are understood. For practical purposes power may be defined as *the ability of a negotiator to influence the behavior of an opponent.*

* * *

There are nine sources of strength that contribute to the overall balance of power between opponents. These are:

1. *Balance of Rewards.* Rewards may be of a tangible or intangible nature. Money, property, rights, and privileges are of a tangible nature. Financial rewards need not be expressed in profit alone but may come about as a result of goals associated with cash flow, liquidity, borrowing power, partial coverage of fixed costs, maintenance of specialized productive resources or return-on-investment targets. Rewards may also be long run— that is, a result of expanded markets, products or channels of distribution.

Intangible rewards may provide an equally important base of power. Among these are benefits that fill needs for safety, love, worth and self-realization. A sales manager's personal need to prove himself may weigh more heavily in the reward structure than the profit to be gained from the sale.

Although reward is a critical element in the balance of power, it is usually analyzed superficially. Rarely is a thorough worth-analysis made to discover the hidden factors in an opponent's reward structure. . . .

2. *Balance of Punishment or Nonreward.* One of the first lessons we learned as children is that parents can punish as well as reward. A seller can punish a buyer by circumventing his authority or by harassing him with minor changes. A buyer can punish a seller by threatening to remove him from a bidder's list or by rejecting a product for minor quality flaws irrelevant to its end use. Deadlock is an interesting form of punishment that leaves both parties in an unpleasant state of uncertainty.

* * *

Punishment and nonreward may be tangible or intangible. When collective bargaining fails and a strike takes place, both parties suffer tangible costs. Psychological punishment may be inflicted by creating tension, uncertainty and loss of confidence at the conference table. The ability to punish or withhold reward goes hand-in-hand with the exercise of influence.

3. *Balance of Legitimacy.* No other source of power is so hypnotic in its effect as legitimacy. We have learned to accept the authority of ownership, tradition, appointment and laws to such an extent that we *fail* to question their applicability in changing situations. . . . Legitimacy is a source and symbol of power.

For the buyer, legitimacy can be enhanced through laws, procedures, procurement regulations or review agencies such as fair-trade commissions. The government exerts influence through its elected role and through the media of public opinion and congressional investigation. A seller can enhance his legitimacy through institutional advertising, trade associations and political pressure. Even the seller's right to a fair profit and the buyer's right to a fair price have a legitimacy deeply rooted in our culture. In each case the principle is the same: the buyer, the seller and the government are building strength on the basis of higher institutional or cultural authority.

4. *Balance of Commitment.* Commitment, loyalty and friendship are benchmarks of power. Those with teenage children are aware that one of the strong bases of parental authority is associated with companionship rather than material rewards. Managers often learn that a mediocre worker who is committed to company objectives may be more effective than a talented but less dedicated man.

In a marriage, the party who cares most about maintaining the relationship gives up a degree of power to the party who is less committed. The commercial and diplomatic world do not differ in this respect. Purchasing executives have long realized that buyer and seller must be committed to each other's long-range interests if a satisfactory business relationship is to exist.

5. *Balance of Knowledge.* Knowledge and the control of information is power. The more a negotiator knows about an opponent's objectives and bargaining position the stronger he is. Knowledge of product, marketplace, legal phraseology and regulations is also a source of strength. By the same token, a thorough understanding of the theory and practice of professional negotiation is an essential ingredient of power.

6. *Balance of Competition.* Competition has an important effect on bargaining power. The seller who can keep his plant busy on other work and the buyer with multiple sources are in a strong bargaining position.

Competition can also be created in other ways. A buyer may increase competition by bringing other economic forces into the transaction. For example, he can urge that the company make a product rather than buy it, or he can entice manufacturers from other fields into the marketplace. Sometimes an end product can be redesigned in order to eliminate dependency upon an exploitive vendor. Competition can be enhanced by providing funding, facilities, tooling and knowledge to otherwise marginal second-source suppliers.

A seller may improve his competitive position by developing a unique knowledge or facility base. He may also purchase other companies, which improves distribution channels and makes him less dependent upon specific customers or seasonal variations.

Last but not least, it is possible to improve one's competitive position by the simple expedient of selecting negotiators who are personally competitive: men who enjoy struggle and have a strong desire to win.

7. *Balance of Uncertainty and Courage.* Security is a goal that humans cherish. We share a desire to avoid risk wherever possible. The person who is willing to accept a greater burden of uncertainty with respect to reward or punishment enhances his power.

Uncertainty may be based on fear and prejudice rather than rational grounds. .   .   . People assess risk differently even when they have access to the same information. A common stock which looks like a speculation to a man who lived through the depression can appear a sound investment to a young man.

* * *

Uncertainty can be created by introducing risk at a personal as well as corporate level. Deadlock introduces the possibility that a good negotiator can lose his reputation. Risk can be heightened by introducing matters in which the opponent's knowledge or ability to grasp a situation is deficient.

Courage plays a part in the decision to make a concession, to hold one's ground, or to force a deadlock. In personal injury work the insurance claims manager can never be sure that his low offer will precipitate costly litigation. Conversely, the claimant can only hope that a final verdict will justify his reluctance to accept an earlier offer. It takes courage to tolerate uncertainty, and we differ in our ability to do so.

8. *Balance of Time and Effort.* Time and patience are power. The party that is most constrained by time limits provides the opponent with a base of strength. It is for this reason that purchasing executives stress the importance of lead time and early-warning inventory systems.

Buying, selling and negotiation are grueling work, and the willingness to work is power. Perhaps the hardest work of all is imposed on us by the demands of planning and deadlock. Both can easily be avoided: one by nonplanning and the other by agreement. The party most willing to work hard gains power. Some people are simply lazy and thereby forfeit this important source of strength.

9. *Balance of Bargaining Skill.* Bargaining skill is power, and that's what this book is all about. The ability to plan, to persuade, to manipulate perceptions, to mobilize bias, to analyze power and decision-making . . . and to understand the theory and anatomy of negotiation constitutes a base of power available to [either party].

NOTES

1. *Satisfaction, Power & The Subprocesses of Bargaining: An Observer's Perspective*

Karrass' model presents a simple truth about negotiation—settlement requires satisfying both parties' needs. That is, unless both parties get more than they believe they will obtain by not agreeing (not more than they give) there will be no settlement. This involves the exchange of "goods" (valued objects) either to obtain some other valued object, or, as Alfred Kuhn has pointed out, to avoid a "bad."

In his words:

> a bad (negative good) is any object or event that reinforces an avoidance response . . . something is a bad if a party is willing to accept a cost to get out of it. . . . Bads include force, violence, bodily injury, pain and destruction of property . . . an insult is a bad, particularly if it diminishes self-esteem or signals an end of a friendship, and so is withdrawal of a good already possessed . . . a stress transaction is one in which a bad is applied unilaterally by A to B . . . along with the express or implied promise that it will be relieved if and only if B does as A requests. . . . In a threat transaction an express or implied promise is made by A that a bad will be applied to B if and only if B does not do as requested. . . . By definition a bad creates an avoidance response . . . B would be willing to give some positive value to avoid its imposition or continuation.[6]

Although Kuhn's terminology is hardly the familiar idiom of lawyers, his concept of a "bad" or negative good helps to explain a basic premise of Karrass' view of the bargaining process. To understand why there is a settlement requires an analysis of the way *each* party perceives the costs and benefits of *both* agreement and disagreement, and what is avoided and gained at each potential settlement point. As Karrass recognizes, this is further complicated by (i) the

6. A. Kuhn, THE LOGIC OF SOCIAL SYSTEMS 194–96 (1974).

nature of the bargaining situation, (ii) its potential for joint gain, (iii) the relations of the bargainers to their clients and each other, (iv) their personalities and self concepts, and (v) the multiple configurations of need, power and perception that the interactions between the parties present. Nevertheless, he sees patterns and common elements in all negotiations. If his model is generally descriptive (which we believe it is), any negotiation should be analyzable in terms of the bargaining subprocesses and dynamics of expected satisfaction and bargaining power which he identifies.

Take the *Agnew* case as an illustration. There were many levels at which agreements were negotiated in the case in addition to the bargain with Agnew. The Baltimore prosecutors negotiated with the "lesser" defendants—Fornoff, Matz, Wolff and Hammerman—and with their lawyers. At the same time there was bargaining between the prosecutors and Elliot Richardson. In addition there were negotiations among the Baltimore prosecutors (*e. g.*, whether to give Fornoff full immunity when his lawyer first broached the possibility of a deal, or be less lenient and wait until he was willing to talk). No doubt there were others.

Consider these negotiations in light of the model Karrass offers. The interactions between the prosecutors and all potential defendants, including Agnew, essentially involved either-or divisions. That is, power, information and status were the goods available for exchange, and to the extent that one side gained, the other lost. As Karrass would predict, the prosecutors' strategies were characterized by secrecy and pursuit of their own—rather than mutual—goals.

At the same time—to use Karrass' terms—"attitudinal," "personal" and "problem-solving" bargaining was going on. For example, the defendants' attorneys had to be convinced that the young prosecutors, Baker and Liebman, were to be taken seriously. Prior to this change in attitude, the exchanges of power and information were very limited. The prosecutors were also concerned about how their actions —which to a considerable extent meant themselves—would be perceived by the public; they were sometimes troubled, other times heady over having the power in their hands to bring down a vice president. We cannot know what sorts of compromises they had to make with themselves, but personal conflicts surely needed to be resolved.

Finally, in their negotiations among themselves the prosecutors had to "work together to solve each other's problems." The issues of how to minimize press leaks, handle timing problems, and decide what should be the bottom line in any deal with Agnew all involved potential or actual conflicts—which were generally resolved with far more open discussion and mutuality than characterized their dealings with outsiders.

Perhaps we make too much of these obvious features of the process. The outcome of the Agnew case is not really explained by saying that each side felt that what it got was more satisfying than what it relinquished. Agnew avoided the greater costs associated with trial and conviction (he entered an ambiguous plea to a less serious charge). He gave up the vice-presidency and possibly any future career in public service. In return for this, the prosecutors gave up the power to bring Agnew and other defendants to trial. They gained in turn an early and certain resolution of what might have been a national crisis. But these trade-offs only partly explain why the case was resolved as it was.

It is difficult to apply the theory of exchange, for example, to Richardson's almost singular goal—Agnew's resignation. Presumably nothing would have been acceptable as a trade-off for this aspect of the agreement: Richardson seemed unwilling to gamble on even a slight probability that Richard Nixon would leave office while Agnew was vice-president. Thus, although the balance of power favored the prosecutors in most respects (rewards, punishment, commitment, knowledge), the balance of time and uncertainty were so significant— at least to Richardson—and so heavily weighted against them that the vice-president found himself with considerable leverage.

There is no question that many of the elements Karrass identifies were present in this situation, yet they are only part of what is needed to adequately explain the outcome. The parties to the Agnew negotiation were motivated by something more than "expected satisfaction," and their agreement was affected by more than the balance of power. The mix of individual needs and aspirations, interpersonal dynamics and situational constraints involved in bargaining make it an elusive process to depict.

---

2.   *Why Parties Settle: The Need For A Participant's Perspective*

It is, of course, not necessary that all the above questions be answered. To be a good negotiator does not require a complete theory of bargaining. Nevertheless, it is useful to think hard about why and how the parties move towards and reach agreement at a particular point. As one economist has stated:

> A theory of bargaining, if it is to be complete, should yield answers to the following questions:
>
> (a) Why do the parties bargain?
>
> (b) What are the essential elements in bargaining and why are they important?
>
> (c) How do the parties determine the extent of their demands through bargaining (benefit levels or goals) and how do they evaluate the terms (benefits) of the bargain?

(d) How are the terms of the agreement influenced by the bargaining process?

(e) Under what conditions is an agreement concluded?[7]

While Karrass offers an answer to the first of these questions and addresses the second and third, he does not provide a comprehensive explanation of why any particular settlement point is agreed upon. That is, his "expected satisfaction" model does not contain a usable theory of convergence. Any overview of the negotiating process as a whole requires some attention to this aspect of reaching agreements. The following discussion, which is admittedly somewhat difficult, attempts to struggle with this need.

Look again at Karrass' example of the tourist and the grocer bargaining over the price of beans. There are any number of possible settlements, but those discussed by Karrass can be represented as follows (we will express each possible settlement in terms of average price per can to facilitate comparison):

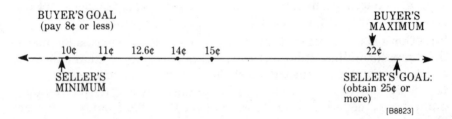

As Karrass points out, settlement is possible anywhere along the solid line—between the maximum price the buyer is willing to pay and the minimum the seller is willing to accept. Karrass tells us how the maximum and minimum were set and shows us a series of offers and counteroffers in which both parties gain in satisfaction until they reach a point (12.6¢ per can) where joint gain is maximized: the best that can be done for both parties through a problem solving approach. Beyond this point the gains of one party would be won at the expense of the other (relative to the first offers)—they would have begun to engage in "share bargaining." This analysis can be followed fairly easily, and standing outside the negotiation, we might recommend to the parties that they in fact agree on that "fair" solution of 5 cans for 63¢. But think for a moment about being *inside* the negotiation. Assuming you were that hungry American tourist, would you necessarily adopt this approach? To what extent could you identify with the grocer's perspective? For example, unless he told you, would you be likely to know his cost? If beans retail at 8¢ in the United States, you might be justified in assuming that the grocer's

7. B. Mabry, *The Pure Theory of Bargaining*, 18 IND. & LAB.REL.REV. 479 (1965).

cost was 8¢ or less, and you might feel that he was being unreasonable if he held out for as much as 12¢. Unless your assessment changed in the course of the negotiation, the possibility of being "taken" might cause you to reject an offer of 15¢ a can, even though you wanted the beans very much and had plenty of money, and even though, *from an objective point of view*, it was a fair price. Similarly, if you were the grocer, you might feel a rich American tourist *should* pay a premium for your foresight in stocking this rare item, and find an initial offer of 8¢ so insulting that you would break off the negotiation. To a greater degree than is suggested by Karrass' analysis, outcomes depend on what the bargaining situation looks like to the parties involved, rather than what an outsider might say it in fact *is*.

You will go into a negotiation with an idea of how much you are willing to pay, give up, or concede—your own "bottom line" or resistance point—but that is not all. You will also have an idea of the best deal you might be able to obtain, based on your assessment of your opponent's bottom line—the least favorable terms he or she will accept rather than "lose the sale" or fail to reach any agreement at all. What you predict will be your opponent's resistance point becomes your own target or goal. As a result, much of your effort in a particular negotiation will be directed toward trying to ascertain your opponent's resistance point while assiduously concealing your own.

Thus, although it is helpful to stand outside a bargaining situation and decide where, with perfect information, a negotiation should come out (as in Karrass' identification of the point where joint gain is maximized), the actual process of bargaining can only be understood by analyzing the perspectives and decisions of each party with respect to their initial goals and resistance points, their shifts *away* from these initial assessments, and their arrival at some mutually acceptable agreement. In short, we need answers to Mabry's last three questions: how the parties determine their own goals and evaluate particular settlements, how the outcome is influenced by the bargaining process itself, and what conditions are necessary if an agreement is to be concluded. Although we can only begin to formulate answers here, even a preliminary response may be useful to you as you begin to confront actual negotiating tasks.

Let us, again, take a simple example. Suppose you represent a dog-bite victim who is suing his next door neighbor for damages in a case where there is no question about liability. The two families have been good friends and your client would not have brought the suit if he had not assumed the neighbor was insured. Nevertheless, relations between the families have been somewhat strained since the suit was filed, and both parties are anxious to settle it. After a discussion with your client, you enter settlement discussions with the following goals:

—$2,000 in damages;

—$500 in costs and attorney's fees;

—An agreement to get rid of the dog or insure that this type of incident will not occur again.

This is the most you think you can possibly obtain. At bottom your client is willing to settle for the agreement and $750, which would cover his actual expenditures for medical treatment, court costs and attorney's fees. *But he wants to obtain as much as possible.*[8] He also wishes to avoid the costs of failing to settle, which include not only monetary costs—such as higher court costs and attorneys' fees, but also delay, a continuance of strained relations, and possible permanent damage to the friendship. Although these cost assessments change in the course of a negotiation, we will assume that they are constant and indivisible, and that the point when they will be incurred—the point where the negotiation breaks down—is what you want to avoid. You do not want to push your opponent to the point of deadlock, and as it is approached, you will modify your demands and make concessions, so long as this does not require going below your client's bottom line. We can represent this graphically as follows:

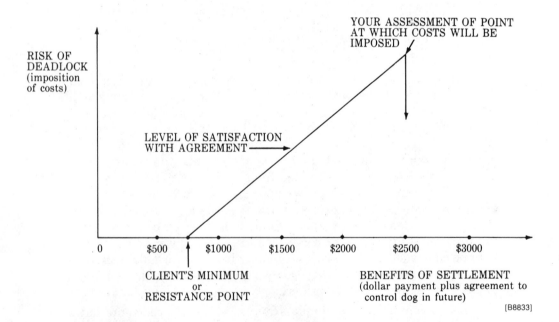

[B8833]

8.   Throughout this chapter we tend to assume that this is the basic orientation of the bargainers. Our experience would suggest, however, that often this is not true. Nor is such an orientation "natural or inevitable." Utility theorists would say that a modification of goals to take account of such values as altruism or fairness involves merely a redefinition of "satisfaction" in a particular case. But where one begins often determines where one ends. However analytically correct, it is an assumption worth being very careful about. *See generally* R. Christie & F. Geis, *supra* note 4; G. Maxwell & D. Schmitt, COOPERATION: AN EXPERIMENTAL ANALYSIS (1975); THE SOCIAL INFLUENCE PROCESS (J. Tedeschi, ed. 1972).

that is, there would be no satisfaction with an agreement under $750, the client's minimum; after that, the level of satisfaction would increase as the dollar payment increased, up to the point of deadlock, where satisfaction would drop off sharply and return to zero. Maximum satisfaction, under this simplified model, would occur at the point just short of deadlock: the most your opponent is willing to pay in lieu of going to trial.

In setting this goal of $2,500 you are, of course, making an estimate of your opponent's resistance point: it may be more than $2,500 and it may be less. You will also be estimating what your opponent will be aiming for—what he or she sees as your resistance point. Assuming you feel that your efforts to this point will have convinced your opponent that your client will demand at least $1,000, you could project a similar function for your opponent:

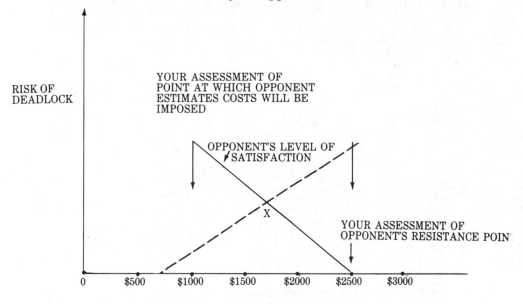

RISK OF
DEADLOCK

YOUR ASSESSMENT OF
POINT AT WHICH OPPONENT
ESTIMATES COSTS WILL BE
IMPOSED

OPPONENT'S LEVEL OF
SATISFACTION

X

YOUR ASSESSMENT OF
OPPONENT'S RESISTANCE POIN'

0          $500 $1000 $1500 $2000 $2500 $3000

BENEFITS OF SETTLEMENT

[B8900]

What this says graphically is that it is your judgment that although settlement is possible anywhere between $750 and $2500, your opponent sees a somewhat narrower range, and many of your efforts will be directed toward making that range *seem* even narrower. On the other hand, if you are wrong in your estimate of the opponent's resistance point, the range may be either narrower or wider than you expect. Thus you will also be trying to discover your opponent's actual limits—the most he or she is authorized to pay—and revising your goals accordingly.

As Karrass suggests, we could plot the opponent's actual target and resistance point on this graph and identify, with perfect information about both sides' expectations, the point where mutual satisfaction would be maximized—presumably where the two lines intersect at point X. The problem, of course, is that in most negotiations in which lawyers engage information is *imperfect*, so that as an advocate you have no choice but to try to maximize your own client's satisfaction. For example, if the costs of deadlock are higher for your opponent than you realize (he or she may expect a jury verdict of at least $10,-000 if the case should go to trial) your opponent might be satisfied with a settlement well above your original goal, and you would be doing your client a disservice if you did not try to find out about and press for that higher (and still mutually advantageous) figure. This situation might be represented as follows, with the solid lines representing your shift away from your original (dotted line) projections:

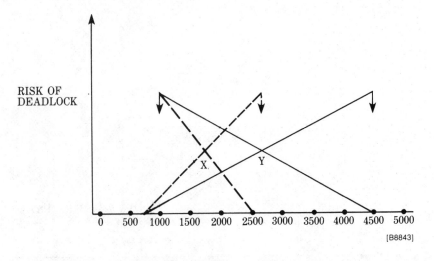

[B8843]

As can be seen from this new figure, even leaving the opponent's target point where it was, the point where joint satisfaction is maximized (y) has moved well to the right, to an amount higher than your original goal. If you had decided to settle on your notion of what was "fair to both parties" (point x) on the basis of your original, erroneous estimate, then, you would actually have settled on terms more advantageous to your opponent. Since you can never be sure of how your opponent perceives a particular negotiation or values certain terms, you can only seek to find that point short of deadlock where your client's gains will be maximized.

Assuming your original estimates are reasonably accurate, however, and a settlement acceptable to both parties can be reached anywhere between $750 and $2,500, how do you get your opponent to agree to a settlement on the high side of that range? Would *you* pay $2,500 if you believed your opponent would accept $1,000, or *knew* he or she would accept $750? This question answers itself, and it also illuminates the basic dynamics in the situation: since your opponent's goal is to pay the least you will accept,[9] you must change his or her perception of your bottom line. You will obtain a settlement upwards of $2,000 only if your opponent believes that a settlement below that figure is unacceptable. On the graph we used earlier, you would be doing everything you could to persuade your opponent that your client's goal and resistance point were far to the right of where he or she had thought they were:

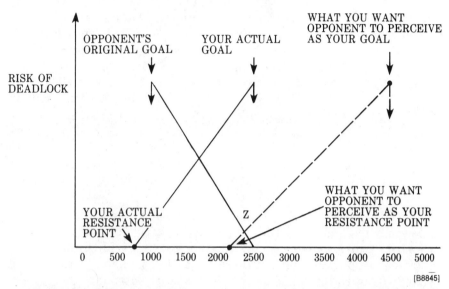

[B8845]

An opponent who believed that your resistance point was $2,200 would feel that a settlement at point z was the best that could be done in a very tight bargaining situation; at least his or her client would prefer that figure to paying the maximum of $2,500, and would certainly prefer it to going to trial. At the same time you would have reached an agreement that would be highly satisfactory to your client. (It would also be possible, as you can see, to establish the relief that your resistance point was $2,500, and because your opponent's perceptions of the *possible* would have changed so drastically during the course of the negotiations, he or she might even feel relief at being able to pay an amount that was within the limits of your authority).

There are, of course, many complications that this analysis glosses over. Even in a suit for damages with clear-cut liability the benefits of the bargain can rarely be expressed in simple money terms. Money is valued very differently by different individuals, and intangibles such as pride, reputation, and relief from anxiety often enter in. Think of how it would complicate the situation we have been dis-

---

9. See our comments in footnote 8, *supra.* We are also assuming that the opponent wants to minimize costs and maximize gains.

cussing, for example, if the dog owner were to refuse to sign an agreement to get rid of the dog or control it in the future. How much is such an agreement worth? Could you accept a somewhat higher settlement—say, $1,000—that did *not* include the agreement, or would you have to go back to your client? Are items of this sort truly nonnegotiable, or might they also be the subject of concessions?

The benefits of a particular negotiation may not only be difficult to measure and compare, but are also complicated by the fact that the lawyer negotiator is working in a representative capacity. Even though you make a conscious effort to suppress them, your own needs and goals will affect what you do in negotiation. For example, if your opponent in the situation we have been discussing had offered $2,000, and you were convinced that further concessions could be won only by the use of tactics that would damage your relationship with this particular attorney, would you be tempted to settle somewhat short of your client's goals? Since your client would find a settlement of $2,000 highly satisfactory, would you feel justified in taking one of your own goals—the maintenance of amicable working relationships —into account? There will be many situations where the demands of your schedule, or your need for control or certainty, will further complicate the task of obtaining the best possible settlement for your client.

In addition, costs in a particular negotiation, like gains, will rarely be easily measured and will frequently be difficult to categorize and compare. Our example assumes a fixed cost that will be incurred at a particular point, but in fact there are costs associated with settling as well as not settling, and calculations of cost enter into the process at every stage. While it is usually true that a party will seek to maximize benefits without incurring the collection of costs associated with deadlock, it is not simply a question of *when* they will be imposed. It is also an object of bargaining to affect the opponent's perception of *what* these costs will be. As a party's estimate of what it will cost to take a case to trial increases, so will his or her calculation of the amount it will be worth paying or giving up to avoid such costs. For example, if the opponent in our hypothetical were convinced in the course of the negotiation that the costs of trying the case—win or lose—would be at least $1,000, he or she would be willing to pay that much to settle. You as the negotiator would thus work to create the impression that the trial would be longer than expected, or that further discovery is necessary, or that some other unforeseen action or complication would increase the costs of litigation. Similarly open to revision is the opponent's estimate of the size of a possible jury verdict, and of the probability that it will be rendered. If trial is seen to involve a greater risk than was anticipated, an opponent will pay more to avoid it.

Perhaps the most that can be said of the kind of cost-benefit analysis we have been pursuing is that in some form it is fundamental in every negotiation. Although not describable in a precise formula, in a rough way it is this sort of balancing which determines whether parties will move from initial positions and finally reach agreement, and each party in a negotiation will be trying to influence the other's perception of the balance. *At a point when further benefits do not seem worth what it will cost to secure them—when net gain reaches zero* [10]*—an agreement will be concluded.*

Both parties must perceive, of course, that they are better off in settling than in not settling: there must be some measure of joint gain. But to a considerable degree the focus of negotiation is on the perception—not the reality—of gain, and a great deal depends on persuading the opponent to accept *your* definition of reality. In this sense negotiation is very much a game, played for information and beliefs as well as for "goods". It is this gamelike quality that accounts for many of the dynamics of the process, and also raises its most puzzling tactical and ethical dilemmas.

C. A DIGRESSION: GAME THEORY AS AN ALTERNATIVE MODEL

A number of commentators have suggested that the "theory of games" offers a more helpful orienting model of bargaining behavior. Although the following material is not from the mainstream of this technical literature, it does offer an introduction to some of the basic features of this perspective.

GOFFMAN, STRATEGIC INTERACTION

85, 89, 93–94, 99–105, 110–111 (1969).

Whenever students of the human scene have considered the dealings individuals have with one another, the issue of calculation has arisen: When a respectable motive is given for action, are we to suspect an ulterior one? When an individual supports a promise or threat with a convincing display of emotional expression, are we to believe him? When an individual seems carried away by feeling, is he intentionally acting this way in order to create an effect? When someone responds to us in a particular way, are we to see this as a spontaneous reaction to the situation or a result of his having canvassed all other possible responses before deciding this one was the most advantageous? And whether or not we have such concerns, ought we to be worried about the individual believing that we have them?

---

10. For a detailed consideration of this "net gain" theory of convergence, see the Mabry article cited in footnote 7, *supra*. You might also be interested in the alternative formulation in C. Stevens, STRATEGY AND COLLECTIVE BARGAINING NEGOTIATION (1953).

In recent years this traditional concern about calculation has been taken up and refined by students of game theory. This paper attempts to isolate the analytical framework implied in the game perspective, and show its relationship to other perspectives in analyzing interpersonal dealings.

* * *

[To develop these themes it] will be useful to follow a custom in game theory and employ miniature scenarios of a very farfetched kind.

* * *

Harry, the . . . spearsman, having strayed from [his own] territory . . ., comes into a small clearing to find that another spearsman from a hostile [group] is facing him from what would otherwise be the safe side. Since each finds himself backed by the other's territory, retreat is cut off. Only by incapacitating the other can either safely cross the clearing and escape into his own part of the forest.

Now the game. If there were no chance of missing a throw, then the first spearsman to throw would win. However, the likelihood of missing a fixed target increases with the distance of the throw. In addition, a throw, as a move, involves a spear easily seen to be on its way by its target. And the target itself isn't quite fixed. It is able to dodge and will certainly try to do so. The greater the distance of the throw, the more time to dodge it and the greater the chance of doing so. (A poison dart silently shot from a concealing bush is a move, too, but one that does not telegraph its puncture, and hence, of course, one that generates quite a different game.) And to miss a throw while the other still has his spear allows the other to approach at will for an easy win. Thus, each player begins at a point where it does not pay to chance a throw and presumably approaches a point where it does not pay not to. And each player, in deciding what to do, must decide knowing the other is engaged in exactly the same sort of decision, and knowing that they both appreciate this.

* * *

Harry, then, will be concerned (and able) to make an assessment of his opponent's situation. The game-theoretical approach suggests a way of describing the other's situation in well-structured terms, in this case, the features of the other's situation that Harry is likely to want to know about.

* * *

. . . Clear recognition is given to the fact that the opponent's assessment of his own situation is an important part of his situation and that human assessments are exactly the sort of thing that Harry can try to fully penetrate and appreciate. This leads to the famous recursive problem. Harry must come to terms with the fact that the assessment he is trying to penetrate, namely, the one that the other is

likely to make, will contain as one of its features the fact that Harry
will try to penetrate it. . . .

* * *

Once Harry sees the need to assess his opponent's view of the
situation, game theory gives him a way of being systematic. He
should exhaustively enumerate the distinctively different courses of
action open to the opponent as a response to each of his own possible
moves, and in light of these settle on his own best course of action.
Further, Harry may find it desirable to work out a strategy, that is,
a framework of different courses of action, each linked in advance to a
possible choice of the opponent, such that howsoever the opponent
acts, Harry automatically will have a considered move with which to
reply immediately. . . .

* * *

Now it is possible to [summarize] the defining conditions for
strategic interaction. Two or more parties must find themselves in a
well-structured situation of mutual impingement where each party
must make a move and where every possible move carries fateful implications for all of the parties. In this situation, each player must
influence his own decision by his knowing that the other players are
likely to try to dope out his decision in advance, and may even appreciate that he knows this is likely. Courses of action or moves will
then be made in the light of one's thoughts about the others' thoughts
about oneself. An exchange of moves made on the basis of this kind
of orientation to self and others can be called strategic interaction.
One part of strategic interaction consists of concrete courses of action
taken in the real world that constrains the parties; the other part,
which has no more intrinsic relation to communication than the first,
consists of a special kind of decision-making—decisions made by directly orienting oneself to the other parties and giving weight to their
situation as they would seem to see it, including their giving weight
to one's own. The special possibilities that result from this mutually
assessed mutual assessment, as these affect the fate of the parties,
provide reason and grounds for employing the special perspective of
strategic interaction. [What especially concerns us here is the problem of "credibility" which this situation presents].

* * *

. . . Harry is concerned to assess his situation and if another
player is part of this situation, this other will be looked to in forming
the assessment. We can think of this second player, the other or opponent, as contributing in two ways to this assessment. First, he can
give off expressions which, when gleaned by Harry, allow the latter
to make some sense out of what is happening and to predict somewhat
what will happen. (In this the opponent presumably is no better than
lesser animals and even inanimate objects, all of which can serve as
a source of information.) Second, the opponent can *transmit com-*

munications, that is, convey linguistic avowals (or substitutes thereof). These Harry can (and is openly meant to) receive, and is meant to be informed thereby. Some special attention should be given to communications in the analysis of strategic interaction, for many games involve this kind of activity.

Certain statements made to Harry by his opponent can have crucial relevance for whatever is gamey in the situation between them. Harry's opponent can make an *unconditional avowal* regarding his intention to follow a stated course of action, affirming that regardless of what Harry does, he is going to do so and so. More important still, the opponent can make a *conditional avowal*, claiming that he will pursue a given course of action if Harry does (or does not) engage in another given course of action. Two basic possibilities are involved here. There is the *promise*, where the outcome conditionally proposed is something Harry can be assumed to desire, and there is the *threat*, where the conditionally proposed outcome is something Harry would presumably like to avoid.

All avowals can be described in terms of their correctness, that is, whether or not what they state accords with the facts. And they can be described according to whether they are believed or not by their maker. Avowals also raise the issue of resolve: that is, does the maker have the temperamental inclination to make every possible effort to carry out his intention? And finally, there is the issue of capability: given a high resolve, does the actor have the resources at his command to execute his design?

Given these independent factors relevant to the significance of avowals, we can begin to see some of the confusions possible in a term like "credibility." When an avowal is made to Harry, he can be concerned about its correctness, the other's belief and resolve in making it, or capability in regard to carrying it out, or—and most likely of all —some unanalyzed combination of these factors. Credibility itself is not to be confused with a more specific phenomenon, trustworthiness, namely, the warrantability of trust, defining trust as the reliance Harry gives through his own actions to classes of the other's avowals based on consideration of the latter's "moral character."

The willingness of an individual to credit another's unconditional and conditional avowals is an entirely necessary thing for the maintenance of collaborative social activity and, as such, a central and constant feature of social life. Nonetheless, this does not tell us why (and where) individuals show this reliance when, in fact, they do.

The issue of self-belief alone (as one ingredient in credibility) presents crucial problems. Surely it is in the nature of words that it will always be physically possible to employ them unbelievingly. And there will always be situations when it will be in the other's interests to lie to Harry. Given these facts of life, will it not be wise for Harry always to suspect the other of misrepresentation, and for the latter to suspect that he will thus be suspected, whether innocent or not? The native spearsmen game provides an example: Harry's opponent, should he speak the language, can say, "Put aside your spear, Harry, and let us discuss a method of getting out of the predicament we find ourselves in, for surely the chance each of us has of getting the other is not worth the cost of failing to do so." But how could Harry possibly know but that as soon as he lowers his spear, the speaker will have at him? Why should Harry accept verbal promises, and why should he who promises bind himself by the ones he makes?

.   .   . To repeat: Since the other's interests will often be served by his making threats and promises, it seems reasonable to assume that his interests will also be frequently served by his making false or empty, that is, self-disbelieved, threats and promises. But it is also reasonable to assume that Harry will appreciate that it is in the other's interests to bluff, and therefore it is wise to discount his statements and not take them at face value. The other in turn, appreciating this view of his avowals that Harry is wise to have, will find himself in a fundamental predicament: whether he believes in his own avowal or not, how can he convince Harry to do so? In short, since words can be faked, what grounds can self-respecting players have for putting faith in any of them?

[To be sure, there are situations where credibility can exist in the absence of trust. For example, if] the other uses words to draw Harry's attention to objective nonverbal evidence as to the correctness of the assertions, then these words ought to be effective regardless of how little Harry may trust mere words; after all, he is only gambling the direction of his attention and may lose very little, should the attended evidence prove unconvincing. (This is not the case, of course, in the famous "Watch out behind you," trap.) Similarly, the other, under pressure to divulge where he has hidden money, or evidence, or anything else that he admits to having hidden, can provide the demanded information, knowing that, and knowing that Harry knows that, the absolute proof of the good faith and correctness of his statements will soon be evident. Providing Harry retains control over the speaker until the information is checked out, Harry may find that the cost of taking the other at his word is only the cost of following directions.   .   .   .

[By the same token, a] joint plan of action verbally proposed by an untrustworthy opponent might be safely given weight by Harry if the plan proposes a sequence of steps simultaneously or alternatively taken by both, such that no *one* step appreciably jeopardizes its taker's position. Thus, our two hostile spearsmen could, following the verbal suggestion of one of them, lower their spears together, leave them on the ground, and both move away, in opposite directions along the circle of the clearing until each described a half-circle and found himself at the other's spear, but now next his own land, not the enemy's—and all this without giving the other enough advantage at any point to render acceptance of the scheme dangerous.

* * *

.   .   . Note that in all these cases, words themselves are not what give weight to promises or threats; what gives credit to avowals is the objective appearance of persuasive evidence that a proposed course of action has been unretractably entered upon or linked to pay-offs which overwhelmingly motivate it. If the player cannot arrange for this evidence, then in many cases no game relevant interaction will be possible between the parties, or least ought not to be.

NOTES

1.   *Game Theory and Lawyer Bargaining*

Many game theorists would blanch at our use of Erving Goffman as in any way representative of their orientation and concerns. He is of interest to us because of his focus on the problems of assessing and developing credibility in negotiating situations. Goffman also offers a way into the game-theoretic perspective which our students have generally found helpful in analyzing this most game-like of lawyer enterprises.

Game theory evolved primarily as a mathematical discipline designed to study decision-making in situations of conflict.[11] Rooted in decision and probability theory it seeks to classify and determine optimal solutions in circumstances in which the actor, in order to achieve as much of a desired end as possible (maximize), must take into account the perspective of others whose goals are different and upon whose actions the final outcome will in part depend. Given (i) two players; (ii) two or more *strategies* (encompassing a series of moves) available to each player; (iii) a matrix of *payoffs* specifying the value to each player of each combination of strategies; (iv) a set of *rules* which delineate the variables the players control; and (v) existing conditions, game theory attempts to offer guidance as to which choices and assumptions about the other's behavior *ought* to be made by each participant. Without tracing the many paths this sort of analysis has followed or the related inquiries it has fostered, it is useful to note some of its obvious limitations as a guide to settlement negotiations among lawyers: (i) it requires the assignment of values to uncertain outcomes; this poses the difficulties always present in measuring the desirability or probability of any set of projected results; (ii) it tends

---

11.   The basic provisions of game theory are set out in M. Davis, GAME THEORY (1973); A. Rapoport, TWO PERSON GAME THEORY: THE ESSENTIAL IDEAS (1966); GAME THEORY AND RELATED APPROACHES TO SOCIAL BEHAVIOR (Shubik, ed., 1964). The basic work was done by J. Von Neuman & O. Morgenstern, THEORY OF GAMES AND ECONOMIC BEHAVIOR (1944).

to ignore "non-optimizing" aspects of behavior—that is, it assumes that decision-makers will pursue a rational or safe course, when they might in fact be willing to take the risks associated with larger gains; (iii) it takes insufficient account of the dynamic factors in such situations *i. e.*, the interdependence of outcomes, the opportunities for bluffing or communication, the changing character of preferences and predictions over time; (iv) it tends to collapse the number of options actually available over the course of the interaction into a few alternatives; and (v) it offers no optimal (or persuasive) solution for many situations encountered in real-life circumstances. Nevertheless, the conception of negotiation as a set of interdependent "moves" which must be made and interpreted by the actors suggests a number of important insights into bargaining among lawyers.[12]

12. For those of you who, like us, need to "do" to understand, the following is a typical game theory problem:

Two automobile-parts manufacturers supply practically all of the market for a given replacement part. Company A has always provided a design that could be used interchangeably on all General Motors cars, while Company B has always designed a part that could be used on all Ford and Chrysler cars.

By modifying his design, each part manufacturer can make his design useable on many of the other models. However, in so doing he will make his product somewhat less than ideal for his primary customer. Thus, if Company A designs a product that also can be used on Plymouths, it will lose some of its advantage in the General Motors field, should Company B decide to invade the General Motors field. Each year the two companies analyze the designs for new models and decide upon the design they will use in the new year. Neither company can know the other's plans early enough to modify its own decisions. Hence neither can select its own strategy to take advantage of the other's decision.

In this example, it is assumed that the unit profit remains constant and that the objective of each company is to maximize its total sales. For simplicity, each company is assumed to have only three alternative designs.

For each pair of decisions by the two companies, there will be a different net result or payoff. In some cases, the combination will favor one company

and in some cases it will favor the other. Sometimes there will be a single preferred strategy for each company; in other situations a mixed strategy will be preferable.

A. *When there is a single preferred strategy*: In this example, if Company A chooses Design a_1 and Company B selects Design b_1, it is estimated that Company A will gain 100,000 sales while Company B will lose a net of 100,000 sales. If Company A chooses Design a_2 and Company B again selects Design b_1, Company A will now suffer a net loss of 20,000 sales to Company B. The payoff for each of the other pairs of decisions of A and B is shown below.

Company B

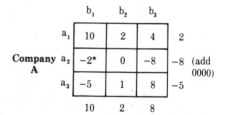

	b_1	b_2	b_3	
a_1	10	2	4	2
a_2	-2*	0	-8	-8 (add
a_3	-5	1	8	-5 0000)
	10	2	8	

Company A

[B8819]

Analysis of this payoff table, or matrix, will show that in this case there is a *single preferred* strategy for each company. Company A can always be sure of gaining at least 20,000 sales if Design a_1 is chosen. If instead, Design a_2 is selected, Company A may lose as many as 80,000 sales if Company B decides on Design b_3. If

* Negative numbers indicate loss of sales by Company A to Company B.

Consider, again, a simple example. Suppose that a lawyer negotiator (N) is trying to decide whether to increase the pressures on her opponent (O) in the course of litigation. She might continue to explore settlement possibilities (approach *A*—accommodative), or

design a_3 is chosen, Company A may lose as many as 50,000 sales.

Similarly, Design b_2 will minimize Company B's losses at 20,000. Selection of Design b_1 could result in a loss of 100,000 sales to Company A, and Design b_3 could result in a loss of 80,000 units. Thus the preferred strategies for both companies will result in an expected gain for Company A of 20,000 sales. The pair of decisions, a_1b_2, represents a "saddle point," which is a point where the largest of the minimum values in all the rows is equal to the smallest of the maximum values in all the columns.

B. *When a mixed strategy is preferable*: If the matrix looks like the one below instead, there is no longer a single preferred strategy for both companies.

Company B

	b_1	b_2	b_3
a_1	2	−4	2
a_2	4	−6	−4
a_3	0	2	1

Company A

[B8832]

Examination of the foregoing matrix will show that there is no single combination of decisions which will always be advantageous to each. Under these circumstances, Company A can assure at least a minimum figure by adopting a mixed strategy. That is, Company A sometimes picks one alternative, and other times another. Company B will be deprived of the opportunity of capitalizing on A's strategy. For example, if B knows from past experience which decision A will make, B can always win. Therefore the only hope of A is to mix his strategies so that B remains in the dark until it is too late for B to change his own plans.

C. *Choosing the best strategy mixture*: It can be shown that, for each game in which there is no one pre-

ferred strategy, the strategies should be mixed in specific proportions which will be determined by the numerical values in the payoff matrix. In order to remove any pattern in the sequence of strategies selected, each decision on a given play should be made by random selection. For example, a single card might be selected from a deck in which the number of cards representing each alternative was in proportion to the ratios of the mixed strategy.

In this example, the proportions or odds for each strategy available to A are shown below.

Company B

	b_1	b_2	b_3	Odds for A
a_1	2	−4	2	1
a_2	4	−6	−4	1
a_3	0	2	1	8
	19	7	4	

Company A

[B8812]

If Company A makes its decision by random choice weighted in the ratio 1:1:8, and Company B adopts a pure strategy of picking alternative b_1 all the time, Company A can expect to gain, on the average, 600 in sales at the expense of B. Similarly, against any other single strategy or any mixed strategy of B, Company A can expect the same gain.

If, however, Company A were to abandon its optimum strategy and instead adopt a strategy of weighting each strategy equally, while Company B employed its optimum mixed strategy, Company A could expect an average decrease in sales of 6,500. This could be worse than settling on Design a_3 permanently, where one could at least be sure of losing no sales regardless of Company B's strategy. Similarly, every other strategy which Company A might select will bring a probable return of less than the optimum mixed strategy described above.

F. Lindsay, NEW TECHNIQUES FOR MANAGEMENT DECISION-MAKING 48–53 (1958).

she might immediately push the case to trial or otherwise increase the pretrial costs of her opponent (approach *B*—adversarial). Suppose further that N believes that approach *B* will force O into an immediate settlement on terms significantly better than N will obtain in any other way. However, N also calculates that if this approach results in pushing the case to trial or causes her opponent to be more aggressive, she will incur a net loss. That is, for N the projected outcome of approach *A* is dependent on the approach taken by O. If O's approach is adversarial (*b*), N will suffer a loss; only if O continues to be accommodative and agrees to prompt settlement (*a*) will N be better off. Assigning a numerical value to N's projected outcomes we can represent them on the following "payoff matrix":

APPROACHES OPEN TO O

	a (accommodative)	b (adversarial)
APPROACHES OPEN TO N A(accommodative)	4	1
B(adversarial)	10	−1

[B8822]

In order to decide which course of action to take, N will have to make the kind of assessment of O's view of the situation which Goffman describes. Suppose that N believes that her opponent sees the possible gains and losses in much the same way as she does (*i. e.*, a greater possible gain, but also a risk of loss associated with the adversarial approach). Separating N's perceptions of O's outcomes from her own by the use of a comma (and placing them on the right) we can add them to the payoff matrix:

O's ALTERNATIVES

	a	b
N's ALTERNATIVES A	4, 4	1, 10
B	10, 1	−1, −1

[B8813]

What the matrix depicts is O's view that if both parties are accommodative, the settlement at point *Aa* will eventually be reached.

If both parties adopt aggressive strategies she anticipates deadlock and a costly litigation which she presumes they both see as undesirable (*Bb*). If she can begin to impose preparation and other costs on O without causing him to respond in kind, however, she expects to maximize the outcomes available to her (*Ba*). This might occur, for example, in a situation in which O feels that if trial looks likely he must associate trial counsel. He might therefore be willing to accept a smaller settlement in order to avoid these costs. On the other hand, if N waits and O takes the initiative, she will have to accept a less favorable settlement (*Ab*). Looked at in another way, N is assuming a bargaining range in which she can gain as much as 10 and as little as 1—her resistance point—and is assuming a similar set of valuations by her opponent.

What does such an analysis add to N's handling of these options? Our experience with law student negotiation suggests some possibilities. First, thinking in these terms forces consideration of the *structure* of the bargaining situation itself. What choices are available? With what outcomes? How are these choices and outcomes likely to be seen/valued by one's opponent? What are the particular vulnerabilities of any choice? In what order will choices be made? For many inexperienced negotiators, the major problem in framing bargaining strategy seems to be in their inability to envision the bargaining situation as a complex of intersecting choices and perceptions; for some game theory may provide a useful way to begin to think systematically about the relationships involved.

Second, the matrix helps to clarify objectives and the *direction* of attempts to influence the situation. In our illustration, for example, N wants O to choose option *a,* or at least to refrain from adopting the more aggressive strategy (*b*). She can accomplish this by making O believe that (i) the outcomes associated with alternative *a* are more attractive to him and the *b* outcomes less attractive; and that (ii) N is more likely to choose strategy *B* than strategy *A*. For example, N might seek to convince O that she is not worried about trial and has as much to gain from litigating the case as settling it, or she might try to persuade O that he has more to lose by going to trial than he had supposed. If N could make these assertions credible, the payoff matrix from O's point of view might look like this:

O's ALTERNATIVES

		a	b
	A	2, 6	−1, 8
N's ALTERNATIVES	B	10, 7	2, −2

O's choices in this situation should be clear. Not only are the outcomes associated with the accommodative strategy almost as attractive to him as the best he can do with strategy *b*: he would also predict that N is much more likely to choose alternative *B*, so he would expect to suffer a loss if he pursues the aggressive strategy. N must take these multiple perceptions into account in any strategy she adopts, and a payoff matrix might help her make objectives and strategies more clear.

Finally, working through a problem in this way underscores *the centrality of credibility* in the negotiating process. Although Goffman identifies a few instances in which credibility can exist without a normative basis—without trust—a great deal depends on a negotiator's ability to persuade his or her opponent that things are as they appear to be. The exchange analogy, then, takes us only so far, for each party is seeking not only to obtain certain "goods" and avoid certain "bads," but also to *acquire the information upon which to make a valid assessment* of the gains and losses a particular bargain involves. Goffman poses the crucial question: How is a negotiator ever to influence his or her opponent in the ways we have discussed if the opponent posits that every statement or action is a strategem? There is no ready answer to this question, yet it is clear that the parties to a negotiation do establish a base of credibility sufficient to support stable, long-term agreements. Communications are believed, acted upon and responded to with communications which themselves generate belief. It seems to us that these consequences, at least in part, are due to (i) mutual self-interest; (ii) norms and self-image, and (iii) trust. Indeed, an effective negotiator will often enlist these factors in the pursuit of his or her ends. But it should at least give us pause that the very existence of the elements in bargaining which make influence and the "creation of belief" possible largely depends on some constraint on their use.

————

2. *The Game as a Research Tool*

Another perspective offered by the sort of analysis Goffman provides relates to its use in compiling experimental data on bargaining behavior. The simple game offers a conflict situation with a manageable number of variables capable of being measured and replicated in successive trials of the same game. For this reason, game models have fascinated researchers interested in isolating influences on choice in circumstances where each player must take the potential choices of an opponent into account. These experiments attempt to simulate social situations (not unlike law practice) in which the pressures toward cooperative behavior and competitive behavior are both very strong, and in which trust is an essential element. The classic formulation is the "prisoner's dilemma," which has been used in a large

number of studies. The basic situation, as well as some of the experimental results, are described in the following summary:

   . . . Two suspects have been taken into custody by the police.
They are interviewed separately by the district attorney, who tries to
convince each one to turn state's evidence in order to obtain a lighter
sentence. Both prisoners know that if neither confesses the worst that
will happen to them is a light sentence for vagrancy. If one confesses
and the other does not, the one who refuses to confess will have the
book thrown at him. On the other hand, if both confess, then both will
be punished with moderate rather than severe sentences. Each prisoner thus has two strategies—to confess or not to confess—and different
payoffs, or consequences, are associated with each course of action.

   Suppose that the payoff matrix shown in [the figure below] obtains for the parties to this dilemma. The dilemma for each suspect
is obvious. If neither knows what choice the other has made, and if
each chooses the alternative most advantageous to himself with no consideration for the other, then both will receive sentences of eight years.
A moment's consideration will reveal why this is so. The rules of the
game, it should be recalled, specify the outcome for each combination
of choices. The strategy picked by A determines the row in which the
outcome will fall and that chosen by B determines the column. The
joint outcome is designated by the point of intersection.

	Prisoner B	
	Does not confess	Confesses
Does not Confess	1 year for A; 1 year for B	20 years for A; 6 months for B
Confesses	6 months for A; 20 years for B	8 years for A; 8 years for B

Prisoner A

Figure: Payoff Matrix for the Prisoner's Dilemma (Adapted from Brown, 1965)

[B8814]

   From A's point of view, the verbal problem-solving process probably goes something like this: "If I do not confess, I may get only one
year. But if B turns state's evidence, then I will get twenty years. On
the other hand, if I confess, I may get only six months, and the worst I
can get is eight years. I had better confess and avoid the possibility
of a twenty-year sentence." If B reasons the same way, then the outcome is a moderate penalty for both.

   If A and B can trust one another, then each is better off not confessing, since the maximum sentence that each can receive is one year.
In the absence of mutual trust, the best they can achieve is a compromise
eight-year sentence. They have then arrived at what can be called a
noncooperative equilibrium point (Shubik, 1934). If the suspects were
to cooperate, in effect to form a *coalition* against the prosecutor, then

they could achieve a better mutual outcome by escaping with only one-year sentences. Effectively, what each has done is to envision the worst thing that could happen to him for either confessing or not confessing. He then selects the lesser of these two evils, thus fixing his strategy. In A's case, this means selection of the row, and in B's case selection of the column, corresponding to "confess."

* * *

[These dilemmas provide a simple set of instances] in which such factors as trust and suspicion can be investigated. . . . [For example, a] study reported by Scodel and Minas (1960) illustrates the procedures and some typical outcomes in this particular experimental setting. In their version of the Prisoner's Dilemma, either money or cigarettes were assigned to the outcomes, and the game was repeated for fifty trials. One interesting feature was that their subjects were actual prisoners from the Federal Reformatory at Chillicothe, Ohio.

Eighteen pairs of prisoners were treated in the following manner. The members of each pair were seated on opposite sides of a partition facing a panel containing a red button and a black button. They were instructed as follows:

> On each trial you will press either the black button or the red button. If you press the black button, two things can happen. If you press the black button and the other person also presses the black button, you get three cigarettes and he gets three cigarettes. If you press the black button and he presses the red button, you get nothing and he gets five cigarettes. Suppose you push the red button. Again two things can happen. If you push the red button and the other person presses the black button, you get five cigarettes and he gets nothing. If you push red and the other person also pushes red, you get one cigarette and the other person gets one cigarette (p. 134).

These various combinations of events can be summarized in matrix form:

Player B

		Black	Red
	Black	3, 3	0, 5
Player A			
	Red	5, 0	1, 1

[B8815]

It should be noted that the matrix shown above was posted on the partition in front of each subject, so that the various options and their consequences to both parties were clearly evident. The results were compared with data obtained previously from college students who had been paid off with pennies (Scodel, Minas, Ratoosh, and Lipetz, 1959). The cooperative solution to this problem is obviously for each player to choose Black, since each will then receive a payoff of three units. By defecting from this cooperative strategy and playing

Red while his opponent is still playing Black, Player B can increase his winnings. Player A can do likewise by switching his play to Red. However, a defensive move made by one player in response to defection by the other will result in both receiving a payoff on one unit. How did the performances of college students in this situation compare with those of actual prisoners?

Among twenty-two pairs of college subjects, a colloborative choice (Black, Black) was made most frequently by only two pairs. In the remaining cases, the subjects behaved as though suspicious of one another and settled for the minimum reward associated with plays of Red, Red. In the group of prison subjects a very similar result was obtained. None of the pairs of actual prisoners displayed collaboration. Among both the college subjects and the prison subjects, the number of competitive (Red, Red) choices increased during the last twenty-five trials as compared with the earlier trials. The investigators concluded that any attempts at collaboration in an effort to maximize joint return were quickly abandoned.

The results obtained in this experiment are consistent with a "rational" solution to the problem, since one cannot really lose by playing Red on a single trial. However, in repeated play, a more reasonable solution would be for both players to switch to Black, inasmuch as this would result in their mutual benefit. Do these results square with what one might predict from behavior theory? It seems at first blush that a collaborative strategy would be more strongly reinforced than a competitive strategy and would, therefore, eventually dominate play. But game theory must be construed within a context of other social variables, and one of these is the prevalent tendency among individuals in our society to compete with one another. The rewards for successful competition, including success at avoiding defeat, are probably more potent in some situations than the reward that one might receive for employing a cooperative strategy that has an outcome of dubious utility.

Without any systematic intervention on the part of the experimenter, as we have already noted, players in the Prisoner's Dilemma tend to become even more competitive as the trials progress. . . .[13]

There are, of course, many problems involved in applying this type of experiment to actual bargaining situations and in assessing the validity and significance of the results themselves. The data used to infer a willingness to exploit or cooperate are ambiguous at best. It may be, for example, that (at least in our own "playing") the most salient factor in experimental games of this sort is their tendency to become boring. As a number of experiments have demonstrated, there is some basis for suggesting that the competitiveness exhibited in these experiments is a function less of the human capacity for exploitation than of the human need to be stimulated. And certainly the media of exchange which are used (*i. e.*, cigarettes, dollars)

13. E. McGinnies, SOCIAL BEHAVI-
OR: A FUNCTIONAL ANALYSIS
417–18, 423–24 (1970).

raise questions about whether the players' judgments accurately reflect the value they place on the consequences. There is artificiality, also, in the limited nature and clarity of the choices with which players are confronted. In most bargaining situations there are continuing trade-offs being made of a mixed exploitative-cooperative kind, and choices are sequential rather than simultaneous, so that either cooperative or competitive behavior may be only one step in a long-range strategy. Moreover, the complexity of the situation tends to blur perceptions of the degree to which exploitation is necessary to achieve results.

It is thus difficult to base generalizations about bargaining behavior on the analysis of experimental games. Whether or not they accurately describe lawyer behavior, however, they do identify patterns that have surprised a number of our students and colleagues (and ourselves):

—Most subjects demonstrate a very low level of cooperative choice.

—The level of cooperative choice is even lower when the matrix offers large *relative* gains. That is, the values of the payoffs are seen in absolute and comparative terms.

—The level of cooperative choice does not change if the other party is cooperative. Many subjects will exploit the pattern of cooperative choices of the other player. This is much less true if (i) there is a likelihood the participants will have social contact with each other after the experiment; (ii) the other participant started with competitive behavior and gradually shifted toward cooperative behavior; (iii) the parties are able to communicate with each other during the discussion (less if they are forced to communicate or the communication is limited to verbal or visual messages).

—The level of cooperative behavior seems to be significantly influenced by personality variables. That is, achievement and power "needs" will generate competitive behavior while persons with high affiliative needs are likely to be more cooperative in their choices. This influence tends to be minimized by changes in the situation (*i. e.*, magnitude of payoffs).[14]

Ask yourself *why* these generalizations might be true and how much they tell you about what you can expect in bargaining with other lawyers. For example, why is cooperative behavior more likely to be reciprocated by a subject if his or her opponent has shifted from a

14. The results and many aspects of this research can be found in the last 10 volumes of the Journal of Conflict Resolution; *see, e. g.*, Braver & Barnett, *Perception of Opponents' Motives and Cooperation in a Mixed Motive Game*, 18 J.CONFL.RES. 686 (1974); Steele & Tedeschi, *Matrix Indices and Strategy Choices in Mixed Motive Games*, 11 J.CONF.RES. 198 (1967). The earlier results and procedures are also summarized in A. Rapoport & A. Chammah, PRISONERS' DILEMMA (1965).

competitive pattern? It may be that the failure to use available power is viewed as a "ploy," so that until there is evidence of a "reason" for cooperation, such overtures are not considered credible. Or it may be that such conduct is seen as a sign of weakness or stupidity and thereby "deserving" of exploitation. Perhaps not using available power merely invites the exercise of a pre-existing individualist orientation in those who find themselves in such situations. The line between explanation and speculation in this area is, to say the least, very hard to draw. Nevertheless, it is well to recognize that many of the variables that characterize experimental games are also present in lawyering negotiations—including an adversarial environment, prior relationships between parties, differential payoffs, and possibilities for both cooperative and competitive strategies. You will undoubtedly develop your own working explanations and predictions of their influence. As you do so, you may find yourself replicating in your own thinking many of the simplifying models with which these social psychologists are struggling.

SECTION TWO.   THE SKILL DIMENSION

A.   ASSESSMENT: UNDERSTANDING THE BARGAINING SITUATION

1.   Determining the Bargaining Range

NOTE, AN ANALYSIS OF SETTLEMENT

22 STAN.L.REV. 67, 70–80 (1969).

Litigants settle out of court for only one reason: Each thinks he obtains through the settlement agreement an outcome at least as good as his estimated outcome in court. Therefore, all settlement negotiation proceeds within the confines of the parties' anticipations of the result of the contemplated lawsuit. Each party's bargaining limit is determined by his evaluation of the probable dollar outcome in court, adjusted for the probable dollar costs of litigation and settlement. Plaintiff will not accept in settlement anything less than his bargaining limit, because he thinks he can obtain that amount by going to court. Defendant will not pay in settlement anything more than his bargaining limit, because that is the amount he thinks he will lose if he defends himself in court. A rational plaintiff and a rational defendant will always settle out of court when defendant's bargaining limit (what he thinks he would lose in court) is greater than plaintiff's bargaining limit (what he thinks he would obtain in court).

In such a situation there is a range of settlement figures within which both parties can and will profitably settle, since at any settlement figure within that range each party is better off than he thinks he would be if he went to court. This "settlement bargaining range" runs from plaintiff's bargaining limit up to defendant's bargaining limit, and its width—the "bargaining span"—is defendant's bargaining limit minus plaintiff's limit. Whether the eventual settlement figure within the bargaining range is more favorable to plaintiff or defendant depends primarily upon which party is the better bargainer. However, so long as a bargaining range exists, both parties are better off settling than litigating. Only if no bargaining range exists, if plaintiff's bargaining limit is greater than defendant's bargaining limit, will both parties prefer to litigate.

Determinants of the Bargaining Limits

In real cases, factors in addition to the parties' estimates of the outcome of the lawsuit affect their determinations of their bargaining limits, and hence affect the settlement bargaining range. This section shows how each of these additional factors should be taken into account by a party trying to decide whether and for how much to settle.

Fixed litigation costs

Suppose defendant and plaintiff both estimate that defendant will be held liable, that they both expect the amount of recoverable damages at $10,000, and that it costs each party nothing to arrange a settlement. In a case in which, under the law of the jurisdiction, each party will be required to bear his own litigation costs regardless of the outcome, the bargaining limits of the parties will reflect their estimates of their respective litigation costs.

Plaintiff estimates his litigation costs—including court costs, attorney's fees, secretarial costs, and other miscellaneous expenses—at $2000. Plaintiff's estimated net recovery in court is $10,000 (damages) minus $2000 (costs), or $8000. If defendant estimates his own litigation costs at $1500, his estimated total payment in court is $10,000 (damages) plus $1500 (costs), or $11,500. The settlement bargaining range runs from $8000 to $11,500. The settlement bargaining span is $3500, equal to the sum of the parties' litigation costs.

* * *

The more common case, of course, places liability for the winner's court costs upon the loser, and in this case the identity of the party who must pay a portion or all of the other's litigation expenses is unknown in advance. To analyze this situation requires estimating the total litigation expenses to be borne by the loser and discounting that amount by the probability that a particular party will lose. . . .

Fixed settlement costs

The foregoing discussion of litigation costs assumes that while the process of litigation costs each party something, the process of settlement out of court costs neither party anything. Negotiation and settlement, however, unavoidably involve some costs: outlays made in drafting and exchanging proposals and counterproposals, the value of time spent by each party in bargaining and strategy sessions, and costs of lawyers' services in bargaining and in drafting and examining the settlement agreement. The magnitude of these costs may vary greatly from one situation to another, and in some circumstances estimated settlement costs may be large enough to preclude settlement.

. . .

To understand how settlement costs affect the parties' bargaining limits, recall the first example in the preceding subsection. Plaintiff and defendant agreed that defendant was liable for $10,000 damages. Plaintiff's net estimated recovery in court was $8000; defendant's total estimated payment in court was $11,500. Now suppose defendant estimates that the process of settlement will cost him about $800. Since defendant is unwilling to spend more in settlement than $11,500 (his expected total payment in court), and since $800 of his settlement expenditures must go to cover his costs in arranging settlement, the most defendant is now willing to pay plaintiff in settlement is $10,700. In more general terms, defendant's settlement bargaining limit equals his expected total payment in court minus the amount of his estimated settlement costs.

* * *

Plaintiff's bargaining limit is computed in much the same way. If plaintiff's estimated net recovery in court is $8000, he will not accept less than a net $8000 in settlement. If his settlement costs are $800, he will accept no less than $8800 in settlement. Plaintiff's bargaining limit thus equals his estimated net recovery in court plus his estimated settlement costs. . . . If settlement costs are high enough, plaintiff's bargaining limit rises above defendant's bargaining limit, the bargaining span becomes negative, and settlement is precluded.

Probable damage award

The assumption so far has been that the two parties have made identical estimates as to plaintiff's damage award in court. In the normal case, their estimates are presumably not the same. The parties may disagree as to the existence of particular facts, the probative significance of the facts on which they agree, the applicable law, or some combination of these. These differences of opinion are bound to result in divergent estimates by the parties of their relative chances of winning or losing, and of the amount of damages the court is likely to award if plaintiff wins. This, in turn, means that the bargaining limits of the parties will be affected by their differing predictions of the courtroom outcome.

* * *

Generally, multiplying a litigant's estimate of the amount of recoverable damages by his estimate of the probability that defendant will be held liable yields a figure that represents the probable damage recovery in court. . . .

Marginal analysis of costs

It has been assumed until now that litigation costs are independent of the probable outcome in court—in other words, that spending more or less money on litigation preparations will not influence either the likelihood that defendant will be held liable or the size of the expected damage award. Litigation expenses, however, will clearly have an effect on the outcome of a great many disputes. Defendant (or plaintiff) can choose to employ a more or less highly skilled attorney, to employ more than one attorney, or to have his counsel spend more or less time doing legal research.

The relationship between litigation costs and the probability of winning in court can be clarified by marginal analysis. Suppose defendant suspects that through some minimal legal effort costing $100 he can reduce from 100 percent to 80 percent the probability that plaintiff will win $10,000 in recoverable damages, so that plaintiff's probable recovery after defendant's $100 expenditure is $8000. Defendant has saved himself $2000 by spending $100, which places him $1900 ahead on the transaction. Suppose further that defendant has reason to believe that by spending $110 rather than $100, he can reduce the probability that he will lose to 79 percent. He will have gained an extra one percent, worth $100, by spending only $10 more. His net gain from spending this last $10 is therefore $90. At any point it is worth defendant's while to spend an additional dollar on litigation so long as this marginal expenditure will reduce his probable losses by more than a dollar: Defendant should continue to spend money on litigation until his marginal savings just equal his marginal expenditure.

Defendant reduces his bargaining limit by reducing the total amount (in probable damages and costs) that he can be forced to pay in court. Likewise, when plaintiff engages in a parallel procedure—comparing marginal increases in probable recovery to the marginal costs of bringing them about—the effect will be to increase his bargaining limit. The combined tendency of plaintiff's and defendant's behavior based on marginal analysis is to decrease the settlement bargaining span.

Marginal analysis must serve to qualify all of the preceding discussion of litigation costs, settlement costs (for it is apparent that a rational litigant should marginally analyze his settlement-cost expenditures as well), and all costs treated below. But the introduction of this technique into the parties' calculations does not alter the basic cost-and-benefit determinants of settlement decisions. The parties must continually determine the best amount to spend and compute the bargaining limits corresponding to the litigation and settlement expenditures they have chosen. At the moment of each decision, all appropriate marginal analyses of the determinative quantities will have been accomplished.

Opportunity costs

* * *

. . . In taking into account opportunity costs associated with different times of payment (whether by settlement or pursuant to court award), the bargaining limits must be adjusted by the difference between the value to a party of possessing the capital longer or receiving it sooner, and the interest, if any, which the court is expected to award.

It has been assumed that each party is motivated solely by economic considerations. If he is not, he should determine what financial sacrifices he is willing to make in order to attain his noneconomic objectives in the dispute and should adjust his settlement bargaining limit accordingly. Further, it has been assumed that each party is indifferent to the size of the risk he faces so long as he knows he is pursuing the course best calculated to ensure the best financial return in the long run. If this assumption does not hold in the particular case, the party should adjust his bargaining limit to reflect his risk preferences.

The party will then determine the respective values of different amounts of information and the expense of acquiring each amount, and will acquire the optimal amount of information upon which to base his actions. He will determine the amount of litigation expenses best calculated to minimize his expected loss or maximize his expected gain, and will use this amount in his computations. He will do the same for settlement costs. Finally, he will determine (if he is defendant) his opportunity costs of settling now as opposed to paying a judgment later, or (if he is plaintiff) his opportunity gains from receiving payment now as opposed to a judgment later.

To compute his bargaining limit, defendant will (1) multiply the expected damage award by the probability that it will be rendered against him, (2) add to the result in (1) the amount of his anticipated litigation costs, (3) subtract his settlement costs, and (4) subtract his opportunity costs of settling now as opposed to paying later.

To compute his bargaining limit, plaintiff will (1) multiply the expected damage award by the probability that the court will award it to him, (2) subtract from the product in (1) the amount of his anticipated litigation costs, (3) add his settlement costs, and (4) subtract his opportunity gains from receiving payment now as opposed to a judgment later.

*   *   *

[In conclusion,] the basic observation developed above merits reiteration: There will be settlement between rational parties if and only if defendant's bargaining limit is greater than plaintiff's bargaining limit. In such a case, neither party has anything to gain by litigation; settlement anywhere within the bargaining range is better for each party than the probable outcome, according to his own estimate, of the contemplated litigation.

NOTES

1. *Determining One's Own Limits: The Least A Case is Worth*

As the above comments indicate, the task of setting one's own outer limit is a complicated yet essential step in preparing for any negotiation. The task of assessing an *opponent's* bargaining limit is basically the same, with the difference being that some of the figures in your calculations—for example, your opponent's actual costs and probability assessments—will be guesses rather than known quantities. Since many of your own figures are similarly uncertain, however, that difference is not so great as it might seem. Comforting as it may be to use concrete formulas and exact amounts, on analysis this aspect of lawyering remains a very intuitive and subjective process.

Despite these limitations, the formula suggested above sets out in simplified form the kind of calculation that must be made in every case. That is, each party determines his or her bargaining limit by adding or subtracting litigation, settlement and opportunity costs to or from the product obtained by multiplying the expected verdict by its probability. You may refine and qualify this model as you acquire more negotiating experience, but it is difficult to imagine an effective lawyer not making such an assessment in preparing for a negotiation. As you engage in your own planning, however, you ought to be aware of some of the problems which such formulas obscure.

Dependence on Subjective Judgments

The decision to settle is a judgment that acceptance of the opponent's final offer is preferable to litigating the case. It requires an appraisal of the value of these two alternatives and, with respect to the trial option, estimates of the likelihood of a number of contingencies. It also involves a determination of the appropriate way to *combine* these probabilities and values. This presents a number of serious conceptual difficulties.[15] The assumption that parties are

---

15. Some of these problems are discussed in Chapter Two *infra* at pp. 177–90 and 219–41.

primarily motivated by economic considerations—or that they are indifferent to different degrees of risk—requires considerable qualification.

Adequacy of Remedy

The foregoing model is limited to a claim for past damages.[16] Additional calculations must be made if damages are of a continuing nature and/or injunctive relief is available. The situation would be further complicated if it was likely that damages would be uncollectible or that an injunction would be difficult and costly to enforce. For example, consider the problems involved in calculating a minimal settlement point in a case where enforcement of the remedy might require continuing involvement and supervision by a court (as in desegregation cases) or where the verdict might include an award of punitive damages. Counsel would have to make a number of additional evaluations and probability assessments.

Type of Case

Beyond these complications, the suggested calculus requires adjustment of estimates to the particulars of each *type* of case. For a criminal defendant, for example, assessing the probable outcome of trial would require judgments about the likelihood of a jury verdict (on any of the included offenses), the length and type of potential sentences (years, fine, etc.), and the probability of their being imposed. The predicted costs of trial would include time in jail awaiting trial. Settlement costs would relate to the likelihood and severity of the sentence the court would impose on receiving a plea. These are difficult calculations and often rely on considerations very different from those to which the reading refers. For instance, if (as we believe) the longer a defendant is out on bail the greater are his chances of probation or a suspended sentence, the opportunity costs associated with an early plea are substantial. Conversely, the involvement of private counsel and the incarceration of the defendant prior to trial often make the fixed costs associated with refusing to plead prohibitive.

The appropriate assessment of such factors in particular circumstances thus requires attention to recurring elements in particular legal disputes. For example, Melvin Belli has suggested that all of the following factors ought to be weighed in personal injury cases: type of accident; the defendant's apparent ability to pay; the plaintiff's apparent need for money; the comparative personality and

---

16. It should be noted that the student note from which this excerpt is taken goes on to analyze disputes involving continuing and future damages, with special attention to the questions of (1) whether and to what extent a defendant will seek to reduce future damages, and (2) how the parties' bargaining limits are affected by their predictions as to the form of the remedy. 22 STAN.L.REV. at 80–88 (1969).

character of the plaintiff and defendant; the comparative intelligence of the plaintiff and defendant and their ability to think, talk and convey the conviction of truth and honesty to others; the character, personality, appearance and intelligence of the plaintiff's witnesses as compared to the defendant's; the comparative capability of the physicians for the plaintiff and defendant; the character of the plaintiff's injury and disability; the plaintiff's age, previous health and accident history; "inflammatory factors" on either side (such as drinking or flagrant violations of traffic laws); "sympathetic factors" for either side (*e. g.,* a widow with children in a death case); race, color and creed as it relates to jury prejudice; special damages (medical, hospital, loss of time); comparative ability of counsel for plaintiff and defendant; and liability as it affects either the chance of winning or the size of the expected verdict.[17] Each of these factors may have a substantial impact on the outcome of a trial, with the result that they must also be considered in deciding what the case is "worth" for purposes of settlement. Such calculations—even with the help of the large amount of statistical data that has been accumulated and analyzed in personal injury actions—involve considerable uncertainty.[18]

Interdependence

The most complex aspect of the calculation of one's minimal settlement position lies in its dependence on the other party's calculations and actions. Analytically it is possible to make assessments of the type discussed above without reference to the expected bargaining behavior of the other party. On further examination, however, the anticipated actions of opposing parties are inevitably intertwined with one's own judgments, for the nature and likelihood of a favorable outcome at trial depends on the intentions and capacities of one's opponent. Thus the costs and benefits of accepting a particular offer must constantly be reassessed as perceptions of both values and

---

17. M. Belli, MODERN TRIALS, VOL. I, 749–52 (1954).

18. It should be pointed out that, because of the expenses involved in making them, in many litigation situations no such calculations are made at all; the case is seen as a type in which the costs of trial are *presumed* to be excessive, and there is frequently a usual or typical settlement point associated with the case "type." Small personal injury or property damage claims ("nuisance cases") are handled by insurance companies in this way; so are a large number of criminal violations arising out of neighborhood or family disputes. Although it would be possible to make the calculations we have been discussing in such cases, they are so rarely litigated that there is virtually no data on which to rely. The decision for counsel is solely whether to settle now or later and what the effects of the passage of time will be. Because there is so much social and precedential support for the "reasonableness and fairness" of standard resolutions for these cases, attempts to alter the usual outcome are generally perceived as "too costly." On the other hand, the opposing party in such cases has little reason to absorb additional costs (since he or she knows they will be settled) and is, therefore, more vulnerable to leverage than if the type of case were not handled in a routine way.

probabilities change. As one comes to believe that a more favorable settlement is possible, the least favorable one would accept in preference to deadlock seems to change as well. Whatever the logic of this reasoning, it is an important source of difficulty in carrying out this generally difficult task.

————

2. *Determining One's Goals: The Most a Case is Worth*

Estimating the point at which one will settle rather than go to trial is, of course, only part of the bargaining situation analysis. There will be a settlement only if your bargaining limit is greater than your opponent's bargaining limit—only if *some* possible settlement is acceptable to both parties. In most instances there will actually be a *range* of mutually acceptable settlement points, and each party will attempt to reach a settlement as near his or her opponent's minimum disposition as possible. Although this should be obvious, some lawyers (and students) frequently enter negotiations without making an effort to estimate the opponent's minimum disposition or the range of outcomes that might be acceptable to both parties. That is, they concentrate on their own limits rather than on the *difference* between the minimal dispositions of both parties. This places additional (and unnecessary) constraints on what can be accomplished in the negotiation itself.

Every bargaining situation can be thought of as a continuum of more or less possible agreements. Consider, for example, a civil case in which a creditor is willing to pay as much as $500 to settle a $1,000 counterclaim filed against him by a debtor who is also willing to pay $500 on the creditor's $1,000 claim. The *bargaining range* would look like this:

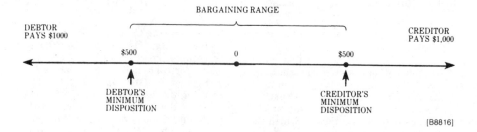

The range here—the difference between the parties' minimum dispositions—is $1,000, and *any* division of that amount, even one in which one party saves or collects $999 while the other saves only a dollar, would be preferred to trial by *both* parties.

In a criminal case the units of exchange are not so easily represented on a linear scale, but there will still be a range of possible dispositions. In the case of a criminal defendant charged with armed robbery, for example, options range from a complete dismissal to a plea to armed robbery. Assume the defendant in such a case is willing to plead, at most, to assault with a dangerous weapon, while the prosecutor will go so far as accepting a plea to taking property without right. This bargaining situation can be depicted as follows:

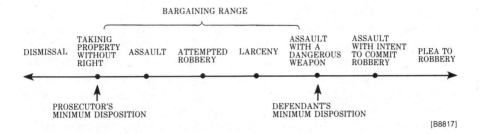

Here, again, there are at least five possible options that would be acceptable to both parties, and a defense lawyer who entered the negotiation concentrating on pleading to assault with a dangerous weapon and *no more* without speculating or attempting to learn about the prosecutor's minimum disposition, would actually negotiate the worst possible settlement for his or her client.

In both of these examples we are dealing with the parties' *actual* bargaining ranges, as they would be seen by an outsider with full information about each side's minimal settlement points. The outcome of the negotiation, of course, will be largely dependent on the range that is *perceived* by each of the parties, and it is this perceived range that must be the focus of negotiation strategies. The decision to accept a particular settlement offer is inevitably a subjective one, not unlike the preferences exercised in a purchase. As Hickam and Scanlon have suggested:

> When a claim is settled something comparable to a sale takes place. The plaintiff sells his cause of action to the defendant for a price (or the prosecutor reduces the charge for the defendant's agreement to accept the consequences of a guilty plea.) The defendant pays that price to regain his peace of mind and to avoid the potential liability, inconvenience and the cost of continuing the litigation. Law suits, however, are not bought and sold at any established market. There is, therefore, no objectively established guide to settlement value . . . Settlement value can only mean that amount which the defendant is willing to pay and the plaintiff is willing to accept in a particular case. A particular defendant, for reasons which appear to him to be sound, may be willing to pay twice the amount which a panel of lawyers would estimate the plaintiff's claim is reasonably worth and twice the amount which the plaintiff is really willing to accept. The double amount is still the settlement value of

that particular case even though no one other than that particular defendant would be willing or would be forced to pay as much.[19]

You should be sure about your understanding of this idea; all of us slip at times into equating success in negotiation with *any* outcome which satisfies the client. Since by definition the client is more satisfied with settlement than non-settlement, client satisfaction cannot distinguish a "good" settlement from a poor one. What is needed is a measure of outcome against what was *possible*—against, that is, the maximum that could have been obtained within the bargaining range. The lawyer who consistently persuades opponents to settle at or near their minimal settlement points is certainly a "better" negotiator than one who is frequently pushed to his or her own limits, even though both are "successful" in avoiding deadlock. Assuming that maximizing the client's interests in negotiation is a desirable norm, thinking in terms of a bargaining range may help keep your efforts focused on this objective.

Bear in mind, however, that these boundaries are not static. While each party enters (or should enter) a particular negotiation with some initial assessments of the bargaining range, those assessments are subject to change in the course of the negotiation itself. The range may expand, contract, or shift for either party as the bargaining progresses. This is not only a result of one party's manipulation of the other's perceptions; a negotiator may revise his or her notions of the bargaining limits in response to changing circumstances. An offer of compromise which falls well within the initial bargaining range, for example, may cause a negotiator to revise his or her estimate of the probable outcome and become less willing to settle at the original level. Expectations in bargaining seem to fluctuate in direct relation to the reactions of one's adversary, and a projected bargaining range, like any other set of valuations, is valid only at a particular point in time.[20]

19. H. Hickam and T. Scanlon, PREPARATION FOR TRIAL 231 (1963).

20. As Ikle and Leites have observed in discussing such preferences in international negotiations:

A "utility" is experimentally determined (and hence operationally defined) by an *act of preference*: if a subject chooses alternative *A* in preference to alternative *B*, *A* is said to have a greater "utility" for this subject than *B*. More precisely, it should be recognized that the "utility" is associated with those characteristics and/or consequences of the alternatives (and the probabilities of their occurrence) that the subject *expects and considers* when making the choice. . . . [W]here

the consequences of choices are . . complex and intuition plays . . . a large role, it is clear that utility thus defined is unlikely to remain stable during the course of negotiations. [This is the case in most negotiation situations.]

* * *

To understand [most real life] negotiations, therefore, we need a concept that takes account of the changes in preferences, in distinction to the *act of preference* which occurs at the time a choice is made and which can be used operationally to define "utility" only at that time. We may define for each negotiator and for a given time in the course of negotiations a "disposition to prefer" as the negotiator's estimate

Indeed, the ability to quickly distinguish real from apparent changes in the bargaining range absorbs much of the negotiator's effort and skill. Ikle and Leites have elaborated:

> As long as both sides try to get an agreement, they will seek to improve the terms for themselves through the modification of Dispositions and estimated Probable Outcomes. If I am the negotiator, I will attempt to modify:
>
> (A) My opponent's Minimum Disposition; *i. e.*, make him believe or feel that he would prefer an agreement to no agreement on terms more favorable to me than he originally thought;
>
> (B) My opponent's estimate of my Minimum Disposition; *i. e.*, make him believe that the terms at which I would prefer no agreement are, in fact, less favorable to him than he had first thought.
>
> If my opponent pays more attention to his estimate of the Probable Outcome than to his estimate of the bargaining range, my efforts will also have to be directed to the former. I might try to convince my opponent that his estimated Probable Outcome lies outside the bargaining range and hence is improbable, or that it would imply an "unfair" division of the bargaining range. . . . [This involves a number of specific tactics] . . .
>
> * * *
>
> I may modify my opponent's Minimum Disposition: (1) By altering the actual situation on which his Minimum Disposition is based. Particularly important are facts that make an agreement seem more urgent to my opponent than he first thought so that he will be willing

that he will prefer one alternative over another if and when he has to make the choice. The most important choice is, of course, that between agreement at given terms and no agreement. Theoretically, we can ask each negotiator at any time during the negotiations what the least favorable terms are at which he would prefer agreement to no agreement. We call these terms— which are often quite vague—the negotiator's *Minimum Disposition* (at time *t*).

* * *

Actually, [parties] often enter negotiations without being conscious of their Minimum Disposition and without making an effort to estimate the opponent's Minimum Disposition. Negotiators frequently seem to be somewhat reluctant to estimate the bargaining range. They may feel that such estimates might reduce flexibility and the capacity to put pressure on the opponent. The tendency not to estimate a bargaining range is also fostered by the fact that real negotiations are im-

mensely . . . complex . . . since most agreements involve a great many bargaining ranges which must be combined into an over-all bargain.

Instead of estimating the bargaining range, a negotiator may estimate a *Probable Outcome, i. e.,* the approximate terms at which he expects agreement. . . .

* * *

[As we have said,] over time . . . the negotiators' own Minimum Disposition and estimated Probable Outcome, and . . . their estimates of the opponent's Minimum Disposition and estimated Probable Outcome [will change]. This change is not a perturbation or a "nuisance factor" that one might want to randomize or hold constant in a study of negotiations; it is the very essence of the negotiating process.

Ikle and Leites, *Negotiation—A Device for Modifying Utilities,* in GAME THEORY AND RELATED APPROACHES TO SOCIAL BEHAVIOR, 245–49 (1964).

to settle for less. The strengthening of forces or military advances during armistice negotiations belong in this category, as do threats (and actions to make threats credible) as to what would happen to the opponent if no agreement was reached. These actions represent bargaining moves in a broader sense and can, of course, be far more important in determining the terms of agreement than the negotiations proper. (2) By pointing out the advantages and minimizing the disadvantages of my proposed terms to my opponent. . . . (3) By conveying to my opponent my (actual or faked) estimate of his Minimum Disposition. (This can easily be illustrated for economic negotiations: I convey to my opponent that I "know" that he can still make a profit if he sells to me for as little as . . . .) This may change my opponent's estimated Probable Outcome in my favor. (4) By portraying to my opponent a certain intrinsic development of the negotiations and convincing him that the *Negotiation Mores* require that he follow this development. For instance, I might demonstrate to my opponent that I made many concessions and convince him that he should reciprocate with a concession. If my opponent reciprocates to the extent of revising his Minimum Disposition, consideration of the Negotiation Mores must have led him to prefer agreement at terms which he originally found unacceptable. Thus, the Negotiation Mores become part of the negotiator's utility: violating them may cause political damage at home, make the negotiator feel badly, or aggravate relations with the opponent and thus spoil future negotiations.

I may modify my opponent's estimate of my Minimum Disposition: (1) By altering the actual situation on which my opponent's estimate of my Minimum Disposition is based. Most important here are commitments, or "burning bridges." If a decision-maker convincingly commits his prestige to a prediction that he will obtain certain terms in negotiations, his opponent may be led to estimate that these terms, or something close to it, constitute the Minimum Disposition. (2) By convincing my opponent that it would be disastrous or impossible for me to agree to less than my proposed terms. I may use legal arguments, thus essentially say to my opponent: "You know that I am constrained by legal norms and I am explaining to you that it would be illegal for me to agree to your proposed terms; hence, I cannot do it." . . . (3) By exhibiting attitudes consistent with a Minimum Disposition more favorable than my opponent's estimate. I may portray coolness towards the negotiations, suggesting that I am about to walk out unless the opponent's proposals become much more favorable for me.[21]

Each of these general strategies relates to changing the preferences and expectations of the opponent, and a number of them involve defending against changes in one's own positions. Since it is obvious that in a sophisticated negotiation *both* parties will be employing such strategies, the task of maintaining even a rough, working estimate of the current bargaining range becomes exceedingly complex. Nevertheless, abandoning the attempt to track these shifting parameters

21. *Id.* at 249–51.

can be a costly error.   Juggling and "using" a bargaining range seems to be the only way to be concrete about where you are and where you might be going.

— — —

3.   *The Uses of Formulas in Assessing the Bargaining Situation*

The complexities of the calculations involved thus far—of recognizing the relevant considerations, and combining your evaluations and predictions in a few figures—may strike you as overwhelming. Your discomfort seems to be shared by a great many practicing attorneys, many of whom rely on various rules of thumb rather than the sort of judgments we have just suggested.   These simplified approaches are generally stated as formulas for computing the "expected damage award" which, when discounted by its probability, corresponds to a case's "settlement value."   In discussions of such formulas in the literature on trial practice it is not always clear whether what is being calculated is a minimal settlement point, a "fair" settlement outcome, or what can reasonably be expected in a particular type of dispute; but whatever their emphasis, these simplified formulas often suggest a pseudo-certainty that can be extremely misleading to both counsel and client.

On the other hand, the use of such formulas—particularly in personal injury litigation—is one of the realities of practice, and must be taken into account by any lawyer negotiator.   In some cases they may be helpful in setting one's own minimum disposition, and they will often be a source of insight into the calculations of opposing counsel in areas where they have become part of the lore of a particular practice.   The following represents one summary of some of these methods:

> Undoubtedly, there are many formulas for settlement.   One of the older methods used by attorneys for plaintiffs consists in the selection of two figures—one the maximum recovery potential and the other the minimum recovery expectation.   Under this system, the plaintiff's attorney then selects a figure midway between these two amounts and submits it as the value of his case for settlement purposes.   Another settlement procedure is the rule-of-thumb "three times specials" method. Under this formula the plaintiff's attorney simply submits an offer of settlement for an amount equivalent to three times the amount of the special damages.
>
> Both of these formulas, however, have been abandoned by most attorneys because of their arbitrariness and lack of accuracy.   For example, under the "three times specials" rule, if the plaintiff has lost an eye and has incurred medical expenses of, say, $500, counsel would arrive at the ridiculously low figure of $1,500.   Applying the same rule, where a professional violinist has sprained his thumb, incurring medical expenses of $10 and lost wages amounting to $300, it would seem absurd to assess his total damages at three times $310 or $930.   In a similar vein, an injury to a limb of a star athlete is worth more than a similar

injury to an office worker. In fact any person with special skills employing the parts of the body that have been injured or destroyed should be entitled to much greater damages than if a similar injury occurred to a person having no special skills involving those parts of the body. Thus, other factors of evaluation must be considered.

The attorney should be careful not to become blindly formula-minded. In view of the many imponderables no formula can be expected to apply mechanically to all cases, even though use of some formula is likely to be helpful as a basis for general evaluation and negotiation.

Value Allocation System

The most realistic method of arriving at the true value of a case for settlement is called the value allocation system. Under this method, counsel must compute the loss of earnings, past and future; the nature and permanency of the injuries, pain, and suffering; the interference with normal activities; and the emotional and nervous effects. Next, verdicts given previously for similar injuries should be researched. Consideration should be given to the jurisdiction involved—whether the verdicts there are usually low or high—and the liability in the case (the settlement figure should be reduced in proportion to the difficulty of showing liability). Finally, a reasonable amount should be added to the initial settlement demand for "horse-trading" purposes. The claims adjuster or defense attorney requires some leeway in the demand so that if he returns with a lower offer, there is room for adjustment both ways.

Point Allocation System

Another realistic method of arriving at the true settlement value of a case utilizes a point allocation system (see Figure 1). This system is now widely used by plaintiffs' attorneys in personal injury actions and has proven itself to be a workable settlement method. The use of this formula is predicated on the allocation of a given number of points for each particular category, with 100 points equaling an ideal or perfect case. From one to fifty points are allocated for liability.

	Factor	Point Scale	Point Value This Case
1.	Liability	50	————
2.	Injury	10	————
3.	Age	10	————
4.	Type of Plaintiff	10	————
5.	Type of Defendant	10	————
6.	Out-of-Pocket Expense	10	————
	Total Possible Points	100	————
	Total Actual Points		————

Figure 1. Formula to Evaluate a Personal Injury Case *

* This formula was devised by attorney
J. M. Sindell of Cleveland, Ohio.

Separate point allocations are made for the type of injury, age of the plaintiff, type of plaintiff, type of defendant, and the out-of-pocket expense, with each category receiving a value of from one to ten points.

Thus, where the liability of the defendant is doubtful, a low number of points will be allocated; where the liability of the defendant is clear, a high number of points will be allocated. Where there is evidence of contributory negligence on the part of the plaintiff, a liability point value of, say, fifteen may be assigned.

Where the injury is slight, two or more points may be assigned. Where the injury is serious or permanently disabling, eight or ten points may be allocated.

Where the plaintiff is one falling in a medium-income group and presenting a pleasant appearance, he may have nine or ten points; whereas if the plaintiff is disagreeable, argumentative, and unfavorable in appearance, he may have merely one or two points.

Where the adverse party is a "target defendant," such as a public utility or large corporation, as many as nine or ten points should be allocated. On the other hand, where the defendant is a highly respectable individual who presents a good appearance and tells a convincing story, perhaps only two or three points may be allocated.

Both the age and the actual loss factors are subject to further division. The table shown in Figure 2 gives point values in relation to age. It is based on American life mortality tables.

Ages	Point Value	Ages	Point Value
1–7	10	40–47	5
8–15	9	48–55	4
16–23	8	56–60	3
24–31	7	61–65	2
32–39	6	66–	1

Figure 2. Point Value in Relation to Age

The theory here is that the younger the plaintiff, the longer will be his life expectancy and, presumably, the greater will be his damages, at least in a case of permanent injury. Therefore, more points are allocated for a youthful plaintiff than for an aged one.

The out-of-pocket expense, as shown in Figure 3, is generally geared to one point for each $100.

Out-of-Pocket Expense	Point Value	Out-of-Pocket Expense	Point Value
$ 1–100	1	$600–700	6
100–200	2	700–800	7
200–300	3	800–900	8
300–400	4	900–1000	9
400–500	5	Over $1,000	10

Figure 3. Point Value in Relation to Out-of-Pocket Expense

Once the point values for each factor have been determined, they should be totaled to reach the point value of the case. Counsel must then determine what this type of case is worth in his particular jurisdiction in order to determine the monetary value of each point. This is done by ascertaining from a survey of recent cases, . . . the highest verdict that has been upheld in the state for a plaintiff with the same injuries, and dividing this amount by the total possible point value—100. Thus, if $70,000 is the highest verdict upheld in such a case, the dollar value per point is arrived at by dividing 100 into that figure. This would result in a monetary value of $700 per point.

This per-point monetary value ($700) is then multiplied by the total actual point value of the case. If the actual point value is 60, for example, the result would be $42,000, or the figure at which a fair settlement should be arranged.[22]

These general formulas can be modified and further refined in a variety of ways. For example, some practitioners will work with an average rather than the highest verdict discussed here, and statistical techniques can be used to differentiate types of injury and other factors in order to obtain a somewhat more reliable base of expected recovery before the dollar value per point is determined. Jury verdict research is typically limited to a particular jurisdiction and may be further adjusted for the peculiarities of a specific locale. Even with numerous adjustments for types of injuries, parties, and jury reactions, however, the limitations of such formulas should be apparent. No case is comparable in every respect to any other, and juries are always made up of individuals who will have their own ideas of what damages should be awarded. In addition, the fact that such formulas supposedly reduce each relevant consideration to a numerical value should not mask the subjectivity and uncertainty that is inevitably involved. It is no easier to assign a point value to liability in a case than it is to predict who will prevail at trial, and the expected response of a jury to a particular human situation will be as difficult to quantify in these terms as any others. More important, perhaps, are the considerations that such formulas do *not* take into account, including the strengths and weaknesses of counsel and a host of intangibles that can affect outcomes. Deciding what money payment or other minimum disposition is worth foregoing the potentially greater benefits of trial, or determining when you may be "pushing too far" are invariably discomforting tasks. No formula is likely to make such judgments a great deal easier.

22. J. Werchick, *Settling the Case—Plaintiff*, 4 AM.JUR.TRIALS 319–22 (1966); *see also* Jury Verdict Research, Inc., PERSONAL INJURY VALUATION HANDBOOKS (published in multiple volumes and updated).

2. Identifying the Available Leverage: Influence and Influenceability in the Bargaining Situation

The negotiator's need to define the bargaining range prior to bargaining requires not only estimates of settlement points, but an assessment of tactics for *affecting* that range. In the literature on negotiation the needs and vulnerabilities of your opponent upon which you concentrate such efforts are referred to as "leverage points," the leverage being the power or influence such factors make available to you. Not surprisingly, this assessment again must be concerned with *those factors that matter to your opponent,* and again requires an empathetic understanding of your opponent's situation. The following selection explores this task in more detail.

FISHER, INTERNATIONAL CONFLICT FOR BEGINNERS

pp. 11, 13–16, 29, 31–33, 36–37, 48–51, 60–63, 68–73 (1969).

[In any bargaining situation, it is essential to bear in mind that it is our opponent's] . . . decision which we want to influence. [A]nd since they are the ones who will have a choice, it is their state of mind which is crucial. The focus of our [effort] is their decision. Our job is to so alter their perception of their choice that they will decide in the way we prefer. How they feel about the choice we will be asking them to make is just as important to us as how we feel about it.

[Our] starting point should, [therefore], be the . . . problems of those we are trying to influence. What is their view of the situation? Can we say anything which will affect that view—affect their . . . problems? If we are trying to influence the Arab states, what domestic political problems do they have? What kind of a decision can we formulate which will be practical for them in their terms?

Since in any international conflict our object is to exert influence on another country to make a decision we would like them to make, our actions, like those of a matador, have meaning only when we know what it is we would like our adversary to do. We must take into account our own long-range values, their view of the present conflict, their political problems, and their desires and fears, and to formulate some things we would like them to decide if we could convince them to do so. What kinds of things do we want? What would it be possible for them to decide? Can we make such a decision look attractive to them, or the consequences of not making the decision look costly?

* * *

1. The Clarity of the Decision We Seek

. . . We are more likely both to know what we want and to get it if we try to write out the proposed decision with such clarity that it is in a form to which the single word "yes" would be an effective answer.

Putting our objective in the form of a *yesable proposition* makes us think through our position and the ways in which we will want to go about exerting influence. Too often our demand—the decision we desire—is vague simply because our own thinking is vague. Events have not forced us to be specific, and we have failed to recognize the impact which a specific offer or requested decision might have. We will almost always have a better chance of getting something we want if we know some specific things we would like to have. . . . Whether or not we intend to communicate the specifics of our demand to our adversary, there is no excuse for not working out in our minds what it is we would like to have them say or do.

* * *

2. The Limited Usefulness of Punishment

Inflicting pain upon an adversary government is, for a number of reasons, likely to be a poor way of getting them to change their mind. The government whose mind we want to change anticipated some costs when they decided to do what we do not like. The costs which they anticipated were not sufficient to deter them. For us to inflict pain may simply be to impose costs which they have already taken into account. To act as they expected is hardly likely to cause them to reverse their position.

Other considerations also suggest that inflicting pain upon an adversary may be worse than useless. There is a common tendency to treat sunken costs as invested capital. The greater the costs we impose upon our adversary, the greater the amount which they will regard themselves as having committed to their present course of action: "Having invested this much in the war of liberation, we cannot quit now. Having lost so many lives and most of our power plants, we should not now abandon the effort."

Everyday experience illustrates the psychological difficulty involved in trying to change a person's mind by increasing the expected cost to him of continuing his actions. If my son is doing something even though I have threatened to spank him ten times for doing it, a threat to spank him twelve times is unlikely to produce better results. If I have decided to build a house at a rather high cost, my contractor knows I will not abandon the enterprise despite marginal increases in that cost.

* * *

One further reason that increasing a threat, marginally or drastically, does not usually work as well as we hope is that our adversaries see that in carrying out the threat we are hurting ourselves, too. To inflict pain involves a cost to us as well as a cost to them. Carrying out a threat is something we do not want to do except to exert influence. The same thinking which leads us to believe that imposing costs on our adversaries will cause them to change their mind leads them to believe that the costs we are imposing on ourselves are likely to make us change our mind. . . .

3. The Palatability of the Choices Offered

The choice we present them must be palatable. This can be represented by the following map, in which the "offer" designates the entire set of circumstances, both good and bad, which the *adversary* believes will come about if they make the decision we are asking them to make, and the "threat" indicates the set of consequences, as they see them, of their not making the decision.

MAP

	DEMAND The decision desired by us	OFFER The consequences of making that decision	THREAT The consequences of not making the decision
WHO?	Who is to make the decision?	Who benefits if the decision is made?	Who gets hurt if the decision is not made?
WHAT?	Exactly what decision is desired?	If the decision is made, what benefits can be expected? —what costs?	If the decision is not made, —what risks? —what potential benefits?
WHEN?	By what time does the decision have to be made?	When, if ever, will the benefits of making the decision occur?	How soon will the consequences of not making the decision be felt?
WHY?	What makes this a right, proper, and lawful decision?	What makes these consequences [acceptable]?	What makes these consequences . . . legitimate?

Every feature of an influence problem can be located somewhere on this schematic map. The nature of a given problem can be discovered through estimating how the presumed adversary would answer the above questions.

[B8825]

These are questions which the [above] map presents. It does not provide any answers. It is a simple scheme which can be applied to any kind of conflict—marital problems, domestic disputes, or business dealings. It is not unique to international affairs.

Even when considering only the threat, there may be more effective means of exerting influence than to change the level of threatened pain. One way to change the threat is to make it more immediate, to change the timing. We may not want the threat to appear as an ultimatum, because then its legitimacy would be reduced and the adversary might balk. But we may be able to advance the time at which the disadvantages of their not changing their minds will take effect. Or we might change the threat so that it will fall more directly on those who are being asked to decide. A lunch-counter sit-in is a more effective way to get a business to desegregate than a street march in part because the threat is calculated to fall directly and immediately on those who are being asked to make a decision. We may change the threat so that instead of imposing costs it appears to deprive the decision maker of benefits he had already anticipated.

.   .   . The irrationality of an adversary does not make the map irrelevant; it makes all the more important our consciously considering how the various elements may look to them. What do they think we are asking them to decide, what do they think the consequences will be, and how do they value those consequences?

*   *   *

4.   The Changing Character of Influence

[These calculations suggest a number of considerations in the ongoing conduct of negotiations. First, our opponent's assessments of the benefits of agreement are continually changing:]   .   .   . We never start out with a clean slate. Any conflict grows out of a situation in which a government had a choice of doing what we wanted them to do but did not do it. In order to exert influence on them, we must change some aspect of the choice with which they see themselves as being faced. Rather than trying to change the threat—the consequences which will follow from their continuing not to make the decision we seek—we may be more successful if we change the decision we ask them to make. That is, we can redefine the demand rather than try to change the consequences they expect from failing to meet our demand. In the short run we will be unable to change their basic values or attitudes.   .   .   . By presenting them with a different proposed decision, we can present them with a decision which we want and which they are more likely to make.

[This approach] can put [a discarded] matter back on their agenda. We have seen that a government tends to conform to a "policy decision" to pursue a certain course of action, even though the costs change. A government which has made a decision is unlikely to reconsider the wisdom of that decision every day. If North Vietnam has decided not to negotiate, a change in the casualty rate will probably not of itself cause any one North Vietnamese official to reopen that decision. On the other hand, if a fresh proposal comes in, a new decision is required. Consider the example of an organization which goes to a congressman with a proposed bill and a petition signed by a thousand voters asking him to support the bill. The congressman says no. The organization will not be likely to achieve success by simply coming back with 1,200 names. But if it comes back with a revised Paragraph 6, the congressman has a new decision to make.

[In addition], changing the demand means that a favorable decision now does not require a reversal of a previous decision. The matter is not only back on the agenda, but in order to decide our way they need not admit that the prior decision was wrong.

* * *

[Beyond the shifting of demands there is also the possibility that the *object* of our influence can change.] . . . The more precisely we can focus attention on those we are trying to influence, the more accurately we will be able to make a judgment about what it is possible for them to do and what is beyond their capacity. Thus as a starting point it is useful to identify the existing object of influence.

The government of North Vietnam, for example, may have trained and supplied the Vietcong, organized, financed, and established the National Liberation Front, and directed the entire effort to overthrow the South Vietnamese government. But these military and political forces having been set in motion, it did not follow that the leadership in North Vietnam was able by itself to call off the entire war of liberation.

This example suggests that in selecting and in shifting the party on whom we try to exert influence, we should look ahead to the decision we want instead of looking back at those who may have caused the situation we do not like. The example also illustrates another common error. What is perceived in Saigon as one adversary may, for the purpose of making a decision, be better understood as two or more separate groups of decision makers subject to one another's influence. Outsiders almost invariably oversimplify the unity of the political body they are trying to influence. Israeli officials often refer to "the Arabs" as though they constituted a single political organization.

If the only decision we can imagine our adversaries might conceivably make collectively is one which we do not want, we should pursue policies which attempt to influence them separately. Analogous to the military policy of divide and conquer, we should divide so they can decide.

Generally speaking, however, our efforts will be less disruptive and more successful if we can identify as the responsible decider a group or official lower in the hierarchy. To seek a decision of a clerk is less likely to provoke a crisis than to seek that decision of a prime minister. At lower levels different officials deal with different problems. The decision we want is more likely to be dealt with on its merits by someone who knows the facts and to whom the facts are important. Political relations are not so vulnerable, since disagreement on one matter is less likely to mean disagreement on another. Further, dealing with a lower official leaves us the chance of appealing to a higher one.

NOTES

1. *Bargaining Power and Litigation: The Sources of Leverage*

Although there are many ambiguities in his concept of power, Fisher does make a number of specific recommendations that we have found helpful to lawyers. There are many opportunities in law practice to choose *which* opponent to make the object of leverage (*i. e.,* counsel or client, principal or agent), and to characterize a proposed outcome in ways which might make it more palatable. As in situations of international conflict, there are inevitable limits on what can be accomplished by threats to inflict further costs or "pain." Such general prescriptions, of course, do not take us very far in devising specific courses of action or making the detailed assessments which must be part of any negotiation strategy. It is necessary to identify the costs and benefits that must be weighed in legal disputes, and the kinds of vulnerabilities that afford opportunities for the exercise of influence. What are the factors that must be taken into account in your assessments of leverage?

Fisher's map of influence suggests that in any such assessment, one must inquire into (i) the operative pressures on each lawyer and party; (ii) considerations of time; (iii) the costs and benefits associated with both agreement and nonagreement; and (iv) the value attached to these various consequences by the opponent. But such a focus on the who, what, when and why of specific outcomes only serves as a starting point. In many instances a number of additional variables must also be weighed in assessing the balance of power in a particular case. The following is a brief discussion of these factors.

Monetary Factors

This refers to dollar outlays associated with the case. Included here are expenses of preparing and presenting the case at trial, participating in negotiating sessions, and developing and maintaining one's negotiating position, as well as the potential costs of an unsuccessful (or successful) trial and/or appeal. Thus such diverse aspects of litigation as discovery rules, the jurisdiction's practice with respect to assessment of costs, and the fee arrangements between opposing counsel and his or her client play an important role in determining each party's vulnerabilities. An attorney on retainer, for example, must absorb the costs of increased time in a case unless they can be passed on under a future agreement. An attorney paid by the hour may have a very different response to actions that increase the expenditure of time.

Relationship Factors

Leverage is also rooted in the value the negotiators place on the opinions of others. A lawyer obviously wants to maintain good client relationships and will seek to avoid situations which threaten the client's confidence in counsel. Thus, encounters which expose the lawyer's lack of skill or loyalty to the client can generate considerable leverage. Similarly, actions which impose time costs or inconvenience on the client produce strong avoidance responses from opposing counsel. This is particularly true if the client has been "oversold." ("Don't worry, I'll have it taken care of in a week; it's just harassment," etc.). No lawyer wants to explain to a client why initial predictions were ill-founded or why he or she is unable to protect the client from undesired expenditures of time or effort. Strategies which involve the client in court appearances will often trigger these avoidance responses.

Lawyers place a similar value on their relationships with judges, clerks, peers, partners, friends, and—in the long run—opposing counsel. They do not want to damage these relationships or suffer even minimal losses in esteem, with the result that the expectations and predicted reactions of a lawyer's reference group will often be an important determinant of conduct. It is for this reason that patterns of personal relationship, group affiliation, and political and social orientation are important sources of information on potential leverage in any bargaining situation.

Norm-Related Factors

Similarly, opposing counsel has values and attitudes which affect his or her actions in any negotiation. Arguing in negotiation that "it isn't fair" or even that "we don't do that sort of thing here" is not always a futile gesture. Such arguments involve challenges to self-images which can themselves generate action and reaction. Professional identity and cultural commitments to reciprocity are major influences on bargaining outcomes and inevitable focal points for potential strategies and appeals. There is virtually no aspect of the process which is not influenced by such normative elements.[23]

Effort Factors

These influences grow out of what seems to be a natural "inertia" in human experience and the need most of us have for predictability in our affairs. Lawyers (like most people) don't like to feel things are "out of control," or to be forced to alter schedules and arrangements. Reentering or prolonging a state of uncertainty thus becomes an additional cost of trial, once a lawyer has anticipated that a case was going to be settled. A lawyer who habitually puts cases aside to work on present matters inevitably experiences "start up" costs when he or she has to get back into the details of a file. As a result, the ability to frustrate expectations or break established patterns can itself be a source of leverage.

23. *See* Gulliver, *Negotiations as a Mode of Dispute Settlement: A General Model,* 7 LAW & SOC.REV. 667 (1973).

Multipliers

The last two sources of leverage are actually variants of some or all of the above factors. They relate to ways in which existing leverage might be enhanced. For example, the possibility of a lost verdict in a personal injury case may involve not only a monetary judgment, but an undesired precedent or increased chances of other such suits being brought. A refusal to compromise, if given publicity, affects attitudes and reactions not only of persons immediately involved, but of a variety of groups and individuals. Leverage is always a function of potential exposures and layers of possible costs and gains.

The timing of one's actions can similarly increase the impact of any exercise of influence. Obviously, *when* one takes a particular action will have very different consequences in different negotiations. The trial literature abounds with discussions of the subtle pressures that can be brought to bear by attorneys who understand the importance of this factor.[24] Given a particular opponent and a particular set of conditions, there will be good times and bad times to seek agreement. Many commentators, for example, feel that an attorney should gear settlement offers to what is happening in his or her opponent's *other* cases, and should time settlement discussions so that future discovery costs become an additional threat.[25] If an attorney is overloaded with litigation or is the sort who likes to pay attention to a few matters at a time, control of timing by opposing counsel—*e. g.*, in deciding when motions must be heard, depositions conducted, or interrogatories answered—exerts pressure beyond the actual dollar costs of those aspects of the litigation.

---

2. *Some Complicating Considerations*

None of the foregoing should be taken as a simple set of prescriptions. To list the possible vulnerabilities of one's opponent is a long way from giving this idea content in particular cases.

First, assessing vulnerability is inevitably associated with one's feelings about taking advantage of it. No simple catalogue of "leverages" quite captures how in any real situation you will actually respond to stress.

Second, these factors only delineate *potential* pressure points. They represent possible costs of going to trial (refusing to settle) or benefits that flow from settlement. These are not necessarily symmetrical. An offer of settlement might be considered more "valu-

---

24. *See, e. g.*, W. Pierson, THE DE-
FENSE ATTORNEY AND BASIC
DEFENSE TACTICS 228, 233–34, 247–
48 (1956).

25. *See, e. g.*, P. Hermann, BETTER
SETTLEMENTS THROUGH LEVER-
AGE 125–36 (1965).

able" in one case because it solves some problem between lawyer and client and yet such considerations might be given very little weight in another context. In specific cases there may be costs of agreeing that fall outside the usual patterns. For example, a lawyer might go to trial to establish the credibility of his or her threats to do so in other cases, or even to impress a client. A settlement can itself impose many of the costs we associated with trial. Thus a complete assessment of influence factors in a particular case requires more than merely identifying leverage possibilities.

In addition, a great deal depends upon the way such leverage is employed against a particular opponent. A threat to impose trial costs may be made so offensively that it makes settling seem *less* attractive—*i. e.*, because it now entails "giving in" or submitting to threats—and even explicitly mentioning other costs, such as damage to opposing counsel's relationship with his or her client, can generate strong resentment or resistance. Identification of possible leverage points is only one part of a very complex assessment.

Third, although, we have attempted to describe some factors which should be considered in most cases, the particular complex of needs and concerns which motivate settlement in many types of cases are not easy to categorize, even under the broad headings we listed. For example, a public prosecutor engaged in plea bargaining in a criminal case may be affected by what could be loosely described as monetary or relationship costs, but these costs are sufficiently different in this context to require a separate analysis by defense counsel. Consider, for example, the following:

> [The rationale behind the decision to accept a plea] differs widely from place to place and jurisdiction to jurisdiction. For instance, a prosecutor's office in a large urban area may have its own idea about guilty pleas concerning looters, rioters, or others involved in "crime in the streets," whereas a rural or small city prosecutor has few problems of this sort and would have a different attitude.

> Public opinion, of course, plays a major role in such cases. If the general public is clamoring for law and order, offenders will be dealt with more harshly. Conversely, if there are so many rioters or looters that the courts and jails become clogged with them, then the prosecutor must take it upon himself to dispose of the cases as expeditiously as possible. Thus, for example, there is a great deal more leverage available to an attorney for an accused rioter if there were many involved in the riot and he offers a plea on the day they all appear. If he drags out the case to an occasion when the courts once again return to the normal load, the prosecutor can take time to try the case and may want to get tough to please the public.

> * * *

> Except in notorious cases such as ones dealing with political corruption, sensational sex or homicide offenses, or large scale narcotic conspiracies, the prosecutor is interested in disposal of cases without trial, even if it means dismissing part of the charge. . . .

When the prosecutor commences a case, he is interested in justice. That means a conviction, if the alleged facts are true as far as he can ascertain. On the other hand, a question is raised as to the type of conviction. This is where the prosecutor's traditional discretion comes into play. At all times, he realizes that a quick disposition, even if it means a lesser penalty than the maximum available, results in savings to the state or Federal Government, because it may eliminate the costs of presentation to the grand jury, the trial itself with attendant fees of witnesses and jurors, and the appeal. In addition, disposition by plea provides a speedy way to prevent potential criminals from being on the streets for long periods of time awaiting trial or appeal. And the state may actually obtain an advantage. For example, a guilty plea to petit larceny and unlawful entry with a jail sentence of 120 days may result in incarceration for a longer period than if the defendant had been committed under a felony sentence of one year.

* * *

A great cause for concern to the prosecutor is tainted evidence which is the product of an illegal search and seizure, or a confession obtained without the proper constitutional safeguards. Many peace officers in urban areas have the training to minimize these problems, but even well-trained officers often blunder in these troublesome areas. And in localities where training is minimal, illegal confessions and unreasonable searches and seizures occur in a large percentage of the cases. If the state commences the case knowing that the tainted evidence may allow the accused to go free, even when all parties know he is guilty, this gives defense counsel considerable leverage in bargaining.[26]

The financial, status, relationship and other costs which we have identified overlap but do not fully describe these sorts of considerations.

Fourth, all of the above factors, no matter how they are described, must be translated into some appropriate unit of exchange. The leverage points we have identified often involve gross costs (*e. g.*, loss of status, uncertainty) and intangible benefits (*e. g.*, future relationships, peace of mind). If they are to have relevance in a particular bargaining situation, these factors have to be converted into objects of value which *can* be exchanged. The richer the mixture of issues, goals or alternatives involved in the negotiation the more readily such exchange equivalents can be found, and the agreement calibrated to the needs and desires of the parties. For example, in a plea bargaining situation involving a charge of manslaughter, where the lesser included offense was simple assault, the parties might not perceive any "room" for the exercise of leverage. Assuming the parties see this as a situation presenting only two alternatives—a plea to assault or a plea to manslaughter—the amount of trading will be minimal; one party will either capitulate to the other's terms on the basis of

26. E. Siler, *Guilty Plea Negotiations*, CRIMINAL DEFENSE TECHNIQUES 13.06 to 13.07 (1976).

some sort of rough cost-benefit assessment or they will deadlock. On the other hand, if bargaining outcomes are *not* limited in reality or a situation can be created in which the needs of both parties can be satisfied, leverage can result in real exchanges. Thus a defendant faced with multiple charges could plead to one or more of them or to lesser included offenses; could voluntarily submit to treatment programs or make restitution; or could cooperate in incriminating others or helping to clear unsolved crimes. In exchange for some or all of these actions the prosecutor could accept pleas to lesser or fewer offenses; agree to recommend a certain sentence or take some other action in regard to sentencing; agree to help the defendant get into specific treatment programs or correctional facilities; agree to help secure dismissal of charges in other jurisdictions; and so forth.[27] Thus the analysis of leverage is closely tied to the analysis of goals and possible outcomes in a specific negotiation.

Finally, leverage cannot be thought of solely in terms of the vulnerabilities of one's opponent. Not only is a similar analysis undoubtedly being made by your adversary but your own vulnerabilities are themselves aspects of any strategy which you plan. To attempt to publicize or exploit an adversary's weakness often suggests that there may be weaknesses in your own position. Moreover, the exercise of leverage is not itself cost-free: timing one's actions to maximize leverage, for example, also requires submitting to these same time constraints. It is always necessary to consider not only what leverage your opponent has against *you* but also what risks and other costs may be involved in using or using up the leverage you have. Very often a bargainer's strategies are repaid in kind. Sauce for the goose can be a main course for the gander.

---

3. *The Elusive Idea of Bargaining Power*

Despite the apparent simplicity of Fisher's prescriptions, the concept of power is surprisingly difficult to define. Some of you may want to reflect further on what power "means." One finds it described in the literature on bargaining as the ability to (i) impose costs or reward another; (ii) exploit advantages; or (iii) engender agreement on one's own terms. On reflection, however, each of these formulations blurs a number of complexities.

First, as Fisher points out, bargaining power is always a function of a comparison by each party of the consequences of agreement against the consequences of disagreement. Stated differently, we can speak of bargaining power as relative to one's "need" for agreement. The more one party perceives the net costs of disagreement exceeding

---

27. This list is taken from A. Amsterdam, B. Segal and M. Miller, TRIAL MANUAL FOR THE DEFENSE OF CRIMINAL CASES § 211 (ALI–ABA, 3rd ed., 1974).

the net gains, the more the other party is able to impose a settlement on his or her terms. Conversely, the less one needs to avoid deadlock (*e. g.*, because of other opportunities or the availability of relatively uncostly resources) the more power he or she has. It is one of the paradoxes of bargaining leverage that the less you need agreement the more likely you are to get it on your terms.

Second, bargaining power must be understood as relational. When used among practitioners, the term usually refers, not only to one party's circumstances, but to the *differences* between them. A party has more power than another if his or her need for agreement is less than the need of his or her adversary. Analytically, this involves a reduction of the cost-benefit calculations of both parties to a single denominator. Difficult as this is philosophically,[28] this rough power computation is, in fact, made by most bargainers.

Third, the idea of bargaining power is not co-extensive with the consequences of one's own choices; not all aspects of one's leverage can be thought of as subject to control. A lawyer may have the ability to force any case to trial (fate control)[29] and because of biases in the system (rules, judges, etc.) be less in need of settlement than his or her adversary. These circumstances, however, can change, (*i. e.*, a different judge might be appointed), and the "power balance" will be altered. Moreover, the power to impose settlement (as compared to deadlock) is always limited by the ability of the other party to resist. However unreasonable the cost-benefit calculation by one's opponent, his or her perceptions limit one's power. It is not unknown to be faced with an opponent who is as "irrational" as a fox.

Fourth, bargaining power refers to conditions which are always changing or changeable even when they are subject to control. Indeed, this is the basis of our suggestion that you need to analyze "leverage" separately from assessments of the existing pattern of minimal settlement points and expectations. Estimates of the costs associated with disagreement or the benefits of agreement at some level of exchange can often be altered by argument and action. Similarly, resources can be used up or enlarged in the course of a negotiation. For example, the introduction of third-party support into a dispute (picketing or other direct action is one example) can be thought of as a type of "resource-creation." That is, one can alter

---

28. There is a great deal of debate in the literature on whether any such "interpersonal comparisons of utility" can ever be made—that is, whether multiple dimenions can be reduced to a single magnitude. It is one of the puzzles of modern scholarship that what we logically know we can't do, so many of us regularly accomplish. Language has its limits as well as its opportunities.

29. A rich source of empirical information on bargaining is the JOURNAL OF CONFLICT RESOLUTION. *See, e. g.,* Buckley and Westen, *Bargaining Set Theory and Majority Rule*, 20 J. OF CONFLICT RES. 481 (1976); Bartenek, Benton and Keys, *Third Party Intervention and Bargaining Behavior of Group Representatives*, 19 J. OF CONFLICT RES. 532 (1975).

one's own and another's ability to absorb the cost of disagreement, or the benefits obtained from any given exchange.

Finally, it is important to remember that we are again speaking of a concept which is perceptual and psychological. Each party's judgment of what is to be gained or lost from accepting a particular demand reflects not necessarily the way things are, but the way they appear to be. For example, a lawyer's minimal settlement point may be much lower than an objective analysis of the situation would suggest because of deep anxieties associated with going to trial. Similarly, a lawyer's judgment of an opponent's willingness to settle or will to resist may be objectively wrong. But as long as such views persist the party's own willingness to settle on any other basis is practically precluded.

All of this is to suggest that we are dealing here with an elusive subject. Nevertheless, judgments about the extent of one's own and one's opponent's bargaining power must be made. From such assessments of how and whether the situation can be changed, settlement points or expectations are formulated.

B. BARGAINING: FRAMING AND IMPLEMENTING STRATEGIES

---

1. Discovery Strategies

WALTON AND McKERSIE, A BEHAVIORAL THEORY OF LABOR NEGOTIATIONS

pp. 61–66 (1965).

Party's first tactical assignment is to assess Opponent's utilities and strike costs and if possible ascertain his resistance point. Party may know that the parties hold differing objectives regarding the resolution of an agenda item; that is, he knows that he is dealing with a [share bargaining] issue. But what is not so obvious to Party is just how important the objective is to Opponent, particularly in terms of how much gain (loss) on the issue would be minimally acceptable to him. Moreover, while a negotiator usually knows whether a strike would be costly to the other party, he does not know *how* costly!

Knowledge about the relevant parameters is critical in deciding whether to maintain or abandon a position. Such knowledge enables Party to make in turn intelligent probability assessments. These assessments tell him how far he has to go in further manipulating the parameters in order to bring about movement on Opponent's part.

They also tell him whether he had better consider altering his own position.

Party has two general ways in which he can gain knowledge about Opponent's resistance point. He can use an indirect route of assessing the factors which underlie each parameter, or he can attempt to obtain more direct clues regarding the resistance point which Opponent has at least tentatively set for himself. Much of the required information for both methods of assessment has to be obtained from Opponent himself. Other information is available through more public channels.

Indirect Assessment. Many factors affecting economic power, and in turn the resistance point, can be assessed by both parties: they include inventories, alternate production or warehousing facilities, market conditions, the percentage of the work force unionized, the size of the strike fund, the numbers involved in a strike vote, mutual assistance arrangements, etc. The "grapevines" supply this information to unions and management with varying degrees of accuracy.

More systematic research methods are often used. For instance, managements frequently hold prenegotiation conferences with their first-line supervisors to get their estimates of how strongly employees feel about certain issues and how willing they are to strike.

*   *   *

Managements sometimes have the industrial relations staff make an analysis of the content and patterns of the grievances processed to various stages of the machinery in order to discover any clues regarding the importance the employees and the union may attach to certain issues. . . . [and] occasionally ask their personnel research staff or some outside agency to administer opinion surveys to their employees to learn how employees feel about issues and striking. . . .

If, with sufficient effort, some knowledge can be gained about issue utilities and strike costs, making the appropriate translations and then computing Opponent's resistance point is more difficult. Actually the problem is even more complicated—it is one of simulating how Opponent interprets these factors and how *he* computes his resistance point. After all, Party is interested in learning what Opponent's resistance point *is*, not what it should be. This being so, it is often more rewarding for Party to try to induce Opponent to betray his own resistance point than it is to attempt to estimate it indirectly.

The validity of the inferences that Party makes about Opponent's position is enhanced, if the former has ever been in the latter's position. Members of management who have been employees or union officials can "put themselves in the shoes" of the union negotiators. Short of this, management can with a little empathy visualize the kinds of factors that would influence feeling in the union organization. Management can examine pattern settlements or precedent-setting circumstances in past settlements. Of course, the union engages in the same kind of vicarious thinking. It seeks to understand management's true position by examining such indicators as the profit and loss statement.

Tactics to Elicit Clues. When we turn to the problem of obtaining more direct clues about Opponent's resistance point, we must consider the ongoing negotiation process. Sometimes the efforts flow along ethically questionable channels and involve cloak-and-dagger operations, *e. g.*, utilizing an informant from Opponent's headquarters or bugging Opponent's caucus room. . . .

Informal conferences with negotiators of the other party are sometimes employed in order to sound them out regarding reactions to various types of proposals. Typically, however, reliance is placed on bargaining-table tactics. Some of these tactics are intended to elicit reactions that become data in estimating the resistance point. The most obvious way is to ask questions designed to clarify both the meaning of the proposal and its underlying rationale. Sometimes Party will direct such questions to some of the "less-coached" members of Opponent's team.

. . . By probing Opponent's team members regarding a specific proposal, Party can determine how well prepared they are, using this information as one basis for inferring how seriously they are advancing their proposal.

Tactics involving personal abuse may be introduced to induce or provoke Opponent into revealing more than he wishes.

* * *

Tactics of exaggerated impatience which make it appear as if the negotiations were rushing headlong into their final stages may force the inexperienced negotiator into prematurely revealing the bargaining room he has allowed himself. That appears to have been the case in the Fanco Oil Company negotiations in which in the very first session the first two remarks below apparently induced the third:

Hayes (U) The morale of our men on the boats is very bad. More than 50% of the men are not paying dues, and I have instructed the delegates not to collect from them. We are not getting anywhere, so I think we may as well adjourn and let matters take their own course. . . .

MacIntosh (U) No sense for further meetings, if we can't agree now on 7 and 7. . . .

Downs (M) If we add $25 monthly income to each man, you would be interested?

Black (U) It makes a lot of difference. . . .[a]

a. B. Selekman, S. Selekman, and S. Fuller, PROBLEMS IN LABOR RELATIONS, 2d ed., (New York: Mc- Graw-Hill Book Company, 1958) pp. 568–69.

In one move Downs offered a monthly increase of $25, virtually everything the negotiating team had to bargain with. What frightened Downs, who was just gaining negotiating experience, was an implicit threat that the independent Fanco union would get discouraged and affiliate with the nearby International Longshoremen's Association. That threat was implicit in the apathy of workers mentioned by Hayes. Still the fact is that this was only the first negotiating session. Furthermore, regardless of how dreaded the consequences of the threat might have been, the threat itself actually was not very credible, because it is unlikely that the officials of the independent union actually had any serious intention of sacrificing an arrangement so beneficial to them.

The tactics discussed above—personal abuse and exaggerated impatience—are not without their risks. In his excitement the other negotiator may take a stronger position than he had originally planned and then become obliged to maintain that position.

Testing techniques are particularly useful for assessing Opponent's resistance point late in negotiations. Sometimes in order to test Opponent's position, Party will suggest calling in a mediator. If Opponent accepts the suggestion, this is taken as an indication that he sees the problem as one of exploring a way by which the positions of the parties can be brought together; he would presumably have some "give" left himself. If he rejects the bid, this may indicate that he has no room to move unless he had reason to believe that Opponent is just looking for an excuse to move all the way himself. Another tactic is for a union to bring the parties up to a strike deadline, arrange a last-minute postponement, and then bargain up to the new deadline in order to test and retest the company's limits.

Tactics to Record and Analyze Reactions. Even in the absence of "baiting" tactics, the verbal and nonverbal behaviors of members of Opponent's negotiating team are often rich with clues about the degree of interest they have in the items being discussed or passed over and about their expectations regarding these issues. The following is an excerpt from a conversation among members of one team as they process the clues available to them:

> . . . soon as he finishes I'll give ya a . . . full report . . . on what took our discussion here and how I think the thing had to go. And it's going all right. *He showed disappointment. Now, a man that shows disappointment, his mind is open on that question.* What's *in* his mind or how far he'll go to buy that we have to find out. . . . But you're not gonna find out now, immediately.[b]

b. Anne Douglas, *Industrial Peacemaking* (New York: Columbia University Press, 1962) p. 576.

In a continuous relationship the negotiators learn in various subtle ways how to assess the position and intentions of the other person. . . .

Several tactics are used to take full advantage of this source of data regarding Opponent's resistance point.

First, Party may have a man-to-man policy in composing his own negotiating team. Many managements find it useful to have one management committeeman for each union committeeman, so that the latter can be under constant observation during negotiation proceedings.

> One newspaper publisher told of a technique by which he organized his team on a two-platoon basis. By rotating committee members, he was able to keep them fresh and alert and in a position to constantly observe the reactions of the union committee. In addition, he assigned technical people who could understand the real meaning of the union's presentation on detailed subjects such as job evaluation.

Second, Party may be even more sophisticated in this practice by making a continually revised assessment about the influence of each member of Opponent's negotiating team. Since negotiations are not an isolated event but occur as part of a continuing labor-management relationship, most members of the negotiating committee are known to the opposite group. Respective individuals work together during contract administration, on problems and grievance handling. This type of familiarity enables each side to better assess the intentions of the other side. . . .

NOTES

1. *Goals and Techniques in Discovery Bargaining*

As we have already mentioned, bargaining for information is a basic aspect of negotiation. The simple strategies Walton and McKersie identify are involved in every phase of the negotiating process. To state that information is important to the negotiator, however, does not take you very far. You need to make judgments about what you want to learn in any particular negotiation. What information would be useful, essential, or irrelevant? By what criteria would you make such choices?

Your response, of course, would vary with the type of case, the opposing party, the stage of the litigation, the particular negotiations involved, the availability of formal discovery devices, etc. For example, consider the difference between what you would want to know as counsel for the defendant in a criminal case seeking reduction of a robbery charge, and what would be useful to you as counsel for the plaintiff in a personal injury action against an insured motorist.

Each case presents a complex of specific assessments—*e. g.*, minimal settlement points, vulnerability to leverage, estimates of the opponent's views of your own limits and vulnerability. Each of these assessments in turn requires information of a very specific nature.

In a criminal case, for instance, you might want to know the prosecutor's caseload, ambitions, peer relationships, experience, knowledge of the case, attitudes toward the offense and contacts with the victim, to name just a few of the relevant factors. You would therefore be interested in how the prosecutor's office worked and the role the particular prosecutor played within it. Similarly, in a personal injury action you might want to know the amount of insurance coverage, the practice of the company with respect to claims above the coverage, how reserves (money set aside for possible payout) are set in each case, what the particular reservation is in your case, how much authority the claims adjuster has, what happens to claims above the aduster's authority, whether the company sees the case as having precedential value, and so forth. Adequately focussing one's inquiries in negotiating requires a good deal of judgment and foresight.

In addition, you will need to develop skill in making direct bids for information during the negotiation. These include, as Walton and McKersie point out, many of the skills we considered in discussing interviewing—careful listening, thoughtful observation of non-verbal cues, the skillful use of questions, and other techniques. Although we don't recommend all of them, the following is a partial list of such devices.

Questioning

Direct questioning in the context of bargaining proves to be a surprisingly effective tactic. When asked a direct question, lawyers seem to have a good deal of difficulty not answering or not revealing some useful piece of information (the Socratic method casts long shadows). John Illich outlines some of the ways questions might be used in bargaining:

> There are numerous advantages to posing questions during the course of any negotiation. Questions can be excellent probing tools to discover additional facts and other information that may only be known to an opponent or otherwise extremely difficult for the negotiator to discover. In addition, they can offer the negotiator more of an assurance of control over the negotiations and may be useful in putting the opponent on the defensive. Attacking the opponent's positions by well timed and phrased questions can often pay rich dividends, and nothing can be more indispensable to cast doubt upon an opponent's position than a timely question.

* * *

> General questions are useful for probing and are best during the early stages of negotiation. As matters unfold, however, it is usually better to refrain from asking them in order not to run the danger of

reopening already agreed upon items, or to unfavorably reflect upon the negotiator's thoroughness of preparation or grasp of the subject matter. In addition, a wise opponent may be able to detect when the negotiator is attempting to strengthen his own knowledge by general questions, and his responses may therefore not be too enlightening.

Specific questions are much safer to venture out with, since they call for fairly confined answers. They're useful in any phase of the negotiation, but more so in the latter stages when the negotiator is more apt to know precisely what he is after when asking. . . .

Whether a question is general or specific, it should be carefully phrased and descriptive in order to have the greatest impact. Descriptive questions will provide the opponent with more of a mental picture of the answer to be elicited. Contrast "Where is the property located?" with "Is the property located near transportation, adequate labor supplies and ample utilities?" The latter question is obviously more illustrative of the negotiator's objectives and thus more likely to draw a productive response. In addition, being a more specific question, it doesn't permit the opponent to ride all over the range with his response and perhaps be evasive or even seize the offensive.[30]

* * *

It is one of the paradoxes of lawyering that vices in one context (such as control) can be virtues in another. Other techniques for obtaining information rely on similar control dynamics.

The Use of Variation

It is sometimes very informative to ask questions on the same subject at different times or to address the same questions to different parties involved in the negotiation. Consistency or inconsistency in the responses can itself be a source of important "clues" to the varying perceptions and preferences one's opponent has brought to the bargaining table. As with most discovery strategies, it is often possible to learn as much from the *way* such questions are answered as from the answers themselves. Did the opponent hesitate before answering or seem surprised by the question? Did the opposing party look at counsel for guidance before responding? Although you will often ask questions to elicit responsive answers, a question may produce information whether it is answered or not.

The Personal Challenge

This approach, often found in the negotiating literature, involves variations of the "baiting" tactics Walton and McKersie describe. The assumption is that very strong feelings, exaggerated disbelief or impatience are so difficult to handle at a bargaining table that the responses of one's adversary will often tell you a great deal about his or her real demands and concerns. For example, a direct challenge to

30. J. Illich, THE ART AND SKILL
   OF SUCCESSFUL NEGOTIATION
   141–45 (1973).

an adversary's position as dilatory may be the only way to ascertain its underlying credibility. A more subtle use of the same tactic lies in calculated understatement concerning one's assessments of the opponent's position or, conversely, concerning one's own position. Losing one's temper similarly can elicit reactions which can tell a negotiator a good deal about his or her adversary. The sort of information that one gets from such reactions, however, is difficult to assess and of questionable validity. We have rarely seen it produce anything but interpersonal difficulties.

Inspection Ploys

A group of approaches not unlike the personal challenge relies on increasing the amount of third party participation in the process. If, for example, there is a question as to the factual contentions being made, either party may suggest an exchange of files or documents or inspection by an outside party. If the question is the degree of commitment to a particular position, the possibility of mediation or arbitration might be opened up. In each instance an acceptance of the proposal is likely to lead to more information; a rejection may give some indication as to the firmness of opposing positions.

Timing Ploys

Another cluster of information-gathering strategies relates to timing. Negotiators will often push a bargaining interchange toward deadlock to see how an adversary reacts under such pressure, leaving some escape route to avoid an actual breakdown of negotiations. Others will offer a quick (and favorable) settlement outcome as a way of getting information, thereafter withdrawing it if it is not immediately accepted. A related approach involves taking actions outside of the negotiating sessions—*i. e.,* filing motions or notices of deposition, marking the case for trial—in order to make such actions a bargaining item in the discussions and elicit the concerns and responses they generate.

* * *

Again, there are problems in every such list. The importance of "information bargaining" should not cause you to ignore some of the inevitable risks that accompany it. No effort to obtain information at the bargaining table is without potential costs. At a minimum such efforts will create pressures on you to disclose information yourself or will themselves reveal clues as to your own preferences, expectations and intentions. More fundamentally, any such tactics can increase the level of suspicion and distrust in the relationship. Although questions are helpful in solving mutual problems and revealing areas of legitimate doubt—as well as in assessing strengths and weaknesses—it is not always easy to use them in a non-threatening way. If you are interested in exploring objections to your proposals or uncovering real areas of difference, you will need to exercise a good deal of skill in communicating your desire for information.

Second, any bid for information depends on your ability and willingness to perceive the "clues" it generates. Most of us hear what we want to hear or, in many instances, don't listen at all. Listening, as you have now been told perhaps too often, requires practice and a degree of discipline which few of us are willing or able to maintain.[31]

Finally, even when discovery tactics are used "carefully," it is always difficult to assess the accuracy and meaning of what you are told. Your ability to understand the motives and dispositions of the person across the table is complicated by the formal quality of many bargaining situations. In addition, the problem of discovering the "true" attitudes and intentions of one's opponent is made even more difficult by the socially sanctioned "right" to conceal or disguise these "truths" about oneself and one's position in bargaining situations. You might give some thought to the difficulties of making inferences and judgments about your opponents and their goals in a situation in which you *know* they may be feigning or pretending—indeed, when feigning or pretending is normatively supported. How accurate are such judgments likely to be? Whatever information you elicit and receive must be *interpreted* before it is of any value to you. Needless to say, there is not always much firm ground on which to base such judgments.

---

2. *The Concealment-Disclosure Problem*

While the foregoing comments assume that opponents will be making efforts to conceal information about themselves and their cases, it should be recognized that some types of information may be readily available. A substantial number of lawyers advocate not only making full disclosure of the evidence that will be introduced at trial, but also revealing an eagerness to settle if the "price" is right. This attitude is especially prevalent in personal injury litigation, where plaintiffs' attorneys frequently prepare a prospectus or "trial brochure" for presentation to defense counsel. The plaintiff's lawsuit is regarded as a commodity to sell and the brochure, as the name implies, is designed to tell the prospective purchaser all he or she needs to know in order to decide whether the case is worth the price the plaintiff is asking. But the brochure is more than a sales "gimmick": it is a relatively complete summary of the evidence that will be presented at trial, albeit from the plaintiff's point of view. Its proponents feel it provides valuable support in settlement negotiations and, as the following excerpts make clear, are willing to discount the risks involved in full disclosure:

> A brochure is a carefully organized, factual and graphic presentation of the most cogent evidence and of the evidence having the most

31. Some of the difficulty involved in careful listening can be alleviated by a systematic review of information obtained throughout the course of a negotiation and, in multi-party situations, by the "one-on-one" observations discussed by Walton and McKersie.

emotional appeal in a personal injury claim for damages; its purpose is to stimulate and justify a prompt and reasonable settlement. The brochure's distinctive function is to ensure that the settlement deliberations of the defense representative will be guided and influenced by a comprehensive and persuasive statement of plaintiff's case, rather than merely by the defense's perspective of the law and facts or an abbreviated report or mere recollection of plaintiff's contentions and demand figure. Of course, the effective utilization of the brochure is contingent on the likelihood of a settlement, the good faith desire of the plaintiff to negotiate a settlement, the good faith desire of the defense representative to consider the brochure, the value of the case, and the skill of the counsel for the plaintiff.

* * *

Most criticism of the brochure method is based on the fear of disclosing vital elements of proof and strategy to an opponent or of revealing weaknesses in plaintiff's case. The replies to these objections are that the use of the brochure is grounded in the philosophy of full disclosure before trial, that under modern discovery rules all relevant material may be obtained before trial, and that it is foolish to rely on the inability of defense counsel to discover weaknesses in plaintiff's case. The possibility that the brochure or some part thereof will be misappropriated or used inconsistently by the other side is conceded. It is contended, however, that this is a calculated risk that may be minimized by ascertaining the good faith of the brochure's recipients and obtaining an agreement as to the conditions of its use.

Some attorneys contend that the use of what is essentially a sales technique does not comport with the professional dignity of a lawyer. The brochure's advocates point out that a settlement is, in fact, a sale of a case; and when a settlement is advantageous to a client it is counsel's professional duty to be an effective salesman.

The brochure itself has been criticized as too formal and inflexible an instrument of negotiation, as one that precludes the adaptability and persuasive impact of personal conversation. This criticism is countered by asserting the persuasive force of a graphic and pictorial representation and by noting that the use of the brochure supplements but does not prohibit personal negotiations.

If the use of a brochure is objected to by defendant's representative as being a biased or unrealistic presentation of a claimant's case, the appropriate response to such an attitude would be not to send a brochure. In fact, however, most defense representatives welcome a carefully prepared brochure, particularly those sections covering matters of evidence, such as medical reports and photographs.

* * *

The enthusiasm of those employing this technique of settlement might be accounted for by the variety of the brochure's functions. Incidental to the primary function of effecting an early and satisfactory settlement, the brochure assures timely and thorough marshaling of the evidence, it tends to disclose latent weaknesses of the case or the necessity for reevaluation of damages, and finally it serves as a basis for the trial brief. In appropriate cases, the brochure is a potentially invaluable tool of an efficient and foresighted trial lawyer.[32]

Despite the enthusiasm of some of its supporters, the "brochure method" is far from universally endorsed by trial lawyers. A treatise for defense attorneys, for example, contains the following admonition:

> It is very seldom wise to disclose too much of your confidential information to your opponent in hopes of frightening him and causing him to make a settlement of the case. Disclosing information from your files is like a two-edged sword. If the information brings about a settlement, everything is fine. If a settlement is not accomplished, the attorney has definitely weakened his defense. His opponent will go over the information furnished with a fine-toothed comb and develop methods for counteracting it. Tell him as little as possible and keep him interested. Let him guess a little bit. It is wishful thinking to believe that by disclosing the entire contents of a file the opposing attorney will become panicky and rush into a settlement. It is best to "play your cards close to the vest."
>
> There is no objection to furnishing the plaintiff's attorney with certain types of information. For instance, if the defense has a report of a reputable doctor to the effect that the plaintiff is suffering from no serious disability, the furnishing of this report may cause the plaintiff to lose faith in his case.[33]

Although an elaboration of these two approaches would require a lengthy discussion, these brief excerpts do present an interesting contrast. Which of them seems to make the most sense? Would disclosure be appropriate in other sorts of cases—*e. g.,* by either prosecutor or defense counsel in a criminal case? Can the difference between the two views be explained by the fact that one is used on behalf of plaintiffs, the other by defendants?

Related to the question of disclosing the "facts" of the case is the issue of disclosing one's own attitudes and aspirations in regard to it. Most commentators recommend not appearing "too eager" to settle. A variation of this advice, which involves *disclosing* an eagerness for trial, is offered by Hermann:

> We have already seen how much settlement leverage one can gain if he can make it clear to his adversary that, unless a favorable settlement is agreed upon, the case will be tried. But this kind of leverage cannot possibly be exerted unless the attorney seeking to employ it impresses his adversary with his complete willingness to try the case in order to achieve a result compatible with his position during settlement negotiations. Regardless of how great a lawyer's trial skills may be, once his opponent discovers that, in this case, he is reluctant to enter the courtroom, his chances of exerting leverage disappear.

---

32. Werchick, *Settling the Case—Plaintiff,* 4 AM.JUR. TRIALS 363–64, 378 (1966).

33. W. Pierson, THE DEFENSE ATTORNEY AND BASIC TACTICS 251–52 (1956).

It follows that if, for any reason (whether ill health, a recent unfavorable verdict or series of unfavorable verdicts, personal problems, or whatever), you wish to avoid trial of a case, don't let your adversary at the settlement table know about it. Do your best to make whatever effort is necessary to give the appearance of eagerness to do battle before judge and jury.[34]

Obviously, prescriptions of this nature raise the issue of feigned vs. actual disclosure. While many lawyers believe that an atmosphere of openness is highly desirable, they also believe that "useful" disclosures should be exploited by any effective adversary. For this reason the appearance of full disclosure is not necessarily the reality, and one must be careful in responding to bids for information, no matter how straightforward the opponent seems to be. At the same time, few attorneys will agree to settlement without having some assurance that they have obtained the kind of accurate and complete information they need to make a full evaluation of the case. Concealment-disclosure choices may be as crucial to the outcome as any other judgments involved in negotiation strategy. They are surely as difficult to make.

————

3.　*The Difficulties of Circumspection*

Although you may decide to disclose some facts about your case, it will be a rare negotiation in which you do not have information to protect. (At a minimum, in most instances, it is safe to assume that full disclosure of one's authority to settle—that is, one's minimal settlement point—would not be advantageous to the client.)

Assuming that you have decided to conceal or create a misleading impression with respect to certain aspects of your case, then, a number of difficulties become manifest. One is the possibility of conveying more information than is intended, or of communicating unintended messages. Another is the problem of generating distrust or hostile reactions to your behavior. To some extent cooperation and information-sharing are normatively supported expectations in a negotiation, and you will be expected—albeit with some license for manipulation—to engage in the give and take of information exchange. Given these norms the following options seem to be available.

Low Activity

One possibility is to participate very little in the negotiation, asking a few questions but chiefly listening. Since people like to talk, the opponent will often fill in the available "information space" with-

---

34. P. Hermann, BETTER SETTLEMENTS THROUGH LEVERAGE 250–51 (1965).

out being fully aware of doing so. This, of course, requires that you disguise your own reactions and convey nothing more than a willingness to listen, and it is worth trying to develop the skill needed to control these aspects of your behavior. To some degree this may involve your becoming conscious of the subtle ways in which you *unconsciously* convey such feelings as surprise, pleasure, interest and belief, in order to mask these reactions when they occur. As difficult as this task may be, if you can succeed in becoming "inscrutable," [35] you will have brought an important dimension of concealment-disclosure strategy under control.

One form of this approach involves "calculated ignorance." The negotiator is inscrutable because he or she has not investigated the case, discussed settlement with the client, or formulated a position. Many criminal defense lawyers, for example, suggest baseline plea agreement with the prosecutor before they have talked to their client. Although there are difficulties associated with such an undirected bargaining posture, it does have the advantage of being unlikely to convey very much information to one's opponent.

Increased Activity

Another way information is concealed in negotiation is by higher activity. A negotiator who fills the air with demands and counterdemands, is unpredictable in his or her emotional responses, or who tends to react quickly in rejecting offers and overtures is "hard to figure." However, the chance that a variety of unintended messages will also be conveyed is substantially increased.

Fending Off Questions and Offers

A third tactic available to counsel relates to the way direct bids for information should be handled. Nierenberg offers the following insights on what he calls "the vital subject of how to answer when questioned":

> These are not offered as suggestions to follow but merely as examples of alternatives that you may have been subjected to or used on others. The field may be divided as follows: (1) leave the other person with the assumption that he has been answered, (2) answer incompletely, (3) answer inaccurately, (4) leave the other person without the desire to pursue the questioning process further.

> **(1) Leaving the Other Person with the Assumption that He Has Been Answered**

> In the questioning process we deal with two sets of assumptions— those of the questioner and those of the person questioned. In answering we should try to handle the questioner's assumptions and attempt to leave out our own. . . .

---

35. We borrow this term from H. Edwards and J. White, THE LAWYER AS A NEGOTIATOR 114 (1977).

(2) Answering Incompletely

An incomplete answer is one in which we cover a much more limited area than the questioner intends. Let us say you have just had dinner at the home of a newly married friend and his wife has cooked the meal. The next day the husband asks you, "Well, how did you like my wife's dinner?" Your answer might be, "She certainly sets a beautiful table. The silver was especially fine. Was it a wedding present?"

Use restricted meanings to the questions asked. Sometimes in a negotiation if details are presented and both sides are concerned that they could never agree on the specifics, they will ask questions which are subject to restricted answers rather than obtain an absolute rejection which they do not want. When, for example, the question was asked of the manufacturer, "Could you handle this order?" the manufacturer, considering a restricted meaning, said, "Certainly we can handle an order of this sort." Neither side was asking or receiving an answer to the question of when delivery could commence.

As previously stated, you should ask questions considering the level that you wish to receive answers on. If you ask a high-level question you will probably get a high-order, abstract answer. A lower-level question will elicit more precise, detailed information. In answering questions, however, this process can be reversed. When you are asked a high-order question, you can give a low-order answer by prefacing your answer with, "Well, to be more fundamental. . . ." When the question is asked, "How do you think the disarmament talks are going?" the answer might be, "As skilled diplomats, our representatives are in direct and constant communication with the representatives of the other side." A low-order question can be given a high-level answer, as when asked, "Why didn't the president of Columbia take more immediate action against the S.D.S. students when they started their disruptive activity?" The answer might be, "Rugged individualism is dead in the United States." . . .

Another method of answering incompletely is to sidestep the question. Let us say that you are a salesman and are in the middle of your presentation. At this point the customer asks, "How much does it cost?" Your object is not to answer at this time; you wish to complete your presentation before revealing the price. You might reply, "The dollar value is what I'm sure you're interested in. Therefore let me round out the details and present the various costs so that I may more fully be able to answer your question." You might also say, "When I've finished my presentation of the entire article, I'm looking forward to asking your opinion of the price." Sometimes use of the restricted meaning can be of assistance; tell him the price of the part that is being demonstrated at the time, then go on with the presentation.

(3) Answering Inaccurately

Use an analogy beginning "As I understand your question . . ." and then set forth your own version of the question; or begin with "A similar situation . . ." and state a situation that you are prepared to compare it to; or set forth a typical analogy to which you would like to relate the question. You can also change the question by substituting a different question. Suggest that you are going to answer and deftly change the subject: "I thought you might say that, and you deserve an answer. But before I reply, let me ask this question." "Yes, I agree with the intent of the question, but let me rephrase it slightly." If the questioner is still unsatisfied and says, "I don't think the answer is pertinent," your answer might be, "Perhaps you're right. How would you phrase it?" or, "How would you have stated it?" or, "Would you prefer that I put it this way?" or, "How would you like me to say it?"

(4) Leaving the Other Person Without the Desire to Pursue the Questioning Process Further

State many answers without committing yourself to any one. For example: "Why can't we improve railroad service?" Answer: "When we consider shifting population, the change in the economic conditions of people in various sections of the area, the failure of the state to supply necessary funds, the federal government's preoccupation with supersonic jets, labor's inclination to give as little for the dollar as possible . . ."

State that the answer to the question is that the question cannot be answered: "That's one of those unanswerable questions." "The future holds the key to that probelm." "It would serve no purpose in this instance to speculate on the future."

Give a "nothing" answer: "That *was* a dinner." "*What* a dress."

Use disarming praise: If the mother of a girl asks a reluctant bachelor, "What are your views on marriage?" he could answer, "If I could only be sure that all mothers looked as charming as you. Tell me, how do you manage to do it?"

* * *

Don't answer: The method used can take many forms: you are distracted; you cause a distraction; you intentionally continue creating a distraction by choosing another question or appointing someone else to answer the question.[36]

A similar pattern of response is available to the negotiator faced with a specific offer or demand. If one really can "brush aside" offers without showing the slightest interest in them, ignore them, or perhaps creatively misinterpret them, the opponent's confidence and feeling of control may be considerably shaken. As with other concealment tactics, however, communications of this type are complicated by the non-verbal messages that accompany them. The slightest hesitation in answering, a change in tone, a lack of eye contact or one of countless other subtle cues can reveal much more than the words themselves. In practice, concealment is a much more complex tactical choice than Nierenberg's tongue-in-cheek analysis would suggest.

36. G. Nierenberg, FUNDAMENTALS OF NEGOTIATING 133–36 (rev. ed. 1973).

2. Demand Strategies

STEVENS, STRATEGY AND COLLECTIVE BARGAINING NEGOTIATION

32–35, 59–66 (1963).

. . . [The large demand functions as a rule] for play of the negotiation game on the one hand, and [as a tactic] utilized for subsequent play within the context of a rules framework on the other. [I will discuss both] the rule-like character of this institutional arrangement [and its tactical implications].

The "Large" Initial Demand Bargaining Rule

The large-demand rule provides that the initial bargaining demand and counterdemand are in excess of the least favorable terms upon which each party is willing to settle, and in excess of what each expects the agreed-upon position to be. Both parties know this.

* * *

. . . [If] one has . . . explained why the parties to collective bargaining elect to negotiate, one has also explained the institution of the large demand as a rule for beginning. This is because the only rule for beginning really consonant with subsequent negotiation is the initial large demand. If there is to be subsequent negotiation, initial demands must permit what is frequently termed 'room for bargaining,' and this the large demand does. Such demands set up a context in which information can be gained during the course of negotiation to elect a firm strategy. Initial uncertainty about the range in which an agreed position can lie makes the large demand prudent, that is, the large demand precludes the possibility of inadvertent commitment to a position either less favorable than that which might have been obtained or to a position sure (it develops) to result in an outcome 'no agreement.'

Another basic consonance of the large initial bargaining demand with the negotiation process is related to the fact that negotiations frequently take considerable time, time during which conditions affecting the negotiations may change. This fact, coupled with the consideration that the practice of adding to demands during the course of negotiation is not itself compatible with the negotiation process, create pressures in favor of large initial demands.

The Minimum Demand or Maximum Offer ('Boulwareism')

The major alternative to the large demand as a tactic for beginning negotiation is the 'minimum' demand or 'maximum' offer, that is, an initial bargaining proposal which is (virtually) identical with the least favorable terms to himself upon which a party is willing to settle. A prominent case in point is the approach to collective bargaining commonly termed 'Boulwareism' (after a chief proponent of the technique, Lemuel Boulware of the General Electric Company).

The central feature of this approach is to meet the union's initial bargaining demand with a single counterproposal to which the company intends to adhere. That is, the union is told that it can accept or reject the company proposal, but come what may, the company does not intend to move from its announced position. With the Boulware approach, the single counterproposal is carefully researched in an effort to come up with an offer which is 'right' by any reasonable standard, which is 'fair,' and which will be considered fair by the employees. Once the proposal is formulated, the technique is to stick to it, not to 'haggle' about it.

* * *

In large measure, the maximum offer (or minimum demand) is not just another way to begin a game of negotiation. It is a technique for converting a would-be negotiation game into one of take-it-or-leave-it. . . . The difficulty is that if either side accepts a 'one-shot' demand or proposal, in the eyes of the employees it might appear as if that side had surrendered. A bargaining technique which completely denies 'victories' will invite interminable prestige fights. It is this basic nonconsonance of the minimum demand with the negotiation which suggests treatment of the large demand as rule for play—rather than just as a tactic used during the early stages of negotiation.

The Agenda Rule—Agenda Set by Initial Demand and Counterproposal

Characteristically in collective bargaining the initial demand and counterproposal set the agenda for each periodic agreement conference. That is, there is no systematic negotiation of the agenda prior to the beginning of substantive contract negotiations.

As with other rules for play of the negotiation game, there are possible alternatives to the agenda rule. In some international negotiations, for example, it is customary to decide upon the agenda itself by negotiation before the beginning of substantive negotiation. In some collective bargaining relationships there are preagreement conference procedures which tend in the direction of agenda negotiation.

The problem of the tactical significance of agenda composition is related to the institution of the 'large demand' since the agenda is brought into being by the bargaining demand and counterproposal. . . .

Additions to Initial Demands

Another aspect of agenda composition is the proscription that, generally speaking, a party to collective bargaining negotiation does not during the course of negotiation make demands in excess of those contained in his initial proposal. This proscription applies both to increasing the magnitude of a given item and to adding additional items to those contained in the initial proposal.

Since negotiation sessions are frequent and the initial bargaining demands can be 'large' in any event, there is no general necessity to provide for subsequent increases in demands. Moreover, the practice of adding to demands during the course of negotiation is not compatible with the negotiation process. How can a party really begin to negotiate until he knows what his opponent's maximum asking price will be? Certainly the basic bargaining processes of changing position, rewarding by concession, threatening by adherence, and so on, could scarcely begin until the total demands to be served during a given play of the negotiation game were on the table.

The above considerations do not rule out the possibility that certain special functions might be served by such subsequent changes in position. One such function, for example, would be the exploitation of information about one's opponent gained during the course of negotiations. The fact that negotiation sessions are frequent greatly reduces the importance of serving this function *vis-a-vis* any particular contract negotiations; that is, it can be served during the next contract negotiations. One legitimate aspect of this function *vis-a-vis* a particular set of negotiations is the case in which the initial demander gets new ideas from the counterproposal—ideas which suggest that some redesign of the initial demand would facilitate agreement.

Much more dubious is the practice whereby a party attempts during the final stages of negotiation to exploit the fact of near agreement by tacking a last-minute demand, as a sort of 'rider,' onto a virtually wrapped-up package. Such an attempt, even if successful, would surely degenerate the atmosphere prevailing during subsequent negotiation sessions. . . . Peters classifies this tactic as, while not perhaps properly considered bad faith, a borderline case— certainly to be regarded as bad practice.

* * *

The Negotiators as Delegates

The negotiators who face each other over the bargaining table are delegates of an organization (or organizations) on each side of the bargaining relationship. Douglas has suggested that the early stages of the negotiation interaction are dominated by the negotiators roles as delegates—that these stages emphasize interparty conflict as contrasted with greater emphasis upon interpersonal (negotiators *qua* negotiators) interaction.

Characteristic features of the early stages may be viewed in this light. Thus there are frequently vigorous speeches in support of firm positions (the large demands) which, it is generally understood, will subsequently be abandoned. At this stage, each party may express surprise and consternation over the proposal advanced by his opposite number. Such manifestations of interparty conflict do not preclude good will and good feeling between the negotiators as individuals. . . .

* * *

The fact that the negotiators are delegates has an important influence upon the size and composition of initial bargaining proposals. Typically, such proposals are initiated by the suggestions of many people. (For this reason alone, demands may be large in the sense of the number of subjects.) Although some screening of suggestions takes place before initial demands are presented, the critical matter of negotiators' relative valuation of these demands, rating them and deciding upon the 'trading value' of each in terms of the others, and so on, takes place in the course of the negotiations.

Constraints Imposed by Information Giving and Seeking Functions of Initial Proposals

The important thing about periodic contract negotiations is their outcome. A party's initial demand and his opposite number's counterproposal are intended by each to influence that outcome from his own point of view. The question is: by what routes is this influence supposed to be operative?

We may begin an answer to this question by recalling [that negotiation tactics in the early stages] involve information giving and seeking functions, functions which are discharged, in part, by the initial bargaining proposals.

It has been suggested that an aspect of [the former]—the security function—is a primary function of the large demand. This is, the large demand serves to shield one's own position while one seeks to determine the real position of one's opponent. . . .

* * *

The security function is . . . one of the considerations in formulation of the initial bargaining position. The other major function is . . . [the] representation of preferences. As summed up by Peters: 'In skillful hands the bargaining position performs a double function. It conceals, and it reveals. The bargaining position is used to indicate—to unfold gradually, step by step—the maximum expectation of the negotiator, while at the same time concealing, for as long as necessary, his minimum expectation.' In this context, a party's maximum expectation is the most favorable settlement he could hope for, his minimum expectation is the edge of the contract zone—he would rather take a strike than go lower. Peters continues that in operating with his bargaining position, the negotiator attempts by indirect means to convince his opposite number that his maximum expectation is really his breaking-off point.

The fact that the initial bargaining proposal serves the function of revealing preferences puts (indefinite) constraints upon the magnitude of that demand. At its largest, the large demand will be of the type that mirrors total constituents' demands (including, perhaps, some demands originated by the leaders and 'sold' to the constituents), or at least all those demands which the negotiator feels he must take seriously enough to make a show of taking to the bargaining table. The process of revealing his maximum expectation will involve the negotiator's relative valuation of the items he initially carried to the table. If indirect means, such as the manner and timing of changes in position, are to reveal a maximum expectation, the initial position itself must be appropriate in the sense of credibility and feasibility.
.   .   .

Typically, elements of bluff and deception will be involved in the early stage of negotiation. This consideration puts constraints upon the magnitude of the initial demand which are similar in nature to those just discussed. For if a negotiator's bargaining position is to serve as an effective bluff, it must be at least credible. Thus if a negotiator intends bluff, he will be dissuaded from asserting a 'huge' demand.

The initial bargaining proposal is an information seeking device. During the early stages of negotiation, each party, in addition to giving information about (and concealing) his own preferences, is attempting to discover the true preferences of his opponent. In part, the negotiator will infer these preferences from his opponent's bargaining position. He will also infer these from his opponent's reaction to his own bargaining position. The parties are at this stage attempting to demarcate the limits of the contract zone.   .   .   .

The fact that the initial bargaining proposal is an information-seeking device also imposes some constraints upon its magnitude. If the initial proposal is so far removed from any possible range of difference in the negotiations as to be virtually meaningless, then it will not invite a reaction or response which will itself be meaningful.

*   *   *

The 'Swap' Theory

This view of the functions of the initial negotiation proposal is related to the matter of nonneutrality of the negotiation agenda.   .   . The notion is that a large initial bargaining demand may facilitate negotiation by providing something to 'swap' during the course of negotiations. Dunlop and Healy have observed that: 'More than one company has "bought" the withdrawal of a union-shop demand for an additional nickel in a series of contract negotiations.'

What the 'swap' theory seems to say, in effect, is that a party to collective bargaining negotiation may increase his negotiation power by increasing the magnitude of his initial demand. Put this way, the mechanism implied would seem to constitute something of a *tour de force*, and it is not immediately obvious how it can work. Why should a party to collective bargaining get more simply because he asks for more? One answer to this question is that such a party does not get more simply because he asks for more—that is, naively including in the package 'demands' manufactured more or less out of thin air will be of no tactical avail. Actually, to be effective, the included items must represent genuine issues, must be 'blue chips' (as the argot of the participants would have it). These are demands which the negotiator might (at least in principle) hope to achieve, demands which in this sense are within the range of expectations with respect to possible (not necessarily likely) outcomes of negotiation.

Another answer to the above question is to be found in the uncertainty which pervades collective bargaining negotiation, and in the fact that there may be a range of positions within which the outcome may lie. A's larger demand may alter B's expectations about the least favorable terms upon which A is willing to settle, and, in consequence, may lead B to suppose that he must concede more to achieve agreement than would have been the case had A's demand been smaller. This is not a trading operation, however. It is use of the communications implications of the size and composition of the bargaining position to convey as high an impression as possible of the negotiator's absolute minimum price.

In any negotiation in which an initial multi-item proposal (demand) adds up as a 'cost package' to more than the cost of the ultimately agreed-upon package, a trade of some sort will appear in the settlement, and these neglected items will, in this sense, have been 'traded' for the included items. This is not really the kind of trading operation envisaged by the swap theory of the bargaining position. It is more a case in which the range of alternatives in the bargaining demand has allowed the opponent a chance to pick his own poison. This itself may facilitate settlement, since concession on one group of items may be preferable to concession on some other group, even though as monetary cost packages they total the same.

But the swap theory implies more than just a range of options from which the opponent may choose. If the dropped demand is relatively unimportant, the mechanism at work is more essentially one of bluff than a trading operation *per se*. A contrives to make B think that, in dropping a demand, he has made a concession, when, in point of fact, the unimportance of the demand to A means that he has given up little. Here the essential feature of the tactic is not so much in the trading operation as in the bluff technique whereby the conceded demand was made to appear *bona fide*.

NOTES

1. *The Dynamics of Demand and Counterdemand*

Although written in the context of labor negotiations, Stevens'
discussion of initial demands applies to almost every type of negotiation in which lawyers engage. In litigation, as in collective bargaining, the demand functions as an information device, concealing and
conveying clues to the preferences and expectations of the parties.
To be effective, it must communicate a believable claim that what is
demanded (or offered) represents the *least* the demanding party will
accept. If it is high enough it will (i) protect counsel from under-
estimations of his or her opponent's minimal settlement point; (ii)
conceal counsel's own minimal settlement point; and (iii) permit counsel to make concessions (and demand counterconcessions) which still
perform these concealment/protective functions. If, at the same time,
a demand is low enough to be believable, it may generate a response
which will provide a clue to the opponent's minimal settlement point,
and may cause opposing counsel to revise his or her estimate of the
best settlement that can be obtained. On the other hand, if the initial
demand is too high, it may (i) be dismissed and have no effect on opposing counsel's decisions; (ii) cause opposing counsel to believe that
threats or other cost-imposing tactics are necessary; (iii) produce an
expectation of deadlock (opposing counsel might then begin preparing
for trial, incurring costs which would later have to be recovered);
(iv) support inferences by opposing counsel concerning counsel's inexperience or inability to adequately estimate the bargaining limits,
thereby raising his or her own settlement expectations; (v) make
counsel appear unreasonable in the eyes of third persons who might
potentially influence the situation (*e. g.*, in many jurisdictions, pretrial conferences are in effect judicially-supervised settlement negotiations, and judges will have their own ideas of what a particular case is
worth.) Conversely, a demand which is too low will usually raise
opposing counsel's estimates of the probable settlement outcome and
may force concessions which approach counsel's minimal settlement
point.

Thus every demand functions as a complex mechanism which
conveys a notion of counsel's view of the situation and probable future
conduct, offers some level of benefit to the other side, and threatens
the additional costs of continued bargaining and a final deadlock.
Indeed, at each stage of the negotiations one can posit a theoretically
optimal demand level low enough to be considered legitimate and high
enough to exert maximum pressure on one's adversary.

Perhaps the best way to illustrate this mechanism is to ask you
to speculate on the choices you would make in a specific bargaining
situation. Assume you are counsel in a personal injury case and you
have estimated (in consultation with your client) that, given all the

relevant factors, a settlement of $20,000 would be a very good settlement and as much as $8,000 would be preferable to going to trial. Suppose further that the opening offer by counsel for the insurance company was $5,000 (with strong accompanying reasons) and after several months of preparation for trial, he or she has made a "final" offer of $8,000. (You have made no counterdemand yet, but have rejected these offers.) What do these demands tell you? How should each be countered? Should you have made a counterdemand? What if both positions had been twice as high?

As you consider these questions (or similar questions with respect to any case you are handling), the fact that initial demands do convey a good deal of information seems obvious. You should also bear in mind, however, that in most instances the demand really *is* a starting point. Despite our emphasis on the demand as indicating a willingness to agree on particular terms and conditions, it is, of course, part of a series of attempts to structure perceptions and to secure agreement. Very soon the parties begin to think of such communications as concessions; that is, after the initial positions on specific issues are set out, it is the *pattern of change* which is read, and such patterns are expected to move in the direction of agreement.[37] It is only in this larger context that any choice of demand tactics can be effectively evaluated.

2. *Some Further Observations on Demand Tactics*

The use of demand analysis in litigation depends, of course, on accurately assessing the bargaining situation and the way it is viewed by one's opponent. With appropriate regard for differences in particular cases, however, it does seem possible to make a number of general statements about the typical expectations and concerns which lawyers bring to demand tactics and strategies.

The Negotiability of the Initial Demand

It is our experience that most lawyers, whatever the type of case, expect the initial demand to be negotiable. That is, it is generally assumed that, no matter how firmly stated, the initial position of every party offers some room for bargaining. The major alternative to this negotiable initial demand is what Stevens labels "Boulwareism"— which involves stating a figure at or near one's minimum disposition and sticking to it. Whatever its function in labor negotiations and other settings, Boulwareism is used infrequently in the settlement of litigated cases, and if it is chosen as a tactic, it presents special problems of credibility. If counsel wants to stick with an early demand it must be bolstered by some specific explanation, such as the unreason-

---

37. *See generally* Liebert, Smith, Hill, & Keiffer, *The Effects of Information and Magnitude of Initial Offer on Interpersonal Negotiation*, 1 EXP.SOC. PSYCH. 431 (1968), and Chertkoff and Conley, *Opening Offer and Frequency of Concession as Bargaining Strategies*, 1 J. OF PERS. & SOC. PSYCH. 181 (1967).

ableness of the client, the amount of work that has been done on the case, or counsel's own considered judgment of what is fair. And no matter how convincing a rationale is advanced, the "take it or leave it" nature of this tactic always poses a greater risk of deadlock.

In most litigation, then, as in the collective bargaining Stevens describes, the "large initial demand" is more of a rule than a tactic, and for many of the same reasons. Melvin Belli states this prescription in the following terms:

> I would suggest that your first demand be sufficiently above your minimum settlement figure to make a reasonable allowance for the following factors:
>
> 1. The margin of error in your own evaluation since you are dealing with intangibles that cannot be put on a precise mathematical table.
>
> 2. Allow a margin for the defendant's judgment as he conceivably may have placed a higher value on the case than you.
>
> 3. Allow a margin for bargaining with the defendant so that you can reduce your demand somewhat during negotiations and still wind up at a reasonable settlement figure. This is an established custom and practice in the business which is expected by the defendant at the time he makes his opening offer.
>
> 4. Allow a margin for a later reduction of demand which will protect the defendant attorney or adjuster with the insurance company management. Since bargaining is customary and the opening demand is usually reduced for settlement purposes, the insurance company executive expects, as a matter of course, that the final settlement will be lower than the plaintiff's original demand. Unless the opening demand is ridiculously low, it is very difficult for a defense attorney or adjuster to explain to the management why he paid the plaintiff's original demand and did not get some concessions by way of settlement negotiations. Keep in mind that the defense attorney or adjuster has a job to do in the scheme of things and needs to look good to his client or boss in a settlement, the same as you wish to look good in the eyes of your client.[38]

It is clear that in Belli's view the large initial demand serves a security function and also gives the parties something to "swap." The initial demand must be large enough to allow you to *appear* to make real concessions to the opponent without actually compromising your underlying bargaining position.

In addition, the potential for a swap affects not only the *size* of the initial demand, but its complexity—the number of issues that are introduced into the negotiation. An encompassing initial demand can be "broken down" and traded-off in the give and take of subsequent exchanges. For example, counsel might accompany a demand concerning payment with a variety of conditions related to releases, apologies,

38. M. Belli, MODERN TRIALS, VOL.
I, 754 (1954).

future contacts between the parties, public disclosure of the results, subsequent review of the agreement, the manner of bringing about a dismissal of the action, and so forth.

The "Excessive" Demand

Many lawyers counsel very high initial demands. This creates "room" for concessions as negotiations proceed. However, one should not take such advice too literally. A demand well beyond what is *usually asked for* (not settled for) in a particular type of case (*e. g.*, neck injury, employment dispute, manslaughter charge), if it is not simply ignored, can either create suspicion about counsel's "reasonableness" (*i. e.*, he or she will be perceived as a type who is trying to "squeeze the last buck"), or be interpreted as a product of ignorance and/or lack of ability. Such judgments may increase opposing counsel's willingness to risk deadlock and go to trial. In addition, when an initial demand bears little or no relation to what are considered legitimate claims, there is little pressure on opposing counsel to reshape his or her own estimates of the probable outcome.

These dynamics have been usefully stated as follows:

> . . . it is probably best that the first offer one makes be a realistic offer. It is only a realistic offer that can create the uncertainty which induces the opposing side to accept it rather than face the possibility of a less desirable result in litigation. The first realistic offer establishes for the other side one of the offeror's limits, and thus gives credibility to a subsequent statement that there will be no further concessions. Such credibility may be lacking if there has been a series of steadily improving offers moving from the unrealistic into the realistic area without clear demarcation. Moreover, if one is dealing with a sophisticated bargaining opposite, a first offer which is realistic can produce professional respect that is advantageous for the remainder of the negotiation.

> For similar reasons, a first offer which is realistic is probably to be desired in business transactions. The unrealistic offer may only convince the bargaining opposite that he is dealing with a neophyte, upon whom it is useless to spend more time. And the lack of procedures comparable to those available in litigation to educate the bargaining opposite in a business transaction makes it worthwhile to convince him that he is dealing with someone with whom it is desirable to do business.[39]

It should be noted that in civil litigation the initial demand is made in the prayer for relief. Although Hermann's reasoning would suggest that the prayer itself ought to be geared to opposing counsel's expectations, excessive prayers do not seem to give rise to the same inferences as do excessive early demands.

---

39. This statement was provided by one of our students. We have been unable to locate its source.

On the other hand, there are many times when even an excessive demand may be not only appropriate but desirable. For instance, if counsel demonstrates his or her good faith and sophistication in conceding that a particular demand seems excessive ("I know this is unusual, but there's real doubt about the witnesses' credibility"), the departure from the typical pattern may give the accompanying statements greater force and believability.

Initiation of Settlement Discussions and the First Offer

Given the difficulty of assessing and framing the "best" first offer to make, some lawyers strongly advocate waiting to respond to the actions of one's opponent. The argument generally runs that initiating settlement discussions will be taken as a sign of weakness, and that the party making the first offer runs a greater risk of revealing prejudicial information and setting an outside limit on what can be obtained in the settlement that may be unduly favorable to the opponent. Hermann presents some competing considerations:

> Whenever there is an attempt to recover for personal injuries it is reasonable to assume that both sides hope for an early, fair settlement. It is just as reasonable to assume that both sides are aware that there can be no settlement without negotiation. But it is amazing how many lawyers, and how many insurance company representatives, are reluctant to take the initiative in getting settlement discussions underway. . . .

* * *

> Preconceptions which inhibit initiation or settlement discussions are invariably expensive luxuries. By sitting down with a pencil and paper and actually calculating the expense of litigation to the claimant, his counsel, and the defense, one can recognize clearly how important it is that settlement discussions be commenced as early in the game as possible. To the extent that any of the reasons for reluctance to initiate negotiations is sound, it is entitled to little weight as compared with the substantial loss that may result from needless litigation. The case for early initiation of settlement discussions is an impressive one, indeed.

> It is worth taking a moment here to point out that the notion that it is a sign of weakness to initiate settlement discussions is little more than nonsense. The keynote of modern negotiation of personal injury claims is directness: the desire of both sides to settle a claim which both know has value is certainly not a secret. The modern negotiator views his adversary's suggestion of settlement negotiations, not as weakness, but as exhibiting a common-sense willingness to work out a settlement.

* * *

> It is always good practice for the defense to sit down with plaintiff's counsel and learn the basis on which plaintiff's counsel believes he is entitled to settlement. It is good for the defense to assume that plaintiff's counsel, unless he is a fool, wouldn't waste his time in seeking settlement. The defense should approach plaintiff's counsel with the idea that he should be heard out because he may be right.

* * *

The negotiator who presses for an early beginning of settlement negotiations, or who seeks to have negotiations continue, is taking full advantage of the informative function of these negotiations: for, during the course of settlement discussions, both sides may learn things about the case that need further investigation, and may discover witnesses whose testimony could not have been counteracted had they first been learned of in the courtroom.[40]

Another commentator, summing up this aspect of negotiation strategy from a defense point of view, makes the following observation:

> Ultimately, of course, the test by which the defendant's counsel should decide whether or not to open settlement negotiations is the effect that action will have upon the price of the settlement. If the experience, outlook and background of counsel for the plaintiff or the circumstances of the case itself are such that the initiation of settlement talks by defense counsel will suggest to the plaintiff's counsel that the defendant is anxious to settle, the result will necessarily be an increase in the price of the plaintiff's case.[41]

Of course, much depends on the particular case and the particular individuals who are involved in the negotiation. But generally, settlement is such a pervasive aspect of the process that if the topic can come up naturally in the course of the interaction between counsel nothing follows from *who* actually brings it up.

The same reasoning would seem to apply to making the first offer, for it is generally recognized that someone has to begin (the first *concession* is quite different). It is usually thought to be desirable to wait for an offer if there is a chance opposing counsel will make a demand that is better than you expected, or to avoid the possibility of making an offer more favorable than your opponent expected. For example, counsel is often advised to wait when he or she does not have full command of the facts of the case or where circumstances might change, on the theory that it is better to fully understand what is in dispute before "laying one's cards on the table". On the other hand, there are circumstances where making the initial offer sets the focus of discussion and ultimately shifts the expectations involved and/or generates useful information about the opponent's preferences. This is especially true when one is dealing with inexperienced negotiators, who are often insufficiently sure of their valuation of the case to react to a first offer without revealing something about their position. In addition, because of the skill needed to handle concessions, inexperienced opponents may become stubborn and find themselves locked in to their initial demands, so that it is better to take the initiative to avoid the risk of deadlock. In general, however, these factors do not characterize the behavior of experienced lawyers and the decision as

---

40. P. Hermann, BETTER SETTLEMENTS THROUGH LEVERAGE 125–26, 128 (1965).

41. J. McConnell, *Settlement Negotiations*, 1 PRAC.LAWYER 34–35 (February, 1955).

to whether to initiate settlement discussions or make the first offer must rest on other considerations.

The Escalation of Demands

This tactic, sometimes used in labor negotiations, involves accompanying the demand with a direct or implicit threat that it may be withdrawn or increased—*e. g.*, "Since I've now had to invest time in preparation of the case my settlement figure must now be higher." Since the costs of failing to agree are becoming higher, not lower, the adversary is placed under considerable pressure.

Despite its potential, however, this device can be used only with considerable caution, and in many situations is considered improper. That is, lawyers see the initial demand as setting the outer limits of what can be asked for in a specific case. In discussions with their own clients, their planning of the litigation, and their bargaining behavior they act accordingly. Shifts upward are viewed with disfavor, and run the risk of breaking off the negotiations. This does not mean that an escalation of demands is not possible, but it does mean that it must be accompanied by an appropriate explanation, such as the need to recoup costs incurred in preparing for trial, the client's increasing dissatisfaction, or new information. If it is properly handled, an increase in demands as the case moves closer to trial can be a very effective way of communicating a willingness to deadlock unless the most recent demand is met, and at least part of this effectiveness is due to the fact that the tactic runs counter to established norms.

Specificity, Clarity, Openness, and Finality

Finally, a word should be said about the actual wording of the demand itself. Every demand or offer can be stated with various degrees of specificity, clarity, and openness. Similarly, every demand can be framed to communicate more or less finality and be more or less explicit about the consequences of refusal. Walton and McKersie's discussion of this aspect of the negotiating process seems particularly helpful here:

> The communications of interest here may have any of four purposes. First, Party may wish to convey firmness in commitment which is complete and which accurately represents Party's present position and future intentions. Second, Party may wish to convey firmness in commitment that is more apparent than real. Third, Party may want to communicate positive flexibility in its current position, such that Opponent can expect Party to make further concessions. This entails a type of "minimal commitment," approaching the form of a promise. Fourth, Party may wish to indicate that his present position might have to be revised to the disadvantage of Opponent. This would require a minimal commitment of a different variety. Throughout the discussions of this section we shall want to keep in mind the above distinctions about purpose.

.   .   . In general the firmer the commitment which Party intends, the clearer the communication he selects; the weaker the commitment, the more ambiguous the communication. However, degree of commitment has several dimensions—we suggest that it has three: .   .   . first, the *degree of finality* of the commitment to a specific position, second, the *degree of specificity* of the position to which the commitment is made, and third, the *consequence* to be associated with a positional commitment, in other words, the threat.

In order to illustrate the importance of these three dimensions, we can analyze the following hypothetical statement by a union negotiator who has received an offer from management late in negotiations: "We must have the 12½-cent package and the seniority provisions which we proposed. We are prepared to strike, if necessary." The above statement is firm along all three dimensions. (1) "We must have .   .   . ." indicates a high degree of finality. (2) ".   .   . the 12½-cent package and seniority provision we proposed" is quite specific. (3) The consequences seem reasonably clear from the phrase, "We are prepared to strike, if necessary." Commitment could be weakened by altering any one of the three dimensions of the statement.

First, less finality in the union's position would be implied if the statement began, "The committee expects management to give more consideration to the .   .   . " rather than, "We must have .   .   . "

Second, less specificity would result if the statement were revised to read: "We must have the kind of package and seniority provision we have been discussing here. We are prepared.   .   .   . "

Third, the statement would be weakened by modifying the consequences linked to the failure to comply with the demand: "We must have the 12½-cent package and the seniority provisions which we proposed, or this committee is going to have to work hard to sell this to the membership." All the union is saying here about consequences is that they will experience difficulty "selling" the membership. This does not obviate the possibility that the membership might vote for ratification even if it isn't exactly "sold" on the package. It certainly does not state that there will be a strike.

What purposes are served by statements such as those above? The first basic statement would be used to convey a firm commitment completely and accurately. However, each of the modifications of that statement contains both a degree of commitment and some qualification or reservation. The apparent firmness still remains, but the real commitment is less than binding. That is, each contains a phrase that can be interpreted in such a way that the party could later abandon the commitment without great loss of face.

* * *

.   .   . [L]anguage offers an almost infinite variety of ways of expressing the finality, the specificity, and the associated consequences of a party's current position. The situation is further confounded by the fact that any given statement comes to carry its own unique meaning in a particular context in a particular relationship.[42]

The *way* in which a demand or offer is made, then, can have important consequences for subsequent bargaining between the parties. If a demand expressing a high decree of finality is suddenly followed by a concession, the party making that demand will find that he or she has a great deal of difficulty establishing the credibility of other demands. Here, as elsewhere in lawyering, control of language is critical in carrying out the tasks involved. It would be a mistake to assume, however, that commitment is conveyed by language alone. The message communicated by a firm demand is always mediated by what the opponent learns from nonverbal aspects of the situation, and is affected by the larger context of the interaction. In any given situation what one party thinks of as a demand may be regarded by the other as a concession, with the very different connotations that flow from those two labels.

3. Concession Strategies

PRUITT, INDIRECT COMMUNICATION AND THE SEARCH FOR AGREEMENT IN NEGOTIATION

1 J.APP.SOC.PSYCH. 205–11, 233–37 (1971).

Picture a pair of negotiators who have been bargaining over an issue for some time. Each has made a few easy concessions from sham positions and is now making a serious or semi-serious effort. . . . [The negotiation is] now at a standstill. Each negotiator is presumably considering the possibility of making a further concession. What kind of arguments might he be using with himself for and against this move?

In support of making another concession are the costs that can result from failure to do so. Cost must be reckoned in terms of (a) the time that will be lost in trying to persuade the opponent to make the next move (time is usually money—delays also lead to weariness); (b) the danger that the opponent will become discouraged and end the negotiation prematurely; (c) the danger that one's own side or the opponent will become so committed to an unviable position that agreement is impossible; (d) the danger that further maneuvering now will leave too little time in the future to work out an agreement; and (e) in a continuing relationship, the danger of antagonizing the opponent and losing good will that is needed for the future (today's opponent may be tomorrow's ally if he is not overly antagonized). On the positive side, it can be argued that making a concession will build

----

42. R. Walton and R. McKersie, A BEHAVIORAL THEORY OF LABOR NEGOTIATIONS 93–95 (1965).

credit with the opponent which may later produce a counterconcession from him. Third parties who are pressing for agreement may also be impressed by the reasonableness of a negotiator who makes concessions and reward him for doing so.

In support of not making a concession are two kinds of "loss" that may be incurred if a concession is made: *position loss* and *image loss*. Together these types of loss constitute what is often loosely called the "weakening of one's negotiation position."

Position loss results from the fact that most negotiations are governed by a rule against withdrawing a concession once it has been made. Negotiators must be concerned about position loss because the possibility always exists that if one holds onto a demand long enough, the other negotiator will accept it entirely. Making a concession precludes this possibility.

Image loss refers to unwanted changes in the way the concession maker is perceived by his opponent, third parties, his constituents or himself. Image loss may take a number of forms:

(1) In pressing his current demand, a negotiator is often trying to convey an image of inflexibility that will move his opponent toward his target. This campaign is likely to suffer if he now demonstrates flexibility by making a concession. Hence he may not be so successful in achieving his target.

(2) A concession may make the negotiator look so flexible or even weak that the opponent's target actually moves in a direction unfavorable to the negotiator or the opponent feels that he can safely commit himself more firmly to his current demand. . . .

* * *

(3) A negotiator may be reluctant to make a concession in the present contest because he fears that it will be viewed as evidence that he will be flexible in *other* contests, involving the same or other opponents. If his current demand has been supported by a strong verbal commitment to make no further concessions, he may be reluctant to concede further for fear of tarnishing the credibility of his commitments in future negotiations. In other words, he fears gaining the reputation of being a bluffer. . . .

* * *

[4] A negotiator may be unwilling to make a concession because he views it as a sign of personal weakness that would cause him to lose his self-respect. . . .

[5] So far in the discussion, we have treated the negotiator as a unit, consisting either of an individual or an undifferentiated group. But in analyzing most formal negotiation, it is profitable to distinguish between the *negotiator*, who is the man on the firing line, and his *constituents*, who usually remain in the background but have an impact on his decisions. Negotiators are often concerned about the image which their constituents have of them. . . .

Changes Over Time in the Advantages and Disadvantages of Concession-Making

As time goes on in a negotiation, changes usually occur in the relative importance of the arguments for and against concession-making listed in the previous section.

The arguments for making a concession tend to become more convincing, for several reasons. Resources and patience become strained. The danger of reaching the deadline without an agreement becomes more apparent. Conflict often becomes more intense, further endangering the relationship between the antagonists. Third parties often exert increasing pressure for agreement. Concomitantly, the tactics that are being used to move the opponent in one's direction often yield diminishing returns. Eventually all of the threats, commitments, and debating points that can be made have been made; and the opponent, while duly impressed, is unwilling to make further concessions.

Paradoxically, as times goes on, many of the arguments for *not* making a concession also become stronger or remain just as strong. One has usually made most of the concessions that are easy to make, so that position loss becomes an increasingly painful affair. The danger that a concession will be interpreted as a sign of weakness and flexibility in this and other contests often remains the same or accentuates over time, because both negotiators become increasingly committed to specific demands and a test of strength develops. Other dangers of image loss are still very much a matter of concern, for example, threats to the negotiator's own self-respect and the respect of his constituents.

With an increase in pressures for making a concession and a concommitant increase or maintenance of pressures for holding firm, the negotiating party finds itself in a progressively deepening *concession dilemma.* . . .

This dilemma is often a *joint affair*, in that both of the negotiating parties are experiencing it simultaneously. When this happens, the negotiations are frequently deadlocked. Neither side is willing to move for fear of either losing a position that may become eventually viable or adversely affecting its image in the eyes of the opponent or third parties. Yet, paradoxically, both parties greatly desire an early agreement, and their resistance points and even their targets may be quite compatible.

The Advantages of Exchanging Concessions

Concession dilemmas are not always resolved. As mentioned earlier, negotiation can end without agreement, even when resistance points are compatible.

When an agreement is reached, we often find that an exchange of concessions has taken place, in other words a mutual de-escalation of demands. Such an exchange may take place on a simple dimension, as when management concedes from 8¢ to 10¢ and labor from 20¢ to 16¢. Or it may constitute a "horsetrade" of concessions on two or more dimensions, as when a supplier agrees to reduce the unit price in exchange for the buyer's willingness to place a larger order. An exchange of concessions can be helpful in resolving the concession dilemma by *materially reducing both side's fear of image loss*. It also has the advantage of appearing equitable.

How can an exchange of concessions reduce the fear of image loss? One of the major concerns in making a concession is that the opponent will rigidify his demands. But this concern is considerably diminished if the opponent concedes too. Another concern is that third parties, constituents, and the negotiator himself will view a concession as a sign of weakness or inability to maintain commitments. But this impression is less likely to prevail if the negotiator receives something valuable in exchange for his concession. He is more likely to be viewed as shrewd than as weak and vacillating. A third concern is that neutral third parties who are trying to produce agreement will view a negotiator who makes a concession as a likely target for unequal pressures to make further concessions. But this concern is of little moment if both sides make concessions at approximately the same time, because both identify themselves simultaneously as willing to make concessions.

* * *

[As desirable as an exchange of concessions may be from the point of view of both parties, it will not take place until the negotiators have worked out (i) some manner of agreement about the *size* of concessions to be exchanged (the problem of position loss) and (ii) some means of communicating a willingness to engage in a concession exchange without incurring image loss. In regard to the latter, it is possible to identify] six approaches to the coordination of concession exchanges. Stated in terms that reflect the viewpoint of a negotiator trying to decide how to get the negotiation moving toward agreement, these are: (a) make a small concession and wait for a counterconcession; (b) overtly propose an exchange of concessions; (c) tacitly communicate a readiness to concede if the opponent concedes; (d) propose an informal conference; (e) transmit a conciliatory message via an intermediary; (f) propose that a mediator be called in and reveal information about own priorities to him. The first two involve direct, and the last four indirect, communication. . . .

Determinants of the Likelihood of Efforts to Coordinate

In trying to arrange for a coordinated agreement, a negotiator always runs the risk of weakening himself in the struggle to dominate and avoid being dominated by the opponent. The chief element of this risk is embodied in the notion of "image loss" discussed earlier. Hence a decision about whether to embark upon such an effort must be carefully weighed. The same can be said about the decision to seek negotiation in the midst of a struggle which is being conducted in other terms.

One set of hypotheses can be derived from the assumption that a negotiator's willingness to run this risk is based on the degree of promise which the struggle to dominate the opponent seems to hold:

(1) A negotiator will be more likely to initiate efforts to co-ordinate an exchange of concessions to the extent that the opponent seems unlikely to make a unilateral concession.

(2) A negotiator will be more likely to initiate efforts to co-ordinate such an exchange, the fewer or weaker the remaining tactics or arguments he has to persuade his opponent to move. (This follows logically from the first hypothesis.)

(3) A negotiator will be more likely to initiate such efforts, the greater the perceived cost of continued struggle.

(4) A negotiator will be more likely to initiate such efforts, the longer the negotiation has already lasted. (This follows from the second and third hypotheses.)

(5) A negotiator will be more likely to initiate such efforts, the greater the perceived danger of alienating the opponent by continued struggle. (Such alienation is one cost of continued struggle.)

(6) A negotiator will be more likely to initiate such efforts, the less important it is to "win" the negotiation.

(7) A negotiator will be more likely to initiate such efforts, the greater the cost of failing to agree by some deadline.

A second set of hypotheses can be derived from the assumption that a negotiator will be more willing to initiate a bid for accommodation to the extent that such a move promises to lead to accommodation and not to a strengthening of his opponent's position in the negotiation:

(8) A negotiator will be more likely to initiate efforts to co-ordinate an exchange of concessions, the more likely it seems that the resistance points of the two parties are compatible. (Attempts at accommodation will seem fruitless unless these basic aspirations appear compatible.)

(9) A negotiator will be more likely to initiate such efforts, the greater the opponent's apparent sentiment for coordinating an exchange of concessions.

(10) A negotiator will be more likely to initiate such efforts after receiving a coordinative signal from his opponent. (This follows from the ninth hypothesis.)

(11) A negotiator will be more likely to initiate such efforts, the less importance he thinks the opponent places on winning the

negotiation.   (The reasoning behind this hypothesis is as follows: when the other is highly motivated to win, he will be relatively uninterested in coordinating a move toward agreement and hence more likely to misinterpret an effort to initiate such a movement as a sign of weakness.)

(12)   A negotiator will be more likely to initiate such efforts, the greater the apparent authority of his opponent.   (By "authority" is meant a negotiator's influence over the substantive decisions made by his own side.   A negotiator with greater authority either is freer to make concessions on his own or has greater influence over the people who make decisions about these concessions.   To the extent that the opponent has little authority, i. e., is a powerless, instructed delegate, efforts to coordinate an exchange of concessions will fall on barren ground and only produce image loss.)

(13)   The greater the *prominence* of a solution to the negotiation, the more likely is a negotiator to initiate efforts to coordinate movement toward that solution.   (The term "prominent solution" is used by Schelling (1960) in the sense of "obvious solution."   An example of a prominent solution would be equal division of one sandwich between two boys of the same age.   The magic of a prominent solution is probably twofold: (a) prominent solutions often seem fair and hence acceptable to oneself; and (b) it may be assumed that the opponent will not concede beyond the prominent solution, so there is no hope to improve on this solution.)

* * *

Practical Implications

The analysis presented so far is filled with practical implications. Yet we must approach the task of spelling them out with some caution because the analysis is tentative and does not pretend to cover every case but rather to state some common trends.   Any effort to derive a set of universally applicable maxims would surely be fallacious.   Nevertheless, with this caveat in mind, it seems worthwhile to mention a few of the more prominent implications.

Because they are based on a rational model, most of the causal hypotheses given in the last section can be converted to advice for a negotiator by substituting the phrase "should be" for "will be."   Thus it can be argued that a negotiator who is interested in reaching agreement should be more willing to initiate efforts to coordinate an exchange of concessions under two conditions: (1) the less importance he thinks the opponent places on winning, and (2) the greater the apparent authority of the negotiator with whom he is dealing.   .   .   . These pieces of advice are based on one or another of the causal propositions presented in the last section.

Quite apart from these causal propositions, which are, by necessity, rather specific in scope, the line of analysis presented throughout this paper can be transformed into some general advice to negotiators who wish to reach agreement at the end of the negotiation trail. First and foremost is the assertion that negotiation is a skill requiring knowledge of a good deal more than how to build a power base, stand firm, and pound on the table. A good negotiator should know the various tactics for moving toward accommodation without serious position or image loss . . ., and he should understand the circumstances under which each is most appropriate. Furthermore, he should be sensitive to his opponent's readiness for accommodation, such that he can move rapidly when the other side indicates (*e. g.*, by a tacit communication) that he is ready and on the other hand, avoid position and image loss when there is no reason to believe that the opponent is ready for accommodation. In addition, he should be sensitive to his opponent's possible need for evidence that he (the negotiator) is interested in accommodation—and be ready to risk some small loss if he suspects that the opponent may be waiting for an accommodative signal. In this connection, a negotiator should probably be alert to the *relative cost of image loss* for himself as opposed to his opponent. If his opponent's losses are greater than his (*e. g.*, because of having more attentive validators or because of being involved in more simultaneous negotiations in which threats or positional commitments are being employed), then it may be incumbent on the negotiator to make the first move toward accommodation.

Not only is it important to have a skilled negotiator on one's own team, but it is often desirable that the opposing team be headed by a skilled negotiator. There are two reasons for this. One is that a poorly qualified opponent will often not understand, and hence not respond to, a negotiator's efforts to coordinate an agreement. The other is that such a negotiator can often not be trusted to observe the norms that regulate tacit communication because he doesn't know them or the implications of breaking them.

———

NOTES

1. *The Dynamics of Concession-Making*

Pruitt's analysis of "concession dilemmas" centers on efforts to coordinate or exchange concessions so that neither side in a negotiation will suffer undue image loss (it is clear that any concession involves at least some *position loss*). Not all concessions, however, involve a painful choice between weakening one's bargaining position or risking deadlock. In the earlier stages of a negotiation, concessions may be an appropriate and even necessary aspect of the bargaining process.

As Pruitt indicates, there are costs of *not* conceding as well as costs of conceding, and at a given point in any negotiation, a comparison of these costs may lead one party to concede whether or not there is an indication that the concession will be reciprocated. Thus if a party who is anxious to settle really does feel that the negotiators are "running out of time" or that the opponent is becoming needlessly antagonized, he or she may decide that these costs are "worth" another concession. There is also the possibility that a unilateral concession will generate pressures for treatment in kind, ultimately producing larger and more numerous concessions from the opponent than verbal appeals. In a criminal case, for example, this would mean that a prosecutor's offer to reduce a manslaughter charge to assault with a dangerous weapon would be likely to alter the defendant's insistence on a dismissal and encourage a plea to some lesser offense. Conversely, an unwillingness to make any concession (or very small, infrequent concessions) would be likely to produce deadlock or an escalation of cost-imposing behavior.

Such reciprocal patterns of "equivalent" concessions are common in many different types of litigation and bargaining situations. Thus, in a personal injury action, a demand of twenty thousand might be reduced to fifteen in expectation of an offer of five thousand being raised to ten. Once one party has "broken the ice" there are normative pressures for his or her opponent to match concessions to some extent. The crucial variable becomes the level at which each party feels the other has made a realistic demand and thereby established the legitimate bargaining range. Image loss in such circumstances seems to have much less importance than Pruitt ascribes to it. If a bargainer conditions continuing conciliation on some signs of response the risks do not seem very significant.

On the other hand, there is also evidence that small, infrequent concessions combined with an unyielding or tough approach produce far more favorable settlements than a conciliatory strategy. One study of bargaining behavior concluded that a more inflexible concession posture produced more favorable outcomes than one more prone to compromise, although in both situations concessions were, in fact, reciprocated.[43] Another experiment suggests that the longer one party is able to maintain a posture outside of even the minimal point at which the other party would settle, the more likely he or she is to obtain a disproportionately favorable settlement.[44] Stated in Pruitt's terms, these studies suggest that a concession is seen by one's adversary as confirming (and, therefore, encouraging) his or her hopes for a more favorable outcome, while intransigence creates doubt that settlement

43. Chertkoff & Conley, *Opening Offer and Frequency of Concession as Bargaining Strategy,* 7 J. OF PERS. & SOC.PSYCH. 181–85 (1967).

44. Hinton, Hamner & Pohlen, *The Influence of Reward Magnitude, Opening Bid and Concession Rate on Profit Earned in a Managerial Negotiation Game,* 19 BEH.SCI. 197–203 (1974).

is possible without concession. The net effect is a convergence of agreement toward the less conciliatory party.

Whether unilateral attempts to communicate a willingness to concede will in fact produce the sort of image loss Pruitt describes is a question that you will, of course, have to answer for yourself. Although researchers speak longingly about more data on this issue, it is not likely that it will arrive on the scene soon enough to help you reconcile these competing explanations of concession dynamics.

––––––

2. *Using Concessions: Problems and Possibilities*

A willingness to compromise is not a matter of simple choice; it is itself a consequence of a variety of pressures and perceptions. The perceived costs of deadlock or continued bargaining, the availability of alternatives, the value of agreement at particular levels of exchange, the degree of adherence to the client's expressed desires, the personal characteristics of the negotiators—confidence, skill, etc.—exert differential influences on both parties.

For these reasons, Pruitt's suggestion that as bargainers we can and should seek indirect commitments to mutual concession seems unassailable. The difficulty is that such efforts require considerable skill, and trust, as well as opportunities for continued coordination between the parties. Such opportunities may not occur if the parties do not know each other well, for as Pruitt's analysis indicates, a number of the strategies for signalling a willingness to concede depend on tacit or indirect communication. Elsewhere in the same article he gives some examples of the subtle forms such tacit communication can take:

> Tacit communications are messages that are passed from one negotiator to the other by innuendo. To understand them, the other negotiator must read between the lines of what is being said overtly. Peters, who first systematically discussed tacit communication in negotiation, called it "sign language." The term "signal" can also be used. In coordinating an exchange of concessions, tacit communication may indicate the nature of an impending concession, the direction of this concession, or simply the fact that some kind of concession may be made.

* * *

> An example of ambiguous tacit communication is given by Douglas who describes a labor negotiator as having taken "too many words to say 'no'." This was presumably a signal that his "no" would become "yes" if a concession were forthcoming from the opponent. Another example from Peters shows a sequence of tacit communications that became increasingly clear. The mediator had just suggested a compromise of 9¢:

> > Frazier and Turner looked each other in the eye. Somewhere a communication established itself without a word between them.

> The question in each other's eye was, "If I move to 9¢, will you move to 9¢?" Frazier said, "Well, we are willing to give it some consideration for the sake of averting a strike." Turner nodded his acquiescence. The tension was gone as he buzzed his secretary to come in and take down a memorandum of agreement.

Peters gives the following example of a tacit communication in labor negotiations whose meaning was quite clear to the recipient. An employer reacted to an offer as follows. "Fifteen cents! You can't really mean it. Why, I wouldn't *even* offer you five cents." In Peters' words, "The union correctly deduced from the word 'even' the thought or message: If you will offer to settle for five cents, we will allow ourselves to be persuaded to grant that amount" (author's italics omitted).[45]

Obviously the subtle clues described in these examples will not always, with all opponents, convey a desire to exchange concessions or even a willingness to concede. The ability to interpret innuendo and nonverbal cues in any context assumes familiarity with usual patterns of communication, and these patterns must be established and understood before subtle deviations from them can be read accurately.

Often, of course, you will be thrown back on direct attempts to gain a concession. That is, you will have to actually make a concession and wait for its reciprocation or make a proposal that concessions be exchanged. Even if such ventures are qualified—*e. g.*, "I'm willing to be more flexible if you are" or "that's how I see it; if you can show me that things are different I'll move. I'm always willing to negotiate"—some of the risks Pruitt identifies will be present. Moreover, you will have to interpret the behavior of your opponent with respect to similar concessions, statements and actions. In doing so, the following dimensions of concession patterns become particularly relevant.

The Character and Context of the Concession

Concessions are always interpreted in context. How much of a reduction in a previous demand does it reflect? How does it compare with the size of prior concessions? What preceded it? In addition, the overall pattern is significant. How many concessions have been made and in what sequence? Have they been made in response to specific arguments or other concessions, or have they simply been made? What is revealed by the rate or timing of a series of concessions? Consider, for example, the following interchange:

PROSECUTOR: I won't accept anything but a plea to manslaughter. There's no sense talking if you're going to insist on a dismissal.

DEFENSE COUNSEL: Well, we'd consider pleading to attempted robbery if an amended charge could be filed.

---

45. D. Pruitt, *Indirect Communication and Agreement in Negotiation*, 1 J. APP.SOC.PSYCH. 205, 218 (1971) (citations omitted).

PROSECUTOR: Look, someone was killed here. I can't talk about robbery.

DEFENSE COUNSEL: Can you talk about assault with a dangerous weapon and attempted robbery?

PROSECUTOR: Not if I expect to have peace in the office. Now are we going to have something to talk about or not?

DEFENSE COUNSEL: If I consider manslaughter what's your feeing about recommendations on sentence?

Ask yourself what is communicated by this pattern of shifting offers. What is it that indicates that defense counsel is not (and was not initially) at his or her minimal settlement point? How much flexibility did the prosecutor communicate? You will find that many of your negotiating judgments will be grounded in just such partial, intuitive inferences.

Similar judgments must be made with respect to what is communicated by your own concessions. Our experience suggests that a pattern of (i) a higher initial demand (ii) reduced only in response to the adversary's concessions (iii) in relatively small increments that (iv) decrease in size as the hoped-for settlement is approached and are (v) consistent with an overall bargaining posture produces the most consistently successful results. But there will be many situations in which the opposite of each of these will be true.

Compliance with Norms and Standards

Since concessions are expected to conform with "common practice," deviations from these norms will themselves have meaning. An obvious example involves the assumption that "one concession deserves another." If a party departs from this norm he or she increases the risk of deadlock but also creates an image of greater firmness and resolve (*i. e.*, "She would not refuse to reciprocate if she didn't really mean it"). Similarly, a departure from being "uninvolved" may communicate more commitment than would usually accompany an early unwillingness to concede (*i. e.*, "If he's really so hung up about it, I'll never get him to change his mind"). All such departures from the usual or typical, however, cut both ways. For example, given the way the give and take of initial bargaining is usually handled, a very quick concession without preliminaries may be seen not as a way of "getting down to cases," but as a sign of vulnerability.

The Accompanying Explanations

The way a party explains a concession and the room this explanation leaves for further compromise is probably key to its effectiveness. With respect to such accompanying statements Thomas Schelling makes the following comments:

> . . . If one reaches the point where concession is advisable, he has to recognize two effects: it puts him closer to his opponent's position, and it affects his opponent's estimate of his firmness. Concession not only may be construed as capitulation, it may mark a prior commitment as a fraud, and make the adversary skeptical of any new pretense at commitment. One, therefore, needs an "excuse" for accommodating his opponent, preferably a rationalized reinterpretation of the original commitment, one that is persuasive to the adversary himself.[46]

The explanation that accompanies a concession should ideally provide a "resting place"—a point which would be viewed as final unless and until it is reinterpreted in the course of further negotiatation. Whatever the forms such explanations take, the justification offered for a particular concession invariably will be assessed by one's opponent, and it is important that the pattern and content of such justifications be well thought out in advance. In working in this area, we have been surprised at how concretely each fallback position in a negotiation can be predicted, and how the statements accompanying it can be planned and practiced. For all their uncertainties, most negotiations follow a number of very well-travelled roads.

4. Commitments, Threats and Promises

SCHELLING, AN ESSAY ON BARGAINING

46 AMER.ECON.REV. 281, 287–89, 290–97, 299–301 (1956), reprinted in
THE STRATEGY OF CONFLICT 21–52 (1971).

How does one person make another believe something? The answer depends importantly on the factual question, "Is it true?" It is easier to prove the truth of something that is true than of something false. To prove the truth about our health we can call on a reputable doctor; to prove the truth about our costs or income we may let the person look at books that have been audited by a reputable firm or the Bureau of Internal Revenue. But to persuade him of something false we may have no such convincing evidence.

When one wishes to persuade someone that he would not pay more than $16,000 for a house that is really worth $20,000 to him, what can he do to take advantage of the usually superior credibility of the truth over a false assertion? Answer: make it true. How can a buyer make it true? If he likes the house because it is near his business, he might move his business, persuading the seller that

---

46. T. Schelling, THE STRATEGY OF
CONFLICT 34–35 (1971).

the house is really now worth only $16,000 to him. This would be unprofitable; he is no better off than if he had paid the higher price.

But suppose the buyer could make an irrevocable and enforceable bet with some third party, duly recorded and certified, according to which he would pay for the house no more than $16,000 or forfeit $5,000. The seller has lost; the buyer need simply present the truth. Unless the seller is enraged and withholds the house in sheer spite, the situation has been rigged against him; the "objective" situation —the buyer's true incentive—has been voluntarily, conspicuously, and irreversibly changed. The seller can take it or leave it. This example demonstrates that if the buyer can accept an irrevocable *commitment,* in a way that is unambiguously visible to the seller, he can squeeze the range of indeterminacy down to the point most favorable to him. It also suggests, by its artificiality, that the tactic is one that may or may not be available; whether the buyer can find an effective device for committing himself may depend on who he is, who the seller is, where they live, and a number of legal and institutional arrangements . . . .

* * *

[Commitment tactics] have certain characteristics in common. First, they clearly depend not only on incurring a commitment but on communicating it persuasively to the other party. Second, it is by no means easy to establish the commitment, nor is it entirely clear to either of the parties concerned just how strong the commitment is. Third, similar activity may be available to the parties on both sides. Fourth, the possibility of commitment, though perhaps available to both sides, is by no means equally available; the ability of a democratic government to get itself tied by public opinion may be different from the ability of a totalitarian government to incur such a commitment. Fifth, they all run the risk of establishing an immovable position that goes beyond the ability of the other to concede, and thereby provoke the likelihood of stalemate or breakdown.

INSTITUTIONAL AND STRUCTURAL CHARACTERISTICS OF THE NEGOTIATION

Some institutional and structural characteristics of bargaining situations may make the commitment tactic easy or difficult to use, or make it more available to one party than the other, or affect the likelihood of simultaneous commitment or stalemate.

Use of a Bargaining Agent. The use of a bargaining agent affects the power of commitment in at least two ways. First, the agent may be given instructions that are difficult or impossible to change, such instructions (and their inflexibility) being visible to the opposite party. . . .

Second, an "agent" may be brought in as a principal in his own right, with an incentive structure of his own that differs from his principal's.　.　.　.

Secrecy vs. Publicity. A potent means of commitment, and sometimes the only means, is the pledge of one's reputation. If national representatives can arrange to be charged with appeasement for every small concession, they place concession visibly beyond their own reach. If a union with other plants to deal with can arrange to make any retreat dramatically visible, it places its bargaining reputation in jeopardy and thereby becomes visibly incapable of serious compromise. (The same convenient jeopardy is the basis for the universally exploited defense, "If I did it for you I'd have to do it for everyone else.") But to commit in this fashion publicity is required. Both the initial offer and the final outcome would have to be known; and if secrecy surrounds either point, or if the outcome is inherently not observable, the device is unavailable.　.　.　.

Continuous Negotiations. A special case of interrelated negotiations occurs when the same two parties are to negotiate other topics, simultaneously or in the future. The logic of this case is more subtle; to persuade the other that one cannot afford to recede, one says in effect, "If I conceded to you here, you would revise your estimate of me in our other negotiations; to protect my reputation with you I must stand firm." The second party is simultaneously the "third party" to whom one's bargaining reputation can be pledged. This situation occurs in the threat of local resistance to local aggression. The party threatening achieves its commitment, and hence the credibility of its threat, not by referring to what it would gain from carrying out the threat in this particular instance but by pointing to the long-run value of a fulfilled threat in enhancing the credibility of future threats.

The Mechanics of Negotiation. A number of other characteristics deserve mention, although we shall not work out their implications. Is there a penalty on the conveyance of false information? Is there a penalty on called bluffs, that is, can one put forth an offer and withdraw it after it has been accepted? Is there a penalty on hiring an agent who pretends to be an interested party and makes insincere offers, simply to test the position of the other party? Can all interested parties be recognized? Is there a time limit on the bargaining?　.　.　. Is there a *status quo*, so that unavailability for negotiation can win the *status quo* for the party that prefers it? Is renegotiation possible in case of stalemate? What are the costs of stalemate? Can compliance with the agreement be observed? What, in general, are the means of communication, and are any of them susceptible of being put out of order by one party or the other? If there are several items to negotiate, are they negotiated in one comprehensive negotiation, separately in a particular order so that each piece is finished before the next is taken up, or simultaneously through different agents or under different rules?

* * *

Principles and Precedents. To be convincing, commitments usually have to be qualitative rather than quantitative, and to rest on some rationale. It may be difficult to conceive of a really firm commitment to $2.07½; why not $2.02¼? The numerical scale is too continuous to provide good resting places, except at nice round numbers like $2.00. But a commitment to the *principle* of "profit sharing," "cost-of-living increases," or any other basis for a numerical calculation that comes out at $2.07½, may provide a foothold for a commitment. Furthermore, one may create something of a commitment by putting the principles and precedents themselves in jeopardy. If in the past one has successfully maintained the principle of, say, nonrecognition of governments imposed by force, and elects to nail his demands to that principle in the present negotiation, he not only adduces precedent behind his claim but risks the principle itself. Having pledged it, he may persuade his adversary that he would accept stalemate rather than capitulate and discredit the principle.

* * *

[Of interest] is the use of casuistry to release an opponent from a commitment. If one can demonstrate to an opponent that the latter is not committed, or that he has miscalculated his commitment, one may in fact undo or revise the opponent's commitment. Or if one can confuse the opponent's commitment, so that his constituents or principals or audience cannot exactly identify compliance with the commitment—show that "productivity" is ambiguous, or that "proportionate contributions" has several meanings—one may undo it or lower its value. In these cases it is to the opponent's disadvantage that this commitment be successfully refuted by argument. But when the opponent has resolved to make a moderate concession one may help him by proving that he *can* make a moderate concession consistent with his former position, and that if he does there are no grounds for believing it to reflect on his original principles. One must seek, in other words, a rationalization by which to deny oneself too great a reward from the opponent's concession, otherwise the concession will not be made.

THE THREAT

When one threatens to fight if attacked or to cut his price if his competitor does, the threat is no more than a communication of one's own incentives, designed to impress on the other the automatic consequences of his act. And, incidentally, if it succeeds in deterring, it benefits both parties.

But more than communication is involved when one threatens an act that he would have no incentive to perform but that is designed to deter through its promise of mutual harm. To threaten massive retaliation against small encroachments is of this nature, as is the threat to bump a car that does not yield the right of way or to call a costly strike if the wage is not raised a few cents. The distinctive feature of this threat is that the threatener has no incentive to carry it out either before the event or after. He does have an incentive to bind himself to fulfill the threat, if he thinks the threat may be successful, because the threat and not its fulfillment gains the end; and fulfillment is not required if the threat succeeds. The more certain the contingent fulfillment is, the less likely is actual fulfillment. But the threat's efficacy depends on the credulity of the other party, and the threat is ineffectual unless the threatener can rearrange or display his own incentives so as to demonstrate that he would, *ex post,* have an incentive to carry it out.

We are back again at the commitment. How can one commit himself in advance to an act that he would in fact prefer not to carry out in the event, in order that his commitment may deter the other party? One can of course bluff, to persuade the other falsely that the costs or damages to the threatener would be minor or negative. More interesting, the one making the threat may pretend that he himself erroneously believes his own costs to be small, and therefore would mistakenly go ahead and fulfill the threat.   .   .   .

One may try to stake his reputation on fulfillment, in a manner that impresses the threatened person. One may even stake his reputation *with the threatened person himself,* on grounds that it would be worth the costs and pains to give a lesson to the latter if he fails to heed the threat.   .   .   .

* * *

Similar techniques may be available to the one threatened. His best defense, of course, is to carry out the act before the threat is made; in that case there is neither incentive nor commitment for retaliation. If he cannot hasten the act itself, he may commit himself to it; if the person to be threatened is already committed, the one who would threaten cannot deter with his threat, he can only make certain the mutually disastrous consequences that he threatens. If the person to be threatened can arrange before the threat is made to share the risk with others (as suggested by the insurance solution to the right-of-way problem mentioned earlier) he may become so visibly unsusceptible to the threat as to dissuade the threatener. Or if by any other means he can either change or misrepresent his own incentives, to make it appear that he would gain in spite of threat fulfillment (or perhaps only that he thinks he would), the threatener may have to give up the threat as costly and fruitless; or if one can misrepresent himself as either unable to comprehend a threat, or too obstinate to heed it, he may deter the threat itself. Best of all may be *genuine* ignorance, obstinacy, or simple disbelief, since it may be more convincing to the prospective threatener; but of course if it fails to persuade him and he commits himself to the threat, both sides lose. Finally, both the threat and the commitment have to be communicated; if the threatened person can be unavailable for messages, or can destroy the communication channels, even though he does so in an obvious effort to avert threat, he may deter the threat itself. . . .

* * *

Special care may be needed in defining the threat, both the act that is threatened against and the counter act that is threatened. The difficulty arises from the fact, just noted, that once the former has been done the incentive to perform the later has disappeared. The credibility of the threat before the act depends on how visible to the threatened party is the inability of the threatening party to rationalize his way out of his commitment once it has failed its purpose. Any loopholes the threatening party leaves himself, if they are visible to the threatened party, weaken the visible commitment and hence reduce the credibility of the threat.

* * *

In order that one be able to pledge his reputation behind a threat, there must be continuity between the present and subsequent issues that will arise. This need for continuity suggests a means of making the original threat more effective; if it can be decomposed into a series of consecutive smaller threats, there is an opportunity to demonstrate on the first few transgressions that the threat will be carried out on the rest. Even the first few become more plausible, since there is a more obvious incentive to fulfill them as a "lesson."

* * *

A piecemeal approach may also be used by the threatened person. If he cannot obviate the threat by hastening the entire act, he may hasten some initial stage that clearly commits him to eventual completion. Or, if his act is divisible while the threatener's retaliation comes only in the large economy size, performing it as a series of increments may deny the threatener the dramatic overt act that would trigger his response.

The Promise

In the commitments discussed up to this point, it was essential that one's adversary (or "partner," however we wish to describe him) not have the power to release one from the commitment; the commitment was, in effect, to some third party, real or fictitious. The promise is a commitment to the second party in the bargain and is required whenever the final action of one or of each is outside the other's control. It is required whenever an agreement leaves any incentive to cheat.

This need for promises is more than incidental; it has an institutional importance of its own. It is not always easy to make a convincing, self-binding, promise. Both the kidnapper who would like to release his prisoner, and the prisoner, may search desperately for a way to commit the latter against informing on his captor, without finding one. If the victim has committed an act whose disclosure could lead to blackmail, he may confess it; if not, he might commit one in the presence of his captor, to create the bond that will ensure his silence. But these extreme possibilities illustrate how difficult, as well as important, it may be to assume a promise. If the law will not enforce price agreements; or if the union is unable to obligate itself to a no-strike pledge; or if a contractor has no assets to pay damages if he loses a suit, and the law will not imprison debtors; or if there is no "audience" to which one can pledge his reputation; it may not be possible to strike a bargain, or at least the same bargain that would otherwise be struck.

Bargaining may have to concern itself with an "incentive" system as well as the division of gains. Oligopolists may lobby for a "fair-trade" law; or exchange shares of stocks. An agreement to stay out of each other's market may require an agreement to redesign the products to be unsuitable in each other's area. Two countries that wish to agree not to make military use of an island may have to destroy the usefulness of the island itself. (In effect, a "third-party commitment" has to be assumed when an effective "second-party commitment" cannot be devised.)

Fulfillment is not always observable. If one sells his vote in a secret election, or a government agrees to recommend an act to its parliament, or an employee agrees not to steal from inventory, or a teacher agrees to keep his political opinions out of class, or a country agrees to stimulate exports "as much as possible," there is no reliable way to observe or measure compliance. The observable outcome is subject to a number of influences, only one of which is covered by the agreement. The bargain may therefore have to be expressed in terms of something observable, even though what is observable is not the intended object of the bargain. One may have to pay the bribed voter if the election is won, not on how he voted; to pay a salesman a commission on sales, rather than on skill and effort; to reward policemen according to statistics on crime rather than on attention to duty; or to punish all employees for the transgressions of one. And, where performance is a matter of degree, the bargain may have to define arbitrary limits distinguishing performance from nonperformance; a specified loss of inventory treated as evidence of theft; a specified increase in exports considered an "adequate" effort; specified samples of performance taken as representative of total performance.

The tactic of decomposition applies to promises as well as to threats. What makes many agreements enforceable is only the recognition of future opportunities for agreement that will be eliminated if mutual trust is not created and maintained, and whose value outweighs the momentary gain from cheating in the present instance. Each party must be confident that the other will not jeopardize future opportunities by destroying trust at the outset. This confidence does not always exist; and one of the purposes of piecemeal bargains is to cultivate the necessary mutual expectations. Neither may be willing to trust the other's prudence (or the other's confidence in the first's prudence, and so forth) on a large issue. But, if a number of preparatory bargains can be struck on a small scale, each may be willing to risk a small investment to create a tradition of trust. The purpose is to let each party demonstrate that he appreciates the need for trust and that he knows the other does too. So, if a major issue has to be negotiated, it may be necessary to seek out and negotiate some minor items for "practice," to establish the necessary confidence in each other's awareness of the long-term value of good faith.

* * *

Preparatory bargains serve another purpose. Bargaining can only occur when at least one party takes initiative in proposing a bargain. A deterrent to initiative is the information it yields, or may seem to yield, about one's eagerness. But if each has visible reason to expect the other to meet him half way, because of a history of successful bargaining, that very history provides protection against the inference of overeagerness.

NOTES

1. *The Problem of Overcommitment*

Commitments, threats and promises are substantially similar. The effectiveness of these tactics depends on their being perceived by the opponent as binding, and each presents problems of credibility. Each, therefore, also presents problems of finding an effective balance between firmness and flexibility.

What Schelling calls a commitment might best be thought of in the context of litigation as a firm demand. It may be a final offer—at or near one's minimal disposition—or it may be an interim statement of position, meant to appear final but in fact subject to revision. If it is in fact final—if a negotiator would rather deadlock than make any further concessions—the range of tactics suggested by Schelling are available to convey that finality. Binding instructions can be given by third parties, publicity can be used to tie the outcome to such factors as reputation and precedent, even the personal convictions and incentives of the negotiator can be brought into play. Assuming a negotiator has accurately assessed his or her own limits—the point beyond which the risk of deadlock is "worth it"—this situation does not pose the danger of becoming too firmly committed to a position which may later have to be abandoned. In regard to other commitments—those which are meant to *appear* but not actually *be* final—the danger of overcommitment is a more complicated problem.

As Schelling points out, the general strategy is to find a justifying principle, a "qualitative" rather than quantitative rationale for one's "resting place." But the types of rationales available for interim commitments or firm demands are of a very different nature from those available in the final offer situation. Since further compromise is preferable to deadlock, it may be necessary to make additional concessions, and the rationale which has been offered for a particular demand must be flexible enough to allow compromise without destroying the credibility of subsequent demands.

The same need to escape from prior commitments also arises in situations where threats have been used to deter or motivate the opposing party. The threat which poses the highest risk of overcommitment in litigated cases is, of course, the threat of deadlock—of going to trial if a settlement offer is rejected. If the threat of deadlock fails to produce its desired result and the party making the threat still prefers some less advantageous settlement to trial, some way must be found to withdraw or qualify the threat without the appearance of capitulation. As with other commitments, this situation frequently presents the opposing party with an opportunity to assist in resolving the dilemma, and the threat statement may best be phrased in terms which leave some room for interpretation.

When one's tactics shift to promises, there are different dynamics, but the same problem of striking an appropriate balance. While threats seek to deter undesirable conduct by the imposition of sanctions, promises hold out rewards for conduct the promisor desires, and to be effective, a promise must be perceived as absolutely binding. The problem is to find ways to convince the opponent that the promise will be kept although it is conditional: that if a particular offer is accepted or a particular concession is made the promised benefits will in fact follow. Since the act for which the reward is promised must precede the bestowal of the reward itself, there is always the chance that the promisor will renege or deliver something less valuable than was promised, and this possibility may keep the promise from having its desired effect. Schelling describes situations where the parties can resolve this difficulty by placing the fulfillment of the promise beyond their own control. More typically, the parties search for ways to establish some appropriate level of trust—to convince each other that there is no "undercommitment" in their willingness to do what has been promised.

———

2. *The Problem of Opposing Counsel's Commitments*

The foregoing difficulties are matched by the need to prevent one's opponent from going too far down the path suggested by his or her own threats and demands. Although specificity has its advantages (particularly if there is a possibility of revising a vague demand upwards), pressures on your adversary to adhere to previous commitments in order to save face or preserve future credibility will rarely work in your favor. As Schelling indicates, it may often be in the interest of both parties to aid one another in revising excessively stated positions.

In part, helping the opponent out of these commitment dilemmas involves reversing many of the tactics Schelling describes. Public statements can be discouraged, demands can intentionally *not* be reduced to writing, and third parties can be specifically excluded. It may be necessary to break off the bargaining sessions in order to allow for the introduction of "new information" or "further discussions with the client," or to find other ways to postpone a final resolution. Humor, tacit communication, even unresponsive answers to direct questions can help avoid an early commitment on sticky issues. In addition, if commitments are made they can be ignored or tactfully misinterpreted. Walton and McKersie elaborate on this technique:

> .   .   .   [Another] line of defense is for Party to ignore commitments or simply not to comprehend them. This has more significance, of course, if Opponent's strategy is one of commitment to Party. If Opponent is committing himself to his principals or to a third party, less is gained by Party's ignoring the commitment.

> Party is presented a difficult choice when he receives a strike threat from Opponent. If Party must make his own commitment, then he acknowledges the threat and proceeds to cite counterpressures which might be taken or costs which Opponent might incur. If these other tactical assignments are not paramount at the time, Party would probably attempt to ignore or minimize the other's commitment.

> Opponent's commitment might be minimized by ridiculing the threat if Party believes it is not backed by real pressure—if he thinks Opponent is using idle threats—or Party might divert attention from Opponent's threat statement by cracking a joke or introducing casual conversation, just as he uses these techniques to head off a commitment before it is made. In some instances Party has no better way of coping with an unwanted commitment statement than by passing it by without flinching or reacting in any other way. Consider the following interchange in which each negotiator is determined to get his own commitment on the table and to ignore the other's. They seem to be talking past each other.

> **Scott (M)** So far, we have offered you 5 cents plus the ½ cent. We have also agreed to raise the third shift differential to 12 cents. Our package cost up to this point is 5.6 to 5.7 cents. Is that what you have, Jim?

> **Watoski (U)** (Ignoring the question just asked.) Our proposal was 9½ cents.

> **Scott (M)** (Ignoring Watoski and checking his figures.) Our offer comes to about 5.6 cents. Our offer on major medical

is still open. (Pause.) I think we've reached a point where I should say what I have to offer. (Pause.) Jim, this is all I have to offer. I have another cent to offer on wages. That's 6 cents. That's all I have, and I'm serious about it. The major medical is still open. (Pause.) I guess that's all I have to say at this point, Jim. We would be willing to make the wage increase retroactive to August 1.

> **Watoski (U)** Let's go over the union agenda. On number 1, since we'll have a one-year agreement, that means the dates will be from August 1, 1961, to August 1, 1962.[47]

In many cases, of course, it will be impossible to prevent the opponent from becoming too firmly committed to a position which must later be abandoned. In this situation, Schelling suggests that a bargainer should search for ways to show the opponent that the desired concessions are consistent with the principles underlying his or her previous commitments. Even where a revision or abandonment *is* in the nature of a capitulation there are ways of minimizing its impact, at least in so far as third parties are concerned. Walton and McKersie explain why this is frequently done:

> Just as one attempts to prevent the other from becoming more than minimally committed, he attempts to make it as easy as possible for the other to revise a previous commitment—without apparent loss of bargaining reputation. . . .

> [L]et us clarify why one party has an interest in accommodating the revising party. For instance, when a settlement represents a defeat for Opponent, why do both parties agree to express it in terms other than those used during negotiation and thereby obscure just what relationship the settlement bears to the earlier positions of the parties?

> We refer to this as letting the other guy "save face." More precisely, it is letting the other guy save his reputation as an effective bargainer. It is still more accurate to state that the parties are refraining from exposing the fact that Opponent abandoned a position previously labeled "final," or "best," or "minimum." Now Party, with whom he is currently bargaining, will know this—which cannot be helped—unless even Party pretends to be fooled. However, others with whom the actually defeated Opponent deals will not have this information on which they could revise their own strategy in negotiating with him. Thus, by this favor, Party makes it easier for Opponent to settle below his earlier commitments.

> There are still other reasons for letting the defeated Opponent save face: Party may otherwise increase Opponent's insecurity with his principals and make him less rational in the future (and hence, perhaps, plunge both parties into a foolish strike); and Party may otherwise set into motion within Opponent a psychology of deliberate revenge.[48]

47. R. Walton and R. McKersie, *supra* note 42, 115–16 (1965). **48.** *Id.* at 116.

The problem is one of saving face. If an avenue of retreat is visible to the opponent a commitment will be seen as less credible. When such avenues are closed, however, the problem of unwanted deadlock becomes unavoidable unless one can revise a formerly firm position. You will find yourself rationalizing away a prior stand which was too firm or contentious—making reference to changed circumstances, the client's revised attitudes, some non-existent concession by your adversary, the public interest and the like—or restating some concession in different terms in order to create a new package. It is not only important that you develop some skill at this complex task, but also that you gain some appreciation of the need for both you and opposing counsel to be allowed to do so.

———

3. *The Threat As A Negotiating Tactic: Some Observations*

When a negotiator reaches the point where he or she does want to communicate a firm commitment—to "hold out" for a specific settlement which seems possible under the circumstances—this firmness can be communicated in a number of ways. A party might (i) demonstrate his or her interest in the particular demand (*e. g.*, by repeating it, raising it at an unexpected point in the discussion, reducing it to writing, or otherwise emphasizing its importance); (ii) relate it to other values, norms and perceptions (*e. g.*, principles, precedents, its effects on other negotiations); (iii) identify it with status and relationship costs (*e. g.*, by bringing in outsiders, making public statements concerning the demand, changing the make-up of the bargaining team,[49] etc.). Each of these tactics rests on the implicit threat that the issue is sufficiently important that the party is willing to deadlock over it.

Similar strategies are available in making any threat credible. Walton and McKersie suggest (i) manifesting a clear willingness to act on the threat (*e. g.*, by expressing strong personal feelings, referring to the intransigence of one's client, apparently ignoring or being unconcerned with associated costs); (ii) making overt preparations (*e. g.*, initiating discovery, marking the case for trial, conducting meetings with witnesses); and (iii) creating and fulfilling minor threats.[50] There is a good deal that can be done both before and during the bargaining session to convince the opponent that one's threats will be carried out. But it is important to recognize that a threat is most effective when it produces the desired result *without having to be carried out*. Even if the threat is one which can be fulfilled without jeopardizing further negotiations—*e. g.*, a threat to engage in extensive discovery or file a time-consuming pretrial motion —once it has been carried out it loses its value as a deterrent or in-

49. These are all part of Walton and   50. *Id.* at 107–11.
McKersie's notion of "underscoring."
Id. at 107–08.

centive for the other party's conduct, except in so far as it lends credibility to subsequent threats and demands. The threat of publicity, for example, is meaningless once exposure has taken place, so it must be made at a time when its deterrent value is strongest.

In addition, a carried-out threat will also have imposed costs on *both* parties. A lawyer-negotiator who threatens extensive discovery or numerous court appearances unless the opponent revises a previous offer may have to incur the costs involved in following through on this threat if it fails to produce the desired result.

These features of this often over-used tactic, and the need to make threats credible, lead us to the following generalizations:

—The threat statement itself should be clear, both as to the action desired from the opponent and the consequences that will follow if the action is not taken. Paradoxically, it is usually most effective if the threat is delivered in a "non-threatening" way—in a way, that is, that does not produce ego-involvement on the part of the opponent. If a threat is made too directly, or in too heavy-handed a fashion, it can push an opponent into taking a more rigid posture than he or she might otherwise have assumed, simply to avoid the feeling or appearance of being "pushed around."

—The threatened consequences must be prospective. This simply restates the point made earlier: What makes the opponent take or refrain from certain actions is the desire to avoid the threatened costs. If the costs associated with the threat have already been incurred, the threat loses its deterrent value. Thus the threat to turn a single claim into a class action is unavailable to one who has already done so, despite the value such a threat would have had if saved for use as a tactic in negotiation.

—The action which the negotiator threatens to take must be consistent with everything known by the opponent, whether that knowledge is gained from the negotiation itself or from outside sources. The threat of taking a case to trial becomes less credible if it is known that the threatening party has never tried a case, unless some rationale can be advanced to make this threat, too, consistent *(e. g.,* an eagerness to try a first case, a desire for experience). Similarly, the action must be within the threatener's capability. The threat of publicity is meaningless in a case which has no news potential.

—The threat must also be consistent with a party's assessments of what the case is worth. It is unwise to make threats you are in fact unwilling to follow through on, since if the desired response is not forthcoming, you will be faced with a choice of failing to carry out the threat or incurring costs which are not worth the expected benefit. Some lawyers will try a "losing" case at times simply to make future threats more credible, but needless to say, this is not a very workable strategy in the long run (it also makes it very difficult to make a living).

—The best threat may be one which can be carried out in increments. Schelling speaks of this in terms of "decomposition" and Walton and McKersie in terms of "creating and fulfilling minor threats." The notion is that if you have taken one or two steps down a path which leads to the imposition of heavy costs (as with the initiation of threatened discovery), your threat to take further steps becomes substantially more credible.

Perhaps we should add to this list one observation on the kinds of threats that should *not* be made. In our experience, threats to impose leverage in general ("I'm going to make you pay for that")— other than the threat of deadlock—ought to be avoided entirely. They are difficult to make credible, extremely hard to control, often produce counterthreats, and more often than not result in more problems than they solve. Indeed, a growing experimental literature casts doubt on the effectiveness of any threats as a bargaining tool.[51] At least, as with the proverbial love-making of porcupines, one should proceed with them very carefully.

5. Supporting Strategies: Strengthening One's Bargaining Position

———

a. The Setting

———

Hardly an article or text on negotiation fails to discuss where and under what conditions settlement should be discussed. Despite the degree of personal preference involved, what emerges from a reading of these sources is the following consensus:

—*It is considered preferable to hold settlement negotiations in one's own office.*

The theory is that being on your own ground (i) creates the psychological advantage of having opposing counsel come to you; (ii) constrains opposing counsel from leaving (i. e., you retain the initiative in terminating discussions); (iii) saves the time and expense of travelling; (iv) gives you the ability to manage the atmosphere of the negotiations; and (v) avoids the inconvenience of being entirely removed from other obligations.

51. J. Rubin & B. Brown, THE SOCIAL PSYCHOLOGY OF BARGAINING AND NEGOTIATION 286 (1975).

On some of these our ideas are neither very clear nor very firm. It would certainly seem that there might be a number of advantages in going to your opponent's office, including (i) the ability to concentrate fully on the interaction; (ii) the fact that opposing counsel, not you, will have to deal with interruptions and the pressure of other duties; (iii) the difficulty opposing counsel would have in refusing requests for documents and other information that is near at hand; and (iv) your concomitant ability to defer your own provision of information. Moreover, if certain aspects of your office environment would reveal weakness—*e. g.*, the ability to withstand a great deal of expense—such a setting is unlikely to bolster arguments based on the need for a high recovery or a quick resolution. Assuming there is some control over the choice there seems little beyond hunch to guide one's decisions on this question.

—*The atmosphere of the negotiation should be comfortable and non-contentious.*

This may offer some guidance as to the physical setting itself, *i. e.*, the arrangement of chairs, tables, lights, etc.; research on the way people relate to space suggests that people are less comfortable with carrying on a conversation across a table. However, there is at least a possibility that such a barrier might make it somewhat easier to stay in the adversary role of negotiator. Generally the notion that personal relations between the negotiators should be non-contentious (and furniture arranged accordingly) seems correct, although it is not difficult to think of situations where quite different attitudes would be appropriate.

The real problem here is that, to a considerable extent, negotiations in the majority of the small cases regularly settled by lawyers are not discussed in offices at all. They are resolved by telephone or in the halls of the courthouse or in less professional social settings. The atmosphere is one of activity, distraction and compelling pressure, with each lawyer judging the other, in part, on the basis of his or her apparent ability to handle such conditions. These situations also require substantial reliance on established norms and procedures, a considerable amount of tacit communication and a great number of very quick impression judgments. We have no ready prescriptions as to the best way to handle these interactions, beyond reminding you again that almost every aspect of one's conduct in such circumstances can convey meaning, and some attention should be paid to indirect as well as direct communications.

b. *The Agenda*

It is similarly very difficult to judge the impact that agenda (order of issues to be discussed) has on negotiation outcomes.[52] Many

----

52. *See* Walton and McKersie, *supra*, note 42 at 127–29. For some of the more general implications of "agenda influence," *see* M. Levine and C. Plott,

lawyers consider agenda control very important but are unable to do more than list the advantages and disadvantages of such efforts; the following is typical of discussions of this aspect of the bargaining process:

> Having the other side accept your agenda has its advantages. It can put the other side on the defensive. Your agenda contains the definitions of your terms in your own way. Therefore, it contains your assumptions. You should remember, however, that your agenda reveals your positions in advance and it may permit the other side to prepare a reaction to the areas that you wish to discuss. You also are not in a position to hear out the other side before presenting your agenda positions. This too is a disadvantage, for the order of procedure, or agenda, has to depend on the strategies chosen beforehand, before you know the actual posture of the opposer. The agenda might very well be considered one of the tactics used in negotiation.

> Try not to permit your agenda to be bound to an arbitrary, uncontrolled arrangement. Many a negotiation has been circumscribed by an agenda based on a printed form, a contract, a lease, a union contract, or merely a chronological listing of issues. This should not be done. Attention should instead be given to the various issues to be discussed so that strategies can be developed. The issues might be listed so that the major ones are discussed first. This will prevent time from being wasted on minor issues, leaving sufficient time to discuss the major ones. As an alternative, minor issues might be listed first so that you can begin the negotiation by making concessions, expecting that as the issues become more important you will get concessions in return. Of course, the fact that you have made concessions may be regarded by your opposer as a precedent and he may expect them to continue. However, minor issues are sometimes easier to resolve, and their resolution creates an atmosphere of good will. . . . [53]

While such pro and con discussions seem to be vaguely unsatisfactory, we find it difficult to come up with any more definitive advice. The few observations we can make on the basis of our own experience seem equally inconclusive:

—*Preliminary interchanges should be considered part of the bargaining process.*

Although cordiality, evenness, and cooperativeness are important objectives of these early discussions, their most important function is the degree of predictability they lend to the interpersonal aspects of

Agenda Influence and Its Implications, 63 VA.L.REV. 561 (1977); L. Walker, J. Thibault and V. Andreoli, *Order of Presentation at Trial,* 82 YALE L.J. 216 (1972).

53. J. Sindell and D. Sindell, LET'S TALK SETTLEMENT 16 (1963).

the exchange. Many of you may be "thrown" by the unexpected in this stage of the process, often conveying more uncertainty, insecurity and concession flexibility than you intend. This is particularly true of telephone negotiations, which are often undertaken without planning or prediction of any kind. Our litany that one needs to think about purposes and possibilities before one acts can readily be repeated here.

—*Except in very large, complex cases, lawyers do not usually negotiate over agenda; agreement as to when new issues are to be introduced occurs tacitly in the course of bargaining.*

This puts a premium on psychological control, which can generate antagonism over the relatively minor issue of what is considered first. Although in some settings an agreement on agenda can effectively preclude certain issues from being "added" or subsequently raised during the negotiations, this is not usually the case in discussions among lawyers. It is extremely difficult to get opposing counsel to "stick" to any agreed-upon plan. For this reason we see little advantage in generating contention on the agenda as an issue.

—*The possibilities of agreement seem to be enhanced when the order of issues introduced moves from the least controversial to the more controversial.*

This advice runs counter to the judgment of a number of lawyers who argue for confronting the most controversial issues first—either to take advantage of the initial predeliction of negotiators to make the relationship work, or because cooperation is facilitated when it is preceded by an initial period of deadlock and posturing for the clients. Our own experience is that success in reaching agreement early in the negotiation reinforces cooperative behavior in both parties and creates a situation where something could now be lost by non-agreement. This *stake* in previous commitments seems of itself to provide an additional motivating factor toward achieving settlement.

—*There is a significant agenda dimension in any stage of negotiation in which the parties are working from a draft.*

Although this usually occurs when a tentative oral agreement is to be reduced to writing, some lawyers start settlement negotiations with written offers or draft agreements. This places the onus on the opposing party to justify departures from this starting point. As a result, many issues are tacitly resolved solely because of opposing counsel's natural reluctance to surface disagreement on a large number of relatively unimportant issues.

—*The most important aspect of agenda control seems to relate not to issues but to timing.*

It may be agreed that some issues will be deferred to other sessions, taken up at the end of the discussion, considered only if time remains, and so forth. Each of these agreements creates particular sorts of deadline or "speed-up" pressures. Many commentators on negotiation have pointed out the strong influences created by a desire to resolve some particular issue before a meeting breaks or is even recessed. So many new variables are introduced once the parties separate that when it is felt agreement is near, most bargainers are loath to allow a break to occur. This deadline effect can be managed in a variety of ways. For example, discussions in the hall prior to argument on a motion are not only subject to interruption by the court call, but change as a consequence of the ruling on the motion itself. Meetings with clients are often set up in advance and lawyers want to report some progress before the date arrives. There are endless opportunities for these kinds of preliminary decisions about what is to be decided when, and they can have a profound influence on the outcomes of bargaining.

c. Arguments

STATSKY, INFORMAL ADVOCACY

Introduction to Paralegalism.
595, 598–608 (1974).*

The following is a summary of eighteen advocacy techniques that paralegals have used in trying to obtain action from an agency. The list is not exhaustive and no attempt is made at this point to evaluate whether or not any particular technique in the list is effective or inappropriate.

—*"Put your cards on the Table:"* be direct and completely above board in telling the agency official what your position is and what you want.

—*"Demand Adequate Service:"* point out to the agency official that the purpose of his organization is service and that this principle should guide his actions.

—*"Seek the Support of Third Parties:"* before you make your position known, gather the support of individuals or groups within or without the agency so that you can demonstrate that you are not alone.

—*"Be a Buddy:"* show the agency official that you are not his enemy and that you respect and like him and that you are aware of how difficult his job is.

—*"Find the Points of Compromise:"* ferret out the negotiable points in the dispute and determine whether you can bargain your way to a favorable result.

—*"Insist on Common-Sense:"* convey to the agency official the impression that common-sense dictates the position you are ad-

* Reprinted with permission of West
Publishing Company.

vocating in addition to or in spite of the regulations or technicalities that might be cited against you.

—*"Demonstrate the Exception:"* insist on uniqueness of your client's situation so that the general rule cited by the agency official to deny your client a benefit is shown to be inapplicable.

—*"Uncover the Realm of Discretion:"* take the position that rules don't exist until they are applied and that in the application of rules, agency officials often have wide discretion in spite of their claim that their hands are tied by the rules.

—*"Ask for Authorization:"* insist that the agency official show you the regulation, law or authority which supports the action he has taken or proposes to take.

—*"Cite the Law:"* show the agency official that you know what administrative regulations apply to the case (and in some instances, you also cite statutes and cases to demonstrate your point).

—*"Redefine the Problem:"* if you can't solve a problem redefine it, if you can still achieve what the client seeks, *e. g.,* stop trying to qualify the client for program "Z" if program "Y" will serve him equally well and the problems of qualifying him for "Y" are not as great as those encountered in continuing to insist on "Z".

—*"Anger/Hostility:"* be completely open about the bad feelings that you have about what is being done.

—*"Preach:"* perhaps the most common way in which people try to change other people is to lecture them, to *tell* them what they should or should not be doing.

—*"Climb the Chain of Command:"* normally everyone has a boss who can overrule decisions made by those beneath him. When you are dissatisfied with the decision or action of an employee, "appeal" or complain "up the chain of command" to the supervisor of the employee, and to the supervisor of the supervisor if needed.

—*"Embarrass Him:"* show the agency official that you do not respect him in such a way that makes him look silly.

—*"Make Clear that You and Your Office are going to Fight this Case All the Way Up:"* make the agency official aware of how important the case is; when you and your office have the grounds to back you, point out that you are thinking about taking the case to a formal agency hearing and that your office may go to court if necessary.

—*"Do a Favor to Get a Favor:"* be willing to do something (within reason) for the person from whom you are seeking something.

—*"Cite a Precedent:"* point out to the agency official (if it is true) that your case is not unusual because the agency has granted clients what you want under the same or under similar circumstances in the past.

Clearly, some of these techniques would be more effective than others. Perhaps some of them should *never* be tried. A great deal would obviously depend upon the circumstances confronting the paralegal at the time. In general how would you assess the eighteen techniques? If you were to list the techniques in the order in which you think that the technique would be effective in *most* situations what would your order be?

* * *

We are going to examine some of the advocacy techniques in the context of the following fact situation:

> You are in your own home or apartment. You receive a letter from the gas company stating that your gas will be shut off in ten days if you do not pay your bill. Your spouse tells you that the bill has already been paid. You call the gas company and when you question the clerk, she says to you, "I'm sorry sir, our records reflect an unpaid bill. You must pay the bill immediately." To try to straighten matters out, you take a trip to the utilities office.

In the dialogue that follows based upon this hypothetical, the complainant is his own advocate, although the techniques that he uses might also apply if he were representing someone else on the claim. "C" will stand for complainant and "E" will stand for the various company employees.

E: Can I help you?

C: Yes, I want to see someone about my bill.

E: I'm sorry sir but the customer complaint division closed at 2 PM. You'll have to come back or call tomorrow.

C: Closed! Well look, I want to see someone about terminating the gas service altogether.

E: All right would you step right over to that desk?

TECHNIQUE: "If you can't solve a problem, redefine the problem" to manageable proportions if on balance it is consistent with your objectives.

The client is taking a risk. He can't get through to the complaint division so he is going to try to achieve his objective through the termination division. He has substituted one problem (getting through the complaint division) for another problem (getting through the termination division) in the hope of obtaining his goal.

E: Can I help you?

C: Yes, I want to terminate my gas if I can't get this problem straightened out.

E: You'll have to go over to the bill complaint division, sir.

C: Look, stop sending me somewhere else! Either I get this straightened out or else!

TECHNIQUE: —"Anger/hostility:" although this is a dangerous tactic to employ, it is a fact of life that some people respond to this kind of pressure.

How would you assess the performance of the complainant thus far? Would you have gone about the matter in the same way? What would you have done differently and why?

C: What the hell is the matter with you people around here? Aren't you here to serve the public?

TECHNIQUE: —"Demand adequate service:" Point out to the agency official that the purpose of his organization is service and that this principle should guide its actions.

E: There are rules and procedures that we all must abide by and. . . .

C: Your responsibility is to take care of the public!

TECHNIQUE: —"Preach:" Perhaps the most common way in which people try to change other people is to lecture them, to tell them what they should or should not be doing.

TECHNIQUE: —"Embarrass him:" Show the agency official that you do not respect him in such a way that makes him look silly.

At this point, has the complainant lost all objectivity? What risks are being taken? Do you think the complainant is aware of what he is doing? If you asked him if he thinks that he is being effective, what do you think his response would be? Is he more involved with the "justice" of his case than with the effectiveness of his approach?

C: I'd like to speak to your supervisor. Who is in charge of this office?

E: Well, Mr. Adams is the unit director. His office is right over there.

C: Fine.

TECHNIQUE: —"Climb the chain of command:" Everyone has a boss who can overrule decisions made by those beneath him, when you are dissatisfied with the decision or action of an employee, "appeal" or complain "up the chain of command" to the supervisor of the employee, and to the supervisor of the supervisor if needed.

E: Can I help you?

C: I want to speak to Mr. Adams about a complaint. Tell him that it is very important.

E: Just a moment. [She goes into Mr. Adams' office for a few moments and then returns.] You can go in sir.

C: Mr. Adams?

E: Yes, what can I do for you? I understand you are having a little problem.

C: It's about this bill. I have been talking to person after person in this office without getting any satisfaction.

TECHNIQUE: "Take the role of the tired, battered, helpless citizen."

E: Well, let me see what I can do. I've asked the secretary to get your file. Oh, yes, here it is. The records say that you haven't paid last month's bill. Our policy here is to terminate utility service if payment is delayed thirty days or more.

C: What policy is that? Could I see a copy of this policy and what law it is based on?

TECHNIQUE: —"Ask for authorization;" Insist that the agency official show you the regulation, law or authority which supports the action he has taken or proposes to take.

What risk is the complainant taking by resorting to this technique? Is the complainant suggesting to Mr. Adams that he does not trust him? Could this "push" Mr. Adams' "button"? How would you have asked for authorization in this situation? Does the request for authorization always have to be made in a hostile manner?

E: Well, I'll be glad to show you the brochure.

C: I would like to see it and also to see the law it is based on. My position, Mr. Adams, is that my wife paid the bill.

E: Well our records don't reflect it. Do you have proof?

C: The cancelled checks have not yet come back from the bank. I would like a xerox copy of your file on me. Under the law, I am entitled to it.

TECHNIQUE: —"Cite the law:" Show the agency official that you know what administrative regulations apply to the case (and in some instances you also cite to statutes and cases to demonstrate your point).

E: You do have this right, but only if you make the request in writing.

C: Let's be reasonable.   I'm making the request in person.
That should be sufficient.

TECHNIQUE: —"Insist on common-sense:" Convey to the agency
official the impression that common-sense dictates the
position you are advocating in addition to or in spite
of the regulations or technicalities that might be
cited against you.

C: Surely, your rule calling for a written request can't apply
when the person making the request is right in front of you.

TECHNIQUE: —"Interpret the law:" Regulations statutes and
cases often are susceptible to more than one meaning; identify and argue for the meaning most favorable to the client.

TECHNIQUE: —"Demonstrate the exception:" Insist on the uniqueness of your situation so that the general rule cited
by the agency official to deny the benefit is shown
to be inapplicable.

C: Don't you have the power to waive this rule in such a case?

TECHNIQUE: —"Uncover the realm of discretion:" Take the position that rules don't exist until they are applied and
that in the application of rules, agency officials often
have wide discretion in spite of their claim that their
hands are tied by the rules.

E: Well, all right, I'll see if I can't get a copy run off for you
while you are here.   But I must point out that it's highly
irregular.   •

C: Now, Mr. Adams.   I understand that you are a very busy
man and that you have responsibilities more demanding
than having to listen to people like me all day.

TECHNIQUE: —"Be a buddy:" Show the agency official that you
are not his enemy and that you respect and like him
and that you are aware of how difficult his job is.

Here the complainant has obviously shifted his tactic; he is no
longer antagonistic.   Consciously or unconsciously, he has made an
evaluation of how successful his techniques have been thus far and
has decided on a different course of action.   What risk is he running
in making this shift?   Do you think that Mr. Adams might conclude
in his own mind that the complainant is a phony?   If so, would it
make any difference?

C: All I want is a thirty day extension of time so that I can collect the proof needed to show you that the bill has been paid.

TECHNIQUE: —"Put your cards on the table:" Be direct and completely above board in telling the agency official what your position is and what you want.

E: Well, we seldom give extensions. The situation must be extreme. I don't know. . . .

C: Mr. Adams, suppose we forget my request for a copy of the records for the time being. All I want is thirty days.

TECHNIQUE: —"Find the points of compromise:" Ferret out the negotiable points in the dispute and determine whether you can bargain your way to a favorable result.

E: I don't think so.

C: Well, Mr. Adams, it's either that or I'm going to go to court. All I'm asking for is some fair treatment. There's a principle involved and I intend to fight it.

TECHNIQUE: —"Make clear that you are going to fight this case all the way up:" Make the agency official aware of how important this case is; when you have grounds to back you, point out that you are thinking about taking the case to a formal hearing, and if necessary, to court.

E: I'm sorry you feel that way, but we have our rules here. It would be chaos if we broke them every time someone asked for it.

C: Good day, Mr. Adams. [you leave the office, resolved never to come back alone].

TECHNIQUE: —"Seek the support of third parties:" Gather the support of individuals or groups within or without the agency so that you can demonstrate that you are not alone.

Has the complainant failed? Was he a "bad" advocate? Has he accomplished anything? Should he give up? Do you think he will? If he doesn't do you think he has learned (or that he should have learned) enough about the gas company to be able to come back next time better equipped to handle his problem? Should he come back? If so, what approach should he take and whom should he see, *e. g.*, the supervisor of Mr. Adams?

NOTE

Despite Statsky's very provocative list, the number of possible arguments and contentions that can be advanced in the course of bargaining is so large that there seems almost no way to adequately catalogue them. They can relate to every matter discussed thus far, including counsel's view of his or her own preferences, expectations and intentions, of the opponent's preferences, expectations and intentions, and of what would be likely to change each of these perspectives. Or they can elaborate arguments and subarguments concerning the costs and benefits associated with each of these features of the negotiating process.

Given this complexity, most writers have found it sufficient to list as many maneuvers and techniques as possible. Chester Karrass, for example, offers the following: [54]

NEGOTIATING MANEUVERS

Timing

Patience
Deadline
Speed
Fait accompli
Surprise
Status quo
Stretchout

Inspection

Open inspection
Limited inspection
Confession
Qualified
Third party
No admittance

Association

Alliances
Associates
Disassociates
United Nations
Bribery

Authority

Limited authority
Approval
Escalation approval
Missing man
Arbitration

Amount

Fair and reasonable
Bulwarism
Nibbling
Budget bogy
Blackmail
Escalation
Intersection
Non-negotiable
. . . Auction

Brotherhood

Equal brothers
Big brother
Little brother
Long-lost brothers
Brinkmanship

Detour

Decoy
Denial
Withdrawal
Good and bad guys
False statistics and errors
Scrambled eggs
Low-balling
Scoundrel

Despite the colorful labels, most of these tactics are self-explanatory or evocative of some familiar image. The "auction" approach,

54. C. Karrass, THE NEGOTIATING GAME 173 (1970).

for example, relates to playing off competitors against each other: a buyer negotiates with two or three suppliers so that each believes that the other is offering a better deal. The "budget bogy" involves an assertion by a buyer that there is a fixed dollar amount available to which the sale must be tailored. Most of these maneuvers are equally available in negotiation among lawyers, and you should be able to relate some of them to our earlier discussions. Each of them requires accompanying arguments at the bargaining table, and the rather simple labels should not obscure the fact that they pose the same problem of evaluation and persuasion involved in any other aspect of negotiation. Nevertheless, such formulations are valuable as checklists, and provide a useful source of ideas in negotiation planning.

We agree with Statsky that it is desirable to have a less haphazard method of preparing arguments to be used in a negotiation, particularly when the negotiators are inexperienced. That is, arguments and positions should be "designed"—weighed, discussed, formulated and reformulated—in much the same way as in preparing for an oral argument before a court. There are many potential ways to come up with such contentions. One that we have found useful involves thinking of arguments that can be made concerning the costs and benefits of both agreement and disagreement—for both parties—on either your own terms or those you expect the other party to propose. Our earlier analysis of leverage might provide a useful guide; arguments can be marshalled around each of the calculations that go into an assessment of the bargaining situation. If this sounds confusing, you might want to review the discussion at pages 50–66, *supra,* where these multiple cost-benefit computations are set out in detail. What is suggested here is that arguments can be developed around each of these costs and benefits.

The Costs of Opposing Counsel's Terms

These contentions make explicit the disadvantages to your client (or yourself) of accepting a particular demand. They may relate to difficulties of administration, the expectations (or even unreasonableness) of the client, your own feelings about an adequate result, the relative value of what is offered and asked in exchange, comparisons with similar agreements (I'll look like I was taken), norms of fairness, attitudes of relevant third parties (my partners wouldn't hear of it), etc. They all take the form, "if you were in my shoes, these are the consequences you'd have to deal with."

Arguments of this type are often treated by one's opponent as an invitation to solve a mutual problem. Thus they can be important levers for generating concessions. On the other hand, in some instances an opponent's cooperation may become a basis for insisting that you make further concessions or accept the original proposal. You are then faced with the choice of conceding or risking your credibility in the remaining (or future) negotiations. Moreover, if they are convincing, such arguments inevitably involve the disclosure of information about your vulnerabilities and difficulties which can itself become the focal point for pressure by your opponent as the negotiations continue.

The Benefits of Your Terms

These arguments focus on the benefits to be gained if opposing counsel accepts your proposal (they may also emphasize the sacrifices you might be making). They relate to the possibility of future profitable relations with you or your clients, the rate and extent of change involved, precedential value in other negotiations, and so on.

The basic problems here are twofold: (i) such statements can often be seen as patronizing or condescending; and (ii) they are often followed by counterproposals suggesting alternate ways to secure such benefits. You may thereby be adding new and unwanted issues to the negotiations.

The Costs of Disagreement or Deadlock

Arguments involving your costs have two goals: they seek to convince the opponent that you have little to lose in going to trial and express your willingness to do so if a better settlement is not forthcoming. For example, you might refer to the factors (judge, jury, facts, law) that indicate there will be a favorable outcome at trial, your own experience and ability in handling them, the low costs involved in preparation and trial time (we've done these before and have most of the basic research under control). Legal services lawyers, for example, often refer to their interest in establishing a legal precedent or in getting experience in order to emphasize the potential "benefits" to them of disagreement. In addition, they will often point out the lack of attorney's fees for their clients if they litigate the case. The same objectives are involved in appeals to standards of fairness (I won't see my client taken advantage of; we'd rather try it), references to the unreasonableness of one's client, feigned anger, ridicule of the opposing counsel's offer, etc. Many negotiators actually discuss the pros and cons of settling as if they were addressing an objective third party in order to demonstrate that they couldn't "sell" the offer to their client.

A second set of deadlock arguments emphasize the costs to the opponent of not settling. Since these involve references to the vulnerabilities of counsel or his client—*e. g.*, relationships, expense, the possibility of an adverse decision at trial—many of them will be seen as implicit or explicit threats and will be subject to all the caveats and conditions we have already discussed.

For some of you this simple schema may stimulate further ideas about what you might say across the bargaining table. Others may not find it useful. But argue something you surely will. Far too many negotiations involve a kind of "name your figure" haggling that rarely produces a good settlement for a particular client. If the parties are truly interested in settling, this approach may eventually turn up a number that is acceptable to both, but then, so might a lottery. Although in many aspects negotiation resembles a game, it should be remembered that it is a game of skill, and not of chance. Despite the adversarial posture of the parties, persuasion—arguments for a good, fair or inevitable result—is a critical aspect of the bargaining process.

6. Problem-Solving Strategies

NIERENBERG, FUNDAMENTALS OF NEGOTIATING

185–92 (1973).

Can we maintain the advantages of competition and at the same time bring about a collaboration in which all parties move toward mutual solutions of their joint and separate goals? . . . [T]he answer is yes. Not only is this possible, but it is feasible even if only one of the two parties has this creative-alternative approach in mind.

The first step is to realize that there must be a better way than the win/lose approach. Let us examine our own attitudes when we are involved in a win/lose situation. What we find occurring within us undoubtedly occurs within our opposer. In the event that we are negotiating with someone who, we feel, wants to win and make us the losers, we find this only strengthens our will to win and forces us to fight harder. Compare this to the reactions that you may have to one who you feel is truly showing you respect and truly attempting to work with you, proposing a number of creative alternatives for consideration to help bring about a resulting solution that might be beneficial to all concerned. Which attitude would you prefer to create after you get over your suspicion?

* * *

[Next one must recognize the degree to which one's own defensiveness may be creating the competitive atmosphere.] . . . Jack R. Gibb states, "If one is to make fundamental improvement in communication, he must make changes in interpersonal relationships." One way to achieve such an improvement is to change defensive behavior into supportive communication that minimizes your opposer's anxieties and enables him to concentrate on what you are saying and attempting to do. Gibb cites six pairs of defensive and supportive categories:

Defensive Climates vs. Supportive Climates

1. Evaluation	1. Description
2. Control	2. Problem Orientation
3. Strategy	3. Spontaneity
4. Neutrality	4. Empathy
5. Superiority	5. Equality
6. Certainty	6. Provisionalism

These six pairs are interactive. Since interpersonal attitudes are often, and sometimes necessarily, evaluative, it may be possible to counterbalance them with attitudes and words expressing empathy, for example. Questions, Gibb points out, often produce defensiveness.

.   .   .

Attempts to control your opposer through speech as well as through nonverbal communication provoke defensive attitudes, while descriptive speech that does not seek to change your opposer but to give him background information provokes no one. Problem orientation also, when it seeks to define a problem and elicit the help of your opposer in solving it, is permissive and allows him to reach his own conclusions.   .   .   .

In short, as Gibb states, "One reduces the defensiveness of the listener when he communicates that he is willing to experiment with his own behavior, attitudes, and ideas. The person who appears to be taking provisional attitudes, to be investigating issues rather than taking sides on them, to be problem-solving rather than debating, and to be willing to experiment and explore, tends to communicate that the listener may have some control over the shared quest or the investigation of ideas. If a person is genuinely searching for information and data, he does not resent help or company along the way." We should discuss our mutual problems, not each other's demands.

Knowing that problems do exist in negotiations between groups, recognizing reasons for their existence, and being understanding of these conditions are useful but they do not help you solve the problems in your negotiations. You must know about and be able to take certain concrete steps to bring about active cooperation between the parties.

The first such phrase is referred to as fact finding. This results from both parties working together to determine the facts. Facts should not be made the subject of negotiations. If they can be initially and independently agreed on, this will eliminate a tremendous number of personalized, emotion-laden attitudes causing conflict. The initial state that tends to separate the two parties is the result of both parties independently arriving at their separate opinion of the facts.

Joint fact finding linked to outside criteria should be the beginning step. Mutual action, in this stage, would facilitate an onward movement in the negotiation.

In taking the second negotiation step, one side should not be requested to present, nor should it present, the "best" or "only" solution to the problem. It should set forth as many creative alternatives as the other team might work with. This in turn will stimulate the other side to approach it in a like manner, and possibly so continuing, the end product will be satisfactory to both. Starting with a mutually beneficial approach in negotiation automatically encourages creativity. Group action is stimulated to looking for alternative ways of coming up with a feasible solution. The knowledge and talent of each member of each group is unlocked, and at the same time each side is prepared to present its needs while helping to meet the needs of the other. Even one-sided disclosing of secrets encourages the other side to be supportive.

During this stage, rather than expressing the fact that differences exist, as suggestions and alternatives are proposed, look for the similarities. Latch on to these similarities and build on them. In most instances, fertile ground for such growth immediately exists.

Bring about involvement of everyone concerned, all members of your team as well as members of the other side. The more people involved in suggestions, the more alternatives set forth, the more successfully differences will be brought out and resolved. When you involve people in seeking a solution to a problem and they make contributions toward its resolution, they can easily become committed to working for its fulfillment.

Attempt to keep the entire group informed of the progress of the negotiation. Let them go through the mental gymnastics that each step entails. We cannot expect members of the opposing group to jump to a conclusion which may have been reached by other members of their group merely because it has been arrived at through the process of negotiation. If they are part of the process and follow the steps through, examining the alternatives and concessions as they occur, the final solution will be realistically accepted.

Having a member of your team who is able spontaneously to recognize a potential stalemate before it occurs or as it is occurring, who is able to step in, suggest alternative ways that might be examined, and state them in a rather abstract, nonevaluative manner so that they do not arouse any emotion, will be of great assistance in working toward a solution. In this role the expert negotiator should not be involved with the contents of what is being negotiated but rather with the alternatives. He should also be able to point out where various courses of action might lead.

To recap the [main elements of this process]:

1. Recognize the shortcomings of and the alternatives to a win/lose approach.
2. Understand defensive and supportive climates.
3. Engage in joint fact finding.
4. Get mutual suggestions of creative alternatives.
5. Involve everyone on both teams.
6. Have an open observer ready for spontaneous, problem-oriented courses of action.

* * *

Being able to come up with creative alternatives is seen as one of the basic concepts of successful negotiation. This allows mutual accommodation where all parties can be the winner. A creative alternative should satisfy some need of each participant in a negotiation . . . [as the following example illustrates.]

* * *

The highest settlement in an antitrust suit was recently made by members of the drug industry for an antibiotic monopoly. The settlement was for $100 million. It was the result of class actions on behalf of forty-three states and certain cities representing the general public and also on behalf of the wholesale and retail druggists. Of the $100 million, $3 million had been allocated to be paid to the drug wholesalers and retailers. It was felt that the wholesalers' and retailers' claim was slight in that if they had been forced to pay more money for the antibiotics, their mark-up was higher—if they had paid less, they would have made less. But after publicity of the settlement came out, the attorneys for that class felt that their clients' claim was worth at least $40 million. After some concentrated negotiations between the lawyers handling most of the claimants and the lawyers representing the wholesalers and retailers, the figure asked for by the wholesalers/retailers was reduced to $10 million. However, this was $7 million more than the allocation in the full settlement.

The drug companies paying the money, when asked for more, refused to go any higher than the $100 million. Other plaintiffs representing the classes of the public refused to give up one cent of the monies that had been allotted to them. A change in the original distribution would have required the further ratification and approval of each different class representing the forty-three states, plus cities, involved in the original settlement. It would have been a long and difficult process. The problem boiled down to how to raise $7 million to complete a final settlement for the $100 million.

This instance called for creative alternatives. A method which seems to stimulate creativity is trying to think in terms of what are the most basic elements that make up the transaction and how are they related. This is in the nature of fact finding. Examining and reexamining the same factors, rethinking, sometimes help uncover creative alternatives. Examining this problem by these methods was helpful. First, time is always a factor and can sometimes be considered as money, and the examination of the time factors involved in this settlement revealed some interesting considerations. Part of the settlement agreement was that the plaintiffs were not to be entitled to any of the money until time for the final appeals had run out. The drug companies did not want one or more plaintiffs causing them additional problems by taking an appeal. Another basic element in any of today's situations involving lawsuits, settlements, etc., is the tax considerations. Many times tax considerations alone will help you solve a particular negotiating problem. It gives different insights for each party and enables you to meet their different needs. One person's tax position may be completely opposite to another person's position, possibly enabling each to complement the other.

In the year 1969, U. S. corporations had to pay a 10 percent surtax. The drug companies had had a particularly good year, and any expenses that they could pay within the year 1969 would be beneficial to their tax position. The plaintiffs' lawyer approached the drug-company defendants with the following propositions: Would they deposit with a bank in the year 1969 at least $85 million of the settlement to be held for the account of the plaintiffs? The bank would hold it for thirteen months, which was the period necessary for the time to appeal to run out. At the same time, the plaintiffs' attorney had found a bank that was willing to take the $85 million for thirteen months and pay about $7 million interest. The drug companies agreed, the attorneys agreed, and finally the wholesalers and retailers agreed, knowing that they would get about $10 million at the end of thirteen months—the $3 million that had been allocated to them, plus approximately $7 million in interest.

No one is without creative alternatives, no matter what his circumstances. . . .

NOTES

1. *The Nature of Problem-Solving Bargaining*

The approach that Nierenberg suggests has been the subject of a great deal of discussion.[55] Stated simply, it focuses bargaining on

55. On problem solving bargaining as a strategic mode, see F. Ikle, HOW NATIONS NEGOTIATE 199–204 (1964); R. Walton & R. McKersie, A BEHAVIORAL THEORY OF LABOR NEGOTIATIONS 46–75 (1965). For the social psychological literature on the same subject *see* C. Rogers, ON PERSONAL POWER (1977); Deutsch, *Conflicts: Productive and Destructive* in CONTEMPORARY SOCIAL PSYCHOLOGY 156–68 (D. Johnson, ed., 1973) and Johnson, *Role Reversal: A Summary and Review of the Research* in the same work at 169–80.

those issues where both parties may have a good deal to gain from agreement and where the gains of one party do not involve a concomitant reduction of the gains of his or her opponent. Whether one emphasizes issues of convenience (continuances, the timing of discovery, etc.) or substantive outcome, there are probably many more problem-solving possibilities in lawyer negotiation than has been recognized. Indeed, problem-solving is part of every settlement, since both parties, for a variety of reasons, prefer agreement to disagreement. The question that Nierenberg raises is how many opportunities are presented in the context of litigation.

Consider, for example, decisions concerning the rate, manner, and timing of payment, the scheduling of events, the degree of publicity the settlement receives, the number of parties to be included, etc. Each of these issues offers the possibility of finding one or more resolutions in which both parties gain more, relatively, than with any alternative arrangement. In negotiating sales contracts, business agreements, etc., these possibilities are even more pervasive.

A number of conditions, however, seem to be prerequisites of problem-solving efforts. First, the parties have to be motivated to proceed in that manner. That is, they have to *see* the potential value in expending the time and effort and incurring the risks involved in trying to approach differences as joint problems to be resolved. Second, they must be possessed of considerable skill. Consider the general steps involved in such bargaining. Issues have to be defined as problems, the parameters of such problems have to be explored from one another's point of view, the relevant facts have to be disclosed, the consequences of a variety of options have to be pointedly examined, and a mutually acceptable solution has to be agreed upon. To carry out this process without breakdown and conflict requires considerable facility with language and interpersonal interaction. Finally, as much of the literature suggests, such efforts require a very supportive climate, which may be a product of attitude as much as skill.

The premise is that problem-solving is not possible in the atmosphere of competitiveness and mutual distrust which characterizes many lawyer negotiations. Morton Deutsch usefully summarizes the research supporting this view:

Typically, a competitive process tends to produce the following effects:

(a) Communication between the conflicting parties is unreliable and impoverished. The available communication channels and opportunities are not utilized or they are used in an attempt to mislead or intimidate the other. Little confidence is placed in information that is obtained directly from the other; espionage and other circuitous means of obtaining information are relied upon. The poor communication enhances the possibility of error and misinformation of the sort which is likely to re-

inforce the preexisting orientations and expectations toward
the other. Thus, the ability to notice and respond by the other away from a win-lose orientation becomes impaired.

(b) It stimulates the view that the solution of the conflict can only
be of the type that is imposed by one side on the other by superior force, deception, or cleverness—an outlook which is
consistent with the definition of the conflict as competitive or
win-lose in nature. The enhancement of one's own power and
the complementary minimization of the other's power become
objectives. The attempt to create or maintain a power difference favorable to one's own side by each of the conflicting
parties tends to expand the scope of the conflict as it enlarges
from a focus on the immediate issue in dispute to a conflict
over who shall have the power to impose his preference upon
the other.

(c) It leads to a suspicious, hostile attitude which increases the
sensitivity to differences and threats, while minimizing the
awareness of similarities. This, in turn, makes the usually
accepted norms of conduct and morality which govern one's
behavior toward others who are similar to oneself less applicable. Hence, it permits behavior toward the other which
would be considered outrageous if directed toward someone
like oneself. Since neither side is likely to grant moral su-
periority to the other, the conflict is likely to escalate as one
side or the other engages in behavior that is morally outrageous to the other side. Of course, if the conflicting parties both agree, implicitly or explicitly, on the rules for waging
competitive conflict and adhere to the agreement then this
agreement serves to limit the escalation of conflict.[56]

These conclusions are based on a number of experiments which
Deutsch and others have conducted to examine the effect that competitive strategies have on bargaining of a problem solving nature.
In one situation where the maximization of joint gain depended on
the development of a cooperative agreement, for example, it was found
that the availability of threat and its use as a tactic not only resulted
in a loss to one or both parties, but also made the process of agreement
considerably more difficult. Deutsch makes the following comments
on these findings:

> Our interpretation of these experimental results places emphasis
> on the assumption that the use of threat strengthens the competitive
> interests of the bargainers by introducing or enhancing the competitive
> struggle for self-esteem. This assumption is based upon the view
> that to allow oneself to be intimidated, particularly by someone who
> does not have the right to expect deferential behavior, is (when re-
> sistance is not seen to be suicidal or useless) to suffer a loss of social
> face and, hence, of self-esteem; and that the culturally defined way

56. Deutsch, *Conflicts: Productive and*   CIAL PSYCHOLOGY 161–62 (D. John-
Destructive in CONTEMPORARY SO-   son, ed. 1973).

of maintaining self-esteem in the face of attempted intimidation is to engage in a contest for supremacy vis-à-vis the power to intimidate or, minimally, to resist intimidation.[57]

In contrast, Deutsch feels that cooperative behavior may frequently lead to better results for both parties:

> In a cooperative context, a conflict can be viewed as a common problem in which the conflicting parties have the joint interest of reaching a mutually satisfactory solution.
>
> . . . [T]here is nothing inherent in most conflicts which makes it impossible for the resolution of conflict to take place in a cooperative context through a cooperative process. It is, of course, true that the occurrence of cooperative conflict resolution is less likely in certain circumstances and in certain types of conflict than in others.
> . . .
> There are a number of reasons why a cooperative process is likely to lead to productive conflict resolution:

> (a) It aids open and honest communication of relevant information between the participants. The freedom to share information enables the parties to go beneath the manifest to the underlying issues involved in the conflict and, thereby, to facilitate the meaningful and accurate definition of the problems they are confronting together. It also enables each party to benefit from the knowledge possessed by the other and, thus, to face the joint problem with greater intellectual resources. In addition, open and honest communication reduces the likelihood of the development of misunderstandings which can lead to confusion and mistrust.

> (b) It encourages the recognition of the legitimacy of each other's interests and of the necessity of searching for a solution which is responsive to the needs of each side. It tends to limit rather than expand the scope of conflicting interests and, thus, minimizes the need for defensiveness. It enables the participants to approach the mutually acknowledged problem in a way which utilizes their special talents and enables them to substitute for one another in their joint work so that duplication of effort is reduced. Influence attempts tend to be limited to processes of persuasion. The enhancement of mutual resources and mutual power become objectives.

> (c) It leads to a trusting, friendly attitude which increases sensitivity to similarities and common interests, while minimizing the salience of differences. However one of the common pathologies of cooperation . . . is expressed in premature agreement, a superficial convergence in beliefs and values before the underlying differences have been exposed.

It can be seen that a cooperative process produces many of the characteristics that are conducive to creative problem-solving—open-

---

57. Deutsch, *Cooperation and Trust: Some Theoretical Notes* in CONTEM- PORARY SOCIAL PSYCHOLOGY 131 (D. Johnson, ed. 1973).

ness, lack of defensiveness, full utilization of available resources. However, in itself, cooperation does not insure that problem-solving efforts will be successful. Such other factors as the imaginativeness, experience and flexibility of the parties involved are also determinative. Nevertheless, if the cooperative relationship is a strong one it can withstand failure and temporarily deactivate or postpone conflict. Or, if it cannot be delayed, cooperative relations will help to contain destructive conflict so that the contest for supremacy occurs under agreed upon rules.[58]

It is of course questionable whether this process can or should be replicated in negotiations among lawyers. Certainly there is a considerable amount of cooperation in most settlement discussions, but there is also a strong overtone of conflict and competition. Cooperation may simply be a device to keep the conflict from degenerating into open aggression and hostility, or it may contribute more than lawyers realize to final outcomes. The answer to this question—as to numerous others that grow out of the bargaining process—will have to be found in your own experience.

————

2. *The Potential for Dissolving Negotiation Conflict*

It may give the notion of problem-solving strategy more content to contrast the way a lawyer committed to such an approach might handle some of the issues we have already discussed. Although it is difficult to speak of a problem-oriented approach as tactical, it certainly suggests a variety of actions that are somewhat different from those we have emphasized thus far.

Demands

We have discussed the choices and communications involved in presenting one's position on matters at issue in a negotiation. In a problem-solving orientation such concerns would be described as problems rather than proposed solutions. They would be "real problems" rather than "firm demands." They would be discussed in terms of specifics and supported by a great deal of disclosure of information. Demands that might increase initial bargaining leverage would be subordinated to those that enhanced mutual agreement and the number of demands would be reduced to manageable propositions.

Concessions

Concessions would not be "read" and scheduled to evoke particular responses. Rather, every effort would be made to surface all the possible options and their attendant difficulties. Attempts would be made to value the actual comparative benefit and loss of a given option and options would wherever possible be modified or separated into discrete components to get agreement where agreement was possible.

58. Deutsch, *supra* note 56 at 164–65.

Commitments

Commitments and threats would be avoided entirely. Even the potential threat of deadlock would be mitigated as much as possible. This could be done by setting long periods of time for negotiations, giving advance notice of major concerns, and evincing a willingness to discuss problems at all times during the course of the relationship.

Agenda

The agenda of discussion would be monitored to provide as much clarity, certainty and success for each party as possible. If solutions to a given problem were not readily apparent both parties would be willing to defer or abandon their consideration. Flexibility rather than firmness would be emphasized.

Arguments

Like commitments, arguments would be avoided. Differing points of view would be presented more as suggestions than contentions and considerable attention would be paid to avoiding differences on abstract principles.

Concealment and Disclosure

Most fundamentally, the entire interaction would be characterized by an open and complete exchange of information. This would include not only accurate expressions of one's intentions and expectations, but also access to the "true facts," to other persons—even to the client—in order to assure the other of the reliability of the information.

This is, of course, only a brief exposition of the possible behaviors associated with such an orientation. You can fill in a good deal of detail yourself, for all of us continually engage in problem-solving relationships in our daily life. It should be recognized, however, that none of these approaches (and none of the writers who argue for them) require total openness, expressiveness or accommodation. Problem-solving, even for its advocates, insists on your opponent considering your problems. In the adversarial context of lawyering, moreover, such possibilities do present dilemmas, and efforts in this direction involve some risks. The disclosure of information can be exploited, and attempts to find initial solutions can be manipulated. Would you be willing to use such overtures tactically, carefully controlling them and with full knowledge of what you expected to gain? Suppose you felt, for example, that by adopting a problem-solving orientation you could increase your potential joint share and thereafter maximize your gains by using a "hard" approach. Would you adopt such a tactic? What are the realistic constraints on doing so?

As these questions suggest, there will be a point at which problem-solving and competitive strategies become mutually exclusive, when efforts to exploit cooperative behavior will be seen as what they are and may lead to a breakdown in relations and ultimately to a worse result than might have been obtained by a strict adherence to either one strategy or the other. Nevertheless, an awareness of the differences between these two orientations should help you in planning any negotiation strategy, and it seems to us that there are a number of ways in which they may be fruitfully combined. Consider the following possibilities:

First, there are a number of actions that enhance neither strategy and can readily be avoided. Gratuitous insults, provocative allusions to contemporary moral, political or social issues, and challenges to certain ritual aspects of the interaction fall within this category. Dress and personal appearance often present choices of this nature, but also raise the question of how far one should go in placating an adversary's biases or inadequacies.

Second, there is usually some course of action which strikes a better balance between leverage and the maintenance of a cooperative relationship than others. It is here that the phrasing, manner, tone, and sequence of some of the tactics we have discussed become particularly important.

Third, attempts to strengthen interpersonal relations and to exert pressure can be sequenced. The "freeze-thaw" pattern is a familiar one in international relations as well as in interpersonal bargaining.

Finally, the responsibility for each approach can be assigned to different persons. The "good guy, bad guy" technique is a troubling example in police interrogation, but the personal difficulties in switching approaches makes assigning different roles to different persons a very reasonable way of maximizing the benefits of both cooperative and conflict-oriented strategies.

In the larger sense, of course, none of these suggestions fully confronts the inevitable tension between an accommodative, problem-solving orientation and one which seeks to maximize competitive advantage. Nor can one merely choose between the two. Each is effective or ineffective (whatever one's goals) only in terms of the particulars of the bargaining situation and the dispositions of one's adversary. A bilateral, open relationship—no matter how desirable—may not be possible without some change in the power relations between the parties. Similarly, where real conflicts of interest exist (as they do), no strategy can alter them. Moreover, the research that has been done on the subject, though inconclusive, suggests that initial overtures of cooperation may not be trusted or reciprocated unless they have been preceded by an initial period of uncooperativeness and pressure. Indeed, it is well to recognize that the strategies we have been discussing may be linked in other complex ways. An increase in cooperativeness and reciprocity also increases the potential leverage that is associated with their withdrawal. Unfortunately, accommodation is sometimes most effective when it is grounded on the possibility that it will be withdrawn.

Chapter Two

ADVISING THE CLIENT

Chronologically, of course, consultation with your client will often precede, follow, or occur during settlement discussions. In compiling this volume we have chosen to order the subject in this way for two reasons. First, although the counseling function pervades much of lawyering and is often the objective of the lawyer-client relationship, the subject is included here because of its close connections to negotiation. The process of helping the client decide whether or not to settle or plead guilty—and exactly what settlement to try for or accept—is one of the most challenging and complex in this area of lawyer work. Second, we have considered negotiation first because giving advice requires that you be able to imagine (and describe to your clients) what will occur in bargaining with your opponents as in every other stage of the case.

In addition, the counseling process creates a relationship with another person or persons. It is affected by emotions, personalities, situations and conceptions of role. With certain clients in certain circumstances you may use some of the skills (and face some of the related ethical dilemmas) we have discussed in the preceding chapter. It is this range of possible relationships—from intimate to distant, from controlling to controlled—that also makes this one of the most difficult of lawyering tasks.

SECTION ONE. PRELIMINARY PERSPECTIVES

BLIND STUDENT SETTLES SUIT—A MOMENT TOO SOON

THE BOSTON GLOBE, Friday, March 23, 1973,
BY KAREN F. OLIVER

New York—The jury was out, and the doctors offered to pay Gail Kalmowitz, who was suing them for malpractice, $165,000.

Miss Kalmowitz, a 21-year-old college student who is nearly blind, had asked for $2 million. Just then, the jury sent word it had reached a verdict and was about to return to court.

"I felt they were coming back too fast and I was afraid that they had ruled against me and I'd lose everything," Miss Kalmowitz said Wednesday. "I didn't want to lose everything because there's so much discrimination against handicapped people in jobs and I don't want to live off my family all my life."

So she accepted the $165,000 in an out-of-court settlement which was approved by the judge and made binding. The jury's verdict, which Miss Kalmowitz learned after the case was closed late Tuesday, was an award of $900,000.

But it was too late. The case was closed forever.

The girl began sobbing. Several jurors also had tears in their eyes.

"I'm not really sorry I didn't wait for the jury," Miss Kalmowitz said later. "I guess I would be, but we've been through a lot and it may have dragged out in court for years. But the $165,000 settlement is immediate. I'm thankful for what I got."

Her suit accused Brookdale Hospital and two doctors of malpractice for administering "uncontrolled amounts of oxygen" to Miss Kalmowitz for a six-week period after she was born prematurely.

The suit said this resulted in damage to her eyes. Her right eye was removed at age 6 and vision in her left eye is so limited that she must use a cane and read Braille in her studies as a psychology major.

NIZER, THE IMPLOSION CONSPIRACY

199–200 (1973).

[In this account of the trial of Julius and Ethel Rosenberg, Nizer discusses two important decisions which had to be made about the conduct of the trial: whether the defendants would take the stand to testify in their own behalf, and whether they would exercise the Fifth Amendment privilege against self-incrimination when asked about their alleged membership in the Communist Party. His description of the way these decisions were made is set out in Chapter Six. Once it had been decided that the Rosenbergs would take the stand, their lawyers—Alexander and Emanuel Bloch—disagreed on the advisibility of refusing to answer on Fifth Amendment grounds. In the end it was Julius Rosenberg, in a late-night conference at the jail, who decided that he would exercise his Constitutional privilege and "take the Fifth." Nizer makes the following comments:]

[A] . . . philosophical question . . . [presented by this incident] . . . was whether a client should be permitted to make a decision of strategy contrary to the judgment of his counsel. Assuming for this purpose that the Blochs had been in agreement and advised not taking the Fifth Amendment, should they have yielded to Rosenberg's contrary view? Did they owe a duty to protect him against himself? Or, as he didn't hesitate to say, "It is my life, and this is the way we'll do it!" Not easy.

I have in the past struggled with this problem. At first, I distinguished between matters which were legal, where I insisted on my view, or the client was invited to get another lawyer whose judgment he would accept, and non-legal questions such as the amount of settlement, in which instance, I offered my judgment, but permitted the

client to decide. I found later regrets by the client, combined sometimes with lack of memory, as to who was responsible for the decision.
So I tried recording the difference of views in writing, and stating
that the client was making the decision despite my advice. Even this
did not avail. When he regretted the result and was confronted with
the letter, he would reply, "I know, but after all, you knew more about
it than I did. Why did you let me do it?"

Perhaps he was right. I have since taken the full responsibility
of decision even in non-legal matters.

But no one could have insisted that Julius Rosenberg should waive
the Fifth Amendment. He considered it intertwined with his liberty
and his life. The Blochs could not be faulted for yielding. Their only
remedy was to withdraw as counsel, if they felt strongly enough, but
this was unthinkable. It would have been desertion in the midst of
battle. Such option was only open to them when they were investigating the facts and interviewing the prospective clients before they
accepted the retainer.

SINDELL, LET'S TALK SETTLEMENT

382–83 (1963).

ATTORNEY: Mr. Wilson, do you recall being taken to the hospital by ambulance?

CLIENT: Sure, but what's that got to do with whether I should
settle or not?

ATTORNEY: Did you refuse the emergency treatment you got,
even though it was rendered by interns and nurses who were strangers
to you?

CLIENT: Of course not.

ATTORNEY: Then later you went to your family doctor and he
wrote out a prescription for you. And then you took it to the drug-
gist to have it filled. You swallowed the medicine every three hours,
as your doctor directed, to relieve the pain and to get some sleep.
Did you argue with the doctor? Did you say "I won't take this medicine"?

CLIENT: Well, that's entirely different.

ATTORNEY: How is it different, Mr. Wilson? How could you
know what ingredients the doctor ordered compounded for you? You
depended upon his advice and skill to help you recover from your
injuries—isn't that the fact? And didn't you trust the pharmacist
you went to?

CLIENT: What right would I have to question the doctor or the
medicine he gave me?

ATTORNEY: Well, Mr. Wilson, that's the point. You accepted
his advice to take the medicine and you did whatever else he told you

to do in order to get better. As your lawyer I, too, have written a prescription for you. My prescription is the advice I am giving you to settle your case, because I feel it will cure your legal ailments.

The analogy is proper. In many cases it will bring the client around to taking your "prescription." You might carry the analogy a bit further by telling the client that some medicines are bitter and difficult to swallow—but all are designed to cure.

SOLZHENITSYN, THE CANCER WARD

86–91 (1968).

"Lyudmila Afanasyevna, instead of your talking to me as if I were a child, can't we converse like two adults? Seriously! When you made the rounds today . . ."

"When I made the rounds today," Dontsova's large face grew ominous, "you created a disgraceful scene. What do you want? To stir up the patients? What notions have you been putting into their heads?"

"What do I want?" He spoke without heat, also weighing his words and sitting back in his chair. "I would only like to remind you of my right to do as I please with my life. A person can do what he likes with his life, can't he? Do you acknowledge this as my right?"

Dontsova studied his colorless curved scar and said nothing. Kostoglotov went on.

"You start with the wrong presumption: Once a patient has entered the hospital, you do all his further thinking for him. All thinking is henceforth done for him by your regulations, your daily consultations, your program, the plan and reputation of your medical institution. And I'm just a grain of sand again, as I was in the camp. Nothing depends on me."

"The surgeon does not operate without the written consent of the patient," Dontsova reminded him.

Why was she talking about an operation? That was something he would not agree to on any account!

"Thanks! Thank goodness for that, though the hospital does this for its own protection. But apart from the operation, you do not consult the patient's wishes about anything or explain anything to him, do you? Just think what a single x-ray does!"

"Where did you get these rumors about x-rays?" Dontsova asked, "from Rabinovich?"

"I don't know any Rabinovich," Kostoglotov asserted, shaking his head. "I'm talking about the principle."

(It was precisely from Rabinovich that he had heard those somber accounts of the effects of x-rays, but he had promised not to betray him. Rabinovich was an outpatient who had already received more than two hundred treatments, who endured them with difficulty and felt that each additional treatment was bringing him closer not to recovery, but to death. Nobody outside understood him—nobody in his apartment, in his building, in the town. Healthy people kept running about from morning to night, thinking about successes and failures that seemed very important to them. Even his family was tired of him. It was only here, on the veranda of the cancer dispensary, that the patients listened and commiserated with him for hours. They knew the meaning of ossification of the flexible triangular arch and the concentration of Roentgen scars all over the radiated areas.)

Imagine! He was talking of principle! That was all Dontsova and her residents needed—to hold discussions with the patients all day along about the principle of the cure! When would they manage to do any curing?

However, such argumentative, stubborn and questioning patients as this one, or as Rabinovich, who drove her to distraction with his interrogations about the course of his illness, were only one in fifty, and the difficult business of entering into explanations with them sometimes could not be avoided. Kostoglotov's case was, moreover, an unusual case in the medical sense as well: It was unusual in the careless, apparently even malicious handling of the case before he came to her, when he had been allowed to reach, indeed had been pushed to, the very edge of death; it was unusual, too, in the decided and extraordinarily rapid recovery that had set in under the x-ray treatment.

"Kostoglotov! In twelve treatments, x-rays have transformed you from a corpse into a living human being. How dare you raise your head against them? You complained that you were not given medical treatment in camp and in exile, that you were neglected. At the same time you complain that you are being treated now and that people are concerned about you. Where is the logic?"

"Apparently there isn't any." Kostoglotov shook his black, shaggy locks. "But perhaps there shouldn't be, Lyudmila Afanasyevna. Man is such a complicated being. Why does he have to be explained by logic? Or economics? Or physiology? Yes, I came to you as a corpse. I begged to be admitted here and lay on the floor at the foot of the stairs—and you have drawn the conclusion that I came here to save myself *at any price.* I don't want to do that—at any price! There is nothing in the world I would be willing to pay *any* price for!" He was hurrying now, something he did not like to do, but Dontsova was bending forward to interrupt him; and he had so much more to say. "I came to you *to relieve my suffering!* I said: I'm in great pain, help me! And help me you did, I'm not in pain any longer. Thank you! Thank you! I am your grateful debtor. But let me go now. Let me return like a dog to his dog house to lick my wounds and rest."

"And when you are stricken again you'll come crawling back?"

"Perhaps. Perhaps I'll come crawling back."

"And we shall have to accept you?"

"Yes! That is where your mercy lies, as I see it. But what you are worried about is the percentage of cures, the records, how you are going to explain that you discharged me after fifteen treatments when the Academy of Medical Sciences recommends no less than sixty."

She had never heard such inconsistent nonsense. Precisely where the records were concerned, it was most advantageous to discharge him now in the "sharp improvement" category. After fifty treatments that advantage would be gone.

However, he persisted:

"It's enough for me that you made that tumor back up, that you have stopped it. It's on the defensive now. And I am too. That's fine. A soldier gets along best on the defensive. As for curing me completely—'to the end'—that is something you won't be able to do anyway, because there is *no end* to the cure for cancer. In general, all processes of nature are marked by asymptomatic saturation, when increasing efforts bring diminishing results. My tumor disintegrated rapidly at first. Now it will do so more slowly; so let me go with what's left of my blood."

"Where did you get all this information, I'd like to know? Dontsova's eyes narrowed.

"I've been fond of reading medical books ever since I was a child."

"Well, what *exactly* are you afraid of in our method of treatment?"

"I don't know what to be afraid of, Lyudmila Afanasyevna. I'm no doctor. It's something you probably know, but don't want to explain. Vera Kornilyevna, for instance, wants to prescribe glucose injections for me . . ."

"They're imperative."

"But I don't want them."

"Why?"

"In the first place, it's unnatural. If I really need grape sugar so badly, let me take it by mouth! What's this they've thought up in the twentieth century? Must every medicine be administered through an injection? Where do you see such a thing in nature? Among animals? In a hundred years this will be laughed at as savage. And how is the needle applied? One nurse hits the right spot, another jabs you all over the arm. I won't have it! And I see, too, that you're getting ready to give me a blood transfusion . . ."

"You ought to be glad. Somebody is giving you his blood. This spells health for you; this spells life!"

"I don't want it. I saw a Chechen get a transfusion here. He was thrashing about on his bed for three hours afterwards. They said it was an 'incomplete match.' On another patient they missed the vein, and he had a big lump on his arm. They've been steaming it with compresses now for a whole month. Not me."

"But we can't give you much Roentgen treatment without a blood transfusion."

"Then don't! Why do you assume you have the right to decide for someone else? That's a fearful right, and hardly ever leads to good. You ought to be afraid of it. It is a right not given even to a doctor."

"But it is the doctor's right. His, first and foremost!" cried Dontsova with conviction. She was very angry now. "Without that right there could be no medicine at all."

"But where does it lead? You'll soon be delivering a report on radiation sickness, won't you?

"How did you know?" She was surprised.

"That's easy to guess."

(It was simply that a thick folder of typewritten pages lay on the table. Kostoglotov had seen the title upside down, but had deciphered it and reflected on it as well.)

"That's easy to guess. A new sickness has appeared, which means a report has to be made about it. But twenty years ago you were radiating some other Kostoglotov who also feared and resisted the treatment. Yet you assured him that everything would be all right, because you did not know about radiation sickness then. I'm in that position now. I don't know yet what to be afraid of, but let me go! I want to get well by my own strength. What if I begin to feel better, eh?"

There is an axiom among doctors: A patient must not be frightened; he must be encouraged. But such an importunate one as Kostoglotov had, on the contrary, to be stunned.

"Better? *You won't be!* I can assure you." She slapped the table with four fingers, as with a fly-swatter, and weighed the blow of her words. "You will die."

She looked at him, expecting him to flinch.

But he only grew still.

"You'll share the fate of Azovkin. You saw him, didn't you? He has the same tumor you have, with about the same degree of neglect. We're managing to save Akhmadzhan, because his radiation began directly after his operation. But you lost two years, think of that! And you should have had a second operation at once along the course of the lymphomatosis, and you didn't; bear that in mind! And the metastases have spread. Your tumor is one of the most dangerous kinds of cancer. It is dangerous because it is fulminant and acutely malignant, that is, it gives off metastases profusely. Its death rate has been ninety percent recently. Does that satisfy you? Here, I'll show you—"

She drew a folder from a stack of others and began to turn the pages.

Kostoglotov was silent. Then he began to talk, but quietly and not at all confidently as before.

"To tell the truth, I'm not hanging on to life so very hard. It's not only that there's no life ahead of me, but there was none behind me either. And if I have the chance to live for six months, I ought to take it. Planning ahead for ten to twenty years is something I don't care to do. More treatment, more suffering. Roentgen nausea will begin, and then the vomiting—what for?"

NOTES

What do these excerpts suggest about the counseling task and its goals, problems and possibilities? How do you conceive of your own role in the process? A variation of these questions was posed to a number of practicing lawyers, and their responses provide some insight into the professional ideal. The questions were as follows:

Which of the following is the nearest description of how you advise and counsel clients?

A. Collect the facts, explain how the law applies, analyze, recommend a best course, or courses, of action and argue for its adoption.

B. Collect the facts, explain how the law applies, analyze, explain the courses of action open to the client and leave the decision entirely to him.

C. "B" above, except with discussion of the ramifications of the course of action and the situation until the client is able to make his decision.

* * *

Should a lawyer—

(1) Arrange for other types of assistance where appropriate, such as psychiatric, welfare, social, medical, etc.?

(2) Concern himself with how his client feels emotionally?

(3) Concern himself with a client's ability to make a decision beyond requirement for minimal mental competency?

(4) Endeavor to put his client "at ease" or in a relaxed frame of mind before he makes a critical decision?

(5) Counsel, or discuss with a client the necessity of adjustment to a changing or difficult situation?

(6) Spend time permitting his client to talk in order to permit the release of anxiety over a situation? [1]

A sizable majority of the practitioners responding to this questionnaire chose "C" in the first group and gave affirmative answers to each of the questions in the second. You might ask yourself whether your own responses would be the same, and what ideals these answers reflect. How far from the ideal are existing practices likely to be? Consider, for example, the following description:

> The institutional setting of the court defines a role for the defense counsel in a criminal case radically different from the one traditionally depicted. . . . [The] variable of the court organization itself . . . grounded in pragmatic values, bureaucratic priorities, and administrative instruments . . . [imposes] a set of demands and conditions of practice on the respective professions in the criminal court, to which they respond by abandoning their ideological and professional commitments to the accused client, in the service of these higher claims of court organization. All court personnel including the accused's own lawyer, tend to be co-opted to become agent-mediators who help the accused redefine his situation and restructure his perceptions concomitant with a plea of guilty.
>
> * * *
>
> The client . . . becomes a means to other ends of the organization's incumbents. He may present doubts, contingencies, and pressures which challenge existing informal arrangements or disrupt them; but these tend to be resolved in favor of the continuance of the organization and its relations as before. . . . The accused's lawyer has far greater professional, economic, intellectual and other ties to the various elements of the court system than he does to his own client. . . .
>
> * * *
>
> The defense attorneys, therefore, whether of the legal-aid, public defender variety, or privately retained . . . ultimately are concerned with strategies which tend to a plea. It is the rational, impersonal elements involving economies of time, labor, expense and a superior commitment of the defense counsel to these rationalistic values of maximum production of court organization that prevail in his relationship with a client. . . . [2]

Is this an accurate description of practices in the courts with which you are becoming familiar? What choices does a lawyer have in such situations?

---

1. P. Hamilton, *Counseling in the Legal Profession*, 58 A.B.A.J. 41 (1972).

2. Blumberg, *The Practice of Law as Confidence Game: Organization Co-optation of a Profession*, 1 LAW AND SOC'Y. REV. 19–21 (1967).

These very different perspectives frame some of the questions on which you might reflect in considering the material in this chapter. First, what is involved in the advice-giving process? What sort of reasoning and attitudes does it require, and what feelings will it produce? Freeman and Wiehofen describe the process as follows:

> Though "advice" may be the first word that comes to mind as equivalent to "counseling," this is too narrow. Counseling can be broadly defined as verbal or non-verbal advice, guidance or direction for a person submitting or constituting a problem. It is a process by which a counselor obtains information and on the basis thereof helps a counselee to solve a problem or develop a new orientation. A fuller definition might be worded as follows:
>
>> "An *interpersonal relationship* characterized by *acceptance and understanding*, whereby a counselor *viewed as competent* seeks to help a counselee, by *intervention* in *a stressful situation*, to *develop insight, work through problems*, make decisions and effectuate solutions, so as to move effectively and creatively *in appropriate directions, within his life* and societal milieu." [3]

Is this what is occurring in the excerpts you have just read? For example, does it describe the way the Sindells communicate their judgments about what is "good for" the client? What assumptions are they making about what clients expect and want?

Second, who should resolve issues that arise in the relationship? Will you be able to give content to the profession's pronouncement that "the authority to make decisions [except in areas not affecting the merits or prejudicing the rights of the client] is exclusively that of the client"? [4] Both the Sindells and Louis Nizer seem to believe that the lawyer may take "the full responsibility of decision even in non-legal matters." Is this consistent with the profession's official position? What kinds of concerns and experiences would lead a lawyer to seize decision-making authority in this way? Think about Kostoglotov's objections to his "treatment" at the hands of Dr. Dontsova, and his assertion that he has the right to decide how he is to live and die. Might clients feel the same way about deciding whether their cases are settled or tried, or what monetary payment is "worth" foregoing other opportunities? What interests are the professionals in these situations protecting when they assume the power to decide? The issue is posed most poignantly when someone like Kostoglotov challenges an expert's authority. But it is also present, and perhaps more difficult to resolve, in those situations where a client wants to be told what to do.

Third, what are the limits on the lawyer's subordination to the client's goals in this relationship? When do counseling, advising, "helping" go beyond the bounds of propriety? What sorts of commitments does this task require?

3. H. Freeman & H. Weihofen, CLIN- 4. EC 7–9.
   ICAL LAW TRAINING 89 (1972).

A familiar example of this problem—and one way of resolving it —is found in Robert Traver's *Anatomy of a Murder:*

> I paused and lit a cigar. I took my time. I had reached a point where a few wrong answers to a few right questions would leave me with a client—if I took his case—whose cause was legally defenseless. Either I stopped now and begged off and let some other lawyer worry over it or I asked him the few fatal questions and let him hang himself. Or else, like any smart lawyer, I went into the Lecture. I studied my man, who sat as inscrutable as an Arab, delicately fingering his Ming holder, daintily sipping his dark mustache. He apparently did not realize how close I had him to admitting that he was guilty of first degree murder, that is, that he "feloniously, wilfully and of his malice aforethought did kill and murder one Barney Quill." The man was a sitting duck. . . .
>
> And what is the Lecture?
>
> The Lecture is an ancient device that lawyers use to coach their clients so that the client won't quite know he has been coached and his lawyer can still preserve the face-saving illusion that he hasn't done any coaching. For coaching clients, like robbing them, is not only frowned upon, it is downright unethical and bad, very bad. Hence the Lecture, an artful device as old as the law itself, and one used constantly by some of the nicest and most ethical lawyers in the land. "Who, me? I didn't tell him what to say," the lawyer can later comfort himself. "I merely explained the law, see." It is a good practice to scowl and shrug here and add virtuously: "That's my duty, isn't it?"
>
> Verily, the question, like expert lecturing, is unchallengeable.[5]

The lawyer in the book goes on to "discuss" possible defenses and, after detailing the elements of an insanity defense, is gratified to learn that the client feels he was *not* in control of his faculties at the time of the offense. Would you do the same? Where would you draw the line?

This may seem to be an easy case. But give some thought to the complexities involved. How will you respond to a client's real need for information as he or she tries to recall relevant details? Is it always possible/desirable to obtain all the facts before you begin to delineate the legal situation?

Conversely, at what point do you become a participant in illegal or immoral conduct? We have already discussed the possibility that a lawyer may create the very dependence he or she seeks to avoid. It is also possible that the same role allocations sufficiently insulate clients from responsibility to make them more aggressive and acquisitive than they might otherwise be. How is a lawyer to respond to this possibility? Client interests will not always be synonymous with your notions of justice and the social good.

5.   R. Traver, ANATOMY OF A MUR-
   DER 32, 35 (1958).

Finally, how does one make the judgments that are asked of a lawyer in this situation—*e. g.*, whether a client should plead guilty or accept a particular settlement offer, or how a particular investigation or negotiation strategy should be pursued? How does one go about "foreseeing" that a jury would award Gail Kalmowitz a verdict five times greater than what she was offered in settlement? What sorts of theories about law and human behavior do such decisions express? By what standards is successful counseling to be judged? In no other aspect of lawyer work is uncertainty so present and so difficult to deal with.

Beyond this, predictions, advice, guidance and support have to be communicated. Even when options are reasonably clear and the consequences of a particular choice can be predicted with some certainty, how are they to be made understandable? How will you go about building confidence and trust in so technical an enterprise? Carl Rogers suggests that every counselor ask him or herself the following questions:

1. Can I *be* in some way which will be perceived by the other person as trustworthy, as dependable or consistent in some deep sense?

2. Can I be expressive enough as a person that what I am will be communicated unambiguously?

3. Can I let myself experience positive attitudes toward this other person—attitudes of warmth, caring, liking, interest, respect?

4. Can I be strong enough as a person to be separate from the other? Can I be a sturdy respecter of my own feelings, my own needs, as well as his?

5. Am I secure enough within myself to permit him his separateness? . . . Or do I feel that he should follow my advice, or remain somewhat dependent on me, or mold himself after me?

6. Can I let myself enter fully into the world of his feelings and personal meanings and see them as he does?

7. Can I [accept this other person] as he is . . . [and] communicate this attitude? Or can I only receive him conditionally, acceptant of some aspects of his feelings and silently or openly disapproving of other aspects?

8. Can I act with sufficient sensitivity in the relationship that my behavior will not be perceived as a threat?

9. Can I free him from the threat of external evaluation?

10. Can I meet this other individual as a person who is in process of *becoming*, or will I be bound by his past and by my past? . . . [Am I] doing what I can to confirm or make real his potentialities?[6]

Think hard about each of the tasks involved in lawyering and the decisions that they require. Are Rogers' questions the central issues for lawyer-counselors as well? If, as we believe, they are, how

6. C. Rogers, ON BECOMING A PERSON 50–55 (1961).

will you "be" in this way and still effectively carry out the technical aspects of the task?

SECTION TWO. THE SKILL DIMENSION

A. ASSESSMENT: FRAMING THE CHOICES

Recognizing that counseling involves an interpersonal process, of course, offers only a general orientation.[11] Where, after all, do you begin? A client has come to you with a partially-stated, partially-defined difficulty. How do you sort out what you are being asked to do in this situation, and how you might respond?

Perhaps it would be useful to divide this task between the tentative judgments the lawyer makes and the more complex process of helping a client choose what he or she wants.[12] Clients come to lawyers for many reasons, but almost always there is some problem to be solved and a request for information and help in solving it. The general structure of what such a "problem-solving" process looks like may be represented graphically as follows: [13]

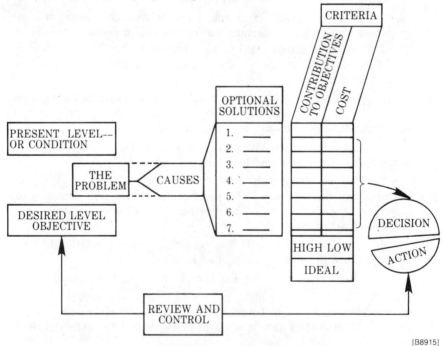

[B8915]

---

11. Notes 7–11 from the original volume have been omitted, along with the material to which they relate.

12. Dealing separately with the judgments a *lawyer* might and (in our view) should make, may appear to be inconsistent with a commitment to

client participation and choice. Nevertheless, in our experience a lawyer

13. See note 13 on page 171.

A similar figure was presented as a model of the lawyer's approach to preparing and investigating a case, and its main elements are used in the chapters on negotiation and advocacy. Strategic prescriptions fit easily into this sort of means-end schema.

It is true, of course, that problems are not actually solved in this way. We generate options and solutions in a much less systematic manner. Moreover, imposing this mode of analysis on a client's problem can not only distort understanding, but can overvalue strategic solutions.[14] Nevertheless, in most cases clients eventually want to discuss their concerns in terms of objectives, causes, costs, consequences and proposed actions. The job of the lawyer-counselor becomes one of (i) translating the problem situation into these terms and (ii) developing a relationship in which the client can meaningfully benefit from this analysis. The following discussions deal more specifically with the first of these interrelated processes.

1. Clarifying Objectives

———

The first step in identifying choices for a client is to clarify what the client's needs and purposes are.[15] As we have previously indicated, the difficulties associated with this process of defining the problem and determining goals are considerable. We note only some of the most obvious complications:

(1) *Goals are inevitably affected by the counseling process itself.* Although a client's objectives can be thought of as pre-existing contact with a lawyer, it is also important to recognize that they are frequently altered in the course of "being advised." A simple model of the purposive client wanting to be told the legal consequences of a planned course of action is not an adequate picture of this complex, interactive process. The advice the client receives will largely depend on what both lawyer and client *have come to understand* about the problem and the client's desires in regard to it. As we said before, what the

who is willing to reach tentative conclusions on the decisions facing a client often offers more real choice to a client than one who leaves the client with no stated views to accept or challenge. Each of the lawyer's assessments, of course, will be altered as the client's preferences and goals become more clearly understood in the course of the interaction.

13. G. Ordione, MANAGEMENT BY OBJECTIVES 11 (1965).

14. Tribe, *Technology Assessment and the Fourth Discontinuity: The Limits*

of Instrumental Rationality, 46 U.S. C.L.REV. 617 (1973).

15. Obviously it is difficult to explore alternatives without knowing the client's objectives:

> "Would you tell me, please, which way I ought to go from here?"
> "That depends a good deal on where you want to get to," said the cat.
> "I don't much care—", said Alice.
> "Then it doesn't matter which way you go."

L. Carroll, ALICE'S ADVENTURES IN WONDERLAND (1865).

client "wants" depends on what he or she can "get." The lawyer's search for available alternatives is always complicated by the fact that the client's goals are not a simple "given" in the situation, but are dependent to a great extent on the lawyer's identification and presentation of the possibilities.

(2) *The client's goals are also inevitably intertwined with those of the lawyer.* Since the lawyer must provide information, structure and projections of the future (which include assessments of the effects of his or her own performance) in order to help the client sort through objectives, the lawyer's own needs and desires are necessarily implicated in the process. The lawyer's need to restructure the problem in reference to the options offered by existing legal institutions necessarily implicates him or her in the content of the decisions that are made. This would be true, as we indicated earlier, even if lawyers made a conscious effort to keep their own needs and desires out of the picture.

(3) *Ends are extremely difficult to state in terms that are sufficiently concrete and tangible to guide action.* Articulating goals such as "maximizing recovery" or "minimizing risk" is of little help to either lawyer or client, and ways must be found to work general statements of objectives into more concrete and particularized goals. Some approaches to this aspect of the task have been suggested in the related context of classroom teaching and the development of educational goals. Consider the following:

(1) *Write down the goal.* Use whatever words are comfortable, regardless of how fuzzy or vague they may be. . . . It doesn't matter how broad the words are because this step is just to get you started and to help you remember what caused you to start analyzing in the first place. . .

Check the goal to make sure it describes an *outcome* rather than a process, so that you don't get bogged down with the problem of means and ends at the very beginning. That is, make the statement . . . read "understand _____," rather than "develop an understanding of _____."

(2) *Write down the things you would want someone to say or do to cause you to agree that he represents the goal.* . . . In other words, decide what you will take as evidence your goal has been achieved. . . .

You can approach this step from the *positive* by writing down the performances you want to see to convince you your goal is achieved, and this is the approach to take whenever you can. When you find yourself unable to make progress, however, you might approach from the *negative* by writing down performances that you don't want to see, performances that would represent non-examples of what someone would have to do to convince you he represents your goals. . .

(3) *Sort the things you have listed in Step Two.* Once you've jotted down the things you think might cause you to agree your goal

has been achieved, you will need to go back over your list and do some tidying up and sorting out. . . . For one thing, you are almost certain to find items that are at least as broad or abstract as the one you started with. . . . [Y]ou may also find redundancies or duplications, things you have said in more than one way . . . you may occasionally find some items that describe procedures rather than outcomes, means rather than ends. . .

. . . Duplications are deleted, as are the items that, on second thought, are unwanted. . . . Each. goal (abstraction) is then written on a separate piece of paper. The process is repeated until every item remaining is either a performance or a non-performance, either a "does it" or a "doesn't do it."

(4) *Make coherent statements to describe what you intend for each of the performances on your list.* These statements describe the outcomes you must achieve to be willing to say your goal is achieved. This step will facilitate your testing of the performances to see if they truly reflect what you mean by the goal, and it will assist you in deciding what to do to achieve the goal better.[16]

Ask yourself whether such a process would also be appropriate in clarifying client objectives. How might it apply to the matrix below, which delineates a broad range of possible client problems?

	Articulated Problems	Unarticulated Problems
Legal Problems	I want a legal separation.	One of the children is in trouble. I need help with that, too . . . The debt problems are getting worse. I need a final resolution.
Non-Legal Problems	The worries are piling up on me, so that separating from my husband seems like a way out.	My husband's drinking has become worse; I wish *somebody* could help with that. I wonder how much of it is my fault.

[B7156]

Following the advice given above, a lawyer might state his or her objectives on the debt problem as follows: (i) increase the client's income or resources (*e. g.*, through government benefit programs, loans, the translation of claims into assets, etc.) so the debts could be paid; (ii) reduce the debt (*e. g.*, by agreement, a court order declaring part or all of the claims unenforceable, bankruptcy) to a level the client can manage on her present income; (iii) reduce and stabilize the rate of payment on the debts at some acceptable level; (iv) obtain an agreement from her creditors to refrain from pressing further; or (v) some combination of the above. A similar list could be generated for

16. This list is adapted from R. Mager, GOAL ANALYSIS 39–63 (1972).

any of the client's other concerns, and would be the starting point for identifying and weighing the risks and benefits of alternative courses of action.

Note that some of these objectives seem to refer to means rather than ends, and some are still relatively abstract. Some will generate different priorities, involve different time frames, and lead to inconsistent courses of action, particularly if pursued at the same time. Moreover, their further specification will surely suffer from some of the problems we described above. Nevertheless, such specification seems useful and possible. Whatever the attraction of "playing it by ear," our hunch is that if you can't count, measure, compare or describe an objective you probably don't know what you or your clients want. Although this may not be an unfamiliar state of affairs, it is a long way from where we (and you) probably want to be.

2. Identifying Alternatives

Once you have a statement of possible objectives, the next step is to identify the options for achieving them. As we have indicated, it is often impossible to think of *all* the relevant alternatives, and the number and appropriateness of various options is always limited by the degree of creativity and innovation a particular decision maker brings to the task. Nevertheless, the range of alternatives you can suggest to the client may largely determine your effectiveness. The following may be of some help in improving your skills in this area.

First, it is almost always necessary to simplify. In a given situation, the alternatives may be so numerous and so complex that we necessarily collapse the number of possibilities we consider. We also narrow the time frame of our inquiries, labelling as possible "alternatives" courses of action which involve a sequence of more or less contingent choices and actions. This may be distorting, but it is an inevitable feature of framing choices. You need not only an awareness that you are doing it, but considerable practice at doing it "better." For example, in our simple debt problem, consider all the possible actions that might be taken to achieve any *one* of the objectives we identified. Take, for example, the objective of reducing the debt. Not only are there many ways to go about it (*e. g.*, raising counterclaims, seeking truth in lending penalties or agreement with the creditor), but also a very large number of possible steps (*e. g.*, threatening to file a claim, filing a court claim, calling the opponent, writing the opponent, contacting the state consumer protection agency). In order to turn these into alternatives which you and the client can consider, some options must be eliminated and some steps subsumed under others.

Second it is generally necessary to work out a rough schema of what is most important to you and your client (*e. g.*, time, contact with adversaries, money, effort, relations with third parties), so that alternatives can be analyzed and compared. For example, the options you find yourself considering may reflect different perceived needs, degrees and types of motivation, and time orientations. They may call for different resources and degrees or patterns of cooperation. They may vary in the amount of resistance anticipated, the direction and sorts of impact that can be expected, and in their complexity, divisibility, cost, risks, and reversibility. You might prefer a course of action with results that are easily measurable or with initial costs that are low and easily limited. Specifically identifying the desirable and undesirable features of various alternatives will produce a checklist which will help you eliminate some alternatives and focus on those that are likely to be most satisfactory.

Third, you will find it useful to specify obstacles. Being clear about what is standing in the way will often lead you to alternative lines of action. For example, suppose a client has related claims which involve violations of both state and federal law. All of the claims can be brought in either state court or federal court, assuming pendant jurisdiction. Given the docket of the U.S. District Court in that jurisdiction, the state court offers a speedier determination and the sort of jury that counsel desires. Federal court, on the other hand, offers far simpler and more effective discovery. Having identified the particular weaknesses of each alternative, is it possible to think of a third option that avoids the deficiencies and offers the benefits of the first two? For example, what if counsel filed the state claim in state court, the federal claim in the U.S. District Court, and used the discovery in the latter to prepare for trial in the former? This alternative, however, raises new problems—possible abstention by the federal court, or dismissal of the state action on the grounds that another action is pending. Counsel might then search for an alternative that responds to these new difficulties, yet combines the benefits of some of the other choices—*i. e.*, filing in federal court first—and so on. At each stage, the "causes" of the projected difficulty are isolated, weighed, and related in ways that suggest altering one or more variables. You will often find yourself using such an approach as you try to think of and evaluate specific options.

Fourth, you can generate possible courses of action by referring to prior accumulated experience. What options were used/considered in the past under similar circumstances? How does the present situation differ? The key to such efforts is the degree to which the prior experience is accessible to you in a form which doesn't overwhelm you with detail. To begin with, your own experience is a rich source of analogies and adaptable solutions. In addition, you may come across further possibilities by "skimming" existing material: books, indexes, law reviews, tables of contents, etc. More often than you might think, these sources provide techniques, tactics, fact patterns, and legal theories which can stimulate new approaches to the handling of a case. Some phrase or example in these commonplace materials can "trigger" a chain of association or an altered orientation to a problem which was never previously considered. For these purposes, form books, treatises, and other practice works are a considerably more significant part of a lawyer's resources than law schools generally acknowledge.

Finally, alternatives often seem to be suggested in the course of "playing" with the problem and its possibilities. What analogue to the problem suggests itself? A game, a road map, a family situation? What if you did the precise opposite of what you have been considering? What would be the worst thing you could do? Which alternatives seem stupid or silly? Such efforts seem to be considerably enhanced by (i) a willingness "to suspend unbelief"; (ii) an imaginative use of metaphor and associative thinking; and (iii) group support. Though it is difficult to be more precise about this approach, it offers a way of bringing intuitive aspects of human intelligence to bear on problems with which lawyers consistently deal.[17]

These suggestions don't go far beyond what most of us consider common sense. Nevertheless, many of you will have difficulty seeing options in particular cases. Common sense, after all, seems to be an acquired competence, and grows only with experience and discipline.

3. Predicting Consequences

———

a. The Nature of Predictive Judgments

———

However one reasons to an understanding of problems, objectives, and alternatives, advice always requires some projection of the future. Not a day will go by in your lawyering experience in which you are not called on to project some future state of affairs and make decisions accordingly. For example:

—A client faced with a criminal charge indicates an interest in pleading to the charge if he can expect a fine or probation;

—A client trying to decide whether or not to accept a settlement offer wants to know what will happen if the case goes to trial;

—A client wishes to call an essential witness to testify at a hearing only if certain facts about the witness' personal life will not be brought out.

In each of these circumstances the decision will be made, in large part, on the basis of judgments of the probable and possible consequences

17. These suggestions are explored in somewhat greater detail in Chapter Four, of Bellow and Moulton, *The* *Lawyering Process* 303–04, 322 and 359–64 (1978).

of the alternatives involved.   How do you decide if there is a "good chance" of getting probation, or how much a claimant might recover in a jury trial, or what opposing counsel is likely to do on cross-examination? Despite the pervasiveness of this need to "know the future," there has been surprisingly little written on predictive judgments in law practice. We seem to cope with the massive uncertainties of advising and representing clients by a combination of hunch and guess, and considerable reliance on a process of negotiated settlement which guarantees that few of our predictive judgments will ever be tested. There is much truth in the view that what lawyers actually do is better explained by their need to give the appearance of certainty than by their efforts to manage the uncertainties themselves.

Insofar as lawyers are systematic about predictions, they rely on relatively straightforward notions of "regularity" [18]—what has happened in the past will generally continue to happen in the future. At least in the area of judicial decision, regularity is a useful assumption. But what about cases of first impression, or those outside of "settled" areas of the law: is past experience of help in deciding whether to file such cases, or how far to pursue them? And what of the other contexts in which lawyers act and in which they must make decisions about future events? Does the same kind of regularity characterize jury decisions, the behavior of a witness on the stand, or the moves of opposing counsel in negotiation? Even if we can agree that knowledge of past occurrences informs these kinds of decisions as well— and may, indeed, be the only basis for prediction—the problems of acquiring such knowledge and deciding exactly how to use it remain. It is one thing to research cases to determine the probability of a favorable appellate ruling, and another to predict the chances of acquittal in your first criminal trial.

To the concept of regularity, then, decision theorists have added other ways in which past experience can be brought to bear on predictive judgments: (i) by establishing that there is "insufficient" data on which to base predictive judgment—*i. e.*, indicating that events are "equally" likely; (ii) by providing a statistical basis for prediction that becomes more and more reliable as the number of specific instances accumulates; or (iii) simply as part of the evidence that underlies the subjective "belief" of a particular decision maker.[19] Furthermore, past experience will support not only judgments on the probability of *recurrence* (what happened in the past will happen in the future), but also inferences of other types. Irwin Bross provides a helpful description of these uses of past data in his summary of "prediction techniques":

> *Persistence Prediction* [rests on the judgment] that there will be
> no change [or change will be very slow in an existing state or cir-

18. Stewart, *Economic Prediction and Human Action*, FUTURES (April, 1975).

19. *See, e. g.*, A. Rapoport, STRATEGY AND CONSCIENCE 22–30 (1964).

cumstance.]. If one wishes to predict the weather tomorrow by this method, one simply describes the weather today.   .   .   .

.   .   .   Despite the use of weather stations and a complicated air-mass theory, in one hundred predictions the scientific weatherman will (on the average) be right in only about ten more cases than a weatherman who used Persistence Prediction .   .   .   .

* * *

A second type of forecasting is [*Trend*] *Prediction*. This assumes that, although there is change, the extent of change is stable. If room temperatures were recorded on successive days as 75, 76, and 77 degrees then the Trend Prediction for the next day would be 78 degrees. In making this prediction we have assumed that the rise of one degree per day will continue.

* * *

[A related mode of forecasting], *Cyclic Prediction*, is based on the principle that history repeats itself.   .   .   .

In Cyclic Prediction, it is assumed that cycles or patterns of events are stable. The method has been used in predicting the return of comets, the occurrence of sunspots, insect plagues, high and low agricultural yield, weather, stock prices, and even (by Spengler) the course of our civilization.   .   .   .   In going from Persistence Prediction to Cyclic Prediction, however there is a utilization of more and more data. The former needs only the most recent occurrence of the event, while in the latter the available historical information is used —in fact, the standard alibi for the failure of Cyclic Prediction is that the record does not go back far enough.[20]

He goes on to identify other bases on which predictions can be made:

Associative Prediction differs from the foregoing in that it uses the data from one type of event to predict a second type. Conditioned response is an example of Associative Prediction. Pavlov made dogs salivate by ringing a bell. To accomplish this, he rang a bell just before feeding and repeated the pattern over a period of time. The association of the two different types of events, ringing of the bell and feeding, is very similar to a casual event chain. In both cases the stable element that is the basis of prediction is the stability of a relationship between two events.

* * *

Such a relationship between events is often expressed by the word "cause." People say that a large national debt "causes" inflation, that overproduction "causes" unemployment, that armament races "cause" war. In everyday life, nasty remarks "cause" hard feelings, and extravagance "causes" ruin.

In all these examples one type of event, the cause, generally precedes the second type of event, the effect. From the point of view of Pavlov's dogs the bell "caused" the feeding. As long as the word "cause" is used in this sense, it serves a useful, descriptive purpose.

20. I. Bross, DESIGN FOR DECI-   STATISTICAL DECISION–MAKING
     SION: AN INTRODUCTION TO   34–36 (1963).

   . . . Unless [however] a great deal of care is exercised in the selection of the "bell," the whole process may degenerate into nonsense. [There must be] demonstration that the events . . . used in exposing the future are relevant [connected] to the events predicted.

Analogue Prediction sets up a correspondence between two sets of events. One of the sets is simple, or at least familiar, and consequently predictions can be made for this set of events. The analogues of these predictions are then made for the second set. . . . [W]hen properly used, analogy may be a powerful tool for prediction. This is especially true if a mathematical analogy (or model) can be constructed. . . . Events in the real world may then be forecast by analogy.

The use of scale-model airplanes in wind tunnels to predict the performance of full-sized aircraft and the use of experimental animals to test drugs destined for human consumption are two examples of Analogue Prediction in the field of science.[21]

In presenting the possible consequences of given courses of action to a client, all these modes of forecasting can be and are employed. We build generalizations from a variety of ill-defined sources—interchanges with others, personal experience, folklore, formal research efforts, assumptions about human behavior—and weave them into models of related variables, factors and influence. In each instance we assume either the continuation of an observed trend or pattern or the underlying validity of the past correlations we have observed.[22]

You will, however, find it difficult to be rigorous and systematic in these efforts. The question for anyone who must give advice on the basis of limited information is whether it is possible and worth the cost and effort to do better. Do we use the information that is available to us in defensible ways? What does it mean to assess the likelihood of an occurrence? It may help you to consider these questions with respect to your own practice if you give some thought to the beliefs in which your predictive judgments are rooted and the

---

21. *Id.* at 36–38.

22. There have even been attempts to turn such observations into "rules" or sets of prescriptions which may simply be "followed" in similar cases, but on first reading, at least, these efforts have a curiously unreal quality, as is illustrated by the typical settlement "formula" we set out at pages 492–95, *supra.* By assigning "points" to such factors as liability, type of injury, age and type of plaintiff, type of defendant and out-of-pocket expenses, these formulas attempt to identify the factors which have influenced jury verdicts in the past and use these same factors to predict the "likely" verdict in a particular case. As we pointed out in discussing the use of such formulas as a means of case evaluation, point allocation systems and similar devices, despite their apparent simplicity, still involve a number of complex judgments. At the same time, by narrowing consideration to a few major factors they may cause lawyers to ignore a host of other variables which may have predictive significance in a particular case. Nevertheless, efforts at prediction in actual practice rarely go beyond the use of such formulas and are sometimes even less sophisticated.

"maps" of the world they imply. The following elements in such beliefs might usefully be isolated:

—The Taken for Granted

These beliefs relate to those aspects of our images of the future which we take as given or consider to have such a high degree of probability that they seem unproblematic. The sun will rise tomorrow; the judge will not descend from the bench and embrace me; the courthouse will be open on Wednesday. Whether relating to the natural or social order, each of these predictions is built on the inference that we experience the world as patterned, regular, and repetitious. Husserl called this the idealization of "and so forth and so on" or "valid until counterevidence appears." It is this realm that gives rise to the feeling that the future is not so arbitrary as to be beyond either knowledge or control. Although what is the "given" at one time may be the "problematic" at another, some experience of "reality" in this sense is a sine qua non of human adaptation.

—The Pattern of Experience

Such features of the world, however, differ with respect to their complexity, accessibility, interrelationship and likelihood. There is too much indeterminancy in human behavior to rely very long on what we are certain of to guide behavior. We act on relative degrees of expectation and information, clarity and ambiguity, hope and skepticism. Thus we inevitably create images of the way the world is likely to work in given situations, how one factor seems to influence another, and how sets of relationships intersect, using prediction techniques of the type described by Bross. In each instance we assume either the continuation of an observed trend or pattern or the underlying validity of the past correlations we have observed. Since I have observed that event B "causes" event A, I can apply that knowledge to all other circumstances similar to event A. Thus we might be willing to state:

—judges will be influenced in their decisions by their social and
 political values;

—litigation outcomes will be affected by the social status and
 power of the litigants;

—the performance and standards of regulatory bodies will tend
 to converge toward the norms of the lawyers rather than the
 claimants with whom they deal.

Whether these statements are true or false, relevant to a particular set of circumstances or not, these sorts of propositions become the basis of many of the causal and predictive inferences we draw. What is involved here is "sampling"—making inferences about the future on the basis of our knowledge of past instances.[23]

Note that the accuracy of such judgments will depend on (i) the correctness of the generalizations; (ii) their applicability to the particular situations; (iii) the extent to which the observations can take into account characteristics of the situation *as it would be seen and experienced by the other person and as it is distorted by the observer's own perceptions and interpretations.* But correct or not and conscious or not, this inference model seems to reflect the logic of the predictive process in which you will inevitably be involved.

b. *Assigning Probabilities*

The extrapolation of trends and similarities, even when expressed in fairly elaborate models, does not take us very far in the realm of practical judgment. If the lawyer-counselor is to make meaningful comparisons of decision alternatives, he or she needs a way to measure the *degree of certainty* that can be attributed to the possible outcomes of the available choices.

Whether expressed in words (very likely, likely, etc.) or quantitatively (*e. g.,* as percentages or ratios) these gradations are often de-

---

23. Bross provides the following examples of this process:

> The [investigator] studies the knife wound in the murder victim's back and announces: "The murderer is left-handed," or you are introduced to a middle-aged gentleman and, after the routine introductions, there is a brief but uncomfortable pause before you ask: "Have you read so-and-so's latest book?"

> These episodes have one thing in common: they involve the process of inference, the procedure for going from a sample (data) and structural knowledge (model) to a statement. In [both] cases, the statement goes beyond the sample. The [Investigator] has not seen the murderer with a knife clutched in his left hand. Similarly, you are not sure that the middle-aged gentleman will be interested in so-and-so's book, but you think from the gentleman's appearance that this book is a likely common ground for conversation.

> All of us are accustomed to making inferences in everyday life, but we usually do the job intuitively.
> ·   ·   ·

*   *   *

> If you will examine [such] inferences—for example, those which lead you to choose a particular topic to start a conversation with a stranger—I think you will find [a] . . . logical pattern . . . . When you are introduced to a stranger you set up a list of alternative statements such as: "X will be interested in books" or "X will not be interested in books." The appearance of the stranger is the sample. Social stereotypes provide the model. If the stranger is a serious-looking, middle-aged gentleman you infer that he will be interested in books.

Bross, *supra* note 20 at 212, 216.

In like manner, lawyers must infer from characteristics of the situations or persons before them the applicability of a number of generalizations about situations and persons similar in a variety of respects (serious-looking, middle-aged gentlemen are interested in books; prosecutors are interested in rapid resolution of cases; lawyer X is likely to respond negatively to "hard bargaining").

terminative in lawyer judgments. Consider the problem of advising
a client whether or not to plead guilty to a criminal charge. Assume
that the case has progressed to the point where the client must decide
whether to plead guilty to a charge of assault with a dangerous
weapon (a lesser included offense) or go to trial. He can, at this
stage, choose the judge before whom he can plead or before whom the
case can be tried, because the rotation of judicial assignments is
known. It is clear that he will want to know more than whether
Judge X or judges with similar backgrounds have, on a number of
occasions, granted probation, or given "light" sentences on such pleas.
He needs to know what the length and likelihood of a jail sentence
would be before Judge X, as compared to other judges, and what the
possibility of an acquittal would be if he went to trial before any of
these judges.

Let us analyze only part of this problem. Assume, for example,
that the client could choose to be before Judge X for either plea or
trial. If he goes to trial there are these possibilities: he may be acquitted, he may be convicted and placed on probation, or he may receive a sentence of up to five years. If he pleads guilty the latter
two possibilities still obtain, but—based on experience with Judge X
—the chances of probation would appear to be greater than if he had
gone to trial. The decisional matrix of the choices facing the client
would look something like this:

	ALTERNATIVES	
PROJECTED **CONSEQUENCES**	GO TO TRIAL	PLEAD GUILTY
ACQUITTAL	possible	no chance
PROBATION	possible	more likely
UP TO 5 YEARS IN JAIL	more likely	possible

[B7859]

If it stops here, this analysis will be of little help to the client.
The information that an acquittal is "possible" if he chooses to go to
trial is relatively useless; the client needs at least a rough idea of *how
likely* this particular outcome is. Similarly, if the chances that he will
receive probation if he pleads guilty are only *slightly* greater than his
chances for probation after trial, he may decide to take a chance, no

matter how slim, on acquittal. Thus we must find some way to predict the *degree* of likelihood—a more exact statement of probability—
as a basis for comparing and evaluating the choice of whether to plead
or go to trial.

If you were counsel, how would you supply these sorts of probability assessments? Is the concept of statistical frequency of any
help? That is, if you know that in a "set" of 100 guilty pleas before
Judge X, 60 of them resulted in probation, could you simply attach a
probability of .6 to this outcome, with a corresponding .4 probability
that at least some jail time will be imposed? Would statistics on the
outcome of trials before Judge X yield probabilities that could be usefully compared to these? Would you need to know the characteristics
of the "set," with either guilty pleas or trials, in order to determine
if the present case was an instance to which these probabilities were
applicable? That is, would it make a difference if the prior cases
involved different charges, or defendants with different criminal records, or diverged along other lines? Can the kind of "certainty" about
probability that is possible in flipping a coin or drawing from a deck
of cards ever be present in such predictive judgments in lawyer work?

While it is clear that such notions of probability cannot simply be
transferred to legal decisions, they may still furnish some useful insights. For example, if you could indeed isolate a relevant "set" of
Judge X's sentencing dispositions, would it not be an important factor
in the prediction? Assume that you could secure information on the
outcomes for all defendants either tried or pleading guilty before
Judge X during the last two years, and that there were approximately
400 cases—300 disposed of by guilty plea, 100 going to trial. Suppose
only 30 of the 100 cases that went to trial resulted in acquittal, and
these 30 cases varied considerably in terms of characteristics of the defendants, seriousness of the charge, etc. Nevertheless, might there
not be some usefulness and validity in attaching a probability of .3
to the chances of acquittal should the trial option be chosen? That
is, might not a statistical frequency, at some point, provide a better
guide than what would otherwise be a "guess" as to how judge and
jury would react to this particular case? Similarly, if you could look
at Judge X's sentencing dispositions regarding a set that seemed to
possess the same characteristics as the case before you (same kind
of offense, young defendant with no prior record and steady employment, no resistance at time of arrest), it would seem that a sharper
idea of the probabilities could be obtained, if only because the analysis
caused you to take such factors into account. Thus, if you could compare members of this "set" who pled guilty against those who went
to trial, you might be able to ascertain that 40% of the former group
received jail time, as opposed to 50% of those who went to trial *and*

were convicted. That is, you might be able to fill in the decisional matrix set out earlier as follows:

ALTERNATIVES

PROJECTED CONSEQUENCES

	GO TO TRIAL	PLEAD GUILTY
AQUITTAL	.3	.0
PROBATION	.2	.6
UP TO 5 YEARS IN JAIL	.5	.4

[B8950]

Ask yourself if this at least clarifies the choices involved. Is it sufficiently reliable to strongly influence the choice that has to be made?

Even if you followed this approach, you would still be left with the problem of explaining this choice to the defendant in a way which makes it clear that you are talking about probabilities—that in his case there will be an "all or nothing" kind of result, and that none of the probabilities approach certainty. You might explain it in terms of *desired* consequences ("you have a 60% chance of probation if you plead guilty, a 50% chance of either getting probation or being acquitted if you go to trial") or the *risks* involved ("you have a 50% chance of jail time if you go to trial, a 40% chance if you plead guilty"). In any case the choice of words itself—the way you characterized and explained your probability assessments—would inevitably influence the client's choices. You would also have to decide how much of the data on which your predictions are based ought to be discussed with the client.

However you resolve these questions, you will want to keep in mind the elusive quality of the projections you are making. Our 400 cases may not afford an adequate basis for prediction: you may want cases covering the last 5 years, or you may want to ignore all but a few similar cases. In addition, you will have to take account of breaks in continuity with the past; if there have been changes in Judge X's circumstances (new rules, personal illness) during or since the period in which the information was collected, the apparent pattern may be misleading. More fundamentally, you cannot be sure that your client's case does not contain a determinative factor for which you did not test (*e. g.*, race), or that there was not some factor or variable, absent in your case, which affected the outcomes in the set with which you made your comparison. From the statisticians' viewpoint, the methods of prediction we applied in this example may be neither *valid* (tested empirically in a sufficient number of cases) nor sufficiently particularized to support the inferences we have made.

Nevertheless, the exercise itself does seem to be helpful, and even rough assessments of numerical probability are often an improvment over methods used in practice. Perhaps this type of analysis will help you to further refine, test and adequately formulate your own predictive judgments.

c. Further Complexities: The Conditional Nature of Lawyer Predictions

It should be noted that we have so far addressed only the assignment of individual probabilities and not their interrelationships— that is, how, if at all, they might be combined. In the plea bargaining case, for example, the probabilities are contingent; that is, the degree of certainty associated with the choice of going to trial involves both the likelihood of being convicted or acquitted *and* the likelihood of probation if convicted. Set up as a stream of *choices* (represented by □) and *chances* beyond counsel's control (represented by O) the decisional problem would look like this:

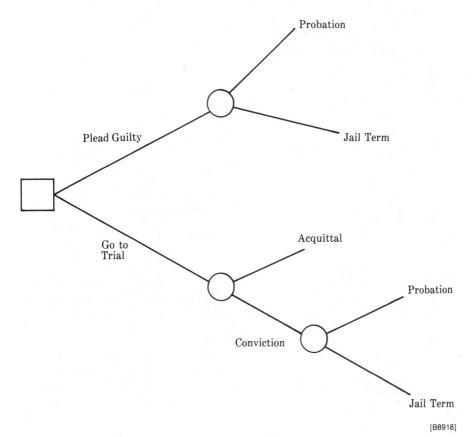

[B8918]

The probabilities associated with the bottom fork depend on two contingencies. Assuming the validity of our initial assessments, is there any way these predictions can be combined? What effect would further efforts (investigation of the case, research on the Judge) have on these assessments?

Some further rules of definition and manipulation from the literature on decision-making may be of help here. First, it is sometimes necessary to assess the probability of an outcome that follows a *sequence* of events. For example, given the information that the probability of conviction if the defendant goes to trial is .7, we might want to assess the probability of the various sentencing options open to Judge X after conviction at trial. Suppose you could attach a probability of .3 to Judge X's granting probation to a defendant in these circumstances, and a corresponding probability of .7 to his imposing a jail term. You could then fill in these probabilities as follows (including the probabilities we earlier assigned to the option of pleading guilty):

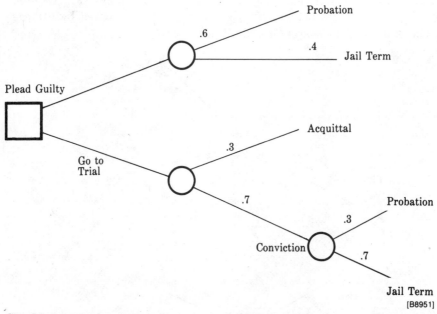

[B8951]

Combining these probabilities in order to determine the chances that the client will be both convicted *and* sentenced to jail becomes a matter of simply multiplying the probabilities of these outcomes:

.7	×	.7	=	.49
probability of conviction		probability of jail term, given conviction		probability of conviction <u>and</u> jail term

[B9003]

We could reasonably say at this point, then, that the chances of jail if the client went to trial were about 50% (or some verbal equivalent), compared with about 40% if he pled guilty.[24]

Second, suppose you could obtain further information that might have a bearing on Judge X's sentencing decision, and the question was whether the new information was worth the cost and effort of obtaining it—*i. e.*, whether it would significantly affect the assessment of probabilities and the consequent decision. For example, suppose that you could wait until a co-defendant pled guilty to see what Judge X did under those circumstances. It is clear that waiting might have certain costs: more time in jail if the defendant is not free on bail, the possible loss of a particular witness, the stresses and strains involved in living with uncertainty. What is needed is a way to make a present judgment of the value of the additional information—a way to ascertain the probability that your client would receive probation (on a plea of guilty) *given* knowledge of the sentence imposed on the co-defendant. These "posterior" probabilities—to use the language of decision theory—can be determined in the following way.

Assume that we are interested in the probability of our client's receiving probation ("light sentence" or L) on a guilty plea, *given* the fact that the co-defendant receives probation (light sentence for co-defendant or C)—expressed in symbols, we are interested in $P(L/C)$. We have already made a judgment that the probability of our client getting probation is .6 under existing circumstances. Suppose we make a further judgment that the co-defendant's chances of probation are quite slim (because of his prior record, greater involvement in the crime, etc.) $P(C) = .2$. However, his chances of probation would be improved somewhat if our client actually received probation. $P(C/L) = .3$.[25] How would our assessment of the probability of probation be altered if, upon waiting, it turned out that the co-defendant did in fact get probation? (Again, you should try to make an intuitive judgment here).

24. This is the concept of conditional probability. It can be simply stated as follows: If A and B are the outcomes of two dependent events, the probability of their joint occurrence is the probability of A multiplied by the conditional probability of B, given that A has occurred, that is $P(A, B) = P(A)P(B/A)$.

25. There are two obvious problems with this ingredient in the formula. First, it is at least as difficult to come up with an estimate of the conditional probability of this event (light sentence for co-defendant *given* a light sentence for our client) as it is to come up with the probability figure with which we are ultimately concerned—$P(L/C)$. Second, if the co-defendant's chances for probation would be improved if *our* client received probation, why wouldn't he delay his own plea and sentencing to take advantage of this relatively likely outcome? As to the first, it seems useful to go through the steps in this calculation anyway, since you may find more and better applications in your own work. As to the second . . . well, perhaps counsel for the co-defendant isn't so sophisticated about probability judgments as you are.

By the application of a simple formula this posterior probability could be determined as follows [26]:

$$P(L/C) = \frac{\overset{.3}{P(C/L)} \times \overset{.6}{P(L)}}{\underset{.2}{P(C)}}$$

$$P(L/C) = .9 \text{ or } 90\%$$

[B9001]

Represented on the kind of decision "tree" we set out earlier, the possibility of waiting for this new information would change the options available at the point of decision:

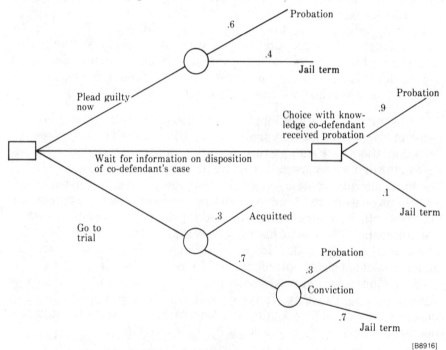

[B8916]

That is, if it turns out that the co-defendant pleads guilty and gets probation (when we expected he would probably go to jail), then our

---

26. What is presented in the text is a simplified version of Bayes Theorem, named after eighteenth-century philosopher Thomas Bayes, who introduced the concept in *An Essay Toward Solving a Problem in the Doctrine of Chance*, originally published in *Philosophical Transactions of the Royal Society* (1763). One of the calculations needed in applying the complete formula is assumed in the problem we discuss. That is, we need to know the probability that the co-defendant will be given probation both *with* probation for our client and *without* it—that is, P(C). This would have to be arrived at in a separate calculation taking the form P(C) = P(L)P(C/L) + P(~L)P(C/~L). To follow through in terms of the symbols used in note 24, *supra*, the complete formula used to determine the posterior probability is

$$P(A/B) = \frac{P(A)P(B/A)}{P(A)P(B/A) + P(\sim A)P(B/\sim A)}$$

estimates of the chances of probation for our own client would have to be increased. The value of the additional information (as indicated above) is so substantial that it might well be worth waiting to find out how the co-defendant is sentenced. Note that the revision would not be nearly as significant if we were waiting for the judge's sentence on a plea in a similar but unrelated case; in the unlikely event that we could estimate that defendant's chances of probation, *e. g.*, .3, the disparities between the two events would be so great that we could not assign a probability to $P(C/L)$ with much assurance.

The same calculations could be made with respect to any case where the decision involves the desirability of further discovery But be careful here. Even if further information would have little impact on probability assessments, there may be a number of other reasons for trying to obtain it. Discovery can generate incidental knowledge of the personalities and attitudes of witnesses, can be a forum for testing and clarifying the strengths and weaknesses of your case, and can function as a significant negotiating tool. These purposes can also be pursued in conjunction with a variety of investigatory decisions, as we have noted before. There are many reasons for "playing for information" in a particular case.

We do not mean to embroil you in the nuances of statistics, nor to suggest that all such judgments need to be quantified. Nor are we trying to place some pseudo-scientific gloss on an enormously difficult and deeply intuitive process. The degree of certainty to be assigned to the mathematical expressions in this realm of choice is always difficult and sometimes baffling.

What we do want to emphasize is the contingent nature of many of the predictive decisions you must make and communicate to clients, the complex relationships between them, and the degree to which you must rely on your ability to obtain and interpret new information as you make them. In formulating these predictions, you may find it useful to (i) use graphic representations of the sequences of decision you face; (ii) test the information you have obtained against your working assumptions; and (iii) attempt to reassess these predictions against each piece of new information you acquire. But you will always have the problem of arriving at a judgment about the future— about "what will happen if"—which can be understood and evaluated by your client. There are few tasks in lawyering in which competence and confidence will so often elude you.

B. ADVICE: HELPING THE CLIENT CHOOSE

---

1. Allocating Responsibility

ROSENTHAL, LAWYER AND CLIENT: WHO'S IN CHARGE

7–20, 27–28 (1974).

There are two ideas about the proper distribution of power in professional consulting relationships. The traditional idea is that both parties are best served by the professional's assuming broad control over solutions to the problems brought by the client. The contradictory view is that both client and consultant gain from a sharing of control over many of the decisions arising out of the relationship. The traditional view has been more systematically elaborated as part of a larger theory of professional service—especially by sociologists specializing in the study of professionalization in medicine. This view is traditional in the sense that it has been the prevailing view since the time of Hippocrates. Even Plato, who argued that free men are entitled to the care of physicians who spend time hearing their patients out and explaining and justifying their diagnosis and proposed remedies, viewed the physician as retaining the position of dominance, using the art of persuasion as a technique of control. The traditional approach to professional control is rooted in and implied by this concept of a profession. Sociologist Howard Becker has characterized what I call the traditional approach in the following terms:

> Professionals, in contrast to members of other occupations, claim and are often accorded complete autonomy in their work. Since they are presumed to be the only judges of how good their work is, no layman or other outsider can make any judgment of what they can do. If their activities are unsuccessful, only another professional can say whether this was due to incompetence or to the inevitable workings of nature or society by which even the most competent practitioner would have been stymied. This image of the professional justifies his demand for complete autonomy and his demand that the client give up his own judgment and responsibility, leaving everything in the hands of the professional.[a]

*   *   *

For formulation of an alternative one must go outside of sociology to the fields of psychiatry and the psychology of bureaucratic organi-

---

a. Becker, *The Nature of a Profession,* EDUCATION FOR THE PROFESSIONS 38–39 (1962). For similar expressions of this viewpoint, see Carr- Saunders & Wilson, THE PROFESSIONS 284; Parsons, THE SOCIAL SYSTEM 441 (1952).

zations.   The first presentation of an alternative approach designed for the doctor-patient relationship, but more broadly relevant to other forms of professional practice, was made in 1956 by psychiatrists Thomas Szasz and Marc Hollender.   They proposed three basic models of the doctor-patient relationship and argued that each was appropriate under certain circumstances and inappropriate under others. Model No. 1 is the active doctor and the inert patient unable to respond to interaction, as when anesthetized in surgery.   Model No. 2 is the guiding doctor and the cooperating patient—analogous to the relationship prescribed by the traditional professional rationale:

> The more powerful of the two parties [doctor, professional, employer] will speak of guidance or leadership and will expect cooperation of the other member of the pair [patient, client, employee].   The patient is expected to "look up to" and "obey" his doctor.   Moreover, he is neither to question nor to argue or disagree with the orders he receives.[b]

Model No. 3 is mutual participation in a cooperative relationship in which the cooperating parties have relatively equal status, are equally dependent, and are engaged in activity "that will be in some ways satisfying to both [parties]."

The contribution of Szasz and Hollender is in suggesting for the first time that even in the "purest" profession, medicine, the traditional rationale of exclusive professional control was neither the only possible basis for consulting interaction nor necessarily the best basis for all therapeutic situations.

It is no accident that the joint authors are psychiatrists.   In psychoanalytic theory a great deal of attention has been given to the norms of therapist-patient interaction in individual psychotherapy. Most psychoanalytically-oriented psychiatrists now take the view that effective psychotherapy requires for its success an active acceptance of personal responsibility by the patient.   The patient collaborates with the therapist in identifying the problems to be treated and shares in decisions about the nature and extent of the treatment to be undertaken.   In other words, the preferred psychotherapeutic model of interaction is one of mutual participation rather than one of guidance-cooperation.   There has not been, however, a consensus on the proper extent of patient control.   One school, under the influence of clinical psychologist Carl Rogers, has taken the relatively extreme position that the most effective therapy takes place in an atmosphere in which it is assumed that the client is capable of making all decisions for himself, with the therapist's task being to provide the client with the op-

b. Szasz & Hollender, *A Contribution to the Philosophy of Medicine*: *The Basic Models of the Doctor-Patient Relationship*, 97 ARCHIVES OF INTERNAL   MEDICINE   587   (1956). The model for No. 2 is the parent-child relationship.   This antecedent also is acknowledged in a paper by Talcott Parsons and Renee Fox, *Illness, Therapy and the Modern Urban Family*, in PATIENTS, PHYSICIANS AND ILLNESS (E. Jaco ed. 1958).

portunity of making responsible choices. Most psychiatrists who favor a considerable degree of patient (client) participation reject this definition of the therapist's task. They point out that the psychotherapist knows more about the "wider context" of the patient's illness than the patient knows himself and that this knowledge must be used to lead (control) the patient to the point where he can assume effective responsibility. Nevertheless, while the extent of client control remains at issue, psychoanalytically-oriented psychiatrists tend to agree that client participation per se is constructive rather than harmful.

Clearly the two conflicting approaches—hereafter to be called the traditional and the participatory—raise a hard issue. Does the professional-client relationship work better when there is primarily professional control or when there is a partnership of control between professional and client? At this point it will help to look more closely at the two approaches, especially at the assumptions used to justify each.

Underlying each approach is a relatively consistent, usually implicit model of how professionals and clients should interact and the justifications for these forms of interaction. Not only does each model lead to different positions on the larger issue of power but to different ideas about how the professional-client relationship should be conducted in specific details. These disagreements can be seen in the contrasting answers that a supporter of each approach would give to the following six questions:

    1. How active should clients be in trying to understand their problem and in trying to influence its solution?

    2. Do professionals usually give effective service?

    3. Do client problems have a single best routine and technical solution inaccessible to lay understanding?

    4. Do professionals give disinterested service?

    5. Are high professional standards set and maintained by professional associations and the courts?

    6. How accessible is effective professional service to paying clients?

[In the following table], two contrasting sets of answers [to these questions] are stated as six basic elements of each model. . . .

	Question	Traditional Answer	Participatory Answer
1.	Proper client behavior?	It consists of little effort at understanding; passive, trusting delegation of responsibility; and following of instructions.	It involves an active, skeptical effort to be informed and to share responsibility, making mutually agreeable choices.
2.	Effectiveness of professional service?	Ineffective professional service is rare.	Ineffective professional service is common.

Question	Traditional Answer	Participatory Answer
3. Nature of professional problems?	They are routine and technical, having a best solution inaccessible to lay understanding.	They involve open, unpredictable individualized choices, understandable to a layman, for which there is no single best answer.
4. Disinterested service?	Professionals can and do make the client's interest their own.	Disinterested professional service is virtually impossible.
5. Professional standards?	High standards are set and maintained by the professions themselves and by the courts.	Standards are neither clearly set nor effectively enforced by either the professions or the courts.
6. Accessibility of effective professional service to paying clients?	Effective professional service is accessible to all paying clients.	Many paying clients have difficulty finding effective professional service.

[Some of these contrasts are explored in more detail below.]

*   *   *

According to the traditional theory the client who is passive, follows instructions, and trusts the professional without criticism, with few questions or requests, is preferable and will do better than the difficult client who is critical and questioning. It is of paramount importance that the interaction between client and professional be stable and free of conflict. This stability requirement is one of the justifications cited for demanding complete client confidence in the professional consultant. Without such confidence the client may disrupt the consultation and undercut the effectiveness of the professional's service. It has been argued by Moore and Tumin that client trust in unvarying professional competence and the certainty of a good outcome is necessary whether or not trust actually is warranted. This assumes, gratuitously, that the public can be kept in the dark if it turns out that professional performance is in reality poor. Most writers who accept the necessity of client trust do not rely on Moore and Tumin's argument. The less cynical view is that most professional performance is in reality of sufficient competence to justify public trust.

The participatory theory promotes an active strategy assuming that it is primarily the client's own responsibility to grapple with the problem. Instead of delegating responsibility to the professional and leaving the decisions to him while being kept only minimally informed, the participating client seeks information to help him define his problem and what he wants to accomplish, rather than waiting to be told how to proceed. Periodically he reviews and reevaluates the steps already taken, and the professional's performance, by questioning and by appraising the consistency and accuracy of the professional's answers. He is aware that there are open choices to be made in solving his problem and expects to have his concerns reflected in the choices made.

The passive client, on the other hand, reacts much as described by a doctor recalling his own behavior at a time when he was seriously ill:

There is a remarkable disparity between the agitated subjectivity of the patient in recounting his symptoms and the detached objectivity with which he regards the steps in treatment. He hires the doctor to attack the disease much in the manner of a Renaissance king hiring Swiss mercenaries, and although he is painfully aware that he also furnishes the battleground, it rarely occurs to him that he might engage himself in the battle.[c]

The passive client's delegation of responsibility and control detaches him from the problem solving process. Only repeated or dramatic evidence of professional nonperformance or misconduct leads to an active reevaluation of the delegation—and the decision whether or not to fire the first professional and delegate responsibility to a second one.

Of course, the active strategy is costly. From the client, it demands energy, intelligence, and judgment. From the professional it demands patience and tolerance built on recognition of an obligation to earn the client's cooperation. The passive strategy makes fewer demands on both parties, but if the professional in fact makes a mistake, it may not be noticed in time to be corrected.

Traditionalists find the notion of an active strategy naïve and possibly dangerous. Take away the professional's role of decision responsibility and the client is more likely to be frightened and resentful. Traditionalists are convinced in fact that people would reject an active problem-solving role even if it were offered to them by an unusually self-sacrificing and foolhardy professional. While participationists concede that most people presently do not push to assert an active role, they contend that clients have never received any real encouragement. On the contrary, they say, clients have been socialized by the traditional theory to think it mistrustful to want influence—mistrust being an illegitimate client response. In the participationist view, if clients don't want decision-making responsibility once it has been effectively offered to them, they can knowingly waive it. But even the chance to forego participatory opportunities is an improvement over the norm of nonparticipation. Traditionalists respond with skepticism about the capacities of most people to make *knowing* waivers. The traditional model implies that there are only two choices for a client: complete trust or uncompromising hostility. The participating model rejects such a clean-cut distinction.

* * *

The participatory theory stresses the uncertainty of the criteria and procedures of professional practice, the dependence of a best course of action on what is important to the client as much as on some objectively right remedy.

c. Paul Williams in WHEN DOCTORS
ARE PATIENTS 225–26 (M. Pinnar &
B. Miller eds. 1962).

If professional problems are essentially closed as traditionalists claim, client delegation is more justifiable. However, if they are essentially open, client delegation limits the client's justifiable influence over the critical choices to be made. Similarly, if professional problems are essentially capable of routinization and the accurate prediction of various outcomes, the client is best served by putting himself in the hands of the professional who has mastered the standard responses. However, if they are in important ways non-routinized, unpredictable problems, the client has a greater stake in seeing that his individual needs are being met.

The traditional theory rests heavily on the need for trust because it is believed that lay clients do not have and cannot feasibly obtain sufficient knowledge for even partial self-diagnosis and remedy. As Alexander Pope observed, "a little learning is a dangerous thing"; the client who thinks he knows better will inflict greater harm upon himself by rejecting good advice than by accepting it unquestioningly. Participationists are more optimistic. One study of the medical knowledge of a sample of outpatients in a hospital clinic has been reported. The researchers found that the patients

> were quite poorly informed about their own condition when they came to the clinic and about ten common diseases.   .   .   .
> [and] they gave little evidence of conscious, aggressive demand for information about their condition from the physician; but there appeared to be an unformulated, latent desire for more information among the majority   .   .   .   physicians apparently cannot judge very accurately the level of medical knowledge in a patient population. The direction of their error was rather consistently to underestimate patient's knowledge.[d]

Participationists are suspicious about the professionals wittingly or unwittingly maintaining client uncertainty and client feelings of incompetence as a means of increasing their own indispensability—their power over the client.

Many traditionalists would not deny that professionals frequently avoid informing their clients, but they feel that most clients prefer it this way. As they see it, clients want simple, reassuring answers. They are afraid of knowing too much lest some news be bad news. Illustrative of traditional thinking is the following advice offered to lawyers by the Wisconsin Bar Association:

> Get at the client's problem immediately and stick to it. Don't bother to explain the reasoning processes by which you arrive at your advice. The client expects you to be an expert. This not only prolongs the interview, but generally confuses the client. The client will feel better and more secure if told

d. Pratt, Seligmann & Reader, *Physicians' Views of the Level of Medical Information Among Patients*, PA-TIENTS, PHYSICIANS AND ILLNESS 222 (E. Jaco ed. 1958).

in simple straightforward language what to do and how to do it, without an explanation of *how* you reached your conclusions.[e]

The participationist counters that people have a greater capacity for confronting reality than they are given credit for—especially when the risks of avoiding reality are made clear to them.

The traditional model assigns the determination of how much information the client should be given about his problem and the possible ways of dealing with it to the discretion of each professional. The professional's judgment may be based on a case-by-case assessment of what each client wants to hear, how much trouble the client is likely to make for the professional in added demands, how much time and energy it is worth spending on the case, how easy it is to communicate with the client, and related factors.

A participatory view of the problem-solving relationship gives explicit and extensive disclosure a central place. Since it is the client who will have to live with the outcome, he should be informed about the risks and benefits of alternative courses of action even if the choice is obvious to the professional and even if the client does not fully comprehend what he is being told. It is not enough to leave the amount of disclosure to the discretion of the professional. The client should be entitled to this information as a matter of course. This information will not only provide psychological reassurance, but will provide a basis for the client's appraisal of the professional's competence to help him. Furthermore, it can be used as a means for sharing decision responsibility with the client. Full disclosure will facilitate the client's ratification of the action taken, thus minimizing the grounds for subsequent client grievances. The discipline of having to hear and understand the information will help the client to feel less estranged from the profession and professional jargon.

* * *

[Although there would be difficulties involved in implementing a participatory model, and it might be a long time before lawyers— and many clients—would feel comfortable with it, it would seem that six] constructive functions may be performed by the participatory model.

The participatory model promotes the dignity of citizens as clients. The desire of human beings to be their own master has been described by Sir Isaiah Berlin:

> I wish my life and decisions to depend on myself, not on external forces of whatever kind. I wish to be the instrument of my own not of other men's, acts of will. I wish to be a subject, not an object; to be moved by reasons, by conscious purposes,

e. Reprinted in J. Goldstein & J. Katz,
THE FAMILY AND THE LAW 87
(1965).

which are my own, not by causes which affect me, as it were, from outside. I wish to be somebody, not nobody; a doer—deciding, not being decided for, self-directed and not acted upon by external nature or by other men as if I were a thing, or an animal, or a slave incapable of playing a human role, that is, of conceiving goals and policies of my own and realizing them. This is at least part of what I mean when I say that I am rational, and that it is my reason that distinguishes me as a human being from the rest of the world. I wish, above all, to be conscious of myself as a thinking, willing, active being, bearing responsibility for my choices and able to explain them by references to my own ideas and purposes.[f]

Client participation in problem solving makes the client a doer, responsible for his choices. The traditional model, on the other hand, encourages passivity, dependence, and an absence of responsibility for choices.

The participatory model increases the chances for client satisfaction in at least two respects. Client participation not only yields satisfactions which come with achieving a measure of control over one's life but participation also reduces excessive anxieties which are the product of uninformed fears and unexpected stress. Dealing with difficult personal problems is a task requiring an individual's intellectual and emotional preparation. A client is faced with a previously unexperienced situation, the perils of which can be magnified out of true proportion unless controlled by a realistic assessment of what may be encountered and the likelihood of experiencing various anticipated dangers. Active collaboration with the professional invites the client to obtain the information necessary to anticipate and cope with the real strains of the problem. Evidence continues to accumulate that client satisfactions are increased by meaningful access to full information about their problems.

The main innovative finding of the research reported in this book is that active participation can actually promote effective problem solving. The traditional model is incapable of explaining this finding. Evidence drawn from the personal injury claims process indicates that clients can supplement the specialized knowledge of professionals, fill gaps, catch mistakes, and provide criteria relevant for decision. Conversely, the collaborative task of having to explain and discuss the problem with the client can help the professional avoid mistakes and focus on the relevant aspects of the problem. While this book does not prove that client participation promotes rational decision, it establishes a prima facie case requiring clear and convincing contrary evidence before it can be rejected.

f.　I. Berlin, *Two Concepts of Liberty*, FOUR ESSAYS ON LIBERTY 131 (1969).

The participatory model serves to protect the integrity of professionals by liberating them from many of the strains and inconsistencies of their traditional ideal. The participatory model reduces the burdens imposed upon the professional by the paternal role. It increases the potential for clients to receive effective service. It removes inconsistencies in the law of professional responsibility, providing the informed consent which can be the only justification for treating, as a matter of law, the professional as the client's agent. It brings professional-client relationships into closer congruence with deeply rooted economic values in our society—the economic norms which prize freedom of contract between supplier and consumer, and free enterprise in a competitive market rather than contracts of adhesion and merchantilist market restrictions. It also brings professional-client relationships into congruence with this society's abiding commitment to democratic values which values are necessarily challenged by the existence within our society of paternalistic institutions.

The participatory model has the potential to increase public respect for the professions and for the institutions of law, healing, science, education and commerce. The model promotes public sophistication about service institutions which increases a true appreciation of their indispensability and invites the more extensive use of these professional services.

Finally, and perhaps most surprisingly to those who see the participatory model as a threat to professionals, it can actually increase the satisfactions of professional practice by freeing professionals both from impossible standards which are bound to be undershot, thereby inevitably disappointing large segments of the public and from the excessive burdens of full responsibility for the solving of the personal problems of individuals. The participatory model invites the professional to assume a broader counseling role than he frequently now assumes and to share in the personal satisfactions and experiences of his clients. It invites personal contact in a society becoming increasingly impersonal. The participatory model liberates the professional from the impossible ideal that he be neutral, disinterested, and passionless. It permits him to articulate and lobby for professional standards and institutions which meet his needs without having necessarily to defend himself against the charges of being selfish, venal, and corrupt. For this freedom, the professional of course pays a price. His preferences are less automatically realized than in a low-visibility vacuum of monopoly professional control. They must win out in the public marketplace of ideas, where they will be challenged by the often competing interests of clients. But this is only fair because clients too must pay a price for the advantages to be gained from participation.

NOTES

Whatever your general orientation toward the counselor's role, you will certainly come to each particular relationship with quite specific desires and expectations. These perspectives will shift as the relationship is "negotiated" and defined. But it will still serve you to give some forethought to how much shared responsibility with the client you will seek.

Rosenthal posits two models: the traditional, in which the professional dominates, and the "participatory", in which some decision-making authority is transferred to the client. He does not discuss the third possibility—expressed so often in the profession's norms—that "the client decides."

Alfred Benjamin's view of the counselor's role provides an interesting contrast here:

[In many situations] . . . the interviewee needs us, and we may need being needed. Engaged as we are in professions focused on the amelioration of the human condition, we obviously need being needed and must always be aware of this need lest it intrude upon our efforts to help the interviewee not need us any longer. We must constantly ask ourselves to what extent we have a need to control his life, to tell him what to do and how to do it; to what extent we can tolerate his disagreeing with us; to what extent we can encourage him to find his own way, not ours, and become self-functioning, independent of us, as soon as possible. . . .

* * *

I feel we can best help the interviewee to help himself through behavior which creates an atmosphere of trust, in which he feels wholly respected. We can best help him through behavior which demonstrates that we consider him responsible for himself, his actions, thoughts, and feelings, and that we believe in his capacity to use his own resources increasingly. In such an atmosphere he can confront himself and those thoughts and feelings which govern his behavior but which he hides, distorts, or denies to himself and to us. We provide information when required; but realizing that this has come from us, we wish to find out how he understands it. We offer the resources at our command and discuss their potential benefit for him, but we believe the decision as to their applicability is his to make. We act in a way that will help him become more aware of himself, his life space, his own frame of reference. We want to help him learn that change is possible but that it is up to him to decide if and when and how to change.

* * *

The interviewer wants the interviewee not to become dependent on him, but to rely more and more on himself. He does not deny his authority but uses it to understand and be understood and to provide the information and resources at his disposal. On the other hand, he does not hide behind this authority to make decisions for the interviewee or to do anything the latter cannot understand or agree with. Although he acts responsibly for himself, he does not take away responsibility from the interviewee. When not sure of his ground, he admits it; and when he is sure, he knows it is *his* ground and not that of the interviewee, who needs to find his own on which to stand firmly.[27]

Ask yourself how closely this matches your own view of the lawyer's role in the counseling process. Do you think it is possible and/or desirable to put yourself "at the disposal of the [client] in the latter's search for solutions"? Is this degree of client autonomy contemplated by the profession's stated ideal? Whether it is or not, many lawyers have a very different view of what *ought* to be the governing norm. Freeman finds lawyers generally to be "authoritarian, directive, parental in their counseling image."[28] That is, their conduct is not only "paternalistic and dominating"—to use Rosenthal's terms—but this approach to counseling is seen as *essential* to doing the job. The following is illustrative:

> Occasionally a client refuses an offer to settle even after counsel recommends acceptance. Your frustration over having worked hard to bring the case to the point of settlement only to receive a rejection from the plaintiff is understandable. You know the law and the chances of success or failure in the courthouse far better than the hesitant plaintiff. Efforts to shout him into reason or threats to withdraw from the case will not conquer his reluctance. It is better to use one of several logical arguments. Try this one, for instance:
>
> * * *
>
> ATTORNEY: Mr. Wilson, I am pleased to report that the insurance company has offered $7,500 to settle your case.
>
> CLIENT: $7,500! I won't take less than $15,000 for myself, and that's final!
>
> ATTORNEY: I'm much inclined to go along with your view if only from a purely selfish standpoint. If I were able to get $15,000 for you that would mean the insurance carrier would have to offer you a settlement of about $23,500. Otherwise there wouldn't be enough to pay your expenses and my fees and still net you $15,000. My fee would be over $7,100 as opposed to $2,500 if you accept their offer. I'd like that as much as you would like to have $15,000 for yourself. But in my opinion it's just not in the cards. The insurance company in this case isn't easy to do business with.
>
> CLIENT: Then you better try my case and teach those guys they can't push me around!
>
> ATTORNEY: Well, let's look at it this way, then. I would rather the company offered nothing. Under those circumstances you would have nothing. Under those circumstances you would have had nothing

---

27. A. Benjamin, The Helping Interview 34–37 (2nd ed. 1974).

28. H. Freeman, LEGAL INTERVIEWING AND COUNSELING 236 (1964).

to lose. I'm truly sorry they offered $7,500; we'll have to take our chances with a jury.

CLIENT: I'll still be able to get $7,500 later, won't I? In case we lose I mean.

ATTORNEY: No, they have the right to refuse to pay $7,500 or any amount if you turn their offer down now. I'm willing to take that chance. Are you?

CLIENT: My doctor told me my case is worth $15,000, from what he knows about cases like mine.

Don't get aggravated. In the first place, doctors seldom stick their necks out on value. In the second place you know the doctor will hedge when the time comes to go to trial.

ATTORNEY: I'm afraid I don't agree with the doctor, but he and you may very well be right. I'll set the case for trial. I just wish they'd taken a position of not paying a dime in your case. You realize, of course, that whatever the verdict is you'll have to accept it. You might also consider that the judge has the power to cut your verdict, even if we should be able to get one above $23,500, down to what he considers to be fair.

CLIENT: You must be kidding me. How can he do that if the jury says I get $23,500?

I suggest that you have handy to read to the plaintiff the statute which gives the court the power to remit. You might point out, too, that the power to add has seldom been used. The very fact that you show yourself willing to give the plaintiff his day in court frequently decides him on settlement.

Another way to convince a reluctant client is to take him to the courthouse. If you have been offered what you consider a satisfactory sum to close the case and the client balks, he may want to use the offer as a jumping-off point. How many times I have heard these words: "Well, if the insurance company is willing to pay $5,000 then they're worried; they'll pay more later." Your past experience with the particular company and their counsel is quite to the contrary, however. You know they have reached the top. Telephone the courthouse and locate a judge who is willing to spend a little time with you and your client. A new force, the dignity of the black robe, can sometimes drive home to the plaintiff that it is better to settle than to wage expensive, unnecessary legal warfare.

* * *

If I have implied that the client alone needs to be conditioned, let me correct this impression. When a client is not receptive to my advice, I frequently consult his or her spouse. I have discovered that women are far more willing to settle than men are. A man is easily tempted to risk everything on the chance that a jury might give him more. Most women prefer having the cash in hand. This is no surprise to those who know that men gamble more than women. It means, of course, that men will require more conditioning. Even if the plaintiff is a woman, you can usually be sure that she will require less conditioning than her husband.

If you have ever held a client conference with a plaintiff wife and later had to re-explain the whole case to her husband, trying to undo the effects of her garbled or incomplete version, you will know why I recommend never to hold a conference on a major decision in her case without her husband's presence. Also, if the husband has a loss of service case, he will be required to sign the release. Schedule such conferences to suit your clients' convenience and work schedule—even if it means that you must get up early or stay at the office a couple of extra hours. Your primary aim is to close cases, and client conferences are an invaluable tool for doing that.[29]

These suggestions, of course, portray a model of the lawyer-client relationship very different from that offered by Benjamin. How do you account for this view? Is it a desirable one? . What values and beliefs does it express? Will these attitudes inevitably develop in relations between skilled lawyers and clients who lack legal expertise?

Perhaps one way to come to terms with these questions is to try to sort out for yourself precisely what kinds of judgments and knowledge are necessarily the lawyer's—not because he or she wants to control, but because they are too "technical" for a layperson. Most lawyers agree that in particular areas of legal practice, such as domestic relations and will drafting, certain decisions *must* be made by the client (for example, few lawyers would attempt to "take away" from the client the decision to file for divorce). In such situations it is recognized that an attorney may be needed less as an expert than as a sympathetic listener, helping the client explore and articulate feelings of which he or she is hardly aware. But once an action is filed, few attorneys with whom we have discussed the issue feel that it is possible or desirable to make the client a fully-functioning participant in decision-making at every stage. This distinction is also adopted by the ABA standards on the allocation of responsibility in criminal cases.[30] The underlying premise is that there are many decisions—such as the precise damages to seek or the order of presentation at trial—that cannot be made by the client simply because of the time and effort that would be required to bring the client to an understanding of the complex factors involved. That is, some of the technicalities of law practice are seen as beyond the skill and judgment of laypersons.

Where the object of counseling is to increase an individual's self-awareness and capacity for personal growth, it is argued, it is clear that it may often be inappropriate for the counselor to tell the client "what to do" or even how to do it. The very function of the counselor

29. J. & D. Sindell, LET'S TALK SET-
TLEMENT 382, 384–85, 308 (1963).
See also, J. Jeans, TRIAL ADVO-
CACY, 464 (1975): . . . "the client
must be conditioned for a settlement
that the lawyer knows is adequate

and which, in the welfare of the
client, must be accepted."

30. ABA Standards, THE DEFENSE
FUNCTION § 5.2 (1971).

in such situations is to help the client develop the resources to think clearly about problems and be able to *make* decisions, whatever the nature of the problems he or she faces.　In the giving of legal advice, however, a distinction is recognized between the "important" decisions—those which affect the client's inmost concerns—and decisions which involve more or less technical aspects of the client's problem.

You should think hard about the degree to which you share this view.　Can you be comfortable with a model in which the client places him or herself in the hands of the lawyer and simply "trusts" that his or her best interests will be protected?　As earlier chapters have indicated, many of your decisions as a lawyer will be influenced by factors related to your own needs and desires, rather than those of the client.　Your discomfort with uncertainty, for example, may lead you to recommend an early settlement in a particular case, when it might be better for the client to postpone settlement until late in the proceedings, or perhaps to take the case to trial.　Given the inevitability of such influences, it seems hard to justify a stance which says "Trust me; I know what's best for you."　If lawyers do not always give disinterested service—and may in fact be *incapable* of giving disinterested service in situations which are, for them, emotionally charged—it seems undesirable to adopt any conception of the lawyer-client relationship which enlarges the already sizable potential for client manipulation.　The passive client who unquestioningly accepts the lawyer's advice, in line with the traditional model, may never know that another lawyer, subject to a different set of influences, might have seen the situation very differently.　A too-passive, "trusting" attitude on the part of clients protects the lawyer from having to look too closely at his or her own reasons for the advice given.

Rosenthal's participatory model offers some counterweight to these tendencies.　In the book from which the excerpts we selected are taken, Rosenthal presents the results of a study on the lawyer-client relationship in personal injury claims.　He concludes that client participation in many aspects of lawyer decision-making is not only possible, but in many cases achieves better results for the client.　Although his conclusions may be limited to the peculiarities of personal injury practice and what may be unique characteristics of the New York City clients he studied, you may find some of his observations helpful in sorting through your own approach to the counseling task.[31]

31.　The methodology employed in Rosenthal's study is summarized as follows:

.　.　.　Characterization of the two professional-client models is drawn from social science literature on the professions and on decision-making and from statements by professionals and laymen.　The experiences and attitudes of clients come from a sample of 60 Manhattan residents who were plaintiffs in relatively serious personal injury claims for which they received some compensation during 1968.　An evaluation of these claims was made by a reviewing panel of three experienced negligence attorneys and two

In order to interpret Rosenthal's findings and relate them to the participatory model he proposes, it is necessary to go back to the six assumptions he identified as supporting the traditional view of the lawyer-client relationship: (i) clients who passively delegate responsibility get far better results; (ii) ineffective professional service is rare; (iii) professional problems have a best technical solution inaccessible to lay understanding; (iv) professionals are capable of giving disinterested service which avoids any conflict of interest with the client; (v) high standards of professional performance are set and maintained by the professions themselves and by the courts; and (vi) effective professional services provided by the professions are readily accessible to the paying public. The study focused on these propositions and compiled data which offered a "direct challenge" to the validity of each of the basic tenets of the traditional model:

> . . . [First] evidence was presented showing that clients who actively participate in the conduct of their claims get significantly better results than those passively delegating decision making responsibility. The main explanations offered are that clients can play a constructive role in appraising and assisting the performance of their attorneys and that continuing client appraisal of lawyer performance is warranted by the frequency with which attorneys perform ineffectively in making personal injury claims. It was shown, [second] that there is no single, routine best solution to clients' legal problems in claims-making because there is so much uncertainty in the claims process and because important facets of the problems and of the criteria for dealing with them are dependent on the unique circumstances and subjective feelings of each client. Furthermore, evidence was presented that these problems are capable of lay understanding not only in that clients tend to be in the best position to identify the criteria for decision most relevant to their own needs but also in that the uncertainty of the claims process can be explained in terms of open choices and the risks of alternative actions at each stage of making a claim and in terms of key institutions of the process which operate largely beyond the control of either client or attorney—insurers, the courts, the doctrine of negligence, judges, and juries. [Third,] a fundamental economic conflict of interest between the negligence attorney and his client was identified. This interest conflict necessarily leads to actions on the attorney's part which often do not reflect the best interests of hte client. [Finally,] evidence was presented demonstrating that the professions and the courts have failed to set or maintain high standards of performance by negligence attorneys or to insure that the public is provided with informed choices in seeking effective professional personal injury claims service. The case

non-attorney insurance claim adjusters. The attitudes and experiences of negligence lawyers come primarily from interviews with 20 lawyer informants and from writings by and about lawyers. These data are supplemented by infor-

mation gained from questionnaires mailed to 48 of the attorneys who represented the sampled clients.

D. Rosenthal. LAWYER AND CLIENT: WHO'S IN CHARGE 5 (1974).

law of professional responsibility fails to protect clients against incompetent attorneys by unfairly treating the client as if he were the informed and responsible decision maker in .the claim while, at the same time, the legal profession denies the client access to the very information which might provide a basis for the assumption of some client responsibility. In sum, clients are forced to delegate decision making responsibility to attorneys who then refuse to accept this responsibility when performance breaks down.[32]

While it is true that some lawyers did a good job for their clients *without* much client involvement, it is not a little disturbing that approximately 60% of the lawyers seemed to perform less well when left alone. Thus the "traditional" model of the lawyer-client relationship not only seems to depart from the profession's norms, but may also fall short of being the best means of providing effective service—the ground on which it is most often justified.

We do not mean, of course, to minimize the complexities here. Some clients do have unrealistic expectations, and there are aspects of counseling decisions which require a lawyer's judgment. Moreover, no client can decide in a vacuum; influence is an inevitable aspect of all advice.

But lines can be drawn to differentiate approaches to these subtleties. It may be that the relationships you choose to establish—to a greater degree than you might like—will do more than your specific case assessments to limit *what* the client can decide.

2. Communicating Your Judgments

WEIHOFEN, OPINIONS [33]

The primary—and usually the only—purpose of an opinion on a point of law is to advise the client concerning his rights, remedies or

32. *Id.* at 144. The evidence supporting the first of these propositions offers a useful illustration of the way Rosenthal reached his results. Clients were first divided into "active" and "passive" categories on the basis of five distinguishable types of client activity: (i) seeking quality medical attention; (ii) expressing a special want or concern; (iii) making follow-up demands for attention; (iv) seeking a second legal opinion; and (v) marshaling information to aid the lawyer. Results in the cases were then classified as "good" or "poor" by a panel of independent attorneys and claims adjusters. Of the clients who were categorized as active, 75% obtained a good result as opposed to 41% of those classed as passive; 25% of the active clients obtained a poor result contrasted with 57% of the passive clients. Rosenthal also concluded that none of the active clients who did poorly did so *because* they were active, and most of the clients in this 25% were, in any event, only minimally active.

This was, of course, a limited sample and there are risks in drawing broad generalizations from this data. On the other hand, it does indicate that a degree of shared responsibility may be beneficial to both lawyer and client, and that a client who stays involved in his or her case as it progresses has a better chance of success than a client who simply "turns it over" to the lawyer.

33. From LEGAL WRITING STYLE 121–28 (1961). While the book from

liabilities. May he take a tax deduction for a certain item of expense? Would he subject himself to liability if he pursued a certain contemplated course of action? Has he a valid claim against another?

But there may also be secondary purposes. The client may want to use the opinion to support his position in a negotiation or a dispute with an adversary party, such as a business rival, a labor union or a governmental agency. He may want to use it in dealing with his own board of directors or stockholders. He may want it for publicity purposes, as to explain his position in a statement to the press. In a large organization, an opinion from the legal department may be designed to guide or protect the administrative official who must make the decision. How the opinion is written may depend to some extent on the purpose for which it is intended.

* * *

Although the internal organization of an opinion will depend somewhat on its purpose, the nature of the subject and the person to whom it is addressed, one general outline that will usually serve would include (1) a statement of the facts on which it is based, (2) the conclusion, giving the answer to the question put or saying what the client should or should not do, and (3) the explanation or documentation of the conclusion reached. In an evaluation of a personal injury case, the opinion will have to consider whether a jury question can be raised, and probably also the extent of injuries and special damages. Often a judgment will be called for on the feasibility of trying to settle the claim, and its value for settlement purposes.

Before writing an opinion on a question put by a client, it is well to discuss the subject with him. After a full explanation of his problem, you may decide that the question that needs answering is somewhat different from the one he originally put.

* * *

Often the full facts cannot be obtained; exactly what happened may be one of the questions in the case. The opinion in such situation should make clear that it rests on certain assumptions and that the conclusions might be different if these assumptions should prove unfounded. For the protection of the lawyer himself as well as for his client, he should underscore his assumptions with such words as "Assuming that the facts stated above can be established" or "If we can prove that."

The detail with which facts are set forth will depend on whether they are disputed and whether a legal conclusion depends upon them.

which this excerpt is drawn is concerned with legal writing rather than counseling, it offers a useful discussion of the importance of communication in either task. This reading again focuses on the lawyer's thought processes in a task—the opinion letter—which is peculiarly the lawyer's responsibility. Subsequent sections make the emotional and personal aspects of this process more explicit.

Irrelevant or incidental information should be omitted, but what is relevant and significant in a given case is a matter of judgment. Concrete data, even though not strictly necessary, may be helpful to clarify and illustrate abstract propositions.

* * *

The nucleus of your opinion is the conclusion. It should be as definite and as clear as you can make it. It certainly should not be susceptible of different interpretations. If you can say without qualification that the answer to the question presented is "yes" or "no," that certain action is lawful or unlawful, do so. But the young lawyer should be aware that the hazards of judicial vagaries, prejudices and plain ignorance are such that he cannot be sure that even the most learned and logical opinion will be followed by the court. He should therefore be chary about offering confident assurance that his client "can't lose." The American Bar Association Canons of Ethics warn us that:

> The miscarriages to which justice is subject, by reason of surprises and disappointments in evidence and witnesses, and through mistakes of juries and errors of Courts, even though only occasional, admonish lawyers to beware of bold and confident assurances to clients, especially where the employment may depend upon such assurances.

In writing your opinion, should you give your conclusion first and then explain how you arrived at it, or should you trace your reasoning and lead up to the conclusion? The answer may depend on the nature of the case and the nature of the client. Perhaps the most important consideration is whether the conclusion is favorable or unfavorable. If it is favorable there is usually no reason for withholding the good news:

> The practice you have been following has been specifically approved by the Commission.

> Durkin Brothers' failure to fill your order of August 1st appears on the facts presented to constitute a breach of contract.

Since, as already said, the client is primarily interested in the conclusion and very little if at all in the legal reasoning, withholding the conclusion may only make him impatient. To find your ultimate answer, he may skip rapidly over the paragraphs in which you present all the arguments and difficulties. He may pay more attention to those difficulties if you tell him at the outset that your conclusion is so-and-so, subject to the conditions and qualifications that follow. He will also be more able to follow your arguments if he knows at the outset the direction in which they are pointed.

If your conclusion is unfavorable, and especially if you fear that your client may be disappointed or annoyed thereby, you may want to lead up to it, first explaining the situation in a way that will permit him to see the logic and inevitability of your conclusion and to accept it when you ultimately state it.

* * *

"I believe" is not an expression that should be used in an opinion. In the first place, it weakens the force of the opinion. Secondly, it is not the correct term for the meaning intended. An opinion should be based on logic and reason, not on faith. "I feel" is subject to the same objection. An opinion should not be based on an intuitive process such as feeling. "I feel" carries the inplication that your conclusion is a mere hunch or guess. The word "guess," of course, should never be used in an opinion; as one writer has candidly said, "it carries professional candor much too far."

"I am inclined to think" is legitimate, when you want to give your tentative opinion, yet serve notice that you are still considering the subject and that your final conclusion may be otherwise. But like all vague phrases, this one may prove habit-forming. Don't be seduced into using it in situations where the reader has a right to have your considered conclusion, and not merely a hint of how you are leaning. The phrase will not serve to evade giving a straight answer, when a straight answer is called for. If you are unable or unready to give a straight answer, say so, explaining why. If you don't have a good excuse, you are, of course, in an embarrassing position. But that is because of your laziness or neglect, and you do not really avoid the blame you deserve by using words that purport to give an answer but really give none. Your reader will probably be no less annoyed by this double-talk than he would by a frank admission that you don't know or have not yet found out.

* * *

The important cases in a lawyer's practice are almost always those in which the outcome is uncertain, because the law, the facts, or both, are in doubt. Cases in which the answers are clear will usually be disposed of quickly; if your client is clearly wrong, you will tell him so and try to settle out of court; if you are clearly right the other side will be anxious to settle. The cases on which you will be spending most of your efforts are those in which there is enough support for each side to encourage it to stand its ground and litigate.

How do you write an opinion when either the law or the possible findings of fact are so dubious that you cannot predict the outcome? The client has asked for and is paying for an opinion, and he is going to be disappointed if you tell him, in effect. "I don't know." On the other hand, you will be misleading him if you pretend to more certainty than the situation justifies.

Here the lawyer may need to be more cautious than in any other writing he does. He may try to find refuge in hedging or Delphic double-talk. But this is at least as likely to disappoint and perhaps annoy as an opinion that ultimately turns out to be an erroneous prediction of what the court would do. Another device is to outline the law on the subject and the facts that would have to be proved if the client is to bring himself within the rule, tacitly leaving it to the client to judge for himself whether he can do so. For example, if asked whether a certain trade practice or agreement would be held to "substantially lessen competition" in violation of the anti-trust laws, or whether profits realized on a sale of certain assets would constitute "capital gains" or "ordinary income" for federal income tax purposes, the lawyer might define the legal terms, illustrate them with examples and with cases, and conclude with some "iffy" sentence, in effect leaving it to the client to figure out whether his transaction is one or the other.

This kind of opinion may sound very learned but it can hardly satisfy a client who is faced with the necessity of making a decision. He cannot help see that he has not been given an answer to his question. Risky though it may be, the lawyer can only give the client his best judgment and hope that the courts will not ultimately disagree. Granting that he can only guess how the courts might hold, his is a more informed guess than the client's would be. He should, of course, make clear that it is a guess. If his conclusion depends upon certain facts, he should make clear, as already said, that it will hold only if these facts can be established.

If the outcome is in doubt because the law is uncertain, he may suggest steps to avoid an unfavorable outcome. Whenever possible, he should evaluate the chances for success and advise his client whether, in the light of the odds, he should stand firm and hope to win, or authorize the attorney to try to effect a settlement. If he can weigh the odds closely enough, he may even be able to suggest a specific basis for settlement.

The choice between different courses of action may involve considerations pro and con that the client will have to weigh for himself. Instead of recommending one solution, a lawyer may have to say to his client in effect: "You can do one of three things. If you do A you will run the following risks, or have to accept the following consequences; if you do B the risks or the consequences will be so and so and you will wind up in such and such a position; if you do C you will encounter the following difficulties. It is your money (or your business or your life) that is at stake and it is you, therefore, who must make the decision." But suppose the client doesn't want to accept the responsibility, and asks the lawyer to make the decision for him? Professor John S. Bradway has given what is probably the best advice: [a]

a. Bradway, HOW TO PRACTICE
LAW EFFECTIVELY, 16 (1958).

If at this point the client insists that the lawyer make the decision, or demonstrates that he is in no position to decide for himself, he places the lawyer in a position where he cannot win. If the case comes out successfully, the client is likely to ascribe the results to the strength of the case itself. On the other hand, if the matter develops unsatisfactorily, the client tends to blame the lawyer for having made the fatal decision. Of course, there are times when a lawyer must assume this sort of responsibility. At least, he must tell the client that he is willing to work with him on solutions A, B, or C, but not on solutions X and Y. The lawyer should not shrink from making these decisions, but he should endeavor to protect himself from unreasonable attack.

If the client to whom you are writing is someone with legal training or experience in the specialized legal subject, such as the trust officer of a bank, you may be able to use technical terms and to discuss in some detail the reasoning by which you came to your conclusion. You may also want to cite the authorities and perhaps quote from them. Indeed, in some cases the best opinion for such a client is indistinguishable from a memorandum of law. If, on the other hand, the opinion is for a layman who is interested only in the practical implications for himself, you will want to tailor your vocabulary and trim your discussion accordingly. Citation of cases will probably be of no interest to him; leave them out.

*   *   *

When the question concerns a statute or regulation, the relevant provisions may need to be not only cited but quoted. In such situations, the words should be quoted as fully as may be necessary—but no more. The language of statutes and administrative regulations is likely to be annoyingly difficult for laymen to understand. If only one clause or phrase needs to be quoted, quote only the essential words, not the whole sentence or paragraph. For your client's purpose, you can probably word the nonessential parts better yourself. . . .

*   *   *

In writing an opinion, a lawyer is writing not as an advocate but as an authority laying down the law. He will typically be explaining fairly intricate technical points to a layman. The most important qualities of style for this form of writing are therefore clarity and simplicity. Here if anywhere you must strip your writing of unnecessarily legalistic and verbose wording and try to put your ideas in terms that are crystal-clear.

NOTES

1. *Formulating Advice: The Language Problem*

However decisional authority is allocated in some aspects of the case, the lawyer will often find it necessary to make an independent judgment of alternatives and consequences. With this responsibility comes the problem of deciding how to communicate these options and predictions to the client in an understandable form. For example, once you have estimated the probability of a favorable jury verdict, what language do you employ to convey that assessment to the client? Should you try to arrive at an exact percentage (you have a 60% chance of winning) or will phrases such as "more likely than not" suffice? How desirable or helpful is it to tell the client of the factors which entered into your choice of alternatives and formed the basis for your predictions?

As an example of this problem, consider the decision concerning whether to accept/make a specific settlement offer, to wait in hopes of an improved settlement position, or to take the case to trial. In some form choices of this sort arise in almost every litigated case, whether civil or criminal.

Assume it is your judgment, after exploration of the available options, that the client should accept a $10,000 settlement offer in a personal injury case. How should this advice be communicated to the client? The following are some possibilities:

—In my considered judgment, it's the best we're going to get. I think you should take it.

—We might get a little more if we wait until just before trial, but that's going to increase my fee, not to mention increasing your waiting time, so you might not be that much better off.

—Now I want to make it clear that we can always take your case to trial, and if we do, there's a *chance* you might get considerably more than that. But it's hard to say what will happen at trial, and there's also a chance that you won't collect anything. I'd say you have at least a 75% chance of recovering *something*, but I can't be more encouraging than that. It basically boils down to whether you want to live with the uncertainty a little while longer, and run the risk of coming away empty-handed, or whether you want the certainty of $10,000 right now. Of course, they may raise their offer before trial, and you could always decide to settle at that point.

The lawyers making these statements may seem to be talking about three different cases, but are in fact making the same predictive judgments and weighing the same risks. Assuming the client did not feel free to ask further questions, how do you think he or she would react to each of these statements? Would the client hearing the first statement be likely to press for taking the case to trial? Is there a greater likelihood for the client hearing the third statement? If so, why?

One important way in which these statements differ is in the number of alternatives the lawyers offer: the first has chosen to limit the choices to "take it—don't take it," without informing the client of the consequences of the latter; the second has decided not to go deeply into his or her assessment of the risks involved in going to trial. The third lawyer's discussion is fuller, but hardly a simple guide for client choice. Is there any way to change these statements to make them more helpful to the client? For example, should the third lawyer detail some of the "problems" that led to the prediction that there was a 25% chance that liability would not be found? Would it be more meaningful to discuss the relation between special and general damages, or the propensities of local juries? Assuming he or she "leans" toward settlement as much as the first lawyer, could such information ever be presented in a way that would not heavily influence, if not determine, the client's decision? If not, might the minimal information involved in the statement be *more* effective in shifting decisional responsibility to the client than a detailed analysis?

In many ways these are questions without answers. The precise wording of an opinion—even in letter form—depends on specifics that can't be captured in a discussion of this sort. What one can do, however, is to recognize the tendencies in given formulations and the degree to which the wording and tone of advice invites the client to disagree, or at least ask questions. No lawyer can say precisely the "right" thing, but advice can be phrased in ways that invite either acquiescence or independent judgment. A lawyer can, with care and patience in using language, provide guidance and direction without implicitly giving orders. As you try to write in the ways Weihofen suggests, you might judge your own work against this demanding standard.

---

2. *Communicating Advice: The Problem of Method*

Communication, of course, is much more than a problem of language. We have discussed this at length in our treatment of client interviewing.* Although there may come a point, in a given interview, where the attorney switches from asking for information to providing it, there are no clear distinctions among the techniques that will be used in the two phases. The client must still be drawn out concerning his or her feelings about the proposed course of conduct, and the attorney's advice-giving may well sound like a slightly expanded version of the responses and leads used in interviewing. It will be necessary to adapt whatever is said to the client's vocabulary, information-level, and frame of reference, and much of what was said about question-formulation and probes will be equally relevant when it becomes the attorney's turn to provide answers. The difference is the degree of initiative and guidance which the lawyer exercises in this phase of the process. Thus we might reiterate some of

* Chapter Three in *The Lawyering Process* (1978).

the familiar "techniques" used in interviewing, and add a few new categories: [34]

Clarification—While clarification is used throughout an interview, it becomes particularly important in the counseling phase of the relationship. It may involve no more than restatement or summary of what the client has said, but may also entail "translating" the client's words into terms that more clearly express what is meant. This not only helps the client develop a clear picture of the problem and his or her desires with regard to it, but is essential if the lawyer is to understand the problem from the client's point of view.

Reflection—Although it must be used carefully, reflection is essential in helping a client decide what he or she wants to do about a problem. While restatement, summary and clarification focus on "pinning down" what the client has said, reflection is concerned with the *feelings* underlying the client's verbal statements. The counselor does not "interpret" the client's statements from his or her own frame of reference (e. g., by attributing motives or attempting to surface subconscious causes), but tries to verbalize the feelings that the client is actually (though indirectly) expressing. It takes a long time to become skilled in using this approach, but if you become comfortable with it it will serve you and your clients well. Reflection may be crucial in the process of sorting out preferences and ascertaining the client's "real" reaction to a proposed course of conduct.

Explanation—This method, which is essential to effective interviewing, also has obvious uses in counseling. No matter how experienced and "decisive" a particular client may be, at a minimum he or she will need a certain amount of information on the legal situation. For many clients, adequate explanation may be basic to their participating fully in the decision process.

Reassurance—When the counselor uses assurance or reassurance, to use Benjamin's terms, he or she gives the client a verbal "pat on the back." While the use of this technique may not be as essential

---

34. The categories listed here are essentially those used by Alfred Benjamin. For a discussion of these and other techniques in a broader counseling context, see A. Benjamin, THE HELPING INTERVIEW 108–53 (2nd ed., 1974).

Some of these techniques may have greater application in the planning aspects of client counseling—such as drafting wills or setting up business organizations—than they do to the litigation model we have emphasized. Nevertheless, we feel that they play a part in almost every lawyer-client interaction. Although we have labeled them "techniques", they also reflect a philosophy that would push techniques aside if they threatened to interfere with real communication between lawyer and client. Moreover, they remind us that responses short of definite, detailed advice may be more helpful to a particular client than explicit instructions, and provide a kind of checklist of things to remember once we do decide that advice is warranted. They suggest, as well, the richness of the options that are available to the counselor.

in legal situations as it is in some others, it can be very effective in encouraging the client to "open up" and express his or her true feelings and desires. It is easy to say something like, "I think you did the right thing," from time to time, and it can greatly facilitate the counseling task.

Suggestion—Benjamin characterizes suggestion as a "mild form of advice."[35] The counselor offers one or more "ideas" or possible solutions, but does so in a way which leaves the client free to accept them, reject them, or use them as a stimulus for his or her own ideas. Suggestion is often appropriate in situations where there are disparities in expertise, and is frequently the means by which problem solving alternatives are introduced and considered. When used effectively, suggestion can be a way to stimulate creative thinking and expand, rather than narrow, the range of possible solutions.

Advice—Here the counselor goes beyond suggestion to a "recommended course of action"; advice essentially involves telling the client what you think he or she should do. It is what many clients would say they go to a lawyer to obtain. Advice can be framed as an ultimatum, can slip into "urging" the client to pursue a certain course of action, or can be very tentative in nature. It can either ensure that the final decision will be made by the client or take that decision away. In some cases, giving advice that will be understood and accepted will require not expressing your own view too soon or too forcefully. In others, it will require just the opposite. You will have to strike your own balance on the difficult questions in this area.

———

3. *The Problem of Uncertainty*

What makes these judgments so difficult, of course, are the risks and uncertainties that attend almost every course of action. As a case proceeds these risk judgments change, often becoming more predictable. How much of this uncertainty should be communicated to the client? At least four possibilities suggest themselves.

LAWYER'S VIEW
OF SITUATION

		Certain	Uncertain
CLIENT'S VIEW OF SITUATION	Certain	(1)	(2)
	Uncertain	(3)	(4)

[B8917]

35. *Id.* at 128.

In box (1) the lawyer is reasonably sure of his or her forecasts, and conveys that certainty to the client. In box (2) the lawyer is uncertain but chooses, for some reason, to conceal that lack of certainty from the client, who is given the impression that a definite result will follow the choice of a particular option. Box (3) involves a situation in which the client is kept in doubt about the outcome of one or more choices, though the lawyer in fact has a more or less definite idea of what will happen. In Box (4) the lawyer is uncertain, and the client knows it. There are, of course, many possible combinations and permutations of these four possibilities.

Honesty would seem to dictate choices (1) and (4). But the problem is more complex. There may be good reasons for conveying more confidence in one's predictions than one feels in some counseling situations, and in others it may make no sense to apprise the client of every conceivable risk, no matter how slight. More important, many of you will feel pressure to "manage" this pervasive aspect of advice giving. Consider, for example, the following analysis of the way communications about uncertainty affect the course of treatment in medical practice:

> Medical sociology is indebted to Talcott Parsons for having called attention to the important influence of uncertainty on the relationship between doctor and patient in the treatment of illness and disease. This is described as a primary source of strain in the physician's role, not only because clinically it so often obscures and vitiates definitive diagnoses and prognoses, but also because in an optimistic and solution-demanding culture such as ours it poses serious and delicate problems in the communicating of the unknown to the patient and his family.

> *   *   *

> [The study on which we base our conclusions involved fourteen Baltimore families, in each of which a young child had contracted paralytic poliomyelitis. The research was conducted over a two-year period.]   .   .   .   By bringing together   .   .   .   interview and observational data from   .   .   .   several sources, it was possible to compare and contrast, at successive stages of the disease and its treatment, what the parents knew and understood of the child's condition with what the doctors knew and understood.

> *   *   *

> Now the pathological course of paralytic poliomyelitis is such that, during the first weeks following onset, it is difficult in most cases for even the most skilled diagnostician to make anything like a definite prognosis of probable residual impairment and functional disability   .   .   .

> By about the sixth week to the third month following onset of the disease, however, the orthopedist and physiotherapist are in a position to make a reasonably sound prognosis of the amount and type of residual handicap   .   .   .

By this time, therefore, the element of clinical uncertainty regarding outcome, so conspicuously present when the child is first stricken, is greatly reduced for the physician, if not altogether eliminated. Was there then a commensurate gain in the parents' understanding of the child's condition after this six-week to three-month period had passed? Did they then, as did the doctors, come to view certain outcomes as highly probable and others as improbable?

On the basis of intensive and repeated interviewing of the parents over a two-year period, the answer to these questions is that, except for one case in which the muscle check pointed clearly to full recovery, the parents were neither told nor explicitly prepared by the treatment personnel to expect an outcome significantly different from that which they understandably hoped for, namely, a complete and natural recovery for the child. This does not imply that the doctors issued falsely optimistic prognoses or that, through indirection and other subtleties, they sought to encourage the parents to expect more by way of recovery than was possible. Rather, what typically transpired was that the parents were kept in the dark. The doctors' answers to their questions were couched for the most part in such hedging, evasive, or unintelligibly technical terms as to cause them, from many such contacts, to expect a more favorable recovery than could be justified by the facts then known. As one treatment-staff member put it, "We try not to tell them too much. It's better if they find out for themselves in a natural sort of way."

Indeed, it was disheartening to note how, for many of the parents, "the natural way" consisted of a painfully slow and prolonged dwindling of expectations for a complete and natural recovery. This is ironical when one considers that as early as two to three months following onset the doctors and physiotherapists were able to tell members of the research team with considerable confidence that one child would require bracing for an indefinite period; that another would never walk with a normal gait; that a third would require a bone-fusion operation before he would be able to hold himself erect; and so on. By contrast, the parents of these children came to know these prognoses much later, if at all. And even then their understanding of them was in most instances partial and subject to considerable distortion.

But what is of special interest here is the way in which uncertainty, a *real* factor in the early diagnosis and treatment of the paralyzed child, came more and more to serve the purely managerial ends of the treatment personnel in their interaction with parents. Long after the doctor himself was no longer in doubt about the outcome, the perpetuation of uncertainty in doctor-to-family communication, although perhaps neither premeditated nor intended, can nonetheless best be understood in terms of its functions in the treatment system. These are several, and closely connected.

Foremost is the way in which the pretense of uncertainty as to outcome serves to reduce materially the expenditure of additional time, effort, and involvement which a frank and straightforward prognosis to the family might entail. The doctor implicitly recognizes that, were he to tell the family that the child would remain crippled or otherwise impaired to some significant extent, he would easily become embroiled in much more than a simple, factual medical prognosis. Presenting so unwelcome a prospect is bound to meet with a strong— and, according to many of the treatment personnel, "unmanageable"— emotional reaction from parents; among other things, it so threatens basic life-values which they cherish for the child, such as physical attractiveness, vocational achievement, a good marriage, and, perhaps most of all, his being perceived and responded to in society as "normal, like everyone else." Moreover, to the extent to which the doctor feels some professional compunction to so inform the parents, the bustling, time-conscious work milieu of the hospital supports him in the convenient rationalization that, even were he to take the trouble, the family could not or would not understand what he had to tell them anyway. Therefore, in hedging, being evasive, equivocating, and cutting short his contact with the parents, the doctor was able to avoid "scenes" with them and having to explain to and comfort them, tasks, at least in the hospital, often viewed as onerous and time-consuming.

Second, since the parents had been told repeatedly during the first weeks of the child's illness that the outcome was subject to great uncertainty, it was not difficult for them, once having accepted the idea, to maintain and even to exaggerate it, particularly in those cases in which the child's progress fell short of full recovery. For, equivocally, uncertainty can be grounds for hope as well as despair; and when, for example, after six months of convalescence the child returned home crippled, the parents could and characteristically did interpret uncertainty to mean that he still stood a good chance of making a full and natural recovery in the indefinite future. The belief in a recuperative moratorium was held long after there was any real possibility of the child's making a full recovery, and with a number of families it had the unfortunate effect of diverting them from taking full advantage of available rehabilitation procedures and therapies. In fact, with few exceptions the parents typically mistook rehabilitation for cure, and, because little was done to correct this misapprehension, they often passively consented to a regimen prescribed for the child which they might have rejected had they known that it had nothing to do with effecting a cure.

Last, it must be noted that in the art (as opposed to the science and technique) of medicine, a sociologically inescapable facet of treatment—often irrespective of how much is clinically known or unknown— is frequently that of somehow getting the patient and his family to accept, "put up with," or "make the best of" the socially and physically disadvantageous consequences of illness. Both patient and family are understandably reluctant to do this at first, if for no other reason than that it usually entails a dramatic revaluation in identity and self-conception. Not only in paralytic poliomyelitis but in numerous other chronic and long-term illnesses, such as cardiac disease, cancer, tuberculosis, mental illness, and diabetes, such is usually the case. Depending on a number of variables, not the least of which are those of personality, the cultural background of the family, and the treatment setting, a number of stratagems besides that of rendering a full and frank diagnosis and prognosis (even when clinically known) are open to the physician who must carry the family through this difficult period. Whereas the evasiveness and equivocality of hospital treatment staff described here may not have been as skilled or effective a means for accomplishing this as others which come to mind, it must in fairness be recognized that there is still little agreement within medical circles on what practice should be in these circumstances. (The perennial debate on whether a patient and his family should be told that he is dying of cancer, and when and how much they should be told, is an extreme though highly relevant case in point.) And perhaps the easiest recourse of the hospital practitioner—who, organizationally, is better barricaded and further removed from the family than, for example, the neighborhood physician—is to avoid it altogether.[36]

You should ask yourself how closely these patterns are likely to mirror motivations and responses in legal practice. Just as observing the effects of a disease on a particular patient can lead to more and more certainty in prognosis, a lawyer's view of what will happen at trial takes more definite shape in the course of discovery, investigation, and discussions with opposing counsel. Should revised predictions always be communicated to the client, or is there a function to be served by keeping him or her in doubt about the outcome? Such problems, of course, must be resolved in the context of specific cases and in reference to the needs and dispositions of specific individuals. But you might want to at least consider the possibility that communications about uncertainty can slip into patterns geared far more to the needs of the professional than those he or she serves.

3. Clarifying the Client's Preferences

BINDER AND PRICE, LEGAL INTERVIEWING AND COUNSELING

148–53 (1977). *

The ultimate decision regarding which alternative should be chosen should be based upon the evaluation of which alternative is most likely to bring the *greatest client satisfaction*. If a decision is to be made on the basis of maximum client satisfaction, there first must be knowledge of the importance or value which the client attaches to each of the consequences involved. Only when the client's values are known can there be a determination of which alternative, on balance, will provide maximum client benefit. However, it is our belief that, by and large, lawyers cannot know what value clients really place on the various consequences. We therefore conclude that

36. Davis, *Uncertainty in Medical Prognosis: Clinical and Functional*, 66 AM. J. of SOC. 41, 42–45 (1960).

* Reprinted with permission of West Publishing Company.

lawyers usually cannot determine which alternative will provide maximum client satisfaction and that decisions should be left to the client.

Our belief about lawyers' inability to know what values clients place on various consequences is derived primarily from our clinical observations of clients' behavior during the decision making process. Our observations in regard to lawyers' inability to know clients' values include the following:

First of all, clients' values are uniquely personal. For example, the value one client attaches to the consqeuence of avoiding the strain of trial is generally different from the value other clients would attach to the same consequence. Second, it is often very difficult, if not impossible, for clients to precisely quantify the value they place on specific consequences. Thus, clients cannot usually say, even to themselves, such things as, "On a scale from one to ten, getting $2500 now has a value of plus 5; avoiding the strain of trial has a value of plus 2; however, giving up the opportunity to obtain an additional $5500 has a value of minus 5;" etc. All that clients can usually do is give general statements of the value they place on the various consequences. Thus, clients can sometimes quantify consequences to the extent of labeling them as "very important," "important," "not so important," etc. However, this quantifying process does not usually allow clients to distinguish between consequences which they see as fitting into the same general category of importance. Thus, typically, clients cannot distinguish between two or three consequences, each of which they see as "important," "not so important," etc. This inability to distinguish between consequences is particularly pronounced when the consequences are of different types. For instance, a client typically cannot distinguish between an "important" economic consequence and an "important" psychological consequence. When asked to rank or weigh the relative importance of such consequences, clients will typically say such things as, "I can't say which is more important. Getting an additional $1500 is important, but it's also important that I not be under a lot of stress. My friends say go for the additional money, but they don't have to face testifying in court. I can't say which is more important; they're both important."

Since clients usually cannot precisely identify for themselves what values they place on various consequences, clients generally cannot convey to their lawyers the unique personal values which they attach to the various consequences. Without access to the specific weights clients attach to the various consequences, lawyers usually are not able to decide which alternative, on balance, will provide *maximum client satisfaction.*

Additionally, in our experience deciding which alternative is most likely to provide the greatest benefit involves another unquantifiable self-assessment which generally cannot effectively be conveyed to the lawyer. Inherent in the weighing process is the consideration of the extent to which the client is willing to risk the negative consequences of one alternative in order to gain the positive consequences of another alternative. The willingness to take the risk depends not only on the weights the client attaches to various consequences, but also on the extent to which the client is "a risk avoider." Even when the odds are the same, and the potential gains and losses are the same, some people are more willing than others to take the gamble. However, the specific extent to which a given client is "a risk avoider," usually cannot meaningfully be conveyed to the lawyer.

In sum, clients are usually unable to communicate a precise description of the weights which they place on the probable consequences and an accurate sense of the degree to which they are "risk avoiders." In our opinion, without access to this information, the lawyer usually cannot determine what course of action would be best suited for the client. We therefore conclude that usually the lawyer should leave the final decision for the client to make on the basis of the client's own intuitive weighing process.

The foregoing analysis has been relatively abstract. At this point, an example may be helpful in illustrating why we have concluded that lawyers generally cannot know their clients' values, cannot know the degree to which their clients are "risk avoiders," and therefore usually cannot make decisions which provide maximum client satisfaction.

The example concerns a basic decision of whether to continue with litigation or settle. The example commences from a point at which the counseling process has already identified all of the pertinent consequences which the lawyer and client believe bear on the decision.

Arnold White has brought suit against the city for false arrest and imprisonment. The arrest occurred because a clerk in the local traffic court failed to note that Mr. White had appeared and paid a traffic citation. As a result of the clerk's error, a warrant was issued. Pursuant to the warrant, Mr. White was arrested as he left for work on a Thursday morning. Mr. White was incarcerated until Sunday evening when his family was finally able to raise money for bail. Before the civil action was instituted, the criminal charges of failure to appear were dismissed.

After the city filed its answer denying liability, each side served two sets of interrogatories and took one deposition. Mr. White's attorney fees and court costs to date have been respectively $640 and $100. The city has now offered $1,000 by way of settlement.

Mr. White's lawyer, Jackie Jones, has carefully analyzed the case and believes there is a good chance of obtaining a judgment for $3500. She believes a judgment for this amount is the most probable result at trial. Additionally she believes there is a small possibility the judgment could go as high as $5000, or as low as $500. In the lawyer's opinion, the city will definitely be held liable; the only issue is the amount of damages the jury will award. The projected additional costs of proceeding to trial, including attorney fees, are $800.

In analyzing the positive and negative consequences of the alternatives of trial and settlement, Mr. White and his lawyer have come up with the following:

SETTLEMENT ALTERNATIVE	LITIGATION ALTERNATIVE
Positive Consequences	Positive Consequences
Economic: (1) $1000 now. (2) No further court costs or attorney fees. (3) No loss of wages for time at trial. Social: (1) Improved relationship with spouse, who opposes putting more money into the suit. Psychological: (1) Avoid concern about the trial itself. (2) Obtain satisfaction of having city admit its error. (3) Avoid concern about ending up with less money than put into case.	Economic: (1) Retain good chance of $3500. (2) Small chance of $5000. Social: None Psychological: (1) Avoid feeling of having "chickened out." (2) Retain good chance of having satisfaction of proving city in error. (3) Satisfaction of having made the best possible effort to obtain reasonable compensation.
Negative Consequences	**Negative Consequences**
Economic: (1) Give up good chance at $3500. Social: None Psychological: (1) Feeling of having "chickened out." (2) Feeling of dissatisfaction because not compensated fairly.	Economic: (1) Give up sure $1000. (2) Take small risk of getting only $500. (3) Loss of additional $150 in wages to attend the trial. (4) Cost of additional $800 in attorney fees and court costs. Social: (1) Continued controversy with spouse about proceeding with the litigation. Psychological: (1) Retain concerns of going to trial. (2) Retain concern of ending up with less money than put into case.

[B8954]

Given the foregoing analysis of the positive and negative consequences, can the lawyer determine which alternative, litigation or settlement, would provide Mr. White with the greatest satisfaction? The answer probably must be "no." There is nothing in the listing of the consequences which provides a basis for evaluating which group of consequences, on balance, will give Mr. White the maximum benefit. There is nothing in the list of consequences that speaks about either the actual or relative importance of any consequence. For example, there is no indication of how important it is to Mr. White that he avoid the dissatisfaction of feeling less than fully compensated. Nor is there any information which provides a basis for deciding whether the alternative of proceeding to trial correlates with Mr. White's sense of what is an acceptable degree of risk to undertake.

However, what about asking Mr. White what importance he places on the various consequences? If the lawyer can ascertain from Mr. White what weights he would place on the various consequences, and what constitutes his sense of appropriate risk-taking, could the lawyer then decide which alternative is best for Mr. White? If Mr. White is like most people, any effort to obtain such information will be quite unsuccessful. Our experience indicates that even if Mr. White thinks carefully about the matter, he will not be able to specify what precise value he would place on each of the foregoing consequences. Mr. White may be able to say that certain consequences seem "important" and others "not so important," but he probably cannot attach precise degrees of importance to each specific consequence.

Moreover, though Mr. White may be able to specify the general importance of each of the foregoing consequences, he probably will not, if he is like most people, be able to distinguish between consequences of similar degrees of importance. Assume, for example, Mr. White attaches great importance to "improved relations with his spouse," to "retaining a good chance of recovering $3500," and to "avoiding the feeling of having 'chickened out'." If Mr. White is like most people, he will probably be unable to say whether the value of "retaining the good chance at $3500," together with the value of "avoiding the feeling of having 'chickened out'," are equivalent to, or greater than, the value placed on "improved relations with his spouse."

Similarly, in our experience, although Mr. White may have some general idea of the degree to which he is a risk avoider, he probably will be unable to say whether he wishes to apply his normal degree of risk avoidance in this case.

What clients generally seem to do in making decisions is to try to take into account the positive and negative consequences of each alternative and then, through an intuitive weighing process, decide which alternative, on balance, seems best. In the course of this intuitive process, the client brings into play his/her own values and sense of appropriate risk avoidance. Thus, in a situation like Mr. White's, this intuitive process might occur along the following lines:

> "Well, let's see, I'd hate to chicken out here, but I might end up with only $500 and I really can't afford that. My wife is really going to be mad if I keep going. If I lose it's going to be a mess, the court costs and attorney fees and a lot of aggravation. But there is a pretty good chance of getting $3500. With $3500 I could really do something. Should I gamble? I wish I knew. Um? $3500 sounds good and the chances are good. I guess I'll go for it."

In an intuitive weighing process such as that just described, there is no attempt to quantify the various consequences, nor is there an effort to systematically rank them. The pros and cons are lumped together and weighed, and the risk factor is also somehow included. The final decision rests on some imprecise accounting concept of what factors, on balance, emerge as important to the decision maker. Since decisions are typically made in the manner just described, we conclude that decisions should be left, in the main, to the client.

In our opinion, there is a second reason why decisions should be left to the client. Generally, it seems a client can best live with a decision, and follow through with a decision, if it is one the client has made. This may be true because a client-made decision usually more accurately reflects client values.

NOTES

1. *The Problem of Values*

Binder and Price add another argument to those we have already considered for the client's "right to decide". Since the lawyer can never know the client's true preferences, it is necessary (and desirable) to leave these rough, intuitive judgments to the client, who will, after all, have to live with them. Indeed, when the element of risk is added—*e. g.*, "do you prefer a settlement of $5,000 to a 20% chance of recovering $40,000?"—the subjective character of the decision becomes clear. Since the client's values are uniquely personal, the decisions must be his or her own.

Whatever your judgment on these assertions (some would argue that this subjectivity justifies more rather than less intervention), they do raise real questions about whether a client can be helped in the process of sorting out priorities. Are there ways to measure and compare values so that, in some sense, client decisions actually do "maximize satisfaction"? Must such choices be left to "intuition"? How can (i) preferences; (ii) predictions; and (iii) goals be combined in a particular case? The following material may at least provide some insight into the nature of the reasoning involved.

Decisions Under Certainty

In many decisions which lawyers help clients reach, risk plays little or no part. A client making a will, for example, may have to choose between leaving the bulk of his or her estate to X or to Y, and whether to use a certain form of trust, but can operate on the assumption that the preferred outcome will result once the choice is made. Even in litigated cases there will be some decisions of this nature— *e. g.*, whether to accept payment "in-kind" or insist on a dollar equivalent, which of a number of treatment programs to enter, etc. Since the outcomes of such decisions are *certain* to follow, the problem is to decide which outcome is preferred. Unfortunately, this is far more complex than it sounds. Anatol Rapoport summarizes some of the problems involved.

* * *

To deserve being called "rational" (as we usually understand the term), decisions must satisfy at least three criteria, namely consistency, instrumentality, and transitivity.

Consistency means that if we prefer outcome O_1 to outcome O_2, we do not at the same time prefer O_2 to O_1.

Instrumentality means that if we prefer outcome O_1 to outcome O_2, we also prefer action A_1 (if it guarantees O_1) to action A_2 (if it leads to O_2).

Transitivity means that if we prefer O_1 to O_2 and O_2 to O_3, we also prefer O_1 to O_3.

In the context of formal theory, these criteria are only a restatement of the definition of a rational decision. In the context of a prescriptive theory, they are rules for ordering preferences and choosing actions. What role do the criteria play in descriptive theory? Clearly they cannot be general descriptions of our gross observations of how people order preferences and choose actions. Violations of these principles are all too common, as the examples we are about to list will show. Confronted with such violations, we could, of course, draw the conclusion that the violators are not behaving "rationally." However, we can usually do better than that. We can often redefine the situation so as to remove the violations. Usually such a redefinition will involve a revision of the list of outcomes, so that outcomes which were first assumed to be simple turn out to be complex. If the redefinition of the decision situation removes the apparent violations of the criteria of rationality, the criteria are thereby vindicated. That is to say, people are seen to act more rationally than it first appeared. We might therefore say that an aim of descriptive decision theory is to describe people's decisions in such a way as to make them appear "rational."

Can such a theory be justified? Is it not true that people often act "irrationally"? We must take care here to distinguish between different meanings of "rational." People do, in fact, often act irrationally in the sense that their actions lead to outcomes which they themselves deplore. However, our definition of rationality was in terms of extremely weak criteria. Such "rationality" is by no means to be identified with prudence or wisdom or intelligence. The criteria we have offered are only different aspects of consistency. They are nothing but a minimal framework within which decisions must be made in order to make *some* sense. They leave the widest latitude to the decision-maker's perception of the situation and to his value system. In this way, the axioms define the task of descriptive theory: to discover the perceptual framework and the value system of the decision-maker, in the light of which his decisions will make sense.

VIOLATIONS OF THE CRITERIA OF RATIONALITY

Consistency seems to be violated when a decision-maker changes his mind for no apparent reason. At times, however, we discover additional features of the situation which make the change of preference understandable. If we can *codify* these features, that is, state a rule which governs the changes of preference, the consistency criterion is restored. What happens is that more outcomes appear in the situation than were originally discerned.

Suppose a man, confronted with a menu, sometimes chooses meat and sometimes fish. We could describe this "inconsistency" to momentary shifts of preference; that is, essentially to whim. Choices dictated by whim are by definition not rational. It may happen, however, that we discover perfectly consistent patterns: The man orders fish only on Fridays and meat on all other days. The two outcomes "eating meat" and "eating fish" have split into four; namely "meat on Friday," "fish on Friday," "meat on non-Friday," and "fish on non-Friday." Of these, the second of the first pair is preferred, but the first of the second pair. The inconsistency has disappeared.

Instrumentality is violated when a decision-maker seemingly chooses an action which leads to a less desirable instead of to a more desirable outcome. Often such decisions cease to appear to be violations if we discover on closer examination that decisions have side effects, not taken into account in the outcomes. If we observe that a firm decides on a course of action which leads to smaller rather than larger net profit, we may conjecture that the decision has other less obvious concomitants. For example, public relations, potential for future growth, etc. When these are taken into account, the action may turn out to lead to the most preferred outcome.

* * *

We can imagine another situation in which . . . transitivity is violated. Suppose our decision-maker is not a single individual but a three-man committee, which makes its decisions by a majority vote. Call the members of the committee Potter, Andrews, and Fox. Let Potter prefer the outcomes . . . the order O_1–O_2–O_3; Andrews, in the order O_2–O_3–O_1; and Fox, in the order O_3–O_1–O_2.

As an illustration imagine that the task of the committee (appointed by the governing board of a country club) is to decide on recommending an expenditure. The alternatives are O_1: to build a clubhouse with a bar; O_2: to build a clubhouse without a bar; and O_3: to build no clubhouse. Potter is a spendthrift. He prefers O_1 to O_2 and O_2 to O_3. Andrews is a teetotaler. He wants a clubhouse without a bar (O_2) but rather than having one with a bar (O_1), he would prefer having no clubhouse at all (O_3). Fox is a tightwad and a sop. He would rather spend no money at all (O_3); but if money is to be spent, he wants a bar (O_1). To him a clubhouse without a bar (O_2) is a total loss. All these preferences are shown in Table 1.

Members of Committee	Decreasing Preference →		
P	O_1	O_2	O_3
A	O_2	O_3	O_1
F	O_3	O_1	O_2

Table 1

[B8953]

We see by the table that the committee prefers O_1 over O_2 by majority vote, since Potter and Fox prefer them in that order. Also O_2 is preferred to O_3 by majority vote, since Potter and Andrews so prefer them. And also O_3 is preferred to O_1 by majority vote, since Andrews and Fox are also a majority. The committee's preference order is therefore O_1–O_2–O_3–O_1. Again the criterion of transitivity is violated.

A similar situation can arise when an individual must make comparisons among objects on several "dimensions" at once. For example, O_1, O_2, and O_3 in Table 1 can be three oranges; and P, A, and F, three different bases of comparison, e. g., price, appearance, and flavor. The oranges are preferred in the order O_1–O_2–O_3 on the basis of price (O_1 being the cheapest), in the order O_2–O_3–O_1 on the basis of appearance, and in the order O_3–O_1–O_2 on the basis of flavor. If the chooser simply counts the number of aspects in which one orange rates above another, he will rank the oranges in the order O_1–O_2–O_3–O_1 and so will violate transitivity.

Thus difficulties arise even in the simplest decision problems, namely, in decisions under certainty. The most common difficulties stem from the presence of incomparable components of outcomes. They arise both in prescriptive and in descriptive theories of rational decision. Attempts to get around such difficulties constitute the so-called theory of utility. In this theory, it is assumed that all aspects of outcomes have a common scale of comparison. That is to say, *numerical* values (positive or negative) are assigned to the aspects, and it is assumed that these values can be algebraically added to ascertain the total utility of an outcome. If the orange chooser can assign such values to price, appearance, and flavor and add them, his problem reduces to that of comparing three numbers (utilities). He can then choose the orange with the largest utility. If utilities of different *people* can be added, the members of the committee can do the same. This is actually done when decisions in boxing matches or in beauty contests are made on the basis of total points assigned to contestants by the different members of a jury.[37]

37. A. Rapoport, STRATEGY AND CONSCIENCE 7–11 (1964).

The problem of "non-comparability", of course, is common in legal work as well. The question is whether there is any numerical value (utility) which can be assigned to each attribute of an alternative that "matters". If this is possible, the client, aided by the lawyer, adds these values and selects the alternative having the highest total.

In many cases, a natural measure of utility is money; delay "costs money" and may be "worth" a smaller settlement figure; even anxiety and inconvenience may have a price tag. In other instances, there is no measure easily translated into quantifiable terms. In either case, the problem of finding and combining measures which truly reflect the client's preferences remains the same.

Let us look at a case involving a choice between two alternatives that must be compared in terms of a number of attributes, only some of which can be quantified. It is a divorce case in which your client, the husband (H), must decide which of two settlement offers he prefers. Assume that either alternative is preferable to going to trial. The choices might be laid out on a matrix as follows:

Attributes of the Outcomes

Alternatives	Alimony	Custody	Visitation	Furnishings
Offer #1	H pays $200/mo.	W	Every other Sunday	W keeps furnishings
Offer #2	H pays $400/mo.	W	Every Sunday, Two weeks in summer	H keeps furnishings

[B8957]

How do you help the client make this choice? Is there any way, when dealing with such intangible and emotion-laden consequences, to help the client sort out the "value" he attaches to each of them? Is less alimony "worth" the furnishings and less visitation? Can the furnishings themselves (which would get very little on the market but are desired by the client) be valued in a way which actually reflects the client's preferences? How does a lawyer give meaning to the "trade-offs" and "equivalents" inevitably involved here?

One approach would be to have the client state his preferences in regard to each of these attributes, then try to rank the attributes in order of importance. But as Rapoport points out, preferences may shift depending on which attributes are compared. Another possibility is to reduce all attributes of the choice to a single attribute which is measurable.[38] Since alimony is expressed in quantifiable terms, this would mean finding out how much more alimony the client might be willing to pay in order to have other perceived advantages

---

38. The authors are indebted for this idea to Professor Philip Heymann of the Harvard Law School, who uses the term "successive limited comparisons" to describe this process.

of the choices involved. (We will assume that dollars do express his utility for money and that he wishes, *other things being equal*, to minimize this expense).

As to the visitation category, the questions for the client would be: "With offer #1 as a starting point, how much more alimony would you be willing to pay each month to have the visitation rights contained in offer #2? Suppose the client says $100 per month. The matrix with this hypothetical option would then look as follows:

Alternatives	Alimony	Custody	Visitation	Furnishings
Offer #1 (revised)	H pays $300/mo.	W	Every Sunday, Two weeks in summer	W Keeps
Offer #2	H pays $400/mo.	W	Every Sunday, Two weeks in summer	H Keeps [B8956]

To equalize the final category, the hypothetical question would be, "With the level of alimony and the visitation rights in **Offer 1**, as we've revised it, how much more alimony would you be willing to pay to retain ownership of the furnishings?" Assuming the client says $50 per month, the matrix would look like this:

Alternatives	Alimony	Custody	Visitation	Furnishings
Offer #1 (Revised)	H pays $350/mo.	W	Every Sunday, Two weeks in summer	H keeps
Offer #2	H pays $400/mo.	W	Every Sunday, Two weeks in summer	H keeps [B8955]

Thus, with every category except alimony equalized, we can identify Offer #1 (which *still* has a lower alimony figure) as the client's preferred alternative. You might not agree with the client's valuations (*e. g.*, you might feel he should be willing to pay more to visit his children more often) and if this exercise were done again, or with a different measure (*e. g.*, numbers of visitations) his decision might be different, but in some sense this choice would reflect his actual values and desires.

Obviously, such an approach is not limited to decisions under certainty: some clients might find it helpful to equalize both risky and non-risky alternatives in this way. On the other hand, there may be very few situations when it can or should be used at all. As Binder and Price point out, clients often do simply throw up their hands and say "I don't know which is more important", and many will quite properly resist attaching a "price" to every attribute of particular choices.[39] Nevertheless, a lawyer skilled and interested in helping

39. The concept of utility, of course, is of considerably greater value in de-   veloping normative models of decision-making than in describing the way

people make decisions is likely to find that *with some clients, in some situations,* it will be possible to help sort our preferences in just such a systemic way. This is simply one example of the kind of approach to this problem which may be worth some experimentation.

Decisions Under Risk

More typically, most of the major decisions that clients must make in litigated cases involve risky outcomes. This adds considerably to the complexity of the decision task. In decisions under certainty, once preferences have been determined the choice is clear; the decision-maker simply selects the course of action that leads to the preferred outcome. When the element of risk is added to the picture, however, preferences have somehow to be combined with probabilities. No matter how much a client "prefers" the consequence of acquittal, he or she might be ill-advised to go to trial if chances of acquittal are slim. The following excerpt briefly describes some of the approaches that have been devised to deal with these problems:

* * *

. . . In decision under risk, as in decision under certainty, the individual knows with certainty all of the alternatives. But in risky decision, at least one of the alternatives leads to a set of consequences with more than one member, the consequences being mutually exclusive. The probability of occurrence of each of the consequences of each set is known. Thus, for example, an individual might be offered a choice between two alternatives with the following respective consequences: (a) receiving with certainty $2, or (b) the probability of .15 of receiving $10 and of .85 of receiving $1. One view of long standing is that such choices involving risk should be made in such a way as to maximize *expected value.* The expected value of a set of consequences is obtained by multiplying each consequence by its probability of occurrence and summing these products across all members of the set. In the example just given, the expected value of the consequence of the first alternative is $2 ($1 \times $2 = 2), and the expected value of the set of consequences of the second alternative is $2.35 ($.15 \times $10 + .85 \times $1 = 2.35). Hence, to maximize expected value the individual would choose the second alternative.

A variety of evidence, however, exists to show that in many decisions under risk individuals do not maximize expected value. Consider, for example, the St. Petersburg paradox (Luce & Raiffa, 1957). How much would you be willing to pay to play the following game: A fair coin is flipped repeatedly. If it comes up heads on the first throw, you receive $2; if it comes up tails on the first throw and heads on the second, you receive $4; if tails on the first two throws and heads on the third, $8. In other words, the payoff is 2^n where n is the number

people actually make comparisons. In addition, utilities, too, are affected by the interaction. See the discussion at note 20 in Chapter One, *supra* at pages 60–61.

of the throw upon which a head first occurs. The expected value may be computed by:

$$\tfrac{1}{2} \times \$2 + \tfrac{1}{4} \times \$4 + \tfrac{1}{8} \times \$8 \quad . \quad . \quad ., \text{ or}$$
$$\$1 + \$1 + \$1 \quad . \quad . \quad . \quad .$$

Since this is an infinite series, the expected value of the bet is clearly infinite. No one, however, has yet been willing to pay anything more than a rather modest sum to play this game.

Consideration of this paradox and of the fact that people buy insurance even though the seller makes a profit led Bernoulli (1738) to suggest that individuals choose so as to maximize not *expected value,* but *expected utility.* Although Bernoulli's suggestion was made more than 200 years ago, the development of the theory of decision under risk has occurred largely within the past 20 years. Major impetus to this development was given by publication in 1944 of *Theory of Games and Economic Behavior* by John von Neumann and Oskar Morgenstern.

The theory of riskless decision assumes that man can weakly order his preferences among all available states. Although in retrospect it appears simple, an important contribution of von Neumann and Morgenstern (1944) was that of pointing out that only a minor addition to this assumption leads clearly to the reintroduction of cardinal utility. The addition involves assuming that the individual can also completely order his preferences among sets of consequences, where the probability of occurrence of each member of each set is known. If this assumption is valid, then it necessarily follows that scales for measuring cardinal utility can be constructed.

Suppose, for example, that one could determine experimentally that an individual is indifferent between the certainty of receiving $5 on the one hand, or on the other hand [a] .3 chance of receiving nothing and a .7 chance of receiving $10. If the utility of $0 is arbitrarily defined as 0 utiles and of $10 as 10 utiles, the utility of $5 may be determined. (Such arbitrary definition is permissible, since cardinal utility is measured only up to a linear transformation.) It is calculated as follows:

$$U(\$5) = .3 \; U(\$0) + .7 \; U(\$10) = .3(0) + .7(10) = 7.$$

The cardinal utility of $5 is 7 utiles. By employing this procedure with varying probabilities and using the utilities previously found, it is possible to determine the utility of any other amount of money and hence to construct a cardinal scale of utility.

Although apparently simple, this conceptual contribution has a variety of important implications. . . .[40]

The ability to construct a cardinal scale of utility, as this discussion suggests, allows us to calculate the "expected utility" of alternatives having more or less risky outcomes. The von Neumann and Morgenstern measure, moreover, takes the decision-maker's attitude toward risk into account, so that it would be unnecessary, once

40. Taylor, *Decision Making and Problem Solving,* in HANDBOOK OF OR-   GANIZATIONS 52–54 (March, ed., 1965).

these utilities are determined, to consider criteria other than maximizing expected utility in making the ultimate choice.

Although one would not go through such calculations with the client, let us consider how this approach might work in practice by looking again at the criminal case we discussed earlier. There our client was struggling with the probabilities of jail or probation on a plea of guilty or on a conviction after trial. Assume (for purposes of simplifying this discussion) that he has now been assured that if he pleads guilty he will either be given probation or the minimum sentence and that our original probability estimates still hold. If he goes to trial he faces the following possible consequences:

> acquittal
> maximum sentence 15 years
> minimum sentence of three years
> probation
> indeterminate sentence (not more than five years at discretion of correctional authorities).

Although we might posit that the client would rank acquittal as the best outcome (1.) and a 15 year sentence as the worst (.0), it is not certain how he would rank the other outcomes, and how *much* he might prefer one to another. If we wanted to ascertain the *extent* of difference between these consequences, we would need a way of translating those preferences into a cardinal scale of values. What von Neumann and Morgenstern suggested as a way to do this was to hypothesize a lottery among these possibilities (called a "standard gamble").

Specifically, the client would be asked what chance of obtaining the best outcome (with a corresponding chance of receiving the worst) he would consider equivalent to each of the outcomes in between. For example, he might be indifferent to receiving a three-year sentence or participating in a lottery giving him a 20% chance of acquittal and an 80% chance of maximum sentence. This alternative would then be assigned a utility of .2. Systematically using this procedure, his utilities for the whole set of outcomes might line up like this:

acquittal	1.0
probation	.6
indeterminate sentence	.3
three year sentence	.2
maximum sentence	.0

His utilities for the possibilities associated with pleading guilty would be:

Probation	.6
Three year sentence	.2

Note that this does not resolve our decisional problem. We are still faced with the following probabilities:

Alternatives	Possible Outcomes	Utility	Prob.
Plea of Guilty	Probation	.6	.6
	Three Year Sentence	.2	.4
Trial	Acquittal	1	.3
	Probation	.6	.2
	Indeterminate Sentence	.3	.2
	Three Year Sentence	.2	.2
	15 Year Sentence	0	.1

[B8958]

If we then calculated the expected utility of these choices, our calculations would look like this:

Alternatives	Possible Outcomes	Utility	Probability	Expected Utility
Plead Guilty	Probation	.6	.6	.36
	Three Year Sentence	.2	.4	.08
				TOTAL .44
Go to Trial	Acquittal	1.0	.3	.3
	Probation	.6	.2	.12
	Indeterminate Sentence	.3	.2	.06
	Three Year Sentence	.2	.2	.04
	15 Year Sentence	.0	.1	.0
				TOTAL .52

[B8959]

If the decision simply involves "maximizing expected utility," the choice would be clear. Since the expected utility of going to trial (.52) is greater than the expected utility of pleading guilty (.44), we would choose trial. But is it as simple as that? If you were the defendant, would *you* be willing to make so important a decision on the basis of these calculations, even if the process by which they were reached seem "rational"?

One of the problems, of course, is that we may have been wrong in assessing the probabilities. As we have discussed, the probability of an event does not inhere in the event itself, but is simply our own subjective "best guess" as to how likely it is to occur. Moreover, probabilities only have real meaning *in the long run.* Any of the possible outcomes could eventuate in a particular case, so that even if our assessments are reasonably accurate, a 10% chance of receiving the maximum sentence might loom very large to our client. These problems, of course, will be present in any approach to decisions under risk.   There are other problems as well.   Rapoport discusses them as follows:

> From the point of view of parsimony, that is, of minimizing the number of independent assumptions upon which to build a theory of rational decision, the advantage of the von Neumann-Morgenstern definition of utility is unquestioned.   The difficult task of assigning numerical values to outcomes has been replaced by a seemingly easier one of *ordering* outcomes.   We must keep in mind, however, that this was done only at the cost of admitting all possible risky outcomes as objects of choice.   This extension of the range of choices makes trivial the task of prescriptive theory.   This is not surprising, since the proponents of the utility theory based on choices between risky outcomes were primarily interested in constructing a *formal* theory of rational decision, not a prescriptive one, least of all a descriptive one.   .   .   .   They *started* at the point where the problem of risky choice had been presumably already solved.   In other words they bypassed rather than answered the question of what it is that people maximize (if anything) when they make risky choices.
>
> In the scheme of von Neumann and Morgenstern, people are simply *assumed* to maximize something and that something is *called* "utility."   The resulting utility theory is a fine starting point for the theory of games, but it is useless as a prescriptive theory of risky choice, as we shall now show.
>
> A decision-maker is faced with a choice of two actions A and A'. Each leads to a set of possible outcomes.   Suppose the decision-maker knows all the probabilities of the outcomes.   He wishes to know what action to take.   An "old-fashioned" utility theory man, invited as a consultant, would first try to ascertain the numerical "worths" of the outcomes.   If he is given these by the decision-maker, he will compute the expected utilities associated with A and A' and will recommend the action with the greater expected utility.   If asked why he recommends the particular action, he might reply somewhat like this: "I always recommend the action associated with the largest expected utility of my clients.   If my clients follow this advice and stick to the principle of maximizing expected utility, then *in the long run* they will have gained almost certainly   .   .   .   more than they would have gained had they been guided by any other policy of choosing among alternative actions."   Thus the "old-fashioned" utility theorist would be doing two things to earn his consultant's fee.   He would be giving advice on how to apply a general principle of choosing among alternatives (whether the advice is sound in all cases is not our concern here) ; and (2) he would be performing a calculation.   (The triviality of this particular problem is irrelevant; in other cases calculations may well need the help of a professional.)
>
> Now let us see what advice the "modern" utility theorist would give and whether he would be earning his consultant's fee.   For him it is possible to ascertain the utilities of the outcomes only if the decision-maker answers *all* questions pertaining to choices among these risky outcomes.   But the choice between A and A' is itself a choice between two risky outcomes.   Therefore the *decision-maker* will have to

tell *the consultant* which of the two risky outcomes he prefers if the
consultant is to estimate the decision-maker's utility scale. But this
is precisely the question which the decision-maker asked the consultant in the first place, namely, whether he should prefer A or A'!
Of what use is this consultant to him?

It is clear, then, that in the context of decision under risk, the
von Neumann-Morgenstern utility theory is useless. It assumes as
given what, according to the theory of decision under risk, is supposed to be calculated from *other* givens. If there is to be a non-
trivial prescriptive theory of risky choices, utility must be defined in
some other way independent of risky choices. Several such definitions
readily suggest themselves. One could, for example, relate utilities
of outcomes to a conventional "basic scale," for example, money, or
labor measured in some conventional units. In decisions made according to democratic traditions, it is usual to rank alternatives according
to the numbers of votes received. This is only an ordinal ordering.
But in interval scale can also be constructed, for example, by taking
into account the actual numbers of votes cast for each alternative.
Alternatives involving quantitatively measurable results (efficiency
of operation, lives saved, degree of approach to specified goals, etc.)
can also be rated numerically on conventionally established scales.

Every one of these methods is based on some agreement, namely,
to take a unit of money or a vote or a percentage point of efficiency
as a utile. .   .[41]

Notwithstanding these reservations, it may be that the process of
attaching standard gamble utilities will be helpful to both you and
your client. The lawyer, like the modern utility theorist, would do
no more than "ask the right questions," but questions are often critical in sorting out preferences. At least you ought to be aware of what
you are up to.

Decisions Under Uncertainty

There are certain kinds of risky decisions where the concept of
"maximizing expected utility" can be quite helpful. Most of the
decision models use examples involving successive tosses of a coin,
or rolls of dice, or selecting cards from a 52-card pack. When there
is a "long run"—when a particular choice can be repeated over and
over again—the concept of probability becomes much more meaningful. Thus an insurance company can take the risk of paying $50,-
000 to a homeowner who has paid only one premium, because statistical probabilities can be relied on to assure that the company will
still make a profit in the long run. From the homeowner's point of
view the situation looks quite different; no matter how unlikely it
is that disaster will strike, that consequence is so grave that avoiding
it is "worth" paying the insurance premium year after uneventful

41. A. Rapoport, STRATEGY AND
CONSCIENCE 19–21 (1964).

year. In entering any *single contract*, then, neither the insurer nor the insured knows what will *actually happen* to a given piece of insured property. It may be totally destroyed in a few months, or it may survive well beyond the lifetime of the homeowner. While the insurance company is making a decision under risk—with known probabilities—the homeowner is essentially making a decision under conditions of uncertainty.[42] What concerns the homeowner is the *possibility* that disaster will strike, and he or she therefore makes provision for that contingency.

It should be apparent that this one-time-only type of decision is what is most frequently faced in legal counseling. There *are* "institutional" litigants; insurance companies can, again, establish standard settlements for certain "types" of claims. But for most individual clients—those in particular need of counseling—the uncertainty of the outcome is an overriding factor.

On the other hand, uncertainty cannot and should not make you powerless to act. If you work hard with the foregoing material, you may find that it makes the following contributions:

—By dealing explicitly with the problem of uncertainty, it affirms that "good judgment" is not synonymous with "being sure," and encourages the decision-maker to be open about the extent to which his or her judgments are based on estimates of likely outcomes.

42. There is a body of material dealing with decisions under conditions of uncertainty, and a number of prescriptive models have emerged. The approaches that have been suggested include the following:

Upon what basis *should* an individual choose among alternatives when he has no knowledge of the probability that any given state of nature in fact exists? One suggestion is that he should *maximin utility*, i. e., that he should choose that alternative which will maximize his minimum utility. In other words, he should consider all consequences of each alternative and then choose that alternative whose worst outcome has the highest utility. (This has been described from another point of view as the *minimax* principle. If one thinks of outcomes as involving possible loss, then one selects that alternative which has as its worst outcome the loss which is smallest, i. e., he minimaxes loss.)

* * *

Both *maximin utility* and *minimax regret* are highly conservative principles in that, with respect to each alternative, they concentrate upon the state having the worst consequence. In contrast, Hurwicz . . has proposed a principle of choice which involves essentially a weighted combination of the best and worst consequences of each alternative. . . . [referred to as] . . . the *pessimism-optimism* index . . .

. . . [S]till another normative procedure for decision under uncertainty [is the] *principle of insufficient reason* [which] states that if there is no reason to believe that one event from an exhaustive set of mutually exclusive events is more likely to occur than another, then the events should be judged equally probable. Acceptance of this principle leads to treating decision under uncertainty as simply a problem in decision under risk. For each alternative all consequences are regarded as equally probable. Hence, the decision-maker can determine the expected utility of each alternative and then choose the one which maximizes expected utility.

Taylor, *supra* note 40 at 56–58.

Unfortunately, we have found none of these usable at all in dealing with the practical problems of decision in lawyer work.

—By requiring clear criteria to be used in choosing alternatives, it emphasizes that no single measure—such as monetary payoff—will be adequate for all decisions, and that some way of incorporating non-monetary values and subjective preferences must be found.

—By focusing on the formulation and evaluation of specific alternatives, it may also stimulate the creation of new options.

—By identifying discreet steps in the decision-making process, it allows complex decision problems to be broken down into manageable components that can be subjected to separate analysis.

—By requiring that assumptions be made explicit, it focuses on the need for full information before a decision is made.

—By attempting to attach degrees of probability to the various outcomes involved in a given choice, it also encourages the collection of data necessary for accurate prediction and for meaningful evaluation of alternatives with uncertain consequences.

Ask yourself whether these considerations are important ones in lawyer-client judgments, and to what extent they can inform choices made on a daily basis. It may be that such an approach is valuable in the context of preparation—drafting pleadings, thinking through general trial or negotiation strategies, or planning—but misleading and disfunctional in the day-to-day intercourse of lawyer work. That is, for a lawyer to think of the choice of question in an interview, the things to say at the bargaining table, the tone of voice to use in an argument in these terms may so "objectify" the interpersonal dimensions of these processes as to restrict one's capacity to act within them. Moreover, going through calculations of this sort in the course of counseling would probably distort the client's attempts to make his or her desires known to counsel. It may be that the very posture that this analysis takes towards judgment limits its usefulness in "common sense" situations.

Nevertheless, whatever "decision rule" makes sense to you or your client, you ought to be aware of the degree to which judgment is a function of taken-for-granted realities. Any mode of practical judgment is a prison if the decider can't step far enough outside it to describe and evaluate its premises and assumptions. If client autonomy is what is truly valued, it may be that lawyers will have to pay much more attention than they have so far to the way client concerns may be realistically translated into practical choice.

———

2. *Alternative Procedures: On Muddling Through and Related Approaches.*

We should not leave this aspect of our inquiries without pointing out a number of other decisional procedures which have evolved from or in response to the models we have been explaining here. Each of these recognizes that human beings are not totally or even largely "maximizers," but have limited capacity, limited tolerance for uncertainty, limited commitment to and need for comprehensive search and evaluation of alternatives. The human animal needs ways of simplifying as well as clarifying choices. From this perspective a number of alternative procedures have been suggested:

Sub-Maximizing

If a careful weighing of all alternatives, variables and probabilities is maximizing, submaximizing calls for doing less than that. While all choice involves something less than the comprehensive deal, submaximizing involves eliminating alternatives that do not satisfy certain minimal criteria or focussing on only the first few that come to mind. For example, if the risk of an unfavorable verdict exceeds a certain level (of probability), or a course of action involves unacceptable costs, that alternative is simply eliminated. In practice, going to trial is often eliminated as a matter of course as too "risky" or too "costly" (the continuation of higher costs, long delays, substantial inconvenience and inadequate training of trial lawyers may be explained to some extent by this attitude) and choices narrowed to how the most favorable agreement can be negotiated without producing deadlock and litigation.[43]

Rule Following

Another approach is to apply pre-established rules of thumb to typical situations. That is, some prior calculus is used as the criterion for judgment and the wheel is not "reinvented" on each choice. Although there are still interpretative and other decisions to be made, the use of prior "tried and true" solutions is a useful way of sorting through the large amount of data and number of choices involved in typical legal decisions. Trial manuals are full of these simple and sometimes useful maxims and bits of folklore. Even if they do no more than provide a quick basis for comparison, such rules of thumb are well worth searching out.

Satisficing

This procedure involves a much more limited search and choice process than we have been exploring. Stated simply, it suggests that the decision maker (i) address only those problems which surface— that is, which generate a need for change of the status quo—and (ii) scan alternatives which come to mind sequentially until one is found which meets the minimal requirements of the situation. The decision maker seeks not the best alternative, but the first one that

---

43. Sub-maximizing also involves dealing separately and early with as many sub-problems as possible. The choices and actions involved provide information and are often less costly and more reversible. Although this can only be loosely called an alternative approach to decision (a decision rule and weighting process is still undertaken within each subproblem), it does express a less global orientation to the problem of judgment than we have been discussing.

"works". Although this approach is rarely prescribed, it may be that this is the way most choices in government organizations, business—and law—are made.

Muddling Through

A final approach, actually a combination of all of the above, attempts to reduce the strain and difficulty of maximization by developing a less comprehensive and more adaptable model known as "muddling through". Its formulator, Charles Lindblom, describes it as follows:

> I propose . . . to clarify and formalize . . . a method [of decision making] described as the method of successive limited comparisons. I will contrast it with . . . what might be called the rational-comprehensive method. More impressionistically . . . they could be characterized as the branch method and the root method, the former continually building out from the current situation, step-by-step and by small degrees; the latter starting from fundamentals anew each time, building on the past only as experience is embodied in a theory, and always prepared to start completely from the ground up.
>
> . . . Side by side, in simplest terms [the two models compare as follows]:

Rational-Comprehensive (Root)	Successive Limited Corporations (Branch)
1a. Clarification of values or objectives distinct from and usually prerequisite to empirical analysis of alternative policies.	1b. Selection of value goals and empirical analysis of the needed action are not distinct from one another but are closely intertwined.
2a. Policy-formulation is therefore approached through means-end analysis: First the ends are isolated, then the means to achieve them are sought.	2b. Since means and ends are not distinct, means-end analysis is often inappropriate or limited.
3a. The test of a "good" policy is that it can be shown to be the most appropriate means to desired ends.	3b. The test of a "good" policy is typically that various analysts find themselves directly agreeing on a policy (without their agreeing that it is the most appropriate means to an agreed objective).
4a. Analysis is comprehensive; every important relevant factor is taken into account.	4b. Analysis is drastically limited: (i) Important possible outcomes are neglected. (ii) Important alternative potential policies are neglected. (iii) Important affected values are neglected.

	Successive Limited Corporations
Rational-Comprehensive (Root)	(Branch)
5a. Theory is often heavily relied upon.	5b. A succession of comparisons greatly reduces or eliminates reliance on theory.

*   *   *

[Thus] a wise decision-maker consequently expects that his policies will achieve only part of what he hopes and at the same time will produce unanticipated consequences he would have preferred to avoid. If he proceeds through a succession of incremental changes, he avoids serious lasting mistakes in several ways.

In the first place, past sequences of policy steps have given him knowledge about the probable consequences of further similar steps. Second, he need not attempt big jumps towards his goals that would require predictions beyond his or anyone else's knowledge, because he never expects his policy to be a final resolution of a problem. His decision is only one step, one that if successful can quickly be followed by another. Third, he is in effect able to test his previous predictions as he moves on to each further step. Lastly, he often can remedy a past error fairly quickly—more quickly than if policy proceeded through more distinct steps widely spaced in time.

Compare this comparative analysis of incremental changes with the aspiration to employ theory in the root method. Man cannot think without classifying, without subsuming one experience under a more general category of experiences. The attempt to push categorization as far as possible and to find general propositions which can be applied to specific situations is what I refer to with the word "theory." Where root analysis often leans heavily on theory in this sense, the branch method does not.

The assumption of root analysis is that theory is the most systematic and economical way to bring relevant knowledge to bear on a specific problem. Granting the assumption, an unhappy fact is that we do not have adequate theory to apply to problems in any policy area, although theory is more adequate in some areas—monetary policy, for example—than in others. Comparative analysis, as in the branch method, is sometimes a systematic alternative to theory.[44]

Which of these approaches best describes the way you and your clients approach choices? To what degree to you "sub-maximize", satisfice or muddle through? Is this what you ought to be doing? Is there an "existing set of choices" with which judgment in legal situations begins? Can/do you use typical solutions to certain problems as the starting point in making choices?

In considering these issues, it is important to remember that the literature on decision theory is highly abstracted from the human situations and relationships in which choices are inevitably embedded. The procedures we have described offer some guidance and are a

---

44. Lindblom, *The Science of Muddling Through,* 19 PUB.ADMIN.REV. 80–81, 86–87 (1959).

check on decisions arrived at in less orderly, more intuitive ways. The best test of their usefulness, of course, will be the extent to which they illuminate the possible, the actual, and the desirable in your work.

4. Coping with Ambiguities and Emotions

SHAFFER, DEATH, PROPERTY AND LAWYERS

94–100, 263 (1970).

Counseling wills clients is a matter of human empathy for a man who is being forced to confront his own death. There is little literature available concerning the testamentary counseling relationship itself. Valuable analogy may be found, however, in Carl Rogers' description of successful, client-centered counseling (in Porter's book on therapeutic counseling):

1. The individual comes for help.

2. The helping situation is usually defined.

3. The counselor encourages free expression of feeling in regard to the problem.

4. The counselor accepts, recognizes, and clarifies these negative feelings.

5. When the individual's negative feelings have been quite fully expressed, they are followed by the faint and tentative expressions of the positive impulses which make for growth.

6. The counselor accepts and recognizes the positive feelings which are expressed, in the same manner in which he has accepted and recognized the negative feeling. In this type of situation, insight and self-understanding come bubbling through spontaneously.

7. This insight, this understanding of the self and acceptance of the self is the next important aspect of the whole process. It provides the basis on which the individual can go ahead to new levels of integration.

8. Intermingled with this process of insight—is a process of clarification of possible decisions, possible courses of action.

9. Then comes one of the fascinating aspects of such therapy, the initiation of minute, but highly significant positive actions.

These are only the first nine of 12 steps described by Rogers. The purpose of the three remaining steps, which I would not claim for a wills lawyer, is to lead the client to a final state of "integrated positive action" and a relaxation of dependence on the counselor. It is quite enough for lawyers to aspire to the "minute but highly significant" moment when the client finds relief in seizing the future through his property. This future includes his own death, of course, but I believe that one way the client reconciles himself to death is by making death a part of his life. This is accomplished when the client plans for death's consequences to his property-personality and to his family.

Testamentary application of the first five steps in Rogers' scheme is a matter of the client's expressing the real reasons he wants to make a will. My study of will-interviews indicates that these reasons will probably be negative. An illustrative, but not exhaustive, listing of the client's feelings is presented below. The accompanying quoted language illustrating these feelings is from my tape-recorded young-family client interviews and from the answers to my questions . . . above, on why people came to hear me talk about wills.

1. He is aware that he might die suddenly. (Young-family client: "What if something happens, supposing, now, when we're going home, there. You know, something happened now.")

2. He is aware that his children might be orphaned. (Young-family client: "It's so—kind of a sad discussion to think who would take care of them. . . .") (Member of audience said he was interested in wills because "I have two sons and I would like to protect their future should I die before they are able to care for themselves.")

3. He is aware that he has liabilities, or projects that must be carried on, and he hopes that supporting persons will carry them on. (Young-family client: Q. "Do you have insurance on your land contract?" A. "No, because I'm sure, if anything happens to us, that her folks will take care of it.")

4. He is afraid that the delays of the law will complicate the support of his family. (Young-family client: "There's a possibility that, if I would just turn over everything to Hanna's parents, that money would be a long time in making that step. . . . It would be tied up for some time.")

5. He is aware that property which is especially significant to him will somehow survive his death. (Young-family client: ". . . as long as the jewelry and the paintings and the art objects go to my daughter. Or my son. The rest of it—I don't care.") (Members of my wills audience said they were interested in wills "for my own benefit" or "to help my husband.")

6. He is aware that his death will sever the expression of his love for his children. (Young-family client: "What would happen to the children immediately? Who would take care of them? Would the state throw them into an orphanage?")

7. He senses that the survival of his property-personality alone will not prevent the family strife that he feels he could prevent if *he* were there. (Members of my wills audience said they were interested

in wills in order "to stop a family fight," or "to be sure of an equitable distribution of my property," or "to leave money where it will be used well," or so that there would be "no misunderstanding among the children.")

8.   He fears that the mysterious machinery of probate will do harm *to him* unless he plans for it.   Probate may be a part of the mystery of death, and planning may be seen as a way to penetrate the mystery.   (Members of my wills audience said they were interested in wills "so I'll know more about what to do for ourselves" or "because [I] would like to avoid having my estate probated" or "because I do not know anything about them and they are necessary" or "to protect ourselves and children.")

* * *

Testamentary counseling is a matter of helping the client to accept, recognize, and clarify these negative feelings.   My observation of will interviews in my own practice, in my students' work, and in the practice of other lawyers, is that this critical beginning is evaded as long as possible and occurs very late in the typical will interview. I have also observed, however, that the interview does not become genuine or meaningful until the reasons for the will are expressed. Therefore, at the very least, lawyers should refuse to aid and abet the process of evasion.   Ideally lawyers should act positively toward guiding the client to an early and frank realization of the fact that his death is involved in testamentary counseling.   I believe that both of these objectives can be accomplished by the reflective system of counseling that Rogers suggests—which is fundamentally a matter of listening closely and empathically to what the client says and of exhibiting to him that what he says and feels is understood.

Once the reasons are expressed, the session often becomes positive.   The client can begin to feel and express what he hopes to gain from the lawyer's services.   This corresponds to Rogers' fifth, sixth and seventh steps.   I have found that young-family clients eventually come to a realization that their small wealth must be applied for minor children, if both parents should die while they have minor children.   In addition, the young-family clients come to realize that the surrogate parents they chose must have broad discretion.   As a result, the clients come to emphasize in their judgment the support of their children over less realistic objectives such as college education.   This is a dogma in planning property settlement—that first things must come first.   The moment in which a client understands this sort of priority and focuses his reasoning around it is suggestive of what Rogers experiences when his psychotherapy patient's "insight and self-understanding come bubbling through."   Here is an example from a young-client interview:

If you are going to put into the terms of the trust that   .   .   . the last four thousand dollars   .   .   .   must be given to each one for their college education. . . . [That] may bind the trustee in a way that is not very good for things you can't foresee now. [Better to] allow the person who has the property to use it more or less as you would, you know, as things come up, he has a chance to do things more or less as if he were their parents. . . .

Another client in that project ended the interview by thanking the students who helped him; he expressed with some satisfaction the decision that he wanted to revoke his present will which set up rigid guardianships for minor children and make a new one. It is important to notice that the clients themselves should arrive at these realizations and these decisions. This can be accomplished when their counsellors are patient, accepting, and gentle. I believe that this kind of lawyer-client relationship produces a positive experience for clients. It is, to paraphrase Rogers, one of the fascinating aspects of being a lawyer.

There are two ways in which consideration of the preceding discussion might be helpful to the practicing attorney. One is that behavioral information should help lawyers to realize how their clients feel, especially about death and the values that death will destroy. Psychology presents a significant amount of information on the subject and promises to develop more as the decade-old effort to explore death as psychologically significant continues in the hospitals and laboratories commanded by that science. The other source of value, less tangible than the first, is a matter of a counseling attitude, an openness, which is more affective than systematic.

Although most lawyers do not realize the influence they exert on clients, the realities and values of the client's situation are heavily influenced by the verbal and non-verbal reactions of the lawyer to what the client says. . . .

This suggests a number of attitudes in testamentary counseling. One is an "experimental mode of inquiry," which is a search for feelings and attitudes as well as for information. It cannot be fulfilled with a fill-in-the-blanks system of will interviews, and lawyers who insist on operating their wills practice as if they were taking driver-license applications should get into another line of work.

The "experimental mode of inquiry" also excludes narrow value systems which reflect what the lawyer thinks the client should do with his property. At the very least, an openness to the client's own feelings and values about property and family requires that the lawyer realize that he communicates his values and attitudes to the client, whether he wants to or not. It may be that a life-estate trust for the client's wife is, in the lawyer's opinion, a poor idea. But the value of the idea should be tested against the way the client feels about his wife, about—for instance—her remarriage after his death, and about her ability to plan for and support their children. It should not be based on a moral absolute which represents the lawyer's own feelings and values.   Redmount [makes the following observations]:

> Poor legal counseling, with the adumbrated view of facts and highly parochial, legalistic conceptions of experience, may be particularly ill-suited to preventive means of dealing with experience.   Failures of perception and a restricted range of information and understanding may make the prediction of other than very narrow issues quite hazardous and unreliable.   The lawyer who is not "counseling-oriented" has the opportunity and perhaps the disposition to be more effective in highly identified matters that require correction.   He is less likely to handle well somewhat unidentified matters that require future planning.

Affectively significant counseling equipment is not altogether the result of attitudes, nor is it altogether the result of study and preparation.   Both sensitivity and information seem to be required, and, although this is not the place for a comprehensive discussion of the process of making counselors from lawyers, it may be helpful to suggest two avenues to more skillful counseling.

One is study.   The literature of counseling, . . . is readily available to lawyers.   Other "helping professions" (medicine, nursing, social work) have been aware of it, and have been systematically developing their own versions for decades.   The legal profession has, meanwhile, neglected its ancient claim to the title "counselor."   That neglect should be redressed in law-school curricula and in the professional reading of those in the practicing profession.

The other avenue is an affective openness, a candor, that is probably inconsistent with the image of lawyers as tough-minded, relevance-centered, masters of order.   If, for example, the "estate planning" lawyer thinks it a poor idea to set up support trusts for wives, and an even poorer idea to attempt to restrict a widow's ability to remarry, rapport would probably be advanced by his candid admission of his feelings and some expression of an honest interest in his client's reaction to them.   The Jungian therapist Marvin Spiegelman expresses the idea:

> I find that the best interpretations come out of what is actually transpiring in the relationship, where both are in the grip of the same complex, which seems to travel back and forth.   The implication of the foregoing is that the relationship itself is central and that the desired objectivity, individuality and understanding come out of the actual experience, rather than out of some presumed knowledge or objectivity (intellectual or feeling) in the analyst.

If the lawyer expresses his negative feelings obliquely (by, say, making faces or shaking his head), the client perceives an obstacle between him and his counselor that he cannot deal with.

* * *

.   .   . Annoyance or impatience or anxiety in the lawyer
.   .   . affects his clients far more than he realizes. It would be
better to "acknowledge one's fatigue, boredom, or anger   .   .   .
where it occurs, and analyze it, jointly." Spiegelman believes that
analysts learn from patients, and most good lawyers would agree
that lawyers learn from their clients. "To learn, one must be ready
to submit to the other and expose one's ignorance."

* * *

[Similarly,] candor, and sympathetic interest, are what Rogers
was talking about when his ideal counselor said to the client that he
wanted "to enter into your world of perception as completely as I am
able   .   .   . become in a sense, another self for you   .   .   . an
alter ego of your own attitudes and feelings   .   .   .." That is a
sound and lofty aspiration for the "counselor at law."

NOTES

1. *Dealing with the Client's Emotions: Some Comments on the
    Importance of Feedback*

Shaffer's discussion of testamentary counseling focuses on a
situation that almost always involves some exploration of the client's
feelings. Even a client who has come to terms with the inevitability of his or her own death may have to sort through a tangle of emotional ties to others and decide on a final ordering of the accumulated
possessions and obligations of a lifetime. In such situations, recognizing the client's emotional reactions and helping to work through
their implications becomes as much a part of the lawyer's job as spelling out tax consequences. Nor is the need for this kind of sensitivity
and skill limited to the estate planning area. Problem, personality
and task combine to create many counseling situations with considerable emotional content.

On a moment's reflection you can think of types of litigation
likely to be especially stressful for clients: Contested divorces and
custody battles, as well as criminal proceedings, come immediately to
mind. But it is difficult to conceive of any area of litigation which
does not have the potential for producing anger, anxiety, and a great
many other emotions in clients: The personal injury client may be
struggling to deal with a drastic change in his or her lifestyle or the
business executive may be facing the prospect of financial ruin. In
addition, as Shaffer points out, a certain amount of emotion is generated by the lawyer-client interaction itself. A client who begins
with a clear notion of the nature of his or her problem and its likely
solution may be angered at the lawyer's "taking over," and another
may assume a very dependent role in the interaction, yet resent that
dependency and fail to follow advice when the session is over. The
lawyer who tries to take every verbal statement at face value and

treat unverbalized responses as acquiescence is merely postponing the necessity of resolving such underlying problems.

It does not do much good, of course, to recognize that emotions can "get in the way" in client counseling unless we can begin to talk about when and how to deal with them. There are a number of difficult decisions involved, including such assessments as whether a particular emotional reaction is clouding a client's judgment or distorting his or her view of the problem, and if it is, whether the lawyer should do something about it. Conceivably one might deal very differently with a client who was being "overly-sentimental" about his or her former spouse than with one who was feeling vindictive. In both instances, however, such feelings—and the lawyer's assumptions about them—can easily distort the interchange. The lawyer may respond more in terms of what he or she seems to be "expected" to feel than in terms of his or her less mediated reactions.

How, then, does one go about—in Shaffer's terms—"helping the client to accept, recognize, and clarify . . . negative feelings"? Does the process at least begin with the kind of "affective openness" discussed by Shaffer? Our own study and experience lead us to believe that it does, but that one must be careful to give specific content to the general terms so often applied to counseling efforts. Being "open" involves listening, acceptance, and something akin to understanding or sympathy—and a great deal more.

Among the helpful insights contributed by the counseling literature—particularly the client-centered model on which Shaffer relies—is the recognition of the extent to which openness is a two-way process. The counselor must not only be open to expressions of the client's feelings about the problem and the lawyer's response to it, but must also be open about his or her own feelings and reactions to what the client is saying. Many in the helping professions would share Shaffer's view that this kind of candor will ultimately lead to a deeper exploration of the client's problem, and lay a more secure foundation for making decisions. But again, this is an area which requires a large measure of skill and sensitivity. Revealing your negative reactions can be destructive as well as constructive, depending on what is transpiring in a particular relationship at a particular point in time. One helpful formulation deals with communications about one person's reactions to another—and efforts to help that other learn and "grow" in the relationship—under the label "feedback". David Johnson offers the following prescriptions for its use:

> The purpose of feedback is to provide constructive information to facilitate another's awareness of the consequences of his behavior on you. It is important, therefore, to give feedback in a way which will not increase the defensiveness of the other person. The more defensive an individual is, the less likely that feedback will be accurate-

ly heard and understood. Some characteristics of helpful, nonthreatening feedback are as follows:

1. *Focus feedback on behavior rather than the person.* It is important that we refer to what a person does rather than comment on what we imagine he is. This focus on behavior further implies that we use adverbs (which relate to actions) rather than adjectives (which relate to qualities) when referring to a person. Thus we might say a person "talked considerably in this meeting," rather than that this person "is a loudmouth."

2. *Focus feedback on observations rather than inferences.* Observations refer to what we can see or hear in the behavior of another person, while inferences refer to interpretations and conclusions which we make from what we see or hear. In a sense, inferences or conclusions about a person contaminate our observations, thus clouding the feedback for another person. When inferences or conclusions are shared, and it may be valuable to have this data, it is important that they be so identified.

3. *Focus feedback on description rather than judgment.* The effort to describe represents a process for reporting what occurred, while judgment refers to an evaluation in terms of good or bad, right or wrong, nice or not nice. The judgments arise out of a personal frame of reference or value system, whereas description represents *neutral* (as far as possible) reporting.

4. *Focus feedback on descriptions of behavior which are in terms of "more or less" rather than in terms of "either-or."* The "more or less" terminology implies a continuum on which any behavior may fall, stressing quantity, which is objective and measurable, rather than quality, which is subjective and judgmental. Thus, participation of a person may fall on a continuum from low participation to high participation, rather than "good" or "bad" participation. Not to think in terms of more or less and the use of a continuum is to trap ourselves into thinking in categories, which may then represent serious distortions of reality.

5. *Focus feedback on behavior related to a specific situation, preferably to the "here and now," rather than to behavior in the abstract, placing it in the "there and then."* What you and I do is always tied in some way to time and place, and we increase our understanding of behavior by keeping it tied to time and place. Feedback is most meaningful if given as soon as appropriate after the observation or reactions occur.

6. *Focus feedback on the sharing of ideas and information rather than on giving advice.* By sharing ideas and information we leave the person free to decide for himself, in the light of his own goals in a particular situation at a particular time, how to use the ideas and the information. When we give advice, we tell him what to do with the information, and in that sense we take away his freedom to determine for himself what is for him the most appropriate course of action.

7. *Focus feedback on exploration of alternatives rather than answers or solutions.* The more we can focus on a variety of procedures and means for the attainment of a particular goal, the less

likely we are to accept prematurely a particular answer or solution—which may or may not fit a particular problem. Many of us go around with a collection of answers and solutions for which there are no problems.

8. *Focus feedback on the value it may have to the recipient, not on the value of "release" that it provides the person giving the feedback.* The feedback provided should serve the needs of the recipient rather than the needs of the giver. Help and feedback needs to be given and heard as an offer, not an imposition.

9. *Focus feedback on the amount of information that the person receiving it can use, rather than on the amount that you have which you might like to give.* To overload a person with feedback is to reduce the possibility that he may use what he receives effectively. When we give more than can be used, we are satisfying some need for ourselves rather than helping the other person.

10. *Focus feedback on time and place so that personal data can be shared at appropriate times.* Because the reception and use of personal feedback involves many possible emotional reactions, it is important to be sensitive to when it is appropriate to provide feedback. Excellent feedback presented at an inappropriate time may do more harm than good. In short, the giving (and receiving) of feedback requires courage, skill, understanding, and respect for self and others.

11. *Focus feedback on what is said rather than why it is said.* The aspects of feedback which relate to the *what, how, when, where* of what is said are observable characteristics. The *why* of what is said takes us from the observable to the preferred and brings up questions of "motive" or "content." To make assumptions about the motives of the person giving feedback may prevent us from hearing or cause us to distort what is said. In short, if I make assumptions about "why" a person gives me feedback, I may not hear *what* he says.[45]

It may be difficult to give content to some of these suggestions in the context of legal counseling, and you may have to test them in a variety of situations before you can tell whether any of them are helpful in your own counseling efforts. At the very least they indicate that thoughtful analysis can be brought to bear on this highly subjective, intuitive process, and that it may indeed reveal ways of relating to clients that are better than others.

———

2. *The Lawyer's Feelings and Needs: The Importance of Self-Awareness*

The notion of interpersonal competence assumes not only a need to respond to emotional reactions in others, but also an awareness of the feelings, traits and attitudes which one typically brings to relationships. One of the variables in any counseling situation will be

45. D. Johnson, CONTEMPORARY SOCIAL PSYCHOLOGY 55–58 (1973).

the personality of the counselor, which in turn evokes specific responses on the part of the client. There is no way to avoid having this kind of "personal" impact, for as Johnson points out:

> When we interact with another person, we have no choice but to make some impact, stimulate some ideas, arouse some impressions and observations, or trigger some feelings and reactions. Sometimes we make the impression we want to, but other times we find that individuals react to our behavior much differently than we would like. An expression of warmth, for example, may be misperceived as being condescending, and an expression of anger may be misperceived as being a joke. A person's interpersonal effectiveness depends upon such things as his self-awareness of his intentions, his self-acceptance of those intentions, his self-disclosure of those intentions to others, his ability to obtain constructive feedback to maximize his awareness of the other's perceptions of and the consequences of his behavior, and his willingness to experiment with new behaviors if the consequences of his present behaviors do not match his intentions.[46]

This is a straightforward point, but one we are often prone to forget. We are not always aware of what we intend, and we often intend something different from what we produce.

Moreover, unconscious—or at least unstated—intentions are almost as numerous as the individuals who have them. They can be related to weaknesses or strengths, hopes or fears, and areas of security as well as doubt. What is important is to realize that they are always present, and that the effective counselor must become aware of them, accept them, and learn to deal with their consequences. Andy Watson has identified a number of needs that are frequently present in lawyers, and has also speculated on their effects on professional relationships:

> The lawyer's contribution to the professional relationship is not only composed of all the personal emotional factors present in the client, but he also provides the complication produced by his need to perform a highly technical task. Because he has selected his own professional activity, there will also be a series of emotional needs, some of which are largely unconscious, which caused him to choose the profession of law. Though we do not yet have well established information about these factors, it would appear that many select law as a vocation because it gives them opportunities to operate from a position of power and authority, as they organize, conceptualize, and manipulate the social forces known as law. To comment about this is not to criticize these impulses, for they are present in every human being in some degree. It is merely to emphasize that each of us in selecting our vocation, responds to inner needs and desires by seeking out tasks which provide probabilities for such gratification. These tasks may be of enormous social value, but the professional role necessitates, or at least makes desirable, some awareness of the manner in which these internal forces may enter into professional activities.

46. *Id.* at 53.

Another emotional factor which will be present in many professionals, is a powerful desire to be helpful to others and thus secure a supply route to sources of approval, affection, or love. All human beings need such guarantees of attachment to the group, and professional activities are one of the surest sources of supply for this need. However, such emotional need may become of such overriding importance, that it can distort the professional relationship and produce inappropriate decisions and actions. One of the burdens of professionalism, is to make occasional moves which by their nature are bound to be unpopular, even when they are desirable and ultimately helpful. This is reflected in the oft repeated protest of punishing parents, that "this will hurt me more than you." No child nor any client can recognize this while suffering pain or frustration, and it is only by hindsight and mature reflection that the truth of the statement and the reason of its offering can become known.

Another important need which can be gratified in the law and which may be a well forged portion of a lawyer's identity, is the wish to create orderliness in ideas, institutions, and relationships. While clearly of enormous social importance, if too urgent a pressure, it can result in premature limitation of hypothesis and result in constriction of viewpoint. No doubt all lawyers recall if their memory is jogged, early frustrations in their legal studies, when they first discovered that the "known certaintie of the law" even when stated by the venerable Coke, is chimerical at best. However, after overcoming initial panic, most learned how to be orderly about disorder, and thus restored a sense of well-being. I would suggest parenthetically, that perhaps some of this need for order, still rests latently in most, where it may occasionally cause problems through forcing premature decisions about clients, their needs, and their wishes.

Because of the psychological components of the lawyer's self-image described above, as well as other and perhaps more subtle ones, each lawyer has tended to select an area of professional activity which best suits the balance of his individual needs. This empirically and perhaps gropingly effected result, has placed each lawyer in his position of best strength as well as greatest weakness. Strength, because it facilitates the use of the sharpest tools possessed; weakness, because it is closest to the built-in blindspots which emanate from the largely unconscious forces which led to the position from which each functions, and by which each is invisibly bound. To get behind this invisible net should be part of the lifetime educational goal of every professional. It is the road to both professional success as well as a sense of personal well-being.

. . . Most lawyers, during the course of their training, have been strongly urged and specifically conditioned, to try to eliminate emotions from their legal task. I would like to take categorical exception to this, and state flatly that such an admonition is not only impossible, but undesirable.

Let me hasten to say, that I do not disagree with the notion that emotions may get in the way and grossly distort the manner in which any task may be conducted. It is simply that they *cannot* be eliminated and furthermore emotions are the principal and most effective tool we have, for knowing what is going on in other people. Assuming that it is inevitable that there shall be emotions involved in one's legal activity, the question then becomes how to best control them. How far may one go without running serious risks of becoming overly involved with clients? How may these emotions be best handled so that the advantages may be maximized in recognizing a client's needs, while at the same time maintaining the psychological distance needed to see clearly what is going on? How may one improve skills for using these feelings?   .   .   .

Because of the factors enumerated above, becoming involved with clients produces high probability that even such concrete matters as choice of legal tactics, whether or not to take a client, whether to negotiate or go to trial, which witnesses to use and which to shelve, which jurors to empanel and which to avoid, and in the last analysis, even which aspect of law to practice, will at least be partially determined by emotions of which the lawyer will be only vaguely aware or completely ignorant.

These omnipresent and disturbing emotional forces in the professional relationship, will place the legal counselor under constant internal pressure to resolve questions in a way which will tend to make him more comfortable, with at least some semblance of control in the variables. In practice, this results in premature decisions with curtailment of fact gathering. Tactical and strategic decisions will be drawn from insufficient and sometimes less-than-optimal data. Decisions of this sort can only result in poor practice which is likely to be less than effective for clients and far from satisfying to the lawyer. Let me emphasize, that these premature maneuvers are not the function of slovenliness, technical ineptitude, or lack of a conscientious interest in clients. Rather, they are due to the inner needs of a lawyer to alleviate anxiety by "settling matters." Also it should be emphasized, that many lawyers do not "feel" this anxiety since their training and experience has provided them with excellent means for avoiding this sensation and thus missing the more obvious clues to conflict in the situation. The desirable approach sounds paradoxical, since the optimal psychological posture for pursuing these professional problems is to be able to sustain comfortably, the discomfort of opened-ended situations.   .   .   . [47]

If Watson is right in asserting that both the professional success and personal well-being of lawyers are dependent, to some degree, on their being aware of their own motivations and emotional reactions, the development of such self-awareness becomes an important goal. No part of the counseling task is easier to state and harder to realize, however, for as Watson points out, we have all been conditioned *not* to allow our emotions to surface, and to channel the anxiety and uncertainty of legal situations in predictable ways. When we are asked to become conscious of our emotions and trace the effects of

---

47. Watson, *The Lawyer As Counselor,*
5 J.FAM.LAW 7, 9–12 (1965).

our anxiety on our relationships with clients, many of us have no idea where to begin.

At least part of the answer may lie in effectively generating and relying on feedback. Those with whom we interact constantly provide information on the way we are coming across to them—whether it be through their verbal and nonverbal responses or the reactions they do *not* have. An openness to this sort of feedback can lead to increased knowledge about ourselves. Actually benefiting from such information, however, requires a good deal of self-acceptance. We cannot accurately interpret reactions to our behavior if we are unwilling to admit that the behavior is present. As Johnson has observed:

> As interpersonal competence is the ability to understand the effects of one's behavior and personality upon others with whom one is interacting, some degree of self-awareness is required to receive information from others as to how they perceive you, and how your behavior affects them. Thus Argyris states that to behave competently in interpersonal situations, the individual must be able to provide and receive information about his relationships with minimal distortion. If a person has a high need to control others, for example, he must be aware of this tendency, and be able to evaluate honestly its effects on his relationships. Argyris states that to minimize distortion of information, the individual needs a relatively high degree of self-awareness and self-acceptance. The more aware and accepting an individual is of those aspects of himself which are operating in a given situation, the higher the probability that he will discuss them with minimal distortion, and the higher the probability that he will listen with minimal distortion. Thus if an individual is aware and accepting of his need to receive affection from others, he will tend to listen to reactions to his attempts to elicit affection which are minimally distorted.[48]

Becoming aware of one's "hidden agenda" and accurately perceiving its effect on others, moreover, only brings us to the harder questions of what to do about it. Interpersonal effectiveness depends, as well, on a person's willingness to "experiment with new behaviors" if the consequences of present behavior do not match his or her intentions. There are, of course, no set formulas for such attempts; being self-aware and acting consistently with one's beliefs is hard work. Nevertheless, it is useful to be reminded now and then that one's own feelings, and the way one handles them, are very much a part of the counseling process.

––––––––

48. Johnson, *supra*, note 45 at 51–52.

Chapter Three

THE ETHICAL DIMENSION

SECTION ONE. ETHICAL ISSUES IN NEGOTIATION

Every bargaining situation offers the possibility of mutual benefit and exchange; but, as we have seen, it also offers opportunities
for taking advantage or exercising coercive power over one's adversary. There are inevitably moral dimensions to these possibilities.

A number of commentators have emphasized the need for a sense
of fairness and constraint in negotiation. As Herrington wrote in
1930:

> One should go into a conference realizing that he is an instrument
> for the furtherance of justice and is under no obligation to aid his
> client in obtaining unconscionable advantage. Of course, in the zone
> of doubt an attorney may and probably should get all possible for
> his client.[59]

The zone of doubt, however, is not so easy to define, and there are
others who would respect not even such minimal limits on adversariness in this context. Indeed, the obligation in Canon 7 to pursue the
"lawful objectives" of one's client at least suggests that refraining
from taking lawful advantage of an adversary, itself, raises ethical
questions.[60]

The following offers an illustration of both sides of this problem.
George Beach represents Mr. and Mrs. Valdez, who have filed suit
against Alloway's Garage alleging that its mechanics negligently
failed to tighten the lug nuts on the wheels of their car. The wheel
collapsed and their youngest son was killed. The insurance company
for Alloway is represented by Sam Kepler.

VALDEZ v. ALLOWAY'S GARAGE

SCENE: *The office of an attorney who is representing a couple
whose son was killed in an automobile accident. The
attorney's investigator enters the office to discuss the
case.*

Eads: Hey, George. You busy as usual?

Beach: Yup. Be with ya in a minute, Ed.

Eads: Hey, I got time.

---

59. Herrington, *Compromise and Contest in Legal Controversies*, 16 A.B.A.
J. 795 (1930). Note that because we
have rearranged the excerpts included
in this volume, the footnotes in this
chapter, though in a numerical sequence in each section, begin with
numbers 59 in this section and 49 in
the next.

60. *See, e. g.*, DR7–101(A)(1), (2), (3).

Beach: Alice? Alice? Take care of these right away, will you please? . . . And, uh, get on this, I need this typed right away, And, uh, when the Valdezes come, show 'em in right away, all right? And Alice, where's the Valdez file?

Alice: Right there on your desk.

Beach: Oh, yeah, yeah, yeah. Uh, thanks.

Eads: Hey, George. You need anything else on Valdez? Ah, how about the mechanic, you know, uh, Rossini, the guy who missed the lug nuts? Maybe I oughta go see 'im again . . . you know . . . just for safety's sake?

Beach: Naw . . . forget it. We already got his deposition. I mean, I don't want you to put any more time into this. I can't afford to put any research into this either. I mean, I feel sorry for the couple, but the case is a dead loser. I mean, there's no use even re-searching it. At best the case is not worth more than . . . ah . . . five thou at best.

Eads: I just thought I'd check by. Nothin's up, I . . . I got things to do. Who you up against on this one anyway?

Beach: A guy named Kepler from downtown. You know him?

Eads: Sure! Hey, he's a biggie. He doesn't miss nothin'. Ah . . . ya know . . . I know his investigator . . . He's pretty tough, too, I hear.

Beach: Damn, just what we don't need . . . Now I know we're gonna hafta settle . . . All right, what the hell . . . I'll see ya tomorrow, Ed, all right?

(*Phone rings. Beach answers.*)

Beach: Yeah? Yeah, Beach here, right Tom?

Alice: Mr. and Mrs. Valdez are here.

Beach: Yeah, yeah, yeah, yeah, right, yeah. Right, okay. Listen, can I get back to ya a little bit later? Okay, fine. All right, Alice, send them in.

(*The following lines are heard over still photos of the Valdez' deceased son.*)

Mrs. Valdez: It was a month ago he died. To me . . . it is still yesterday.

Mr. Valdez: He was our only son, Mr. Beach. That's all that matters to us. Not the car.

Mrs. Valdez: I tell him, "take off your seat belt. That way you sleep better . . ."

Mr. Valdez: They say . . . with a seat belt, maybe he survive. But who knows? . . .

Mrs. Valdez: He's gone . . . our only child . . . our litt . . . our little boy . . . our future . . . all gone.

(*Picture reverts back to Beach's office.*)

Mr. Valdez: You see how she is, Mr. Beach . . . We do not want to live this thing again. If there is any other way . . . we do not want the court . . .

Beach: Maybe they'll settle . . .

Mr. Valdez: Yes, that would be best.

Beach: But . . . we're gonna be lucky to get one or two thousand . . . I mean, maybe enough to cover the medical bills . . . uh . . . maybe a little bit more. But, like I told ya, it's the seat belt issue. Uh, we can't get around that.

Mr. Valdez: Get whatever you can, Mr. Beach. For me, I must consider what is best for my wife . . . for both of us. We do not want the court.

Beach: Look, I see what'cha mean. Um . . . I'm gonna do my very best for ya, Mr. Valdez. I can shave my fee a bit to, uh, help stretch things.

Mr. Valdez: Thank you, Mr. Beach. Oh . . . Mr. Beach . . . there is one more thing.

Beach: Yes?

Mr. Valdez: The other attorney . . . the lawyer in the big office downtown . . . he talk with us? After we came to see you, I think?

Beach: You mean Kepler?

Mr. Valdez: Sí . . . he knows about us . . . he say in the talk that we have.

Beach: You mean about your illegal immigration?

Mrs. Valdez: We're afraid . . . he can send us back.

Mr. Valdez: We don't want to go back, Mr. Beach.

Beach: Look, don't worry. I'll handle it. I see Kepler this afternoon.

Mr. Valdez: Thank you.

> SCENE: *The office of the attorney who is representing the defendant insurance company.*

Kepler: This is a pre-negotiation memo . . . date it March 10 . . . the case is *Valdez v. Alloway's Garage.*

I spoke this morning with Mrs. Green, chief adjuster for Mutual Insurance Company. I informed her that plaintiff's failure to use a seat belt would not bar recovery in this particular instance since the accident occurred immediately *after* the effective date of the new comparative negligence statutes. However, plaintiff's attorney may not realize that contributory negligence no longer bars his client's claim.

While this is bound to come out in trial, I think we should attempt to settle this quickly before it comes to their attention. Mrs. Green reported that Mutual is worried about setting a precedent in this case, and they wish to settle out of court. They've authorized me to offer up to $20,000 for that purpose.

Have you got all that, Miss Riley?

Secretary: Yes, Mr. Kepler.

Kepler: In my opinion, we can settle for less. The plaintiffs are here illegally . . . On the other hand, the case is loaded with problems that make its outcome at trial uncertain from our point of view. Hold, uh, hold up a second . . . do you have the *Valdez* file with you?

Secretary: Yes, Mr. Kepler.

Kepler: In particular, I'd like to see Investigator Clark's report . . . (*She hands it to him.*) We'll continue now . . . Investigator Clark's memo of February 2nd indicates a key witness for our client, a mechanic by the name of Rossini, has changed his story from an earlier deposition. His most recent version directly undercuts our client's position in this case. He now says the Valdezes definitely asked for full inspection and that there was none done. I do not know if the plaintiff's counsel is aware of this change . . . but Rossini is quite frightened about his part in this action. (*Phone intercom buzzes.*) That'll be all, Miss Riley . . . at least for now.

Kepler: Yes?

Receptionist's Voice: Mr. Beach is here.

Kepler: Oh, thank you. Would you direct him to my office, please?

(*Beach knocks on door.*)

Beach: Sam.

Kepler: George. How are you? Have a seat.

Beach: Fine.

Kepler: Have a seat, George.

Beach: Thanks.

Kepler: How long is this going to take, George? I have another appointment . . .

Beach: Oh, no, it won't take long. Ah, we can get right to the point; ah, my client would like to know whether or not you were thinking of, like, settling the case.

Kepler: Ah yes. Of course settlement is always best whenever feasible. But to be perfectly frank with you, I don't know whether we can reach an agreement in this matter. Now, I'm speaking from the perspective of my client, you understand, not for myself.

Beach: What's the problem?

Kepler: They're under pressure. They don't want to get a reputation for settling this type of case out of court for a very high figure

. . . which is what you're asking them to do in this case. It's their policy to try the case where the facts appear to relieve them of liability, as in this instance.

Beach: Oh, sure, but the, ah, jury is going to be very sympathetic to the Valdezes . . . you know that. Look, even so, uh, would your client consider, uh, *any* offer?

Kepler: I doubt it very seriously. Of course, if you could give me some reasonable ball-park figure. For example, medical expenses. I could ask them for that.

Beach: Uh, what figure are you talking about, exactly?

Kepler: Oh, say . . . two thousand dollars.

Beach: Two thousand dollars? . . . You can't be serious! I can't accept that! This is a wrongful death case, maybe ya forgot that. My clients lost their only son. You gotta go a little above that!

Kepler: Now you see why I don't think we'll reach a settlement in this matter. I've laid all my cards on the table. I hope you'll be equally frank with me.

Beach: Look, I know we've got a problem. The seat belt issue would legally bar any recovery before a judge, but I can't go back to these poor people who've lost their only son with nothing but medical expenses. And you never know before a jury. They may ignore any contributory negligence claim.

Kepler: We're prepared for that.

Beach: And let me tell ya something else. Your case isn't as strong as you think. You got a witness that no one's gonna believe.

Kepler: Who's that?

Beach: Rossini . . . the mechanic . . . the guy who missed the lug nuts? . . .

Kepler: Rossini? I don't know what you hope to find there. His deposition is solidly on our side.

Beach: Yeah, but the deposition just doesn't ring true. I'm gonna give 'em a lot of trouble on cross-exam. I mean, we're not gonna give up everything just to avoid a showdown in court! I can tell ya that right now!

Kepler: Now wait a minute. Don't get hot with me! I told you I'd see what I could do. I'm in a difficult position myself. I know your clients are here illegally . . . and I don't want to hurt them or anyone else, but I have a duty to my client . . . to keep them informed of every facet in this case. Now you can't expect me not to raise that fact with them. And once they have that information . . . well, neither one of us are in any position to control how they're going to use it. I don't think we want that to happen . . . do we?

Now, look, George, I don't want to be hard-nosed about this. I wanna settle this matter. I'm prepared to call my clients and ask them for medical expenses and enough for you to make a nice fee. Now tell me, George, what authority do you have to settle this case?

Beach: Well, I could, ah, settle because of the . . . ah . . . special circumstances here . . . I could . . . ah . . . settle for . . . three thousand dollars?

Kepler: Let's see what I can do.

Beach: I, ah, hope this won't take too long.

Kepler: No, it shouldn't take too long. Oh . . . ah, I assume the three thousand dollars is a firm offer?

Beach: Yeah, that's right.

Kepler: Okay.

(*He leaves office, and returns shortly.*)

Kepler: Good news. I'm authorized to settle this case for $3,000.

Beach: Say, that *is* good news. This is gonna make the Valdez family very happy, and it's gonna save your client a lot of time and trouble.

Kepler: I'm surprised. I didn't think we'd be able to reach an agreement on this one.

Beach: Will you draw up the papers and, ah, drop 'em by my office tomorrow?

Kepler: Oh, by the way, remember I'll have to deduct expenses in this case. I've had over $500 in deposition costs.

Beach: I thought we had an agreement! $3,000! That's what you said, Sam.

Kepler: I'm not changing anything I said. I assumed you knew that my client's legal expenses would be deducted. You know, I'm surprised you're not aware of that practice.

Beach (*leaving office with a sigh*): Just send me the papers.

Kepler: Miss Riley, would you come in please? I'd like to dictate a follow-up memo on the Valdez case.

NOTES

1. *Relationships with Adversaries: The Guidance of the Code*

In the course of representing Mr. and Mrs. Valdez, George Beach has probably violated a number of provisions of the Code of Professional Responsibility:

—He has misrepresented his belief that the case is "worth" four or five thousand dollars, telling them that they would be lucky to collect two thousand dollars.[61]

61. Although this is a common practice and understandable—since it insulates   the lawyer from "excessive expectations"—misstatement of one's valua-

—He has (or may have) accepted less for his clients in order to guarantee his fee.[62]

—He has undertaken a matter "which he knows or should know he is not competent to handle." [63]

The first two of these propositions raise relatively straightforward applications of Code provisions we have already discussed.[64] The last statement, however, raises many problems and deserves some elaboration. Beach has not found an important change in the law relevant to the case,[65] and has not learned that an important witness has changed his account of the facts.[66] He does not counsel his clients about the obvious vulnerabilities they face because of their immigration status and is apparently unable to handle Kepler's improprieties with respect to the problem.[67] He is obviously unaware of local practice with respect to the deductibility of costs from settlement agreements, if such a practice exists.[68] As we have indicated elsewhere,

---

tions seems to us clearly to violate counsel's obligations of loyalty to his or her client. *See* ABA Opinion 82 (1932). This was explicitly stated in former Canon 8, which read:

A lawyer should endeavor to obtain full knowledge of his client's cause before advising thereon, and he is bound to give a candid opinion of the merits and probable results of pending or contemplated litigation.

The framers of the new Code apparently believed that this obligation is subsumed under Canon 5 and Canon 7.

62. The transcript is ambiguous here. The fee-settlement arrangement, however, is always a potential source of conflicting interests between lawyer and client. Suppose, for example, that Beach had said he would not accept less than three thousand dollars "in order to guarantee a decent fee." Note that by so doing he would have increased the recovery of the clients. Would such a tack be proper? How is what Beach did different? Look again at DR5–103(a); *cf.* Butler v. Young, 121 W.Va. 176, 2 S.E.2d 250 (1939) (upholding a contingent fee arrangement under which the attorney could approve any settlement sought by his client); Ward v. Orsini, 243 N. Y. 123, 152 N.E. 696 (1926) (upholding a similar arrangement in which the attorney's fee would be higher if his client settled without the attorney's approval). The view of the ABA Committee on Professional Ethics seems to be contrary to these cases.

63. *See* DR6–101(A).

64. See our discussion on client loyalty in Chapter 2 (of *The Lawyering Process*) at pages 52–57.

65. *See* EC6–2, 6–4.

66. You might ask yourself what he should have done and in what ways his actions were negligent. See Chapter Four in this regard. For a discussion of the general standards governing malpractice, see Chapter Two at pages 79–80.

67. For example, Mr. and Mrs. Valdez might have been able to adjust their status before he entered into the negotiations. Similarly, Beach might have responded more forcefully to Kepler's veiled threat. Again, ask yourself if such failures can be considered "incompetence." Did Beach have any obligation to report Kepler if he believed the statement was a threat which violated DR7–105? *See* DR1–103(A). Compare his obligations with respect to reporting the possibly illegal immigration status of his clients. DR4–101(C)(3); DR1–102.

68. Note that Kepler noticed the deposition and paid the initial costs. But Beach's clients probably had to pay for a copy unless there was some agreement on this with the reporter beforehand. Beach and Kepler are both entitled to reimbursement if they laid out these costs. DR5–103(B). Indeed, they could not advance such expenses unless (i) they were related to

neglect of a lawyer's obligation to "represent [his] client competently" is not the "same as negligence" and "usually involves more than a simple act of omission." [69]   Would you agree that Beach's apparent failure to do more research into the applicable law, or to request correction of the depositions,[70] is enough to violate his ethical obligations?   What weight should be given to the fact that his economic circumstances made him unable (or unwilling) to spend the time?   Certainly he is not relieved of his responsibility because the case involves a contingent fee, or because it is only one of the many cases he is handling.   If he is overextended or insufficiently experienced, he is required to associate counsel in the case.[71]   But what are the implications of such a view of ethical responsibility?   Is this requirement a necessary safeguard of competence or will it often result, where experienced counsel is unavailable, in effectively precluding the client from getting any representation at all?   Jeanne Kettleson makes the following observations about a similar problem in legal aid practice:

> .   .   .   Not only does the Code of Professional Responsibility contain no obligation to provide access to all clients who seek service, it prohibits practices which result in clients not being "fully" served. These prohibitions fall into three main areas.

> First, taking on very large numbers of clients is prohibited whenever this would result in a violation of Canon 6 obligations to provide competent representation.   Given the high caseloads in the NLS office, it's possible—even likely—that this is occurring.

> The ABA Committee on Ethics and Professional Responsibility recently addressed this issue directly in Informal Opinion 1359 (1976). Responding to an inquiry from a legal services office in which staff attorneys were faced with "unmanageable caseloads", the Committee stated that "the refusal by directors of legal services offices to establish priorities could result in Code violations if it causes 'inadequate preparation' or 'neglect' by a staff lawyer within the meaning of DR6–101." DR6–101 provides that a lawyer should not "handle a legal matter without preparation adequate to the circumstances" or "neglect a case entrusted to him".   The Disciplinary Rule makes no exception for inadequate preparation, neglect or delay because a legal services lawyer has too many clients.

litigation costs (rather than living expenses), *see* ABA Opinion 288 (1954); *but see* In re Ratner, 194 Kan. 362, 399 P.2d 865 (1965); (ii) the client is ultimately liable for them. DR5–103(B); ABA Informal Opinion 1283 (1973) (applying this limit to the named plaintiff in a class action litigation). Do these seem like sensible, desirable, or enforceable restrictions?

69.   ABA Informal Opinion 1273 (1973) (lawyers may not be disciplined for

lack of ordinary or due care); *but see* ABA Informal Opinion 1368 (1976) (suggesting that attorneys must at least make case by case judgments).

70.   If the applicable state rule placed a duty on Kepler to "supplement" the response, of course, no such request would be required.   *See, e. g.* Mass. Rules of Civil Procedure 26(e)(2).

71.   DR6–101(A)(1); EC6–3; 6–4.

Second, even if service in the NLS office raised no problems of competence, the failure to set limits on caseload probably results in violations of DR5–105A which in essence prohibits accepting any employment which would adversely affect existing clients. Present clients concerned with prompt and well-prepared service have demands on the legal staff. If the staff handles more cases than its resources permit, the interests of one of these groups will be sacrificed. In addition, EC5–14 states that maintaining independent professional judgment precludes "acceptance or continuation of employment that will . . . dilute the lawyer's loyalty to a client." Whenever acceptance of a new client necessitates delaying or putting less effort into prior clients' cases, such a dilution of loyalty arguably exists.

Third, the office's practices appear to violate Canon 7 obligations of individual loyalty to the client. Besides placing additional strictures on inadequate preparation, Canon 7 requires that clients be made fully aware of the options that are available to them. EC7–8 provides, "A lawyer should exert his best efforts to insure that decisions of his client are made only after the client has been informed of relevant considerations" . . . and EC 7–7 provides that in any area affecting the merits of a case or substantially prejudicing the rights of a client, " . . . the authority to make decisions is exclusively that of the client, and . . . binding on his lawyer".

* * *

The practice also runs contrary to Canon 2 aspirations, particularly EC2–2, which states that: "[T]he legal profession should assist laymen to recognize legal problems because such problems may not be self-revealing and often are not timely noticed." . . .

[T]he Code does not seem to permit the trade off of quality for quantity that NLS made, even though the resources available were woefully inadequate to meet the needs of the community it served. Here I find myself in agreement with the profession's norms. To provide far less service than an individual client needs without even letting the client know seems an unacceptable way of "solving" the problem of limited resources.

* * *

It is my belief that, if we think hard about the choices limited resources force us to confront, we will find that minimal service to large numbers of clients is not an effective way to affirm the kind of human relationships that led us into this work, to generate additional resources, or to change conditions for those we serve. Certainly, in not even informing our clients and their communities of what such choices involve, we violate a trust at the programmatic level which few of us would violate in person-to-person contact. . . .[72]

Is this a fair reading of the applicable Code provisions? Should a different standard be applied to Beach if he were honestly motivated by a desire to maximize the availability of service?[73] Is

---

72. Kettleson, *Caseload Control*, 34 NLADA BRIEFCASE III, 112–13 (1977).

73. Such a "dual standard" has apparently been rejected by the ABA. *See* ABA Informal Opinion 1359 (1976).

the lawyer being asked to be a guarantor of the outcomes of his or her work? How is a determination of adequate preparation otherwise to be made?

However you resolve these questions, you should note that all the above comments relate to whether Beach has done *enough* for his clients. Note that, beyond filing an action which he apparently believed to be without merit,[74] he has not acted in ways which contravene possible obligations to those other than his clients. Kepler, on the other hand, might be criticized for having done "too much." In contrast to Beach, however, very few of his actions would seem to run afoul of the existing provisions of the Code of Professional Responsibility.

Consider the following aspects of Kepler's conduct. First, he does not reveal the changes in Rossini's statement. However, if he has not made a "false statement of fact," he does not have an obligation to disclose weaknesses in his case. The Committee on Professional Ethics stated in Opinion 314:

> In practice before the Internal Revenue Service, which is itself an adversary party rather than a judicial tribunal, the lawyer is under a duty not to mislead the Service either by misstatement, silence, or through his client, but is under no duty to disclose the weaknesses of his client's case .   .   .   .   Nor does the absolute duty, not to

In 1974, lawyers for the New York Legal Aid Society struck to obtain better working conditions, including lower caseloads. Their conduct was considered to raise questions under DR6–101(A)(3) and DR1–102(A). *See* N.Y. County Opinion 645 (1975); *cf.* Freedman, LEGAL ETHICS, N.Y.L.J. (June 25, 1975) (arguing that the opinion failed to recognize that the attorneys' actions might have been warranted by violations of the rights of existing clients and potential violations of the rights of future clients).

74. In retrospect, it was the case that (i) Rossini was a witness favorable to Mr. and Mrs. Valdez; and (ii) their claim was not barred by contributory negligence. Note, however, that Beach believed the opposite of each of these propositions to be true. Was he acting properly in filing the action? DR7–102(A)(2) provides that a lawyer shall not:

> Knowingly advance a claim or defense that is unwarranted under existing law, except that he may advance such claim or defense if it can be supported by good faith argument for

an extension, modification, or reversal of existing law.

See also DR7–102(A)(5); Rule 11, Federal Rules of Civil Procedure (providing, inter alia, that an attorney signing an unverified pleading certifies that there is "good ground" for it and that it "is not interposed for delay." Has Beach violated these provisions? Are these standards subjective or objective? An attorney who makes a false statement in a pleading violates DR7–102(A)(5). What do these rules add to the obligation of candor? In ABA Informal Opinion 1271 (1973) the Committee on Ethics and Professional Responsibility held that it was not improper to file a pleading in a divorce action despite the fact that there was a complete defense of recrimination available to the defendant. The committee reasoned that the defendant might not choose to assert the defense. *See also* N.Y.County Opinion 281 (1930); *but see* In the Matter of Greenbaum, 161 A.D. 558, 146 N.Y.S. 969 (1914). Does such a distinction comport with the objectives purportedly served by the above rules?

make false assertions of fact require . . . the disclosure of his confidences, unless the facts in the attorney's possession indicate beyond reasonable doubt that a crime will be committed. A *wrong, or indeed sometimes an unjust, tax result* in the settlement of a controversy is not a crime.[75]

Look carefully at Kepler's statements and ask yourself if they would constitute misrepresentation at common law. Are they "false" within the meaning of the Code? Our guess is that they would not be so held.

Second, he does not correct Beach's misconception of the law. However, although there is some authority to the contrary, his obligation to disclose legal authority against him seems to be limited to disclosures to the court.[76]

Third, Kepler engages in what appears to be "low balling"— that is, he adds an extra demand after the agreement is reached. If this were done consciously, it might be considered an implicit "false" statement, but in general, the mere fact that Beach was misled would not condemn Kepler's conduct.

Finally, Kepler takes advantage of his adversary's inexperience and secures an agreement (we will assume) which even he considers to be an unfair result. Again the Code seems to place no clear prohibition on such consequences.[77]

Only Kepler's threat to reveal the Valdez' immigration status seems explicitly to violate any Code provision (he could not do through his client what he could not do himself). DR7–105 provides that "a lawyer shall not present, participate in presenting, or threaten to present criminal charges solely to obtain advantage in a civil matter." However, the language of this provision would have to be stretched to cover deportation (non-criminal) proceedings, and Kepler's statement would have to be held to have been a threat to act—rather than a prediction that the information would be likely to come out at trial. The restrictions on "hard bargaining" are very few indeed.

How is one to understand such a conception of the lawyer's role? One way to conceptualize the scope of permissible conduct in negotiation is to see the line drawn by the profession as dividing legality

75. ABA Opinion 314 (1965) (emphasis added); *see also* Maguire, *Conscience and Propriety in Lawyer's Tax Practice,* 6 TAX COUNSELLOR'S Q. 493 (1962); S. Williston, LIFE AND LAW 271–72 (1940). It has been held that the identity and whereabouts of an eyewitness could be withheld even in an action against a minor. *See* N.Y. County Opinion 309 (1933).

76. *See* DR7–106(B)(1); ABA Opinion 280 (1949). There is some authority, however, prohibiting a lawyer from inserting a clause declared to be against public policy in a lease or contract. *See* N.Y.City Opinion 722 (1948). Can this be reconciled with the general rule?

77. *See* EC7–10; DR7–101(A)(1); DR7–101(B)(1). Do any of these support an opposite conclusion? There are cases saying a default judgment will be set aside if it appears that an attorney has "taken advantage" of another attorney's error or negligence, but this has not been applied to analogous situations.

and illegality. Short of this boundary the decision to forego advantage—even what is believed to be unfair advantage—is the client's, not the lawyer's. Applying this standard to Kepler's situation would seem to entail the following propositions. As you review the applicable provisions, ask yourself whether you agree.

—If he remains in the case, he must seek settlement in his client's behalf in accordance with their wishes, irrespective of his personal views of its fairness.

—Subject to limits on expressly or impliedly making false statements with respect to the owner's mistaken beliefs about the extent of his liability, he may not correct Beach's misapprehension on a matter beneficial to his clients.

—He may not, without his client's permission, temper his advocacy or in any way "hold back" in the face of his opponent's disadvantages.

Kepler could urge his clients to forego their advantages and, were Mr. and Mrs. Valdez unrepresented, he could suggest to them that they "need" legal advice. In general, however, he would have to assert his client's advantages not only within but up to the bounds of legality.

Compare this view with the following formulation of the lawyer's obligation:

> From a long range point of view, as distinguished from concern with the immediate case only, you have an interest in avoiding customary use of methods designed to win cases on grounds that may be regarded as unfair, though legal. A reputation for this type of practice becomes a handicap to you in representing your clients in future cases, since even your more substantial contentions come to be viewed with suspicion by judges familiar with your reputation. The duty of supporting the client's cause is sometimes so forcefully stated as to support the argument that as a trial lawyer you are obliged to assert every legal claim or defense available, except those you reject on tactical grounds relating to the immediate case. But the aim of the trial system to achieve justice, the interests of future clients, and your legitimate interest in your own reputation and future effectiveness at the bar compel moderation of that extreme view.[78]

Does this accurately describe the professional norm? Can you reconcile the idea that "personal reputation" is an appropriate consideration, with DR5–101 disapproving judgments influenced by "personal interests"?

If such restraint is not permitted under the Code, Kepler is finally left with only three options. First, he could try to avoid employment in this type of situation. However, this hardly seems a realistic option to a person in his position. Second, he could seek to withdraw. If the client freely consents, this would be an appropriate solution

78. R. Keeton, TRIAL TACTICS AND METHODS 3 (2d ed. 1973).

when a lawyer has strong personal feelings about proceeding in a given case.[79] Given the likely reaction of his clients, however, withdrawal is a large order for someone in Kepler's position.[80] Third, he might continue in the case while trying to mitigate, to some extent, the degree to which he would have to take advantage of a vulnerable adversary. That is, he could seek the client's permission to forego the advantage or lessen its potential influence.

None of these possibilities, however, will offer much solace to an attorney who wants to feel he or she is "doing justice" in the individual case as well as in the aggregate. Boswell's advice notwithstanding,[81] most of us know an unjust outcome when we see one. We are also unable to derive much satisfaction from the allusions to stoicism, humanity, the larger good, or—most recently—friendship, that are advanced to justifying our participation in it. All of these arguments leave unchanged the same paradoxical situation: while the lawyer's partisanship may not extend to assisting clients in conduct that violates the law, short of that stricture it must be pressed with indifference to its harsh consequences on others, whatever the client's "need" or "moral entitlement" to the benefits gained.

---

2. *The Larger Puzzle: Power, Vulnerability, and Regard for Adversaries*

The moral issues involved in "taking advantage" are, in some ways, obvious. Deception and coercion may be justified, but they would seem to require stronger warrant than the rules of the game, or a facile assertion that when such conduct is engaged in by lawyers it is not "really" lying or undue pressure. Judge Rubin puts it well:

> Is the lawyer-negotiator entitled, like Metternich, to depend on "cunning, precise calculation, and a willingness to employ whatever means justify the end of policy?" Few are so bold as to say so. Yet some whose personal integrity and reputation are scrupulous have instructed students in negotiating tactics that appear tacitly to countenance that kind of conduct. . . .
>
> * * *
>
> Let us consider the proper role for a lawyer engaged in negotiations when he knows that the opposing side, whether as a result of poor legal representation or otherwise, is assuming a state of affairs that is incorrect. Hypothesize: *L*, a lawyer, is negotiating the sale

---

79. *See, e. g.,* EC7–9; DR2–110(A), (C). The problem of withdrawal is discussed in more detail in Section Two. It is not entirely clear whether Kepler could withdraw in the absence of consent.

80. *But see* the comments of William Simon in Chapter Two, of *The Lawyering Process* at pp. 103–106 and 110–112.

81. Boswell: "But what do you think of supporting a cause which you know to be bad? "

Johnson: "Sir, you do not know it to be good or bad til the Judge determines it."

J. Boswell, THE LIFE OF JOHNSON (1791).

of his client's business to another businessman, who is likewise represented by counsel. Balance sheets and profit and loss statements
prepared one month ago have been supplied. In the last month, sales
have fallen dramatically. Counsel for the potential buyer has made
no inquiry about current sales. Does L have a duty to disclose the
change in sales volume?

* * *

. . . [L]et us consider another hypothet. L, the lawyer, is
representing C, a client, in a suit for personal injuries. There have
been active settlement negotiations with LD, the defendant's lawyer.
The physician who has been treating C rendered a written report,
containing a prognosis stating that it is unlikely that C can return
to work at his former occupation. This has been furnished to LD. L
learns from C that he has consulted another doctor, who has given
him a new medication. C states that he is now feeling fine and thinks
he can return to work, but he is reluctant to do so until the case is
settled or tried. The next day L and LD again discuss settlement.
Does L have a duty either to guard his client's secret or to make a
full disclosure? Does he satisfy or violate either duty if, instead
of mentioning C's revelation he suggests that D require a new medical examination?

* * *

The professional literature contains many instances indicating
that, in the general opinion of the bar, there is no requirement that
the lawyer disclose unfavorable evidence in the usual litigious situation. The *racontes* of lawyers and judges with their peers are full of
tales of how the other side failed to ask the one key question that
would have revealed the truth and changed the result, or how one side
cleverly avoided producing the critical document or the key witness
whom the adversary had not discovered. The feeling that, in an adversary encounter, each side should develop its own case helps to insulate counsel from considering it a duty to disclose information
unknown to the other side. Judge Marvin Frankel, an experienced
and perceptive observer of the profession, comments, "Within these
unconfining limits [of the Code] advocates freely employ time-honored
tricks and strategems to block or distort the truth."

* * *

To most practitioners it appears that anything sanctioned by the
rules of the game is appropriate. From this point of view, negotiations are merely, as the social scientists have viewed it, a form of
game; observance of the expected rules, not professional ethics, is
the guiding precept. . . .

* * *

The profession seldom confronts the necessity Vern Countryman
and Ted Finman say the attorney-at-law must consider: "the need,
if conflicting interests are to be protected, for the lawyer to serve as
a source of restraint on his client, and, indeed, on himself." The
lawyer is a professional because his role is not merely to represent
his client as a mercenary in the client's war; he is also "a guardian
of society's interests."

In an unpublished paper, Dean Murray L. Schwartz, of the University of California Law School, succinctly proposed three possible standards of the relationship of the lawyer's value structure to that of his client:

(1) A lawyer should do everything for his client that is lawful and that the client would do for himself if he had the lawyer's skill;

(2) A lawyer *need not* do for his client that which the lawyer thinks is unfair, unconscionable or over-reaching, even if lawful;

(3) A lawyer *must not* do for his client that which the lawyer thinks is unfair, unconscionable or over-reaching, even if lawful.

"It will be giving away no professional secrets," he continues, "to tell you that the first standard of behavior is the one that is largely applied in a contested judicial matter." He thinks that the second standard is "officially recognized as appropriate for non-litigated matters" though the authorities cited in this paper and my own experience make me think this observation overly generous to the profession. The third, he correctly finds, "no part of official doctrine."

A lawyer should not be restrained only by the legal inhibitions on his client. He enjoys a monopoly on the practice of law protected by sanctions against unauthorized practice. Through a subpart of the profession, lawyer-educators, the lawyer controls access to legal education. He licenses practitioners by exacting bar examinations. He controls access to the courts save in those limited instances when a litigant may appear *pro se*, and then he aptly characterizes this litigant as being his own lawyer, hence having a fool for his client.

The monopoly on the practice of law does not arise from the presumed advantages of an attorney's education or social status: it stems from the concept that, as professionals, lawyers serve society's interests by participating in the process of achieving the just termination of disputes. That an adversary system is the basic means to this end does not crown it with supreme value. It is means, not end.

If he is a professional and not merely a hired, albeit skilled hand, the lawyer is not free to do anything his client might do in the same circumstances. The corollary of that proposition does set a minimum standard: the lawyer must be at least as candid and honest as his client would be required to be. The agent of the client, that is, his attorney-at-law, must not perpetrate the kind of fraud or deception that would vitiate a bargain if practiced by his principal. Beyond that, the profession should embrace an affirmative ethical standard for attorneys' professional relationships with courts, other lawyers and the public: *The lawyer must act honestly and in good faith.* Another lawyer, or a layman, who deals with a lawyer should not need to exercise the same degree of caution that he would if trading for reputedly antique copper jugs in an oriental bazaar. It is inherent in the concept of an ethic, as a principle of good conduct, that it is morally binding on the conscience of the professional, and not merely a rule of the game adopted because other players observe (or fail to adopt) the same rule. Good conduct exacts more than mere convenience. It is not sufficient to call on personal self-interest; this is the standard created by the thesis that the same adversary met today may be faced again tomorrow, and one had best not prejudice that future engagement.

Patterson and Cheatham correctly assert that the basic standard for the negotiator is honesty. "In terms of the standards of the profession, honesty is candor. . . ." Candor is not inconsistent with striking a deal on terms favorable to the client, for it is known to all that, at least within limits, that is the purpose to be served. Substantial rules of law in some areas already exact of principals the duty to perform legal obligations honestly and in good faith. Equivalent standards should pervade the lawyer's professional environment. The distinction between honesty and good faith need not be finely drawn here; all lawyers know that good faith requires conduct beyond simple honesty.

* * *

[The same standards should apply to the results of a negotiation.] While it might strain present concepts of the role of the lawyer in an adversary system, surely the professional standards must ultimately impose upon him a duty not to accept an unconscionable deal. While some difficulty in line-drawing is inevitable when such a distinction is sought to be made, there must be a point at which the lawyer cannot ethically accept an arrangement that is completely unfair to the other side, be that opponent a patsy or a tax collector. So I posit a second precept: *The lawyer may not accept a result that is unconscionably unfair to the other party.*

A settlement that is unconscionable may result from a variety of circumstances. There may be a vast difference in the bargaining power of the principals so that, regardless of the adequacy of representation by counsel, one party may simply not be able to withstand the expense and bear the delay and uncertainty inherent in a protracted suit. There may be a vast difference in the bargaining skill of counsel so that one is able to manipulate the other virtually at will despite the fact that their framed certificates of admission to the bar contain the same words.

The unconscionable result in these circumstances is in part created by the relative power, knowledge and skill of the principals and their negotiators. While it is the unconscionable result that is to be avoided, the question of whether the result is indeed intolerable depends in part on examination of the relative status of the parties. The imposition of a duty to tell the truth and to bargain in good faith would reduce their relative inequality, and tend to produce negotiation results that are within relatively tolerable bounds.

But part of the test must be in result alone: whether the lesion is so unbearable that it represents a sacrifice of value that an ethical person cannot in conscience impose upon another. The civil law has long had a principle that a sale of land would be set aside if made for less than half its value, regardless of circumstance. This doctrine, called lesion beyond moiety; looks purely to result. If the professional ethic is *caveat negotiator*, then we could not tolerate such a burden. But there certainly comes a time when a deal is too good to be true, where what has been accomplished passes the line of simply-a-good-deal and becomes a cheat.

The lawyer should not be free to negotiate an unconscionable result, however pleasing to his client, merely because it is possible, any more than he is free to do other reprobated acts. He is not to commit perjury or pay a bribe or give advice about how to commit embezzlement. These examples refer to advice concerning illegal conduct, but we do already, in at least some instances, accept the principle that some acts are proscribed though not criminal: the lawyer is forbidden to testify as a witness in his client's cause, or to assert a defense merely to harass his opponent; he is enjoined to point out to his client "those factors that may lead to a decision that is morally just." Whether a mode of conduct available to the lawyer is illegal or merely unconscionably unfair, the attorney must refuse to participate. This duty of fairness is one owed to the profession and to society; it must supersede any duty owed to the client.

* * *

It is to serve society's needs that professions are licensed and the unlicensed prohibited from performing professional functions. It is inherent in the concept of professionalism that the profession will regulate itself, adhering to an ethos that imposes standards higher than mere law observance. Client avarice and hostility neither control the lawyer's conscience nor measure his ethics. Surely if its practitioners are principled, a profession that dominates the legal process in our law-oriented society would not expect too much if it required its members to adhere to two simple principles when they negotiate as professionals: Negotiate honestly and in good faith; and do not take unfair advantage of another—regardless of his relative expertise or sophistication. . . .[82]

Can you answer this critique of existing negotiating norms? What changes would it envision in the conduct of Beach and Kepler? William Muir adds the following to these speculations:

Tocqueville . . . observed that "men are not corrupted by the exercise of power . . ., but by the exercise of power which they believe to be illegitimate." His point was that political persons were not debased by the inescapable necessities of coercive power—dispossession, detachment, remorselessness, and madness. Rather, they were corrupted by their inability to reconcile these implications of exercising coercive authority with their personal congenital standards of decency. Politicians were bewildered by the conflict between the practices of extortion and the principles of civility; they found their belief in the nobility of their cause and their instinct for innocence working at cross-purposes; they were impaled on the dilemma of power—they had either to violate their most profound codes of self-restraint or suffer political defeat.

Tocqueville's insight was that the process of corruption by power started with feelings of profound guilt at having to act harmfully.

82. Rubin, *A Causerie on Lawyers' Ethics in Negotiation*, 35 LA.L.REV. 577, 580, 582–86, 588–93 (1975).

Persons with authority constantly bore the burden of feeling they had double-crossed one set of obligations or another. The corrupted man of power, Tocqueville argued, was the one who overcame the moral conflict raging within him by annihilating his civilized principles. By simplifying the complexity of the codes to which he was responsive, he rid himself of the paralyzing agony of deciding between irreconcilable obligations. He denied the principles of legitimate conduct in order to flee from his sense of wrongdoing. The result, however, was the subversion of human self-restraint and an unconditional victory for the demon of politics. The ideals, the noble "cause" of political action, might well remain in the mind of the politician. But if he obliterated the ethical guideposts of human remorse and sympathy, he then expunged the very perspective which might have prevented him from succumbing to the bad effects of coercive power. In the long run he would come to destroy all tender sensibility and to harm the very hostages—mankind, civilization, and its gentling institutions—which he had set out to save in the first place.[83]

He also points out that the very possession of power can turn the power-holder into a victim:

The extortionate model makes it possible to see the pitfalls of coercion more clearly, particularly the paradoxes of coercive power:

1. *The paradox of dispossession:* The less one has, the less one has to lose.

2. *The paradox of detachment:* The less the victim cares about preserving something, the less the victimizer cares about taking it hostage.

3. *The paradox of face:* The nastier one's reputation, the less nasty one has to be.

4. *The paradox of irrationality:* The more delirious the threatener, the more serious the threat; the more delirious the victim, the less serious the threat.

How do these four paradoxes apply to the policeman? How may they help explain his professional development? The answer may appear obvious. The policeman's authority consists of a legal license to coerce others to refrain from using illegitimate coercion. Society licenses him to kill, hurt, confine, and otherwise victimize nonpolicemen who would illegally kill, hurt, confine, or victimize others whom the policeman is charged to protect.

But the reality, and the subtle irony, of being a policeman is that, while he may appear to be the supreme practitioner of coercion, in fact he is first and foremost its most frequent victim. The policeman is society's "fall guy," the object of coercion more frequently than its practitioner. Recurrently he is involved in extortionate behavior as victim, and only rarely does he initiate coercive actions as victimizer. If he is vicious, his viciousness is the upswing of the vicious cycle inherent in an extortionate relationship.

83. W. Muir, Jr., POLICE: STREET CORNER POLITICIANS 271–72 (1972).

Contrary to the more unflattering stereotypes of the policeman, it is the citizen who virtually always initiates the coercive encounter. What is more, the citizen tends to enjoy certain inordinate advantages over the policeman in these transactions. The advantages derive from the four paradoxes of coercion. The citizen is, relative to the policeman, the more dispossessed, the more detached, the nastier, and the crazier. Add to these natural advantages the fact that most police-citizen encounters are begun under circumstances which the citizen has determined, and the reader may begin to feel some of the significant limits placed on the policeman's freedom to respond in these encounters. The policeman is the one who is on the defensive. What is interesting about him is that he demonstrates how difficult it is for the self-restrained person to defend himself against the bully. What will distinguish one policeman from the other are the techniques he invents to defend himself in his position of comparative vulnerability.

The irony of the policeman's lot is that his authority, his status, his sense of civility, and his reasonableness impose terrible limits on his freedom to react successfully to the extortionate practices of others. His alternatives are sharply foreclosed; he works within a much smaller range of choices than do his illegitimate and nonofficial adversaries. If Lord Acton was right that power tends to corrupt, at least it is also arguable that the corrupting influence of power stems from the way that the power of a powerful person attracts the practice of coercion against him, placing him on the defensive. Power tends to confine, frustrate, frighten, and burden the consciences of its holders.[84]

Is this the situation of lawyers? To what extent is it inevitable? To what extent rooted in present conceptions of the lawyer's role?

Surely the possibility of an alternative to "adversariness" will be attractive to many of you. In the long run, it is hard to imagine that either society or the bar will fare well in a system which sets no constraints on its members short of the law itself. Given its many traps for the vulnerable and the unwary, one suspects that the system's "success" (or acceptance) depends primarily on the unwillingness or inability of large numbers of people to use it.

Why not have a different ethics of negotiation, then? Is the problem one of fairness to clients? Or does it lie in the claim that "a lawyer [or client] who looks at himself as an instrument for the furtherance of justice [is unlikely to fare well] when pitted against [someone] willing to take whatever he can get and use any means he can get away with"?[85] This concern seems to suggest that violations of a more cooperative norm would be inevitable. Is this necessarily true? The degree to which many potential adversaries evolve cooperative modes of interaction suggest that it is not. Where par-

84. *Id.* at 44–45.

85. V. Countryman and T. Finman, THE LAWYER IN MODERN SOCIETY 281 (1966).

ties (i) share values; (ii) enjoy some equality of bargaining power; and (iii) anticipate continuing relationships, they rarely adopt an excessively adversarial posture. On the other hand, what if these factors are not present? Think hard about the disparities in wealth, power, access to advice, confidence and skill that exist in our social world. What do these mean for a lawyer representing clients like Mr. and Mrs. Valdez? Can we realistically deal with the problem of coercion without a radical change in the circumstances which produce such vulnerabilities?

Beach's conduct may be understood as a reaction to his own lack of power as well as the powerlessness of his clients. Kepler's conduct may be seen as a response to these same vulnerabilities. How can these extreme disparities be redressed? For Beach, the profession would merely suggest hard work and experience. For Kepler, the advice would include circumspection and restraint. For both the following adaptation of Muir's comments would be worth repeating:

> In a nutshell, the conclusions are these. A policeman becomes a good policeman to the extent that he develops two virtues. Intellectually, he has to grasp the nature of human suffering. Morally, he has to resolve the contradiction of achieving just ends with coercive means. A patrolman who develops this tragic sense and moral equanimity tends to grow in the job, increasing in confidence, skill, sensitivity, and awareness.

> Whether or not he develops these two virtues depends on the choices he makes among alternative means of defending himself against recurrent threats. Those self-defensive reactions to violence and madness influence the very core of his being. The responses he has to make to what I have called "the paradoxes of coercive power" challenge his basic assumptions about human nature and his conventional notions of right and wrong.

> Achieving a tragic sense and a moral calm under the threatening circumstances of patrol work depends in part upon developing an enjoyment of talk. Eloquence enriches his repertoire of potential responses to violence and permits him to touch the citizenry's souls— their hopes, their fears, their needs to be something worthwhile, their consciences. Equally important, a policeman's penchant to talk provides him the chance to associate with his fellow officers. . . . In being thrust together in training and in squads, policemen have unique opportunities to talk out the intellectual and moral issues inherent in the paradoxes of dispossession, detachment, face, and irrationality—the four paradoxes of coercive power. . . .

> On the other hand, in the paradoxical circumstances in which the policeman is forever working, of being powerful but not absolutely powerful, the absence of either the inclination or the opportunity to talk is likely to isolate him from both the public and his fellow officers. This isolation impedes developing a tragic outlook in combination with a moral equanimity about coercion. As a result, he tends increasingly to habits of avoidance, brutality, or favoritism. In turn, these unacceptable performances tend to compound moral and in-

tellectual disorientation, leading to ever increasing isolation from human companionship and, eventually, to personal deterioration.[86]

It may be that lawyers as well can cope with the problem of powerlessness by maintaining such associations. However, nothing in these prescriptions speaks to a change in the social circumstances which would make Mr. and Mrs. Valdez less vulnerable. Nor do they offer any alternative to help Beach become more like Kepler, or to make Kepler more open and humane. It does not minimize the difficulties to hope that our social imagination might reach much, much further.

SECTION TWO. ETHICAL ISSUES IN ADVISING THE CLIENT

Basic to all the ethical issues we have thus far considered is the ambiguous moral relationship with clients.[49] On the one hand, client loyalty is the justification for everything the lawyer does, whatever the moral questions it may produce. The lawyer serves clients, not abstract ideals of justice or fairness. On the other hand, the client is the source of most of the profession's moral dilemmas. If clients were less self-interested and ungenerous, how much easier the job of representation would be. What requires us to give their interests priority?

Once again the analogy to medicine may be helpful. Patients have been said to have the following legitimate expectations:

> The rights implied by . . . the . . . concerns involved in medical care may be put under four heads: lucidity, autonomy, fidelity and humanity.

> *Lucidity.* The patient has a right to know all relevant details about the situation he finds himself in. This follows from the significance of the situation of medical care for his understanding of what he is and what he might become. Thus lucidity is not just an instrumental benefit, contingently useful to the patient, to his doctor or to some third persons in maximizing this or that set of goods. It is a constitutive good and therefore a right, since it is crucial to a fully human process of choosing one's goods and in the process of choosing what kind of person one will be. To deny a patient an opportunity for lucidity is to treat him not as a person but as a means to an end. And even if the ends are the patient's own ends, to treat him as a means to them is to undermine his humanity in so far as humanity consists in choosing and

----

86. Muir, supra note 83 at 3–4.

49. For contrasting visions of this relationship see the following reviews of Dean Freedman's LAWYER'S ETHICS IN AN ADVERSARY SYSTEM (1975): Greenbaum, *Review Essay: Attorneys' Problems in Making Ethical Deci-* sions, 52 IND.L.J. 627 (1977); Kunstler, Book Review, 4 HOFSTRA L.REV. 895 (1976); Rotunda, Book Review, 89 HARV.L.REV. 622 (1976); Weiss, Book Review, 44 GEO.WASH.L.REV. 202 (1975).

being able to judge one's own ends, rather than being a machine which is used to serve ends, even one's own ends.

Further, an offense against lucidity denies the patient the opportunity to make out of the significant situation in which the patient encounters the doctor a human encounter, a human relation—that is one in which the parties to the relation may equally engage their major capacities, their capacities for intelligence, choice and affection. Denial of lucidity is a sufficient condition for a relation of dominance, and that in itself is a violation of right.

Autonomy. A patient has a right not only to be free from fraud in the relation of medical care, but free from force, violence as well. Thus if a patient, though fully informed, is subjected to a treatment against his will, this too violates his rights. Similarly if the doctor is forced to perform services against his will, this violates his autonomy. Admittedly, no more controversial philosophical notion exists than of this liberty. The intuitive notion is of liberty to dispose of one's self, that is of one's person, one's body, mind and capacities according to a plan and a conception fully chosen for one's self. The idea is one of being one's own man, and from that position entering into relations of friendship, love, generosity and service. In the relation of medical care this means that both patient and doctor fully define their relation to each other, neither being imposed on as a resource at the command of the other.

Fidelity. Dealings among persons create expectations, reliance and trust. Where each party acknowledges not only that his conduct causes expectations to arise in his counterpart, but acknowledges also that these expectations are justified, that is he ratifies them, then deliberately to disappoint such expectations is a form of deceit. It is a form of deceit which is so clearly identified that it has its own name, faithlessness. Thus, lying is a form of faithlessness because the use of language not only generates expectations, but acknowledges those expectations as justified. There is perhaps usually a conventional element to fidelity. The expectations one acknowledges are rarely specified in full in the particular encounter. Rather there is a more or less implicit incorporation by reference of a whole conventional system of expectations. This is the case in the relation of medical care, where the patient relies and the doctor allows him to rely on a tradition of loyalty to his interests.

Humanity. This is the vaguest of the four concepts. The notion is that over and above a right to be treated without deceit or violence, a person has a right to have his full human particularity taken into account by those who do enter into relations with him. It may be that a man has no right to any affirmative consideration at all, but once we have been drawn into a significant nexus, my wants, needs and vulnerabilities may not be ignored even if my right to autonomy is fully respected and I am treated with complete candor. This too is an important element in the concept of personal care.[50]

50. C. Fried, MEDICAL EXPERIMEN-
TATION: PERSONAL INTEGRITY
AND SOCIAL POLICY 101–03 (1974).

Again, in thinking through what is involved in counseling, ask yourself if these values express your own commitments to clients. Can they legitimate whatever consequences result from this sort of loyalty? Would they apply even when an institutional rather than an individual client is involved?

In the following transcript, such a situation is presented. Glenn Sparks is the recently appointed president of Electro Corporation, a large enterprise engaged in manufacturing electrical appliances. Helen Wilson is house counsel to the corporation. The transcript should be read against lawyer-client transactions occurring in other contexts as well.[51]

IN RE ELECTRO CORPORATION

SCENE: *The president of a large corporation calls the general counsel to his office to discuss some business matters.*

Secretary: Office of the General Counsel.

Sparks: This is Glenn Sparks. Ask Mrs. Wilson to come in right away.

Secretary: Yes sir.

Receptionist: He's waiting for you.

Sparks: Where the hell did you dig this up?

Wilson: We found it by accident. It surprised me too.

Sparks: Why didn't you find it six months ago before I took over?

Wilson: It was a fluke. Normally no one would be looking for something like this, Glenn. When we started to prepare the SEC registration statement on that new stock issue, we just hired a new attorney. I asked him to track down all possible contingent liabilities, just to give him some practice. Of course, he reviewed the abstract of title. That's when it turned up.

Sparks: So you're telling me that the corner of our main plant sits on Katchitorian's property, huh?

Wilson: I'm afraid so.

Sparks: That S.O.B. He's fought this company for years.

Wilson: The defect qualifies as a contingent liability. It'll have to be disclosed in the registration statement.

Sparks: Damn it. Katchitorian will be all over us the minute the word gets out . . . No one else knows about this but you and me. Is that right?

---

51. In particular, you may want to read the discussions of advice to clients in Chapter Three (of the Lawyering Process) at pages 247–65 and 270–72. On ethics in counseling, in a variety of contexts, see Krash, *Professional Re-* *sponsibility to Clients and the Public Interest: Is There a Conflict?* 55 CHI.BAR RECORD 31 (1976); Paul, *The Responsibilities of the Tax Adviser,* 63 HARV.L.REV. 377 (1950).

Wilson: Um, the lawyer who found it, but no one else, and I doubt anyone will be looking for it. The irony is that in another six months it would solve itself. We'd be able to acquire clear title by adverse possession.

Sparks: Six months! We can't delay the stock offering that long.

Wilson: Well, that would solve the disclosure problem.

Sparks: Yes, but what would happen to stockholder confidence? All of a sudden, for no apparent reason, the industry's leading corporation delays an offering that everyone's already expecting. Do you realize what that could mean to the company?

Wilson: It's a messy situation, Glenn. I think you should take it back to the board.

Sparks: The board? I can't do that. I've got the board's approval. The details are my responsibility. You know my policy, we can handle this at staff level. I'll be damned if I'm going to go back and tell them our factory is sitting on someone else's property.

Wilson: Well, I can't approve the registration statement, not unless everything's there.

Sparks: There's a way out of this. You won't have to approve, Helen. I'll retain outside counsel to handle this. That was our original plan, anyway.

Wilson: But what about accounting? They still might want to talk, and if they ask me directly, I'll have to tell the truth.

Sparks: I'll tell them to talk to the outside firm. They won't know anything about it. If they insist on seeing you, well let's hope that they don't ask you the direct question. Then it won't have to come out, will it?

Wilson: I'll do whatever you want me to, Glenn, but I want you to know the liabilities at issue here, and I also want to make it clear to you that I will have to respond if I'm asked. Frankly, I'm most worried about the board, about not telling them.

Sparks: I understand, Helen . . . I'm taking you off the registration altogether and we'll let our accountants and the outside attorneys hammer it out. That'll get you off the hook, won't it? Does it sound okay to you?

Wilson: Alright. If they don't come looking for me, I won't go looking for them.

Sparks: Okay, that takes care of that problem. Now I've got another one for you.

Wilson: The registration statement?

Sparks: No, it's about that other matter you've been pestering me about. That lawsuit. You know, the toaster that started the fire, where the fellow got burned?

Wilson: Oh yes. I was going to ask you about that.

Sparks: I ordered an engineering review to see if the filament could actually reach a temperature hot enough to start the fire.

Wilson: What did they find out?

Sparks: Well, there may be a problem. It's not that clear, but the tests seem to indicate about ten percent of the toasters coming off the line are below our safety levels. The engineers need to run more tests, but that'll take time. We're going to have to stall.

Wilson: Um, the plaintiff's attorney will start discovery any day, Glenn. We can't delay indefinitely.

Sparks: I know, I know.

Wilson: Well, we just can't risk it. If it gets out that non-union truckers delivered the shipments, you know what that means.

Sparks: That'll lead to the under the table payments.

Wilson: From a highly irregular corporate slush fund.

Sparks: I'm trying to stop that, Helen. We don't need payoffs to stay on top.

Wilson: It's got to stop. That's for sure. We could have some problems with criminal liability here. I've been saying that for years.

Sparks: I really inherited a mess here. It's been going on for so long, it's hard to change.

Wilson: It could hurt the company if it gets out, Glenn. Even if you put a stop to it before then, the accountants might want to look at this as well.

Sparks: I know, I know. This is all top priority with me—you know that—but I can't perform miracles. We've got to stall for time.

Wilson: Then why not settle this one? You're going to buy a bunch of lawsuits if this goes to court.

Sparks: Oh, I doubt it. Most people won't have the kind of injuries this guy did. And we're going to settle this one, just as soon as he decides he can't hold us up.

Wilson: Well, I'm sure he'd be willing to adjust the damages. I think it's a mistake for his lawyers to start taking depositions.

Sparks: I talked this over with Ned Franks, our insurance lawyer. I'd like the two of you to work together and delay it for a while. Raise every technicality and objection you can to the discovery request and make it expensive. I doubt the plaintiff is ready for a real fight when he sees that it's going to be an expensive, long, drawn-out litigation. I'm betting that he'll settle for something more reasonable.

Wilson: I told Franks to tell plaintiff's attorney that his time will be well compensated in the event of a settlement.

Sparks: Did he think that would work?

Wilson: Yes. And he's a good judge of things like that. I told him I'd do whatever I could to help out.

Sparks: You can help me too, Helen. Stay on top of this mess, will you? Keep me informed. I'd really appreciate that.

Wilson: Will do.

Sparks: Thanks, Helen.

NOTES

1. *Relations with Clients (The Counseling Phase)—The Guidance of the Code*

When pressed to give advice that a client may not want to hear and decides not to follow, the lawyer has a limited number of options: he or she may (i) do nothing; (ii) withdraw or resign; (iii) argue for his or her position; (iv) act to prevent the course of action the client has chosen; (v) alter the advice; or (vi) pursue some combination of these. As in a number of areas, the Code provides only partial guidance as to when any of these options, may, must or must not be pursued.

The Failure to Disclose to the Board

In the instant case, it is clear that Wilson acts improperly in not making disclosure of her judgments to the Board. No matter how close her working relationship with Sparks, the ABA pronouncements on this subject make it clear that the client of a lawyer employed by a corporation is the corporate entity and not its officers.[52] Note that there is no similar obligation to the shareholders of the corporation or its creditors. You might ask yourself what functions such an abstraction serves, and whether it makes sense in the

---

52. EC 5–18. The text is as follows:

A lawyer employed or retained by a corporation or similar entity owes his allegiance to the entity and not to a stockholder, director, officer, employee, representative or other person connected with the entity. In advising the entity, the lawyer should keep paramount its interests and his professional judgment should not be influenced by the personal desires of any person or organization. Occasionally a lawyer for an entity is requested by a stockholder, director, officer, employee, representative or other person connected with the entity to represent him in an individual capacity; in such case the lawyer may serve the individual only if the lawyer is convinced that differing interests are not present.

See also ABA Opinion 202 (1940) ("Since the board of directors of the trust company is its governing board, we think A with propriety may and should make disclosures to the board of directors in order that they may take such action as they deem necessary to protect the trust company from the wrongful acts of the executive officers").

context of the day-to-day relations of practice. It is Sparks with whom Wilson works, and (like many corporate counsel) to whom she feels primarily responsible. Should this make a difference in sorting out the ethical obligations involved? [53]

The Advice—Disassociation Continuum

The precise content of Wilson's obligations to the Board and others, however, is unclear. There seem to be four unlawful courses of conduct in which the Corporation is engaged: (i) the issuance of a false registration statement; (ii) the use of non-union truckers; (iii) payoffs to union inspectors who overlook the contract violations; and (iv) continued manufacture of products of which a high percentage are known to be defective. Assume that (i) and (iii) are violations of the criminal law; (ii) involves a breach of the collective bargaining agreement and (iv) constitutes gross negligence. Each of these poses a number of difficult judgments for counsel.

First, what advice may Helen Wilson give? A lawyer may not "counsel or assist his (her) client in conduct that the lawyer knows to be illegal or fraudulent." [54] Clearly she could not advise her client to make criminally-sanctioned "payoffs" even if the fine would not exceed the cost of changing the firm's practice.[55] But what about advice that it would be in the company's best interests to violate the collective bargaining agreement, or to continue to assume the risk that some purchaser will be badly injured by a defective toaster? The Code and opinions are surprisingly silent about whether advising a client to commit a *civil wrong* is unethical. In general, the prohibition against illegal or fraudulent conduct does not seem to extend to "ordinary" negligence or breach of contract.

Ask yourself if this seems justifiable to you. Why shouldn't a lawyer be prohibited from advising or doing anything he or she believes to be likely to be declared unlawful by a court? [56] What interests are served by insulating this sort of "lawlessness"?

Similar issues arise with respect to the line between advising and "supplying information." Suppose Wilson merely informed Sparks about existing law enforcement policies, the kinds of audits that are usually conducted, and the likely penalty if the company is

---

53. *See generally*, Rotunda, *Law, Lawyers and Managers*, THE ETHICS OF CORPORATE CONDUCT 127 *et seq.* (1977).

54. DR 7–102(A)(7).

55. *See, e. g.*, N.Y.County Opinion 27 (1913) (improper to advise a client to do an act "punishable by fine" even if the lawyer thought "it would be better for the client to pay [the] fine

. . . than to obey [the statute's] direction.").

56. *Cf.*, DR 7–101(B)(2) ("a lawyer may . . . refuse to aid or participate in conduct that he believes to be unlawful, even though there is some support for an argument that the conduct is legal"). An alternative formulation would change "may" to "must" in this provision.

caught?[57]   For example, she tells him that if the company waits a period of time without informing Katchitorian, it will not be liable for what is clearly a trespass on his property.   How does this differ from telling a client what a fine is likely to be, when you know that this will be determinative of the client's actions on the issue?   At what point does merely giving information to a client become improper?   Monroe Freedman offers the following analysis of this type of problem:

> Assume that a man consults a tax lawyer and says: "I am fifty years old. Nobody in my immediate family has lived past fifty. Therefore, I would like to put my affairs in order. Specifically, I understand that I can avoid substantial estate taxes by setting up a trust. Can I do it?" The lawyer informs the client that he can successfully avoid the estate taxes only if he lives at least three years after establishing the trust or, should he die within three years, if the trust should be found not to have been created in contemplation of death. The client then might ask how to go about satisfying the Internal Revenue Service or the courts that the trust was not in contemplation of death.

> At that point, the lawyer can either refuse to answer the question, or he can tell the client, first, that he should never again tell anyone that he is concerned about an early death, and, second, that he should write letters and have conversations with relatives and friends indicating that he is setting up the trust for reasons that have nothing to do with imminent death or a desire to "put his affairs in order". On the assumption that virtually every tax attorney in the country would answer the client's question (and subsequently present in court the letters and the testimony about the client's conversations), I concluded that it should not be unethical for the lawyer to give the advice. Although I did not articulate it at the time, I also had in mind the "I am a law book" rationale, that is, that the attorney would be doing no more than informing the client of what is in the applicable statutes and court decisions. After considerable reflection, I now consider that decision to have been wrong. The lawyer in the tax case is, purely and simply, the active instrument in establishing—and, ultimately, presenting—a fraudulent case.[58]

Do you agree with Freedman's conclusion?   What would his judgment be about the way Wilson handles each of the unlawful activities in which the client is engaged?   For example, did Wilson overstep his boundary when she informed Sparks that the defect in title would be cured by a six-months' delay?

---

57. N.Y.County Opinion 27 (1913) (". . . it is the lawyer's duty, when asked to advise, to instruct the client as to the measure of the penalty prescribed by law; but he should stop there.").

58. M. Freedman, LAWYERS' ETHICS IN AN ADVERSARY SYSTEM 71–72 (1975).

You might contrast these two problems with a third issue: whether and how Wilson must disassociate herself from these acts of illegality if Sparks determines to continue them. A lawyer may not "engage" in "illegal conduct" or conduct "involving dishonesty, fraud, deceit or misrepresentation." [59] Does her remaining with the company implicate her in Sparks' plans to issue the registration statement or to continue to use non-union truckers? [60] Again, the Code and opinions *seem* to make two distinctions in dealing with this issue. Withdrawal is probably required only if the unlawful continuing activity is criminal.[61] And even with respect to criminal activity, Wilson can probably continue to represent the company on other matters if she does not assist in any way in the continuing illegality.[62] Only the decision to refer the matters to other counsel raises a disciplinary question: She cannot "circumvent" a disciplinary rule through the actions of another.[63]

As you look at the relevant Code provisions consider carefully whether we have read them too liberally. Do you agree with the latitude they seem to offer? Can you reconcile this apparent license with the following:

> A client may wish to pursue a course of conduct which is not consistent with or cannot be realized within the limits of established law or precedents. When he is asked to provide such a plan, the lawyer is faced with the difficult task of determining the fine line between avoidance and evasion of the law and of creating new law which will be accepted by the courts as a sound piece of private legislation. He must develop a plan which involves the proper use, rather than a misuse, of law   .   .   .   .
>
> The problem is not often perceived in these terms for two reasons. The courts are concerned only with the legal effectiveness of a plan and not with the legal or professional quality of the lawyer's work, and they seldom hold him to account for misuse of the law. The lawyer's duty to

---

59. *See* DR 1–102(A)(4); DR 7–102(A)(8); *Cf.*, DR 1–102(A)(3) (qualifying "illegal conduct" with the phrase "involving moral turpitude." Whether there are limits beyond illegality is somewhat unclear. *See generally* DR 1–102(A)(5) ("A lawyer shall not . . . engage in conduct that is prejudicial to the administration of justice."); EC 1–5 ("A lawyer should maintain high standards of professional conduct and   .   .   .   should refrain from all illegal and morally reprehensible conduct."); EC 9–2 ("When explicit ethical guidance does not exist, a lawyer should determine his conduct by acting in a manner that promotes public confidence in the integrity and ef-

ficiency of the legal system and the legal profession.").

60. Bear in mind that "total disassociation" would involve leaving her job. This is a different choice from that faced by a firm in an analogous situation. *But see*, Rotunda, *Law, Lawyers and Managers*, THE ETHICS OF CORPORATE CONDUCT (1977).

61. *Cf.*, DR 2–110.

62. EC 7–5.

63. DR 1–102(A)(2); *see also* ABA Opinion 95 (1933).

his client insulates him from criticism by the court, except in cases of the most flagrant abuse. Courts almost always speak in terms of the actions of the parties, not of the lawyers, even though they are responsible for the parties' conduct.

Equally as important—and perhaps the court's attitude is partially responsible—lawyers rarely acknowledge their own responsibility for misusing law. They can too easily rationalize it away, because both the client and the lawyer use law. The client uses it in a beneficial sense, to obtain a benefit, in a particular situation, as when he enters a contract. The lawyer's use is an instrumental one, for he uses it as an instrument to achieve the goals of his client.

The plans which involve misuse of law typically fall into three basic categories: (1) plans which so clearly violate the law that the courts strike them down without hesitation; (2) plans which seemingly comply with the law, but in fact are inconsistent with its purposes; and (3) plans in which the parties by agreement supplant a general rule of law with a private rule. . . .

To view the duty of the lawyer in the use of law as that of the responsible exercise of power is to provide a basis for resolving problems of the misuse of law because most of the problems arise out of a misguided sense of loyalty to the client. The duty of the responsible exercise of power serves to bring this duty of loyalty into proper perspective in two ways. First, it serves to make the lawyer aware that part of his duty of loyalty is to enable his client to be his best self. "It is the lawyer's duty to keep the client from putting a black mark on his business record and never to yield, nor to permit his client to yield, to the purpose or intent of following a course of persecution or oppression or of any form of fraud or injustice." Secondly, the duty of the responsible exercise of power by the lawyer gives him a basis for the exercise of independent judgment. The pressure on the lawyer to satisfy his client is enhanced not only by the duty of loyalty, but by his need to make a living. Just as the lawyer needs a basis for acting for his client, the duty of loyalty, he needs also a basis to refuse to act improperly, the duty of the responsible exercise of power.[64]

Is this satisfactory guidance for the questions Wilson faces? In the circumstances set out in the transcript what more could/should she have done?

The Failure to Disclose the Illegality Beyond the Board

A related, but different set of issues is presented by the question of whether Wilson, if the board refuses to do so, may, must or may not inform (i) the S.E.C.; (ii) the local prosecuting authorities; (iii) the Union; (iv) the party in the law suit against the corporation; (v) any member of the consuming or investing public of the corporation's continuing and planned actions. The problem, of course,

---

64. L. Patterson & E. Cheatham, THE
PROFESSION OF LAW 148–49 (1971).

lies in the fact that, despite the confidential nature of the information, there is continuing future action contemplated. If the same acts were already completed, DR4–101(A) & (B) would bar disclosure.

In the larger work from which these excerpts are drawn, we review the opinions on this issue and the slippery line they draw between past, continuing and future activity.[65] In addition, note that the exemptions in Canon 4 *permit* disclosure only where an intention to commit a "crime" is involved or where disclosure is "permitted under Disciplinary Rules or required by law or court order." [66] Thus, it might be that with respect to the defective toasters (an issue which we have assumed involves only civil liability), Wilson is precluded from disclosing the danger or in any way warning the public. With respect to the illegal payoffs (assuming commercial bribery is criminal), counsel apparently *may* reveal the wrongdoing. Again, ask yourself whether these distinctions seem sensible and justifiable. Have any of your attitudes toward client loyalty changed as you have deepened your own actual experience with clients?

An additional perspective is added to these questions if you imagine that some public authority has indicated that the lawyer should disclose the information. Suppose, for example, that a court ruled that the corporation was obligated to respond to a discovery request concerning all illegal activity and the corporation determined not to do so.[67] Or what if, in a disciplinary proceeding against counsel representing the insurance company, Wilson were ordered by a court to reveal the test results she had learned from Sparks. Compare your reactions to these questions to your response to the following developments in the securities field:

> The SEC traditionally took the position that, while the securities lawyer had a duty to the investing public as well as to his client, his primary duty was owed to his client. In contrast to [the] standard for accountants, the SEC traditionally has not expected lawyers . . . to criticize publicly their clients' securities practices or to disclose anything beyond what is authorized by their clients. . . .

> During the last few years [however] the traditional view of the securities lawyers' responsibilities and duties . . . has been eroded by the SEC and, to a lesser degree, by the federal courts. No longer are sanctions and liabilities reserved for securities lawyers who are active participants or prime movers in blatant frauds. No longer is

65. The Lawyering Process 254–60. *See also*, Dallas, *The Attorney-Client Privilege and the Corporation in Shareholder Litigation*, 50 SO.CAL.L.REV. 303 (1977); Hinsey, *Auditors, Inquiries and Lawyer Responses*, 62 A.B.A.J. 1572 (1976).

66. DR 4–101(C)(2). *See also* DR 7–109 (A); DR 7–102(A)(3).

67. See DR 1–103(B); EC 1–4; ABA Informal Opinions 1203 (1972); 1210 (1972).

it clear that the securities lawyer owes his first and primary allegiance to his client.   .   .   .

The most widely publicized example of the new trend in standard of care and priorities of duties for securities lawyers was the SEC's complaint, filed in February, 1972, against National Student Marketing Corporation (NSMC) and eighteen other defendants including four individual attorneys and two prominent law firms. The charges against the attorneys arose from the merger between NSMC and Interstate National Corp., in which the Interstate shareholders exchanged their shares for approximately 1,650,000 shares of NSMC stock. Just before the merger closing, NSMC's accountants submitted a "comfort" letter to counsel for both parties that adjusted NSMC's nine months' earnings downward by $784,000 and converted a reported $700,000 profit into a net loss. Counsel for both parties declined to insist that the contents of this letter be publicized, declined to insist that Interstate's shareholders (whose approval of the merger had been solicited based on the erroneous profit report) be resolicited, and proceeded to consummate the merger. Immediately following the closing, 77,000 shares of NSMC common stock were publicly sold by former Interstate directors for $1,900,000.

The Commission charged NSMC's lawyers with violations of four different sections and Interstate's lawyers with violations of two different sections of the Securities Act of 1933 and the Securities Exchange Act of 1934. According to the Commission, securities counsel for both parties should have disclosed the contents of the "comfort" letter to NSMC and Interstate shareholders as well as to the investing public, and should have insisted that NSMC's nine months' financial statements be revised and that Interstate's shareholders be resolicited. Moreover, the lawyers should have refused to issue their opinions, which were a condition to the closing, that the merger was lawful. Had the clients refused to revise the financial statements and resolicit the shareholders, the lawyers should have ceased representing them. And most remarkably, the SEC asserted that the lawyers should have, "under the circumstances, notified the plaintiff Commission concerning the misleading nature of the nine month financial statements."   .   .   .[68]

Look carefully at DR4–101(C)(2); DR7–102(A)(5), (8); DR4–102 (A), (B); DR1–102(A)(5). How far is the SEC position from the mandates of the Code? What if Wilson had merely chosen not to look for contingent liabilities as thoroughly?[69]

68. Lowenfels, *Expanding Public Responsibilities of Securities Lawyers: An Analysis of the New Standard of Care and Priorities of Duties*, 74 COLUM.L.REV. 412 (1974); *see also* SEC v. Spectrum, Ltd., 489 F.2d 535 (2d Cir. 1973).

69. See ABA Opinion 335 (1974) ("if any of the alleged facts, or the alleged facts taken as a whole, are incomplete in a material respect; or are suspect; or are inconsistent; or either on their face or on the basis of other known facts are open to question, the lawyer should make further inquiry."). The committee indicated, however, that this responsibility was not one of the "mandatory obligations imposed by the Disciplinary Rules."

Note that a securities lawyer usually writes the registration statement and renders an opinion that the registration statement complies with existing legal rules. Should this make his or her obligations different from those of a tax or personal injury lawyer? Would it matter whether, as the S.E.C. claims, the securities law could not be effectively enforced without such obligations in the Bar?

The ABA has responded to the "new trend" as follows:

1. The confidentiality of lawyer-client consultations and advice and the fiduciary loyalty of the lawyer to the client, as prescribed in the American Bar Association's Code of Professional Responsibility ("CPR"), are vital to the basic function of the lawyer as legal counselor because they enable and encourage clients to consult legal counsel freely, with assurance that counsel will respect the confidentiality of the client's communications and will advise independently and in the client's best interest without conflicting loyalties or obligations.

2. This vital confidentiality of consultation and advice would be destroyed or seriously impaired if it is accepted as a general principle that lawyers must inform the SEC or others regarding confidential information received by lawyers from their clients even though such action would not be permitted or required by the CPR. Any such compelled disclosure would seriously and adversely affect the lawyers' function as counselor, and may seriously and adversely affect the ability of lawyers as advocates to represent and defend their clients' interests.

3. In light of the foregoing considerations, it must be recognized that a lawyer cannot, consistently with his essential role as legal adviser, be regarded as a source of information concerning possible wrongdoing by clients. Accordingly, any principle of law which, except as permitted or required by the CPR, permits or obliges a lawyer to disclose to the SEC otherwise confidential information should be established only by statute after full and careful consideration of the public interests involved and should be resisted unless clearly mandated by law.

4. Lawyers have an obligation under the CPR to advise clients, to the best of their ability, concerning the need for or advisability of public disclosure of a broad range of events and circumstances, including the obligation of the client to make appropriate disclosures as required by various laws and regulations administered by the SEC. In appropriate circumstances, a lawyer may be permitted or required by the Disciplinary Rules under the CPR to resign his engagement if his advice concerning disclosures is disregarded by the client and, if the conduct of a client clearly establishes his prospective commission of a crime or the past or prospective perpetration of a fraud in the course of the lawyer's representation, even to make the disclosures himself. However, the lawyer has neither the obligation nor the right to make disclosure when any reasonable doubt exists concerning the client's obligation of disclosure, *i. e.*, the client's failure to meet his obligation is not clearly established, except to the extent that the lawyer should consider appropriate action, as required or permitted

by the CPR, in cases where the lawyer's opinion is expected to be relied on by third parties and the opinion is discovered to be not correct, whether because it is based on erroneous information or otherwise.

5.   Fulfillment by attorneys of their obligations to clients under the CPR best serves the public interest of assisting and furthering clients' compliance with legal requirements.   Efforts by the government to impose responsibility upon lawyers to assure the quality of their clients' compliance with the law or to compel lawyers to give advice resolving all doubts in favor of regulatory restrictions would evoke serious and far-reaching disruption in the role of the lawyer as counselor, which would be detrimental to the public, clients, and the legal profession.   In fulfillment of their responsibility to clients under the CPR, lawyers must be free to advise clients as to the full range of their legitimately available courses of action and the relative attendant risks involved.   Furthermore, it is often desirable for the lawyer to point out those factors which may suggest a decision that is morally just as well as legally permissible.   However, the decision as to the course to be taken should be made by the client.   The client's actions should not be improperly narrowed through the insistence of an attorney who may, perhaps unconsciously, eliminate available choices from consideration because of his concern over possible personal risks if the position is taken which, though supportable, is subject to uncertainty or contrary to a known, but perhaps erroneous, position of the SEC or a questionable lower court decision.   Public policy, we strongly believe, is best served by lawyers acting in conformance with their obligations to their clients and others as prescribed under the CPR.   Accordingly, liability should not be imposed upon lawyers whose conduct is in conformance with the CPR.[70]

Does this adequately answer the S.E.C. position?   How would you reconcile the competing interests here?

Resistance to the Law Suit

The obligations the S.E.C. imposes on the lawyer as a securities counselor are also usefully contrasted with Wilson's responsibilities under the Code with respect to the pending litigation against the corporation.   What is apparently planned is: (i) resistance to each discovery request to the limits of the rules; (ii) delay; (iii) refusal to concede liability despite Sparks' acknowledgement that the toaster

---

70. Statement of Policy Adopted by the American Bar Association Regarding Responsibilities and Liabilities of Lawyers in Advising with Respect to the Compliance by Clients with Laws Administered by the Securities and Exchange Commission (1975).   There has been a great deal of heated debate on this subject within the profession. *See, e. g.,* Goldberg, *Policing Responsibilities of the Securities Bar: The At-*torney-Client Relationship and the Code of Professional Responsibility, 19 N.Y.L.F. 221 (1973); Shipman, *The Need for S.E.C. Rules to Govern the Duties and Civil Liabilities of Attorneys Under the Federal Securities Statutes,* 34 OHIO ST.L.J. 231 (1973); Sonde, *Professional Responsibility: A New Religion or the Old Gospel?,* 24 EMORY L.J. 827 (1975).

was probably defective; (iv) a veiled bribe to plaintiff's counsel. Except for the last of these,[71] it is hard to find specific condemnation of such conduct in the Code. Counsel is entitled to raise every defense, procedural and substantive, permitted by law. The only limits on this conduct are that the conduct not serve "merely to harass or maliciously injure" the opposing party and that the claims not be "unwarranted." Again, you should ask why the strictures on the sort of tactics Sparks wants to use should be so narrowly drawn. What would be the consequences of a different set of rules to govern this situation?[72]

Several commentators have suggested that, however necessary such an adversarial orientation might be in litigation, it has no place in determining the obligations of the lawyer-counselor.[73] Ask yourself if this seems to be correct? How might such a distinction be administered? Abe Krash, for example, makes the following observations:

> It has been suggested that a distinction should be made between acting as an advocate for a client with respect to past conduct and advising a client as to his future conduct. An advocate, it is said, is entitled in a courtroom to present every contention, regardless of its consistency with the public interest, whereas an adviser as to future conduct has a responsibility to take account of the public interest. This difference in a lawyer's responsibility has been particularly urged in connection with representation of clients seeking or opposing legislation.
>
> In practice, it is extremely difficult to apply this distinction. Many firms represent clients as a General Counsel, defending their clients' past conduct and rendering advice as to future transactions. Moreover, as The New York Times case makes clear, it may be exceedingly difficult in a situation involving proposed conduct to assert with confidence that the public interest requires one thing but not another. To take another example: Assume that an opinion is requested of counsel concerning the legality of a proposed merger under the antitrust laws. If the client determines to proceed with the transaction notwithstanding counsel's opinion that the merger is likely

---

71. DR 5–107.

72. The literature on the "delay" problem, for example, raises a number of possibilities and problems that might arise from stricter standards and sanctions. *See generally, A Program for the Elimination of Litigation Delay*, 27 OHIO ST.L.J. 402 (1966).

73. It should be noted that the Code has few provisions which deal explicitly with the lawyer as *advisor*.

See generally Schwartz, *The Missing Rule of Professional Conduct*, 52 L.A.B. BULL. 10 (1976). Nevertheless, a number of commentators have expressed the view that there are important differences between the ethical problems of the lawyer as advisor and the lawyer as advocate. *See, e. g.*, Brown & Brown, *What Counsels the Counselor? The Code of Professional Responsibility's Ethical Considerations —A Preventive Law Analysis*, 10 VAL. U.L.REV. 453 (1976).

to be adjudged illegal, the lawyer who rendered the opinion is certainly not disabled from representing the client in the event the merger is challenged. A competent adviser would, of course, point out to his client that not all that is legal is wise; and that short term profits may lead to long term difficulties. Moreover, I suspect that most lawyers feel freer than the lawyers of a generation ago to point out to a client the public policy implications of a proposed course of conduct. However, I remain of the view that the ultimate policy decision must be made by the client. Further, I am of the view that the solution to this problem is not to impose on counsel the burden of representing interests othet than those of his client, but rather to take appropriate steps to insure that all interests are effectively represented.[74]

Does this seem correct? How is the problem of delay different when a lawyer is in a non-litigation situation? In what form do such issues even arise?

----

2. *The Larger Puzzle: The Lawyer's Responsibility for Consequences.*

We thus come a full circle to one of the questions with which we began: Can a good lawyer be a good person? Indeed, why do we keep asking such a question? Why is it not enough to say with Charles Curtis, "an honest man is not responsible for the vices or the stupidity of his calling, and need not refuse to practice them"? Surely one of the reasons lies not in our moral ambiguities but in our status as professionals. As Burton Bledstein, commenting on the meaning of professionalism in nineteenth century America, has stated:

> [The professional strove to realize] the radical idea of the . . . liberated person seeking to free the power of nature within every worldly sphere, a self-governing individual exercising his trained judgment in an open society.

*   *   *

> Utilizing his trained capacity, the professional person interpreted the special lines along which such complex phenomena as a physical disease, a point of law, a stage of human psychological growth, or the identity of an historical society developed in time and space. The professional did not vend a commodity, or exclusively pursue a self-interest. He did not sell a service by a contract which called for specific results in a specific time or restitution for errors. Rather, through a special understanding of a segment of the universe, the professional person released nature's potential and rearranged reality

74. Krash, *Professional Responsibility to Clients and the Public Interest: Is*   *There a Conflict?*, 55 CHI.B.REC. 31, 37 (Special Centennial Issue, 1973).

on grounds which were neither artificial, arbitrary, faddish, convenient, nor at the mercy of popular whim. Such was the august basis for the authority of the professional.

The jurisdictional claim of that authority derived from a special power over worldly experience, a command over the profundities of a discipline. Such masterful command was designed to establish confidence in the mind of the helpless client. The professional person possessed esoteric knowledge about the universe which if withheld from society could cause positive harm. In the cases of the doctor, the lawyer, the engineer, and the chemist, the consequences could be lethal. No less, however, did society require the minister to recite knowingly at the grave, the teacher to instruct intelligently in the classroom, the national historian to discover a meaning that related the present to the past. Laymen were neither prepared to comprehend the mystery of the tasks which professionals performed, nor—more ominously—were they equipped to pass judgment upon special skills and technical competence. Hence, . . . professionalism required amateurs to "trust" in the integrity of trained persons, to respect the moral authority of those whose claim to power lay in the sphere of the sacred and the charismatic. . . . .

* * *

The person who mastered professional discipline and control emerged as an emulated example of leadership in American society. He was self-reliant, independent, ambitious, and mentally organized. He structured a life and a career around noble aims and purposes, including the ideal of moral obligation. But [on the other hand] the professional person absolutely protected his precious autonomy against all assailants, not in the name of an irrational egotism but in the name of a special grasp of the universe and [in] . . . the service of mankind.

* * *

[With this as a backdrop] what formed a [professional] career was not disconnected ends, not conditioned habits, not *ad hoc* actions, not practical good works, not an infinite series of jobs, but the entire coherence of an intellectually defined and goal-oriented life. . . .

For the careerist by definition committed himself totally, not merely to private concerns, personal results, particular accomplishments, and the welfare of neighbors. He committed himself to a continuous performance in the service of universal ends. Horizontally the careerist . . . fought, energetically competed, wasted the obstacles in the way, and overcame all impediments, especially his own inertia. Vertically he escalated, mounting the successive platforms of achievement. The "promise" of a professional life made the difference in [his] struggle to triumph over inability and inefficiency, to conquer partisanship and subjectivity.[75]

75. B. Bledstein, THE CULTURE OF
    PROFESSIONALISM 87, 91–92, 89–
    90, 111–112 (1976).

Much of our satisfaction, our self-image, and our claims to privilege reside in the public's and our belief in this assertion. We want to *both* do well and do good—to believe that we can reconcile a vision of social justice with our personal actions.

As each of the preceding transcripts have amply demonstrated, however, such a resolution is very, very difficult to discern. Consider, for example, Mark Green's efforts in this regard:

. . . When, if ever, should a lawyer tell a client that a proposed argument or tactic is unjust? Is this judgment his to make? When, and by what standards, should a lawyer refuse to represent a particular client? Can the law-for-hire ethic provide just law?

These questions do not particularly trouble many lawyers, who simply assume that a lawyer is an advocate doing everything possible for his client to prevail, period. It hardly requires explanation that attorneys should zealously promote their clients' interests. But less appreciated is the fact that lawyers and law firms have public obligations as trustees of justice. They constitute a "profession," which by self-definition is a "higher calling" involving more than merely making money. (The word "profession" comes from the Middle English word to "profess," which originally meant taking a religious vow.) There is considerable language in court decisions, ABA formal opinions, the Canons of Ethics, and scholarly writings to the effect that lawyers take vows as officers of the court not to abuse the legal process for client benefit. Paradoxically, the vigorous representation of a client is seen as a subordinate obligation to the process itself, for a lawyer furthers justice by advocating one position in an adversary context.

* * *

This is not always self-evident in the behavior of Washington lawyers. It is a matter of personal choice, not professional compulsion, that Tommy Austern intimidates FDA staff, engages in ex parte contacts to influence agency decisions, uses the "work product" standard as a cover for running the Tobacco Institute's computer, and refuses to acknowledge that smoking can be hazardous. No ethical obligation required Lloyd Cutler to meet privately with Senator Kefauver's opponents, to bring the representative of a powerful constituent to his meeting with Congressman Van Deerlin, to acquiesce in client schemes that would deprive South American peasants of low-cost drugs or foist hazardous drugs on foreign consumers, or to oppose, systematically, nearly every automobile-safety improvement on behalf of Detroit.

There are many more examples. James McKay, rather than quitting the Plumbing Fixtures Manufacturers Association account or reporting its criminal conduct, at best merely swallowed hard and closed his eyes. Stanley Temko directed a delaying action that permitted the continued marketing of a drug known to be dangerous by his client and presumably by himself. Jack Schafer continues to represent ITT despite its apparent irresistible impulse to fix public policy unethically or illegally. Ernest Jennes engages in ex parte lobbying seeking to influence pending cable-TV cases. In all these situations, intelligent lawyers—choosing their clients and their techniques, often in a unique position to influence corporate policy for the better—should be held accountable for the results of their advocacy.

*   *   *

[Indeed, the counterarguments, some of which follow, have a hollow ring] . . .

● *It is up to the adversary system, not the lawyer, to uncover the truth.* This is largely true where the adversary system exists. But what of where it doesn't?

*   *   *

In Congress, the absence of any formal adversary system is obvious. Thousands of corporate lobbyists, often lawyers, patrol Capitol Hill corridors to watch out for hostile legislation. Randomly someone from a union or citizens' organization may oppose business on a particular bill; essentially, this is like prescribing aspirin for cancer, since such groups simply lack the resources to look at more than a small fraction of the fifteen thousand bills introduced each session of Congress. Members of Congress themselves can barely keep up with the deluge of work and requests cascading over their slender staffs. "If you aren't independently wealthy," complained ex-congressman Allard Lowenstein,

> you can't have a staff that is capable of putting things together much beyond what you can come up with from the sources available to everyone—the executive departments, the lobbies, the staffs of congressional committees, the Library of Congress. That's one reason why the lobbies are so influential. They have people who are able to spend all their time collecting data on why pollution is good for River X. What Congressman can match that?

This situation leads to the breakdown of the pluralist model of competing "factions"—the political analogue of the adversary process. Political scientist Henry Kariel attributes this breakdown to a system biased against unorganized groups or those in the process of formation. Consumers are hard to organize because of what economists call "the free-rider effect": achievements such as fair labeling or stronger bumpers are "public goods" which any single consumer can receive even if he or she does not work to secure them. Also, although employment is of overriding concern to a union employee, or profits to a manager, a consumer issue is only one of the many concerns confronting citizens. Unlike labor or management, consequently, consumers have not forged themselves into a powerful political group. Nor have poor people, who lack the resources and time to lobby effectively. "Precisely because our institutions are formally open to participation by all elements in a society," explains author-lawyer Simon Lazarus of this phenomenon, "they are vulnerable to domination by the most powerful elements in society."

● *Who can say what the "public interest" really is?* There is some merit in this question. Few were satisfied with Justice Potter Stewart's now famous statement that though he couldn't define pornography, he knew it when he saw it. There is no talmadic definition of what the public interest is in every situation; and since personal subjectivity makes lawyers, who deal in the concreteness of precedent, uncomfortable, they ridicule the notion that this talisman can be used to evaluate client conduct.

But that line-drawing is difficult does not mean that no line can ever be drawn. Otherwise, scrambling into the safety hatch of "who can say," lawyers would cease to function as independent professionals. . . .

To be sure, instances come to mind in which the public interest is unclear. . . .

* * *

But when it is argued that the oil-depletion allowance is essential to a healthy oil industry, or that GM sharply competes with other auto firms over price, safety, and pollution controls, few people are fooled—and certainly not their lawyers.

• *It is guilt by association (what Edward Bennett Williams calls "guilt by client") to tar a lawyer with the views of his client.* Thus, when the ACLU defends Nazis or Communists from unconstitutional infringements, it is wrong to perceive the lawyer as endorsing his clients' policies; rather, he is upholding constitutional safeguards due any citizen.

Yet this contrasts with a corporate lawyer who on a continuing basis advises his client not merely on constitutional safeguards but also on policy matters. As Lloyd Cutler has written, the Washington lawyer "is not limited, as in the courts, to defending what has already occurred. He has the opportunity of advising his client what ought to be done—how best to accommodate its practical problems to the emerging demands of the public interest." What if the client ignores its lawyer's counsel, or what if the lawyer advises not what ought to be done but what the client can get away with? It seems illogical to criticize, say, a corporate polluter but not the Washington lawyer whose perennial strategies may *permit* the pollution. After years of representing only corporations, "advocacy of one interest necessarily entails the neglect of or opposition to other interests," Congressman Abner Mikva has argued, "and [a lawyer] cannot escape the social, political, and economic consequences of his choice."

* * *

Lawyers continue to argue that they should not be judged by their corporate clients, even though they may perennially earn the incomes of business from business. But from Hoyt Moore's bribing of a federal judge for Bethlehem Steel (he avoided conviction because the statute of limitations had run out; the bar never moved against him) to the directorships held by lawyers in client firms (a director becomes legally responsible for certain business activity), it seems reasonable to associate a corporate lawyer with a client he continually advises in nonadversarial forums.

* * *

There is a significant difference between a lawyer who just once represents an individual accused of a *past* violation and a lawyer who on retainer represents a corporation that *repeatedly* and continuously is in legal trouble. It is one thing to defend Upjohn, which continually sells a dangerous drug, or to represent Continental Baking, which seems to violate the antitrust laws with the regularity of the vernal equinox. If a court assigned a lawyer the former case, it would be unethical to turn it down; but it is not unethical to drop a recidivist client, especially in a retainer-relationship in which the attorney on an ongoing basis is supposed to counsel his client against illegality.

It is unpersuasive when Washington lawyers compare themselves with courtroom advocates to justify their lobbying activities. When Ralph Nader criticized law-firm lobbying for "cutting down consumer programs in their incipiency or undermining them if they mature," the late Thurman Arnold dissented. He spoke of the "necessity of having representatives on both sides of a case" and thought that Nader was effectively saying "that we should get rid of skilled advocates because they confuse the court." Both sides? The court? Congress is not a court with a pristine adversary process but a place of politics. To defend oneself in court, an individual almost always needs a licensed lawyer; but every citizen has the license to try to influence legislation, and in Congress a lawyer is more a luxury than a constitutional requirement of justice. It is not unusual for a Washington lawyer to defend an unpopular client in court, but heads would no doubt turn if Lloyd Cutler lobbied for the Black Panthers in Congress. Why? Because the lawyer has more latitude in choosing whom he represents in the legislative forum than in a courtroom—and consequently is more responsible for the results.

* * *

What can be done about a one-sided process in which giant companies hire Washington law firms to rationalize all client misbehavior regardless of the public cost? Since we are dealing with nongovernmental institutions on matters often involving subjective judgments, there is no simple remedial law, no undisclosed panaceas to resolve this dilemma entirely. Still, the present way is not the only way.

Some radical critics would apply an antitrust analogy to the legal profession. Several Chicago state legislators, for example, recently urged a strict size limit on law firms—the theory being that smaller firms would be less likely to exhaust, delay, or inundate weaker opponents into submission. Or perhaps, no law firm could represent a business client with over, say, $100 million in assets for more than seven years. To be sure, there would be lost expertise and burdensome start-up costs every seven years for the new law firm, but it might be less likely that lawyers would find themselves indentured to dominant clients, so integrated with them that the lawyers would no longer even be aware that they had lost their professional independence. These ideas are worth exploring, but until their effects are more sharply framed, not yet worth implementing. Three more practicable approaches could reform the way Washington lawyers work.

● To a serious extent, the governmental and legal system themselves tolerate if not encourage lawyer chicanery ("I have news for Dean Burch," a lawyer has already been quoted as saying, "I'm going

to try a case . . . and take advantage of every rule that's there").
The rules governing legal advocacy can be revised to make lawyers more responsive to the process and more open in their dealings. For example, to reduce the tactical delaying of corporate lawyers, administrative-law judges and courtroom judges should insist that strict deadlines for submissions be met and that obvious dilatory action will be referred to bar associations for sanction. Bar grievance committees, which serve a quasi-public function of overseeing a profession licensed by the state, should contain not merely in-bred brothers-at-the-bar but also some public, nonlawyer members as well; perhaps then the practices of corporate lawyers may begin to come under the kind of scrutiny reserved for ambulance-chasers and those who convert client funds.

Greater disclosure about the activity of lawyers could discourage secret influencing and better educate the public about the lawyer's role and function. The 1946 Lobbying Registration Act is, by consensus, more loophole than law; it should be amended so that whenever a lawyer-lobbyist contacts a member of Congress or his/her staff on behalf of a client (except for mere requests for information), that lawyer should register as a lobbyist and provide information about purpose, expenses, and fees. The same should be true of the regulatory and executive agencies. Meetings should be logged between Washington lawyers and their official counterparts. And regulatory agencies should require their regulatees, who by definition are in the "public" sector of the economy, to list all their legal fees (as the CAB now does). These measures emphasize the fact that information is a predicate of reform and underscore the Brandeisian wisdom that "sunlight is said to be the best of disinfectants."

• *Since part of the problem is that wealthier Americans nearly monopolize legal talent, lawyers must be encouraged to represent the now unrepresented.* This involves expanding legal services for the poor, encouraging the establishment of prepaid legal-service programs for the middle class, creating a Consumer Protection Agency to advocate consumer interests in Washington agencies, permitting foundation-supported public-interest advocates to lobby by changing the tax code, allowing plaintiffs' lawyers who bring successful lawsuits against the government to collect their legal fees from the government, and providing more funds to dues-supported citizens' groups. The responsibility for these advances is shared by the government, which can pass needed laws, by the bar, which should rewrite an "ethical" code that now frustrates access to lawyers, and by the public itself, on whom dues-supported groups depend. To the extent that the adversary system of justice truly works, Washington lawyers will be less able to prevail by default.

• Whenever and if ever any of the above changes occur, Washington lawyers will continue to have a public obligation to oversee client conduct. For they can no longer shield themselves behind the excuse of a malfunctioning adversary process—malfunctioning precisely because these lawyers represent one sector of society while they loftily urge that all are entitled to a lawyer. Sirhan Sirhan is not Upjohn and the courthouse is not the Congress or the Federal

Power Commission.   The making of this distinction should lead to a new lawyers' ethic: *when a Washington counsel, on a continuing retainer for past and future legal liability, represents a corporation in a, civil or legislative proceeding, he (or she) should make a judgment about the likely impact on the public, and if the client desires tactics based on political influence or seeks a demonstrable though avoidable public harm, he should quit the account.*

This ethic would encourage a lawyer to make his own moral judgment about whether and how to represent clients based on a sliding scale of considerations: for example, is the proceeding civil or criminal, nonadversarial or actually adversarial, abusive of judicial procedure or not, concerned with an alleged past or continuing violation? After weighing factors like these, an attorney may choose to represent such firms, and to accept responsibility for the continuing results; but he is also free to refuse to do so, and to decide what to do with his one professional life. For there is nothing in the Code of Professional Responsibility that says a lawyer *must* represent the House of Morgan or GM.   Even the Canons of Ethics say, "He has the right to decline employment," and "If a client persists in . . . wrong-doing, the lawyer should terminate their relation."

A lawyer can also simply conclude that certain business defenses can harm society more than any conceptual contribution made to the adversary process.   Or he can decide initially that corporate law firms in general, whatever their legal wizardy and genteel advocacy, are institutions with negative social balance sheets.

This new ethic is no Rosetta stone instructing all lawyers what to do in all situations.   Like any ethical judgment, it is subjective and personal, not universal, though the lawyer may wish others to follow his example.   It is an ethic that throws the lawyer ultimately back on his own subjective references, his own view of "the public interest."

This is surely not new. What is the adversary process itself but a social judgment that legal combat is in the public interest because it leads to justice—a conclusion the author shares but one which, for example, China and Herbert Marcuse do not. Nor is it a neutral principle that lawyers will represent those who can pay and not represent those who cannot. This means-test effectively excludes a large class of Americans from access to legal services; it is very much a value choice. So is the new ethic of conscientious refusal. As the concept of a good German has changed, so will the concept of a good lawyer. Lawyers chafe at the accusation that they are merely hired guns following orders, but it is not surprising that some now agree with Washington lawyer Joseph Califano when he says, "I think we are going to have to start making moral judgments on our clients."

It is obviously academic to fear that all lawyers, following this guide, will rush out to conclude simultaneously that, say, an IBM doesn't deserve representation. The military draft would have collapsed if all draftees had declared themselves conscientious objectors, but military officials knew that statistically this could not happen. Any single lawyer conscientiously refusing an IBM would be secure in the knowledge that the computer giant would not go unrepresented.

Why then bother to refuse?, some might plausibly ask. The reasons are both ethical and practical. Ethically, it can be immoral to become an executioner, even though society can always find someone to lop off heads. "Someone else will do it anyway" is a standard that obliterates individual choice and can rationalize any evil. And practically, GM retains a Lloyd Cutler, and the Tobacco Institute a Covington & Burling, presumably because they can do things other lawyers cannot. To the extent that lawyers refused to expend their skills on *pro malo* advocacy, certain clients would have to use lawyers of lesser ability to make their case—a case which might not then prevail. This situation could send a message to the business sector that the best lawyers would not be merely message-takers and spear-carriers. Ideally, this spreading feedback could, to some extent, deter and reform corporate misbehavior.[76]

Think hard about this analysis and the criteria it offers. In light of your own clinical experience would you be able/willing to act on it?

Consider first how one decides who should be represented. Does one look to the sorts of claims and interests involved? The influence the potential client has? Whether the client has acted in ways that appear to have been "improper" in the past? In terms of some ultimate vision of just social relationships?

It might be argued that one should represent those less likely to be represented by others, or less financially or otherwise advantaged. Certainly we would join Green in urging that lawyers turn their efforts to those unable to obtain or afford counsel. But should this be taken as an affirmative *moral* obligation for any individual—a requirement you would advance as binding on every individual lawyer? Although there is a deeply rooted religious ethic in our tradition that might support just such a moral ideal, it seems to have little hold on our felt commitments. It is no accident that Green limits his prescriptions to "encouraging" lawyers to represent the now underrepresented.

The same problem of criteria attends the question of how clients, once accepted, are served. Are there certain means or ends which are inadmissible? Is there a way of defining "public interest", "public harm", "harm to others" in ways that provide guidance and justification? What goes into the posit of "demonstrable but avoidable" public harm?

Green seems correct in pointing to the moral responsibility that the power to refuse and withdraw—to say "no"—places on counsel. Fidelity to a client is only meaningful if it involves "obligations freely chosen"—if it expresses one's relationship to self and others as well as to the particular relationship. But Green also states that such decisions are "subjective and personal, not universal"—that the law-

---

76. M. Green, THE OTHER GOVERN-
MENT 269, 273–77, 279–81, 285–88
(1975).

yer is inevitably thrown "back on his own subjective preferences, his own view of the public interest." If this is the case, what justifies the lawyer in refusing to carry out a client's wishes or determining that a corporation has a "negative social balance sheet", or in particular circumstances, attempting to be an "example" for others? Our hunch is that the problem here may lie in too narrow a view of what must change if any vision of the "public interest" is to be clarified. Consider whether it really is possible to resolve the issues Green raises without

—far greater limits on the exercise of private corporate power;

—far less inequality in wealth, income and security within the country;

—a different cultural orientation toward cooperation, acquisitiveness, and participation in social life.

You may, of course, add to this list, criticize or modify it, or hopefully develop a very different one of your own. To tease out the implications for social structure and experience toward which Green's arguments lead is, fortunately or unfortunately, another book.

But surely his concerns would require some larger social and ethical vision. Unless the political and professional can be seen as less firmly separate, no such vision seems possible.

†